P9-CJF-239

The Politics of
FAT

The Politics of

FAT

Food and Nutrition Policy in America

Laura S. Sims

DISCARD

M. E. Sharpe
Armonk, New York
London, England

363.856
S614p

Copyright © 1998 by M. E. Sharpe, Inc.

All rights reserved. No part of this book may be reproduced in any form
without written permission from the publisher, M. E. Sharpe, Inc.,
80 Business Park Drive, Armonk, New York 10504.

Library of Congress Cataloging-in-Publication Data

Sims, Laura S., 1943–
The politics of fat : food and nutrition in America / by
Laura S. Sims.
p.   cm.
Includes bibliographical references and index.
ISBN 0-7656-0193-1 (cloth : alk. paper). —
ISBN 0-7656-0194-X (pbk. : alk. paper)
1. Nutrition policy—United States.   2. Food—Fat content.
3. Lipids in human nutrition.   I. Title.
TX360.U6S58   1997
363.8′56′0973—dc21
97-26608
CIP
Printed in the United States of America

The paper used in this publication meets the minimum requirements of
American National Standard for Information Sciences—
Permanence of Paper for Printed Library Materials,
ANSI Z 39.48-1984.

EB (c)   10   9   8   7   6   5   4   3   2   1
EB (p)   10   9   8   7   6   5   4   3   2   1

¹/99

DEDICATION

". . . for Roots and Wings."

To Mother, with love. . .
for giving me deep roots and fledgling wings,

For my children—Jonathan, Amy, and Andrew
to whom I pray I have given both strong roots and soaring wings,

And for Toby,
with whom I share both spreading roots and steady wings, truly
the "*wind* beneath my wings. . ."

Contents

List of Tables and Figures

Tables

Figures

Preface

Government policies exert a profound influence on consumers' food choices. In recent years, a number of authoritative reports (many released by the federal government) have warned consumers of the health damage that can result from eating high-fat diets. Yet for over half a century, the government has supported policies that favor the production and pricing of these same "high-fat" foods. This policy irony is further complicated by market forces that cater to meeting consumer demands for tasty, convenient foods (many of which are high in fat) that fit into their time-stressed lifestyles.

Policy results from the collective actions of *people* working with and through their government to realize certain goals. What emerges as policy is actually a result of people's beliefs, aspirations, and personal experiences that are channeled to transform the machinery of government into overarching directives that govern many facets of our everyday lives. People's food choices are influenced—some would even say, constrained—by actions of the federal government.

The study of nutrition policy is a vibrant field, and this book is meant both to describe and to analyze that richness of experience. This book was written to capture the exciting, exhilarating moments of food and nutrition policy making, as well as the boring, often laborious and tedious, aspects of the process.

First, I present an overview of public policy and the policy-making process, accompanied by a description of the process and events related specifically to food and nutrition. Then, I systematically review each segment of the food system—from agricultural food production, to food processing and manufacturing, to food marketing and distribution, and finally to food consumption—and relate government's involvement in specific aspects of each segment. Five case studies are presented, each a significant policy event, told in a more personal, less pedantic style to help the reader learn how the government works (or doesn't work) to affect the foods we eat, what's in those foods, and what we learn about those foods. My hope is that the reader will emerge with a better understanding and appreciation of the public policy process and how governmental policies affect our food choices.

Acknowledgments

It is said that a "journey of a thousand miles begins with a single step." While the writing of this book has often seemed like a never-ending journey, the first steps were taken over a decade ago.

My interest in nutrition was fueled by a love of science coupled with a passion for studying people. As a public health nutritionist trained in the 1960s, I saw that government intervention was clearly a factor in affecting people's lives. As a member of the founding class of W.K. Kellogg Foundation Fellows in 1980, I focused on the role of national nutrition policy as a factor determining food consumption behavior, and my self-directed "study" became the "first step" toward this book. Then, again, in 1992, as a Fellow with the National Center for Food and Agricultural Policy, I began the process of shaping this book. Fellows from both groups have continued to advise me in the conceptualization and writing of this book, for which I am very grateful.

Honed, edited, and pruned numerous times, this book bears the imprint of numerous conversations and readings with noted scholars in public policy, with government bureaucrats, with policy makers, with industry spokespersons, with lobbyists, with public health practitioners, with nutritionists and food scientists. Notable among the many who have shared so generously of their time in the preparation of this book are Paul Thomas, Bruce Silverglade, and Sandra Shepherd. Numerous others have given of their time to review and discuss preliminary drafts, including (in alphabetical order): Stephen Abrams, Scott Barao, James Barney, Geoffrey Becker, Susan Conley, Carol Tucker Foreman, Christopher Hassall, Peter Barton Hutt, Lynn Larsen, Terry Lutz, Marshall Matz, James Russell, Terry Smith, James Stephenson, Linda Weinberg, and Susan Welch, as well as several anonymous reviewers. Thanks are also due to Sheryl Rosenthal, Susan Mayer, and Anna Arrowsmith for research assistance. To these individuals I owe my deepest thanks for insights and revelations. Any errors of judgment or fact, of course, are my own responsibility.

I greatly appreciate the support of my colleagues in the Department of Nutrition and Food Science at the University of Maryland College Park. And a great round of applause is due my family for their patience with me while I continually reminded them that I needed to "finish *The* book." Thanks are especially due to my husband, Hank Sims, whose unfailing encouragement saw this project through to completion.

Laura S. Sims
May 1997

PART I

OVERVIEW AND APPROACH

Chapter 1

Dietary Fat as a Public Policy Issue

What's political about food? my friends often ask.
Listen up. Almost everything about food is political.
—M. Burros*

This book describes the connection between federal policies and the foods we eat. Government-sponsored reports repeatedly warn us of the dangers of consuming foods high in fat. Yet for more than half a century, food and agricultural policies have been in place that favor the production and pricing of those foods that our health policies now recommend restricting. This imbalance of policies is further compounded by the fact that most people really *like* and *prefer* high-fat foods to low-fat fruits, vegetables, legumes, and grains.

Despite growing public awareness of the health dangers of high-fat diets, the amount of dietary fat consumed by Americans has only slightly decreased in recent years. Many believe that long-standing government policies have favored the production of high-fat foods, thus creating a situation where these less healthful foods are more plentiful and cheaper for consumers than their lower-fat counterparts. Others maintain, however, that it is our history and culture that are mainly responsible for our food choices, and that, government policies aside, we'll continue to eat as we like. Indeed, research has demonstrated the physiological connection between dietary fat's contribution to the flavor of foods and our "addiction" to fatty foods.

American consumers are increasingly confronted with a plethora of food choices. It is estimated that most modern supermarkets offer more than 20,000 different food items. Even though we face an almost overwhelming array of foods from which to choose, the assortment of different foods that we consume is often constrained by powerful influences on the food system—marketing orders, commodity price supports, regulations, laws, educational programs, even tax incentives—which act in

---

*M. Burros, *Eating Well Is the Best Revenge*. New York: Simon & Schuster, 1995. p. 321.

concert to circumscribe the number and type of foods that are available to us at prices we can afford.

The Politics of Fat tells a fascinating story, based on the power of economics and the findings of science, all compounded by the pleasures associated with eating. Consumers have gotten the message: "Eat low-fat!" And the food industry is scrambling to meet market demand by creating new foods and novel ingredients, all subject to government's regulatory approval. Yet current federal policies are often either working against consumer concerns and the potential marketplace response, lagging behind these influences, or ignoring them altogether.

The main purpose of this book is to examine whether current food policies have failed to keep pace either with the marketplace or with consumer concerns about diet and health, with the potential result the undermining of the health of Americans. A major question addressed by the book is whether federal policies have created an environment whereby health-promoting food choices are easier, or more difficult, to make. In fulfilling this purpose, we will also explain how government policies are operative at virtually every stage of the food system and show the interaction between the government and market forces in influencing consumers' food choices.

Why Dietary Fat?

This book tells the fascinating tale of fat—the kind in food and the kind we eat, not the kind on our bodies. This is *not* a book about obesity or losing body fat, albeit dietary fat is certainly a major contributor to that condition. Dietary fat is, in fact, a symbolic representation of public policy in the arenas of science, health, economics, and consumer behavior. Dietary fat serves as a symbol of the "schizophrenia" within federal public health agencies and the dominance of agribusiness interests at the U.S. Department of Agriculture that promote production of high-fat foods on the one hand and dispense information that admonishes consumers not to eat "too much" dietary fat on the other. Further, the issues concerning dietary fat demonstrate the viability of the Advocacy Coalition Framework,[1] a public policy analytical tool that describes the role of entrenched interests; the role of government bureaucrats as members of advocacy coalitions; and the role of scientific evidence, policy analysis, elections, and the media—all of which act in concert to alter the climate for reforming the status quo.

This chapter will discuss fat as a chemical component of our bodies and as a food ingredient. Further, we will show how dietary fat consumption has been implicated as a serious health risk. Because of dietary fat's role in contributing to the risk of chronic disease, it has an underestimated impact on national economic costs and thus becomes a public policy issue.

Fat as Chemical—An Essential Physiological and Culinary Component

Lipids—or by their more familiar name, *fats*—are chemically a family of compounds that are soluble in organic solvents (like alcohol or ether) but are not soluble in water. (Think of an oil and vinegar salad dressing. The oil is not soluble in the water-based vinegar; upon standing, the two separate into distinct layers, with oil on top and vinegar on the bottom.) Technically, lipids include triglycerides (which most people think of as fats and oils), phospholipids (of which the emulsifier lecithin is one), and sterols (of which cholesterol is the best known). Further, fats are lipids that are solid at room temperature, while oils are liquid at room temperature.

Fats serve a variety of functions, both in our bodies and as a food ingredient.[2] For the purposes of our discussion in this book, these functions have been divided into two main categories: (1) in our bodies, where the roles of fat are physiological or nutritional, and (2) as a food ingredient, where fat has a culinary role.

Physiological (Nutritional) Functions of Lipids

Triglycerides are the major form of fat in the body. Triglycerides in the body are used to store and supply energy, to protect and insulate body organs, and to aid in the absorption of fat-soluble vitamins. We require only a minute amount of fat, but our bodies cannot function properly without it.

Dietary fats supply more calories (the measure of energy value) per unit weight than any other nutrient. Lipids provide 9 calories per gram of weight, while carbohydrates and proteins supply 4 calories per gram, and alcohol provides 7. Another way to think of it—a tablespoon of oil supplies 124 calories, a tablespoon of sugar only 50. While one tablespoon of butter contains 11 grams of fat and has 100 calories, whole-wheat bread contains little fat, and one slice supplies 80 calories.

Fat is the body's chief storage form for the energy from food when consumed in quantities not needed for immediate use. In addition, body fat is concentrated in certain places in the body primarily as "fat pads" to protect vital organs, such as the liver and kidneys. Some fatty acids from foods may be incorporated into cell membranes, where they may affect what enters the cell as well as control what is transported between and within cells.

Among all the different fats in our food supply, two have been labeled essential" because they cannot be manufactured from other substances by the human body itself. These substances must be supplied and consumed "preformed" in the food fats we eat. These fatty acids are linoleic acid and alpha-linolenic acid, found mainly in plant seed oils and "fatty" fish, such as salmon, tuna, and sardines.

Dietary fats also serve to transport the fat-soluble vitamins—vitamins A, D, E, and K—throughout the body, thus making them available for various physiological purposes. Eating a small amount of visible fat or foods that contain fat is absolutely essential so that the body can use these vitamins efficiently. This premise applies regardless of whether these four vitamins are taken in the form of supplements or in foods.

Culinary Functions: Fat as Food Ingredient

Many foods naturally contain fats, with familiar fare like meats, dairy products, poultry, fish, nuts, and vegetable oils supplying most of the fats Americans eat. Whole grains and vegetables contain only small amounts of fats when not swimming in salad dressing or cooked in fat. Further, most fruits—with the exception of avocados, coconut, and olives—do not contain fat. Many food favorites hide their fat; fat is a necessary ingredient to make baked goods flaky and tender, and fat is used to give fried foods their crispy texture and familiar flavor. Grocery staples such as butter, margarine, shortening, and oil are almost all fat.

The properties fats impart to foods—their flavor, texture, and aroma—are what cause certain foods to be preferred and enjoyed. Many of the aromatic compounds that give foods their distinctive flavors are fat-soluble, and fat is the vehicle that carries these dissolved substances to the sensory cells in the mouth that discriminate taste and smell. Oil-based flavorings are often used in baking or in making candy. Heating spices in oil intensifies the flavors of an Indian curry or Mexican dish far more than simply adding them at the table. Thus, many highly flavorful foods are associated with a high fat content.

Fats in foods provide a wide variety of oral sensations. Food scientists use the term *mouthfeel* to describe the rich, smooth, creamy sensation that fat gives to many foods such as ice cream or custard. Dairy fat in ice cream contributes to the smoothness of the product by preventing the formation of large ice crystals.

Triglycerides and other lipid components in foods are responsible for the textures we associate with our food favorites. The most tender cuts of meat are usually also high in fat. The marbling of meat—where fat is interspersed within the muscle—contributes to its tenderness because the fat melts during the cooking process. In contrast, low-fat meats, such as flank steak or

Figure 1.1 **Functions of Fats in Foods**

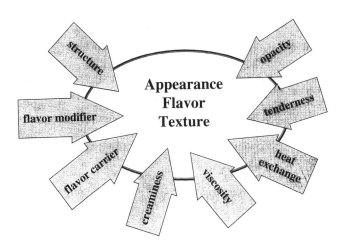

Source: American Journal of Clinical Nutrition: 62, 1176S, November 1995.

brisket, require special preparation techniques—such as marinating or slow, moist cooking—to ensure tenderness.

Fats have specific functions in baked goods, such as pie crusts, cakes, cookies, and pastries, without which these products would not exist. Certain properties of fats in bakery goods are responsible for the sensation of freshness and moisture. In products such as cakes, fats help to produce a high, fine texture. When fats and sugar are "creamed" or mixed together (the first step in mixing many cake batters), fats trap tiny air bubbles that help the batter to rise. Fats also help keep doughs and batters from separating and falling, and fats coat the proteins in flour to make a tender or flaky product. Figure 1.1 illustrates the different functions of fats in foods.

Edible fats and oils are excellent cooking media. They can be heated to above 100°C to provide rapid cooking (without the steam associated with boiling water) and simultaneously impart surface texture (crispness) and flavor to fried food. This fact may explain, in part, why some foods offered in various "fast-food" franchises in the United States—such as "french fries"—are so popular with consumers.

Consumption of Dietary Fat

The relationship between human beings and the food they consume goes far beyond the animal instinct to eat. For people, appetite is not simply a physiological drive toward food but, rather, a complex set of physical, emotional, and cognitive stimuli that direct the response to food. Early species of *Homo sapiens* learned what foods were edible or poisonous, which tastes each food conveyed, which foods had to be "cooked" or treated in certain ways to make them palatable and chewable, and how to store foods so that nourishment would be available when no food was readily obtainable by hunting or crop cultivation.

Obesity researchers tell us that the human preference for dietary fat was probably inherited originally from our ancestors who survived as hunter–gatherers. When plant foods were unavailable, our ancestors relied on their internal fat stores or adipose tissue to get them through long periods of food deprivation. Thus, they naturally began to seek foods that contained greater amounts of dietary fat in their drive for basic survival because fats provide more than twice the amount of calories as an equal amount of carbohydrates.

Factors Influencing Food Choices

Those factors that influence how much and what kinds of food people choose to eat are displayed in Figure 1.2. In general, these two sets of factors can be further categorized as those external to the individual (and thus applicable to groups of people) and those that are idiosyncratic and specific to the individual. The outermost of the concentric circles is ringed by the terms food, agricultural, and trade policies, which, when abetted by technology, contribute most directly to what foods are available for consumption. These policies, in turn, are directly affected by consumer demand, in terms of both the quantity and quality of certain food products. It is here that the government exerts its most direct influence on food choices—that is, by influencing what foods are *available* for purchase and choice.

Most of us eat foods from a core group of about 100 basic food items, which account for 75 percent of our total food intake. We may think we buy—and report that we buy—foods for their sensory appearance, freshness, safety, nutritional quality, healthfulness, convenience, or price. Those factors undoubtedly affect our food purchases, but we are still constrained in our choices by the routines, habits, and associations that have surrounded our interactions with food throughout our lifetimes.

Group Influences

Early humans learned the joy of social interaction and the sharing of food as one of the experiences in which such interaction could take place. Certain foods began to be associated with certain desirable characteristics—for example, meat with strength. Equally, certain foods began to be associated with certain tribes or groups of human beings, usually based on those con-

Figure 1.2 **Influences on Food Choices**

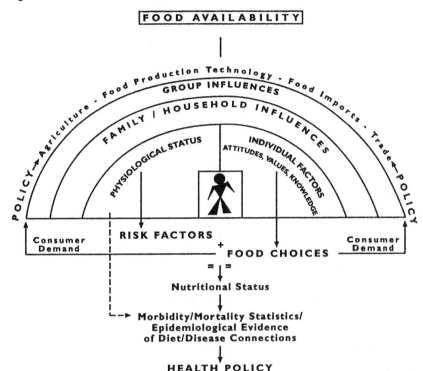

sumable items that were available and edible. This is also how certain religious beliefs came to be expressed through ceremonial rites involving the preparation and consumption of food.

Specific foods or dishes serve an important function for certain groups of people by providing them with a sense of identity and "shared" focus. Often specific food choices and preferences are symbolic of a group's cultural identity and/or social status or "class." These food preferences shared by certain groups often evolve from those foods that are available to be grown or raised in that particular environment. For example, it is difficult to raise fresh produce in arctic temperatures, and such foods are not available for consumption unless technology has intervened to make them so.

Although human beings have certain "built-in" preferences as well as the physiological apparatus to discern the tastes of bitter, salty, sweet, and sour, such innate responses are capable of being modified through exposure and conditioning. This allows some people—even entire cultures—to learn enjoy very sour or hot, spicy foods, such as jalapeño peppers and curries. It has also been suggested that the use of certain spices evolv warm climates as a means of masking off-flavors produced by contamination or spoilage when foods were improperly stored without refrigeration.

Food "taboos" practiced by certain religious groups also serve to mark identity with a particular group. Further, such practices as sanctioned by religious authorities often evolved from past experiences with food safety. It is said that the avoidance of pork products by both the Jewish and Muslim religions grew not so much out of any particular religious observance but because in the hot climates of the Middle East, fresh meat products, such as pork, simply could not be stored or saved for any length of time without risking contamination by some food-borne organism. Further, meat from pigs was more likely to carry the organism causing trichinosis. Thus, it was simply "easier" to ban the consumption of such products altogether on religious grounds than to "regulate" the slaughter and ensure the safety of the meat as it was brought to market and sold to the consumer.

Because humans from birth through childhood depend for their survival on nurturance provided by other members of their species, usually caregivers within the family or household unit, nourishment almost inevitably becomes associated with powerful emotional attachments. Food preferences are learned early as social and cultural dictates and are refined through interactions with parents and friends.

A number of factors at the level of the household or family affect food intake of individuals. Chief among these is the size of the household and its composition because it is at the household level where most food-purchase decisions are still made. The economic resources available for food purchases obviously affect what foods are purchased and in what quantities certain foods are purchased. It should come as no surprise, therefore, that the largest food assistance program, the food stamp program, certifies eligibility for participation in the program at the household level.

Many households serve those dishes (particularly for certain holidays) that are part of their cultural heritage and identify them as members of a particular ethnic group. College students away from home for the first time often complain about the quality of the food they are served, mainly because it has not been prepared in the manner to which they are accustomed. "Family favorites" are the mode by which individuals align their food preferences with certain household traditions. And it is often these family "comfort foods" that come heavily laden with dietary fat.

Internal, Idiosyncratic Factors Influencing Consumption of Dietary Fat

Immutable Factors. Our genetic makeup determines our nutrient requirements. Further, genetically defined characteristics such as age, gender, food allergies and sensitivities, and predispositions to certain diseases, such as diabetes, cannot be modified by external factors. In point of fact, these immutable characteristics dictate the quantity of nutrients essential to life and specify the types of foods that can be tolerated to deliver these nutrients.

For example, one's gender affects nutrient requirements directly. Women need more calcium throughout their lives and more iron and folic acid during their childbearing years. Men, because of their larger body size, often require additional quantities of calories, protein, and certain vitamins.

One's chronological age, another genetic determinant of sorts, is likewise a major factor affecting nutrient needs. Infants and young children need proportionately more protein and calories *per unit of body weight* than they do at any other point in their lives. However, because of decreased physical activity as well as a lower metabolic rate, elderly persons need fewer calories and B vitamins as they age. However, these physiological differences that influence nutrient needs explain very little about the food choices people actually make.

Some researchers believe that metabolic factors may play a role in dietary fat consumption. Eating fat may be an addictive behavior with a pleasure response modified by what scientists call "the endogenous opiod peptide system."[3] Thus, preferences for fat are not merely psychological; a physiological or metabolic component may be involved. Reducing dietary fat intake does not result simply from modifying behavior patterns. Interventions to educate people to consume less fat must also recognize and deal with what may be a powerful physiological component.

There may also be gender differences in preferred food sources of dietary fat. Men and women typically admit to liking their dietary fat in different forms. In one study, men and women listed "top ten" favorite foods. Women were more likely to express preferences for doughnuts, bread, and chocolate, while men listed steak, hot dogs, sausage, and eggs. The picture that seems to be emerging here is that men select protein/fat sources, such as meat, while women select carbohydrate/fat sources, such as doughnuts, cookies, and cake.

There is also a link between preferences for high-fat foods and obesity. Overweight people show elevated preferences for fat-rich foods. The higher the subject's body fat, the fattier the foods that person preferred. Conversely, in sensory evaluation studies, anorectic patients liked intensely sweet stimuli but disliked foods rich in fat.[4]

Consumers have told us that taste is probably the most important consideration when they shop for food. According to the Trends Surveys conducted by the Food Marketing Institute, taste was rated very important

90 percent of shoppers, followed by nutrition (74 percent), price (69 percent), and product safety (69 percent). These ratings have remained relatively consistent in surveys conducted annually since 1990.[5]

It used to be that scientists considered taste an acquired preference, a trait modifiable by factors such as accommodation, familiarity, or training. Researchers have now confirmed that genetics also influences our tasting abilities.[6] Persons with more densely packed taste buds on their tongues are "supertasters" and react more intensely to food flavors. While taste buds do not react to any flavor of fat, they react to its touch, sending that information through the trigeminal nerve to the brain. Fat molecules press against the taste buds, producing a tactile sensation that is interpreted by the brain as viscous, slippery, or greasy. Supertasters are sensitive to food fats and generally tend to eschew fatty foods throughout their lives. Most of us, however, are regular tasters, who truly like and enjoy the flavors that fat conveys in food.

Modifiable Factors That Influence Individual Food Choices. Just as certain immutable, physiological characteristics determine our *requirements* for certain nutrients, other factors—those under our direct control—are responsible for most of our *food choices*. These factors include one's beliefs, attitudes, and health concerns as well as one's knowledge of food and nutrition. One's lifestyle and health behavior patterns are usually greatly influenced by one's education, occupation, and disposable income.

Taste and habit are probably the two most powerful influences on food behavior. Our food habits are formed early and by a complex array of factors over which we usually exert little control. Psychosocial factors also strongly influence food choices. Individuals' positive or aversive food or eating experiences may make certain foods especially palatable or nauseatingly unacceptable. Likewise, simple familiarity with certain foods probably plays just as important a role in determining food choice in adulthood as it does during childhood. This is why changing adults' food habits in a more healthful direction is a formidable challenge to all who undertake it.

Food has psychological uses for some people, as an instrument to express certain emotions, such as coping with stress and tension by eating or not eating, or by eating certain "comfort foods" and avoiding others. Some of us even display our creative talents through the preparation of intricate or unusual dishes. Food likes and dislikes are the most important determinants of our personal food choices. But what influences food-related behavior is a much more complex story, which must be relayed in the context of our "national preference" for foods containing dietary fat.

Individuals' knowledge and attitudes about dietary fat also influence their dietary patterns. Fat is the number one nutrition concern of consumers, according to the 1995 Food Marketing Institute (FMI) Trends Survey. This has remained at the top of nutrition concerns since the 1990 FMI survey. Further, in the Food Marketing Institute/*Prevention* magazine Shopping for Health Survey, fat content is the primary reason consumers gave for not purchasing certain foods; 77 percent of shoppers stopped buying food products because of the amount of fat listed on the nutrition label.[7]

Although consumers profess to be aware of the link between diet and health, many are confused when it comes to applying the principles of healthy eating to limiting their consumption of dietary fat. Recently, when people were asked why they did not include foods they knew were healthful components of a good diet (such as vegetables, low-fat and nonfat milk, and whole-grain breads and cereals), they said these were foods they didn't like. Likewise, when asked why they didn't reduce their intake of less healthy foods (e.g., whole milk, high-fat cheeses, and fatty meat), respondents said they liked these foods *too* much.

When asked about their attitudes about eating, over 90 percent of consumers surveyed said they found eating "enjoyable." But behind that positive view of eating, there are some surprising concerns. Many Americans do not find eating pleasurable because they worry about fat, cholesterol, or weight gain or they feel guilty about eating the foods they enjoy. Food choices are made because Americans are searching for "good" foods, and trying to avoid "bad" foods. Most Americans are motivated to eat healthfully, but their interpretation of how to accomplish this often conflicts with their statement of how they enjoy food. As a result, many are eliminating certain foods, then feeling deprived, then splurging and feeling guilty. Most Americans have the basic knowledge to make healthful food choices but fail to understand and practice the basic nutrition principles of balance, variety, and moderation.[8]

Americans have a "love/hate" relationship with dietary fat. They want the flavor, the familiarity of high-fat foods, but they are increasingly aware that consuming too much dietary fat has negative health consequences. Survey data show a widespread *verbal* commitment to eating for health, but food consumption data show that declining consumption of beef, eggs, butter, whole milk, and other traditional contributors of dietary fat has been countered somewhat by an increasing consumption of cheese, premium ice cream, croissants, and rich desserts.[9]

Consumer awareness of the dangers associated with high-fat diets is at an all-time high. Despite some optimistic reports to the contrary, consumption of high-fat items has remained strong. Consumers find it difficult to adhere to dietary recommendations that call for consuming less fat. Why? Forces that compel us to head for the high-fat choices are strong. They include taste (low-fat foods simply aren't as tasty or appealing), expense (lower-fat foods and foods made with fat substitutes still cost more), and availability (lower-fat foods may be more difficult to obtain and prepare).

Dietary fat is indeed *powerful*. It is the substance in food that makes it "taste good," makes us feel "full" and "satisfied" after eating, and gives tender texture to pastry and other baked goods. Foods high in fat are those that "taste good," but many aren't "good for us," according to most dietary advice we receive. Thus, we *want* to eat high-fat foods, and they are widely available for us to choose.

Trends in the Consumption of Dietary Fat in the United States

Food Supply Data

Several types of data are used to document trends in the use and consumption of dietary fat. "Food supply" or "food disappearance" data furnish information about the gross *availability* of fats for human consumption. Data on production, imports and exports, military use, and beginning and year-end inventories are aggregated to describe the U.S. food supply. Per capita data are used with tables of food composition to estimate the nutrient intake of each individual.[10] Over the past twenty years, food supply data show an overall increase in the availability of total fat, nearly all of which can be accounted for by the increased use of polyunsaturated vegetable oils. Further, vegetable oils have partially substituted for fats from animal sources, such as lard. (At issue, frankly, is whether these oils are actually consumed. Vegetable oils have been used increasingly in recent years for frying foods served in fast-food restaurants. Operators of these establishments report that they discard about 50 percent of the oil they use.)[11]

Results from Dietary Surveys

As part of the National Nutrition Monitoring System, a number of government agencies routinely gather information about the food intake of the U.S. population. Five national dietary surveys were conducted in the 1970s and 1980s—the National Health and Nutrition Examination Surveys (NHANES) conducted by the National Center for Health Statistics (NCHS) in the Department of Health and Human Services (DHHS), and the Nationwide Food Consumption Surveys (NFCS) and Continuing Survey of Food Intakes by Individuals (CSFII) surveys conducted by the U.S. Department of Agriculture (USDA). Unfortunately, these surveys employed different sampling approaches, different methodologies for collecting dietary data, and different methods of interviewing and coding. Therefore, it is difficult to draw definitive conclusions about trends in American consumers' self-reported dietary fat intake.

However different their methodologies, these surveys do show that Americans have changed their consumption of dietary fat in recent years—both in the amounts consumed and in the food sources of that fat. The good news is that many have decreased their intake of total fat. In the 1977–78 Nationwide Food Consumption Survey, Americans were consuming approximately 41 percent of their calories as fat. The largest contributor to dietary fat was the meat, poultry, and fish group, followed by fats and oils, then dairy products.

In the mid-1980s, the figure for total fat consumption had decreased to 36–37 percent, and in the latest figures (1994), fats accounted for 33 percent of calories in the diets of Americans.[12] However, only about one-third of adults consume 30 percent or less of their calories from fat, the figure recommended as optimal by most health authorities.

American diets are changing in content and variety; also changing is where the foods are purchased and eaten. For example, Americans are eating more grain products, mainly as "mixtures" such as sandwiches and pizza. The consumption of these types of foods has increased 115 percent since the late 1970s and now accounts for one of the major sources of dietary fat. Further, over 50 percent of Americans eat away from home on any given day. Foods eaten away from home accounted for more than 25 percent of total calories and fat intake.

Saturated fat intake has decreased from 15 percent of calories in the late 1970s to 13 percent in the mid-1980s and to 12 percent in 1990. The meat group is the major dietary source of both total fat and total saturated fat. Milk and dairy products, as well as the fats and oils group, contribute significant amounts of total fat to the diet, paralleling the contribution from the bread group (which most people don't think of as a source of dietary fat) in the form of popular breakfast foods such as croissants and doughnuts, as well as baked desserts, such as cakes, pies, and cookies.

A meta-analysis study was conducted on 171 studies of fat intake published between 1920 and 1984.[13] The results of this study, when combined with more recent survey data, support an overall conclusion that there has been a weak trend toward lower intakes of dietary fat in the American population.

The "Low-Fat" Lifestyle

When people want to shift to a "lower-fat" diet, how do they do it? Nutritionists usually advise cutting down on "high-fat" foods and choosing more grains, fruits, and vegetables. Unfortunately, many find making this generic type of wholesale change difficult and unsatisfying. Adaptation to a low-fat diet does work, but it takes time (usually eight to twelve weeks) and is usually a function of how often lower-fat foods are consumed.[14] Further, the consumer must be vigilant and knowledgeable about the foods to choose. When dietary advice was first issued about limiting fat consumption, beef and whole milk were among the first products to show a decline in consumption. USDA data from the mid-1980s showed that while women were increasing their intake of fresh vegetables (usually in the form of salads), their fat consumption did not proportionally decline. Why? Because they were pouring on the salad dressing! The *type* of fat they were using had changed, but the *amount* had not.

Researchers at the Pennsylvania State University recently asked consumers who had successfully reduced the amount of fat in their diets how they did it. Of the nine fat-reduction strategies identified, those that accounted for the most significant reductions in fat intake included the following—decreasing fat flavorings, such as spreads and dressings; decreasing "recreational foods," such as snacks and high-fat desserts; decreasing cooking fat; replacing meat with more grain-based entrées and mixtures; changing breakfast from eggs and meat to cereal and fruit; and using fat-modified foods.[15]

Typical consumers want to change their diet, but not too much. Those who wish to switch to a healthier, low-fat diet usually recognize that they will probably not be on any regimen for long unless it contains some of their food favorites. So the demand has been created for products that are lower-fat versions of the ones with which people are familiar. Consumers want to "change without changing." For example, instead of giving up chocolate-chip cookies for fruit snacks, many people opt for popular low-fat brands of cookies (like SnackWell's®). What may happen, however, is that they end up eating the whole box instead of one or two cookies, resulting in decreased fat consumption but certainly not decreased calorie intake. According to the NPD Group, which has been conducting surveys on eating trends in America since 1980, 86 percent of Americans consume at least one low-fat or no-fat food every two weeks, and "better-for-you" foods (e.g., lower-fat versions of products) now account for nearly one-third of all grocery purchases.[16]

Food processors are responding to the demand for low-fat versions of longtime favorites. On average, more than a thousand new low-fat and fat-free products have been introduced annually since 1990, according to the International Food Information Council. And most of these foods are designed to taste identical to their full-fat counterpart.[17]

Clearly, advances in technology and new ingredients are a driving force behind the development of high-quality fat- and cholesterol-reduced foods, and the market for these types of foods is driven by high consumer demand. As the demand increases, food processors face a challenge to deliver well-rounded flavor and mouthfeel as well as reduced fat and calories in new products. This trend of "getting the fat out" has become a multibillion-dollar phenomenon, and the use of "fat replacers" has become the food industry's method of choice for delivering the taste, but not the calories, of fat in food favorites.[18] And of course, all such food additives are subject to the regulatory power of Food and Drug Administration (FDA) policy making. The story of the regulatory process for one fat replacer in foods, olestra, is the subject of a case study in this book.

I have just made the argument that although making major dietary changes is quite difficult, there has been a slight decrease in the amount of dietary fat consumed by most Americans since the 1980s. In the final chapter of this book, I will discuss whether government policies (such as those presented as case studies in this book) are linked to such dietary shifts.

Health Aspects of Dietary Fat Overconsumption

The main reason why fat is the subject of this book is that overconsumption of this dietary favorite is one of the greatest menaces to the health of the American people. The top ten leading causes of death in the United States are heart disease, cancer, stroke, accidents, lung disease, pneumonia/influenza, diabetes, liver disease, arteriosclerosis, and suicide. Of these, five (the top three, plus diabetes and arteriosclerosis) are associated with dietary excesses or imbalances.[19] The major dietary components correlated with U.S. mortality are dietary fat and excess calories. Since much of the excess caloric intake is in the form of fat, it can be concluded that consuming too much dietary fat is indeed one of the major causes of death in the United States today.

A seminal study recently attempted to identify and quantify the major factors that contribute to death in the United States.[20] Recognizing that the effects of dietary factors and physical activity patterns were virtually impossible to distinguish, they were considered together as a single entity. However, even with this qualification, the conclusions of the study were staggering—300,000 (14 percent) of the 2.1 million deaths in 1990 could be attributed to poor diets and/or inadequate physical activity! As the surgeon general so clearly stated in 1988, "For the two out of three adult Americans who do not smoke and do not drink excessively, one personal choice seems to influence long-term health prospects more than any other: what we eat."

The main conclusion [of this report] is that overconsumption of certain dietary components is now a major concern for Americans. While many food factors are involved, chief among them is the *disproportionate consumption of foods high in fats.*"[21]

The most recent report of the Joint Nutrition Monitoring Evaluation Committee, established by both the U.S. Department of Agriculture and the Department of Health and Human Services, the two most prominent government agencies involved with food and nutrition issues, issued a startling indictment of dietary fat. The 1991 report stated that the principal nutrition-related health problems in the United States today (coronary heart disease, adult-onset diabetes, hypertension/stroke, and certain types of cancer) are *all* attributable to overconsumption of fat, saturated fat, cholesterol, and sodium.

An even more emphatic statement was made by the authors of Eat for Life, the National Academy of Sciences' Food and Nutrition Board's "Guide to Reducing Your Risk of Chronic Diseases": "Without a doubt, *fats* and cholesterol are the single most important group of nutrients to limit in your diet if you want to help to reduce your risk of chronic disease."[22]

Each year, all diet-related diseases cost our nation over $200 billion in direct and indirect costs. Population-based interventions to encourage Americans to reduce dietary intake of saturated fat may prevent tens of thousands of cases of coronary heart disease (CHD) and save billions of dollars in related costs. If Americans reduced the average amount of saturated fat in their diets from the current level of about 12 percent of total calories to 9 percent, about 100,000 first-time coronary events (such as heart attacks, which are estimated to cost some $13 billion in health care) could be prevented by the year 2005.[23] Another estimate shows that if Americans reduced their daily intake of saturated fat by only 8 grams (from 13 percent of calories to 10 percent)—the amount in an average-sized doughnut—2.3 million fewer Americans would have heart disease and the health care system would save as much as $24 billion annually.[24] What more evidence is needed to show that dietary fat is indeed a menace to health? With such compelling economic implications at stake, dietary fat is assuredly an important public policy issue—for *all* Americans, not just for a select few.

Policy Aspects of Dietary Fat

Dietary fat makes a perfect topic for the study of nutrition policy because governmental actions affect the supply and demand for foods containing fat at virtually every point along the food chain. Starting at the beginning where food is produced, feed grains, such as corn and soybeans, are supported by an elaborate system of governmental price supports and commodity subsidies. These commodities are then transformed into popular foods, such as meats and dairy products, whose production is supported by government-approved price supports, import quotas, pricing policies, and the like. Even at the food-processing and distribution stages, governmental policies such as grading policies, standards of identity for processed foods, marketing orders, and food-labeling regulations act in concert to influence the types of foods made available for consumer purchase. At the consumption stage of the food system, the government is again involved: government agencies issue dietary guidance materials giving advice to the general public about what they should eat, thus indirectly influencing consumer demand for certain food items. The irony in all this is that governmental actions that are more directly related to food consumption usually take the form of consumer information campaigns, less "powerful" policy tools than government-sanctioned efforts affecting the supply of food.

How did this story on "dietary fat in the policy arena" get started? The earliest federal nutrition policies were designed to strengthen the agricultural production system and to ensure a consistent and adequate food supply. As a result, food production increased, and farmers began to produce more food than could be consumed. In these early years, foods that were high in dietary fat (e.g., dairy products, meat, oils) were a symbol of prosperity and a prominent contributor to the economy.

The image of certain nutrients has changed over time, and fat is a good example. At the turn of the twentieth century, those individuals who were heavier, even obese, were perceived as being more affluent and prosperous. Lean, gaunt looks were associated with being poor and unsuccessful. Further, actuarial statistics kept by life insurance companies suggested that leaner people were more prone to develop tuberculosis, a primary cause of mortality at the time. Hence, heavier individuals were thought to be more resistant to this dread disease and were rewarded for their obesity by being levied lower life insurance premiums.

As research garnered evidence about the deleterious effects of dietary fat on human health, fat's favorable reputation began to tarnish. Even the food industry was caught in this shift. Rather than continuing to process only those tasty, high-fat foods, the food industry responded by creating a variety of ersatz fat substitutes carrying the mouthfeel of their genuine cousins. Where was government? Its primary actions in recent years have been to continue supporting research, in a documentable but minor way, and to issue dietary advice to consumers, such as, "Avoid eating too much dietary fat." However, the fundamental, more "powerful" governmental actions, at the level of food production and processing, prevail to keep high-fat foods plentiful and affordable.

Some maintain—and it is also the conviction of this author—that "government's role is to make health-promoting choices *easier* and health-damaging choices *more difficult* to make."[25] There are those who believe that if we know what to do to improve the health of Americans, we should enlist the power of government to enable that to be done. However, others feel that the government has no business intervening or altering personal lifestyle habits. Those who support this view assert that the matter of dietary choices is purely a personal one. They say that government's responsibility is to provide the public with science-based dietary recommendations, which consumers can choose whether or not to follow.

In the past, governmental actions have largely concentrated on supporting the more entrenched, powerful forces on the "supply side" of the food chain, resulting in economic incentives, subsidies, price supports, and market orders for producing, processing, and marketing a variety of foods, many that are high in fat. Government has listened to market forces and rewarded economic incentives for producing high-fat foods more consistently than it has attended to the demands from health professionals for policies that would make following a low-fat diet easier. History and tradition also play a powerful role. It is obviously much more difficult to "undo" existing governmental laws and regulations (many of which were enacted in the 1930s and 1940s) than it is to modify or initiate new actions in response to the latest scientific thinking. Such policies are backed by the fact that high-fat foods appeal to most people—they like them; they choose them.

For the most part, current government policies are designed to support those private-sector decisions that reinforce and make easier those behaviors that are health-damaging. The ubiquitous nature of convenient, tasty high-fat favorites, and the millions of dollars spent to advertise them, have far exceeded any government-supported efforts to educate the public about the longer-term, not immediately evident, benefits to health of consuming a lower-fat diet. Governmental policies affecting the "demand side" of the equation have mainly taken the form of weaker policy actions, such as providing education and supporting research. Strategies that are designed to change personal well-entrenched behaviors have a much more difficult task than strategies that positively reinforce current—albeit harmful—habits. This is indeed the case with nutrition education campaigns that seek to change the American public's love affair with high-fat foods. Educational strategies are, by their very nature, usually less forceful and ultimately less immediately successful than broad-based structural or environmental strategies, especially when they are overwhelmed by billions of dollars in food advertising, much of it for high-fat foods.[26]

This book focuses expressly on *public policy* (i.e., the role of government)—and how it affects the food we eat. What is the appropriate role of government in influencing consumers' food choices, and what form should this involvement take? In this book, I will answer these questions by describing how the government has intervened to affect the kinds and amounts of food produced. I will describe the nature of agricultural policies as well as regulatory actions that affect the kinds of foods, and food ingredients, that are offered to the public—some of which are more health-damaging than others. We will also comment on the effectiveness of government-sponsored informational campaigns that are designed to influence consumers' "demand" for more healthful foods. Further, I will show that government policies have consistently lagged behind science and have failed to keep pace either with the marketplace or with consumers' diet and health concerns.

Chapter 2

Policy Making—The Art of Sausage Making

If you like laws and sausages, you should never watch either one being made.

—Widely attributed to Otto von Bismarck

Policy—the very word conjures up images of government, marble-columned buildings, stuffy politicians, smoke-filled rooms. While such may be the substance of mental caricatures, policy is actually all about *people*! Policy is made *by* people *for* people. The derivation of the Greek word, *polis*, conveys the notion of a person as *citizen*. Policy—in some form or another—affects each of us in our everyday lives, touching us in the most unexpected moment or the most mundane of circumstances. Who among us hasn't experienced the vagaries of a check-cashing "policy," a merchandise return "policy," or, for the university reader, a course drop-and-add "policy"?

While the more general term *policy* can be applied to any set of rules for activity, *public policy* is the term used when the government is involved. Public policy is what government *does*, the action that a government takes (or does not take) to respond to a problem. A public policy may also be called a law, a rule, a statute, an edict, a regulation, an order. The policy may be very specific, as in a law that might make it illegal for stores to sell cigarettes to minors, or it can be stated in rather broad and general terms, as in the myriad regulations that govern interstate commerce. However, if it is determined that a problem is outside the scope of governmental control or is not resolvable by intervention, a public policy can certainly involve a decision to do *nothing*.

Public policy is composed of two elements, the first of which is an officially stated intention or goal to address the problem. The second element states the means that government proposes to use to achieve those goals; these techniques can take the form of rules, procedures, or sanctions, which use either reward or punishment techniques. There may be many public policies to pursue many goals, but there are very few methods of control that government can employ to fulfill those purposes.[1]

One need not look far to witness the wide-ranging effects of public policies. Public policy affects virtually every aspect of our everyday lives—from what we earn (and then the amount withheld for taxes!) to where we can afford to live, to what we wear, and, yes, to what we eat and drink. In sum, policy is about those rules and guidelines developed to meet people's needs; public policy evolves when government is involved, presumably acting in the best interests of its people, the citizens of the land.

The Policy-Making Process: Government in Action

Public policy making is a dynamic, evolving process that results when individuals and groups force government to act. As Charles Lindblom has observed, "[Policy making] is a complex analytic and political process to which there is no beginning or end, and the boundaries of which are uncertain."[2] Policy making is a continuous process, subject to evolving scrutiny, tested by time, and evaluated by experience. Indeed, many participants are involved in this process, some more powerful than others, who by compromise and consensus work to attain mutually agreed-upon goals. The policy-making process, by definition and by the nature of the process involved, can be—and probably should be, to ensure fairness to all viewpoints—time-consuming and deliberate. Anytime one group focuses attention on how government should be involved to meet an existing need or solve an identified problem, competing groups or forces should be able to voice concerns and be assured that such concerns will be heard and respected in the discussion. "A policy is never static. It is continuously shaped by the process that forms it as it moves from conception to adoption, implementation, evaluation, and reformulation. Its beginnings are in the past and its development depends on the attention of those who care about it, despite hostile or indifferent environments. A policy may not so much end as be transformed by the social climate and specific organizational environment under which it evolved."[3]

Policy making is not as enigmatic a process as many think, nor is it perfect. The process remains basically the same, no matter what the issue. Legislative policy flows from the political decisions of ordinary citizens (whether farmers or advocates, producers or consumers) and their organizations, through the ballot box in which all voters may register their choices, to the political parties as an instrument of power, to the strategies and tactics of particular bills. Policies reflect people's ability to harness the power of governmental action to respond to their organized and articulated needs. Thus, policy, in essence, is built on the will and desires of certain groups of people who have been able to direct the force of government in a particular way.[4]

Incrementalism in Policy Making

Incrementalism has been defined as "decision making through small or incremental moves on particular problems rather than through any comprehensive reform program."[5] This definition certainly applies to the usual course of policy events in the areas of food and nutrition. Generally, incrementalism favors reliance on past experience as a guide for new policies, careful deliberation before policy changes, and a rejection of rapid or comprehensive policy innovation. Public officials strongly favor making and changing policy incrementally. As Charles Lindblom has stated, "Policy making typically is part of a political process in which the only feasible political change is that which changes social states by relatively small steps. . . . Hence, decisionmakers typically consider, among all the alternative policies that might be imagined to consider, only those relatively few alternatives that represent small or incremental changes from existing policies."[6]

Incrementalism as a mode of public policy change permits policy makers to draw upon their own experience in the face of unfamiliar problems or new challenges and encourages the making of small policy changes "at the margins" to reduce anticipated, perhaps irreversible, and politically risky consequences. But incrementalism can also inhibit innovative thinking and stifle new solutions to issues. If policy makers treat new issues and deal with new scientific developments in the same old, familiar ways, we are doomed to repeat our failures of the past. We must encourage and reward creative, innovative thinking so that effective, responsive policies can result.

This warning is especially salient when it comes to changing or forming new policy solutions to food and nutrition issues. The times are *not* the same as they were in the 1930s, when direct governmental assistance to farmers and consumers was warranted; in the 1950s, when new technologies were encouraged and strictly regulated; or in the 1980s, when governmental actions were minimized and the marketplace was relied upon to provide all the answers. New, courageous, strategic thinking and policy decisions—such that the power of government will be creatively used to improve the health of the American public through their food choices—will be needed to guide food and nutrition policy into the next millennium.

Federalism in Policy Making

Defined as "the division of powers and functions between the national government and the state governments," federalism is one of the most fundamental influences on public policy.[7] In effect, writers of the Constitution created a "confederacy" of two sovereigns—the national government and the state governments. For nearly a century and a half after the Constitution was ratified, virtually all of the fundamental policies governing the lives of American citizens were made by the state legislatures, not by Congress. Federalism also restrained the economic power of the national government, creating a system of strong state and weak national government. It was not until 1937 that a Supreme Court decision permitted the national government to regulate local economic conditions in a case involving interstate commerce.

Federalism has also allowed a great deal of variation from state to state in the rights enjoyed by citizens and in the roles played by governments. During the past half century, we have moved toward greater national uniformity in state laws, but even today federalism continues to permit significant differences among the states.

The concept of "conjoint federalism" most appropriately describes the nature of federal and state responsibilities in food and nutrition policy.[8] The federal government establishes laws, regulations, and national standards, but the responsibility for implementation and enforcement is usually handed off to the states. In some cases, concurrent enforcement efforts can occur. States may impose more stringent food inspection codes, for example, than stated in federal policies. State attorneys general were most active in the food-labeling debate in the late 1980s and freely exercised their right to strongly enforce state statutes and local ordinances. Other related issues such as the inspection of food-handling operations, the licensing and credentialing of nutrition service providers, and the delivery of federal food assistance programs are all under the jurisdiction of state and local authorities.

The Stages of Public Policy Making

The public policy process describes how government deals with public problems.[9] The process of policy making is actually a very dynamic one in which a number of participants—including those outside the government (such as influential professional organizations, consumer advocacy groups, and trade associations) as well as those within government (such as legislators, bureaucrats in the executive branch, and their research and investigative groups)—work toward attaining mutually satisfactory goals by compromise and consensus.

Policy researchers and policy makers alike have broadly embraced the "stages" heuristic to describe the public policy process. The most authoritative statements describing this approach can be found in Charles O. Jones's *An Introduction to the Study of Public Policy*[10] and James E. Anderson's *Public Policymaking*.[11] This model of policy making (illustrated in Figure

Figure 2.1 **The "Policy Stages" Model**

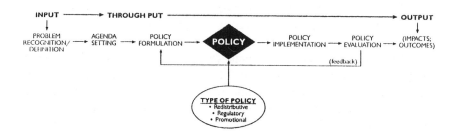

2.1) describes a linear process, starting with problem recognition and definition, followed by agenda setting, policy adoption, implementation, and evaluation. This series of stages is set within a broader environmental context characterized by federalism, political institutions, public opinion, and other constraints. Each of the stages in the process involves distinct periods of time, political institutions, and policy actors. The model does not explain *why* policies take the shape they do, but it is useful for examining those factors that are active at each stage of the policy process.

The following discussion elaborates on each of these stages in terms of the actors involved and the nature of the policy process at that stage. Further, the interaction of government institutions with forces outside the government (such as interest groups and influential parties) at each stage as they formulate or change policy is described.

Stage 1: *Problem Recognition and Definition*

The development of a public policy begins with recognizing that there is a problem that can be solved or alleviated by governmental action. This situation occurs when some highly undesirable social condition exists but has not yet captured widespread public attention, even though some experts or interest groups may already be alarmed by it. The extent of hunger and malnutrition among America's children has consistently been one such issue.

Ethical and ideological perspectives play an important role during this first stage because groups with different perspectives will "see" and define problems differently. In order to put such views in proper context, various types of information are required. These include data or results drawn from scientific research studies, social indicators such as demographic changes and trends, and results of program evaluations or demonstration projects. A sound knowledge base is important at this stage to accurately document the nature and the extent of the problem.

Stage 2: *Placing the Issue on the Political Agenda*

After the problem has been recognized and defined, the proposal may be placed on the policy agenda, depending on the strength of the political forces behind the proposal and policy makers' perception of its importance. The process by which issues compete—successfully——for the attention of policy makers is called agenda setting. Charles O. Jones has referred to this phase as "the politics of getting problems to government."[12] The process of agenda setting is much like "gatekeeping," with the policy makers deciding which items go onto the agenda and which do not. Moving an issue onto the public agenda may, in fact, be the most difficult step in achieving policy change. An issue may be so sensitive that policy makers or public attitudes work to keep it from reaching the agenda-setting stage. In other situations, an issue may be perceived as a problem by only a small number of people who lack the political clout to get the issue onto the instiutional agenda. Yet in other circumstances, the agenda-setting process may take place quickly; major catastrophes—such as earthquakes, riots, and famines—frequently trigger public outcry to such an extent that the issue is pushed almost "effortlessly" onto the policy agenda.

The mere recognition of a problem that can be alleviated by governmental action is not always sufficient to ensure that the issue will be placed on the policy agenda. Given the tremendous number of problems clamoring for the attention of policy makers, getting a problem on the policy agenda is a major challenge. A problem is placed on the policy agenda when there is a convergence of public attention, political interest in responding to public concern, and "policy entrepreneurs" who are able to channel the political energy toward policy changes.[13]

In order to get an issue on the public policy agenda, attention must be drawn to certain scientific facts in such a way that one or more reasons provide an incentive for governmental action. The media provide a forum by which attention-hungry policy makers can join forces with other interested parties, both within and outside of government, to take action on issues of shared interest. The media have often been instrumental in bringing public attention to problems defined by professionals and are useful at this stage for galvanizing public interest in the problem. If the general public becomes convinced that a problem exists, it will more often generate attention from public officials. As demonstrated by analyses examining the hunger problem in the United States, if people lose interest or public officials no longer want to deal with the problem, attention is diverted elsewhere and policy initiatives are no longer supported, even if the problem continues to exist.[14]

Stage 3. *Policy Formulation*

In the third stage of the policy-making cycle, an issue placed on the policy agenda is further defined, additional information about the problem is collected and discussed, alternative solutions are considered, and a preferred choice of action is decided upon. Decision makers—with the input of interest groups, policy experts, and constituents—debate and bargain over alternative policy formulations, selecting an alternative or a combination of alternatives to respond to the problem. Public policy is shaped by groups that have deployed their resources to influence the form, pace, or direction of policy making in ways that will enhance—or at least not harm—their own interests. The business of policy making often involves an ongoing struggle among conflicting values, vested interests, and ambitious personalities. Setting policy almost always involves striking a balance between the scientific evidence and the values, priorities, needs, and concerns of stakeholders and constituents. A complex balancing act is usually required to satisfy consumer concerns, industry interests, scientific principles, and budget realities.[15]

The debate and shaping of public policy take place, of course, within the general social, political, and economic environment of the United States. They occur, as well, within a context specific to each policy area. These contexts include the institutional context (the unique features of the American political system and the public's perception of the appropriate role of government), the economic context, and the demographic context.[16] While it appears that interest on the part of the American public in food and nutrition is at an all-time high, there continues to be spirited debate as to *how* and *whether* the federal government should influence America's eating behavior in a more healthful direction.

It takes at least two elements to formulate new public policy—a sound information base, coupled with a supportive political climate. Good, hard facts, presented in a persuasive fashion, are usually necessary to convince policy makers that a problem exists. Such evidence—drawn from scientific research data, program evaluation results, or amassed testimonials—should describe the nature of the problem and promote the reasons for government action as the best means to resolve the problem. But information alone usually won't be sufficient to force policy makers, anxious to win the next election, to act. Policy making also requires a "supportive political climate." This means that the general public (or at least several policy makers' local constituents) must be generally supportive of the actions proposed (or at least not violently opposed to them).

Information-driven academics and pragmatic politicians regard the roles of sound information and a positive political climate very differently. Many academics see policy making as a systematic, rational process of finding the best solution to a social problem; they place a premium on the power of information and analysis to influence decisions. Action-oriented politicians (usually those more responsible for implementing policy rather than studying it) tend to think of policy making as a "pragmatic art" and value the fact that decision making occurs in the context of uncertainty, conflicting values and interests, and incomplete information. This view relies on the force of the "political climate" and supports the value of compromise, negotiation, and incremental solutions as part of the decision-making process. Research, analysis, and the "right" information represent only one group of inputs to the policy-making process. Other factors such as personalities and personal agendas contribute to a dynamic, often unpredictable, process in the view of the pragmatist. These two perspectives were dramatically illustrated in the tensions between the White House "policy wonks" and the congressional "pragmatists" in the struggle to control the direction of health care reform.

Historically, most enacted policies follow public opinion. Different types of policies may be enthusiastically supported, merely accepted, or vociferously opposed by the public, thus lending another element to be considered in the implementation of public policy. Many express amazement that public policy is ever formulated in the first place given the complexities of the process.

Lawmaking and Representation: Role of the Legislative Branch

In this country, most policy formulation is in the form of legislation. Laws that initiate, modify, authorize, and appropriate funds for all programs and services administered by the federal government are passed by the Congress, the central core of the legislative branch. Although Congress is usually thought of as an amorphous institution, one must not forget that Congress is, first and foremost, *people*. The members of Congress—all 100 senators and 435 members of the House of Representatives—have stood for election to office. It is their responsibility to assume three roles: a lawmaking role, a representative role, and a constituency service role. While in Washington, they are collectively making and passing laws, but it is the effectiveness with which they perform the representative and constituency service roles for which they were primarily elected to office and by which they stand for reelection.

In addition to the 535 members of Congress, there are nearly 12,000 staff assistants who work with members in various capacities, from answering constituent mail to tracking legislative initiatives, from bartering on issues (on behalf of their employer) to actually drafting legislation. The legislative branch also counts among its members those individuals who work on congressional committees and various research arms of Congress (such as the Congressional Research Service, the Congressional Budget Office, and the General Accounting Office).

The Legislative Process

The general process through which a bill passes on its way to becoming a law is shown in Figure 2.2. Actually all of the specific steps can be combined into six major phases—introduction; committee action; scheduling for vote in either the Senate or House; decision; conference (if the House and Senate versions of the bill differ); and finally, executive action by the president of the United States. Although congressional procedures may seem overly complex, technical, and time-consuming, these very characteristics encourage parties to achieve consensus and compromise. Such procedures also serve to protect the interests of minority views by giving them the means to affect the course of legislative decision making. Members of the public—whether they be concerned citizens or paid lobbyists—can take the appropriate actions if they know the steps in the legislative process as well as key decision makers and their responsibilities at each step of the process.

In any given year, between ten thousand and fifteen thousand bills are introduced in Congress. Because of the volume of work and the potential for chaos in such a large legislative body, certain rules and procedures—as well as personalities of the lawmakers—influence how the system works. Party leadership, the committee structure, and procedural rules all greatly affect the legislative process. Obviously, the number of members who vote to support a bill is essential to passing legislation. However, it is more often the passion of a bill's sponsors about the topic and their ability to propel it through complicated committee discussions and floor voting procedures that determine whether or not any particular piece of legislation will eventually be passed.

What has just been described is the rational, ideal model for policy making. All too often, policy making depends on capturing the force of raw emotion (either positive or negative) to create an action. Lobbyists know that if a legislator cares passionately about their issue, they can harness that extra measure of energy to capture yet another vote. Thus, the "making" of public policy involves bringing together those individuals and groups (even the media) who together want to change the status quo in the direction that they deem desirable, and will work to do so.

The policy formulation stage results in ... *policy*! This can come in the form of legislation, regulations, executive orders, or "policy statements."

Figure 2.2 **How a Bill Becomes Law**

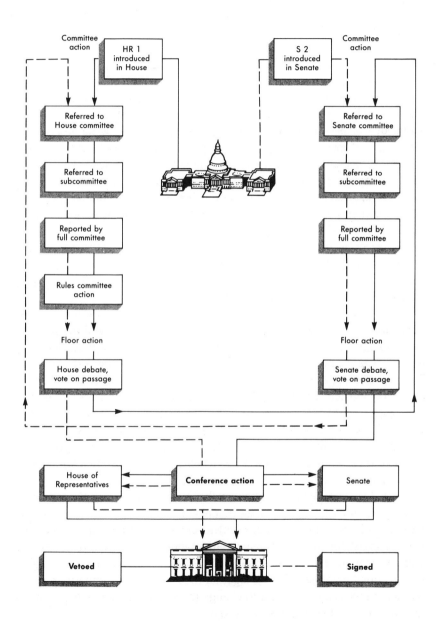

Source: Guide to Current American Government, Congressional Quarterly: 119, 1996.

Although policy can assume any number of forms, it must be publicly exhibited and articulated to be valid.

Types of Policy

Early on, I described public policy has having a goal statement accompanied by a suggested means by which government action could be used to achieve that goal. These means of government action, or "techniques of control," have been classified by Theodore Lowi into four primary types— distributive, redistributive, regulatory, and promotional.[17] All such policies, according to Lowi, are coercive because they seek to alter individual and societal conduct. Each type of policy has a different way of controlling behavior and has different implications both for the way the policy-making process works and for the implementation of those policies that result.

Distributive policies are aimed at promoting private activities that are argued to be desirable to society as a whole and, at least in theory, would not or could not be undertaken without government support. Such policies provide subsidies for those private activities and thus convey tangible government benefits to the individuals, groups, and corporations subsidized. Formulation and implementation of distributive policies are likely to be accompanied by relationships between the recepient and congressional representatives or government bureaucrats that are disaggregated or individualized, that involve "logrolling" (i.e., the trading of votes or exchanges of support among legislators), and that are usually removed from the public's attention. The key decisions—i.e., who is to receive benefits and how much they are to receive—are usually made by legislators who have a considerable interest in ensuring that recipients can clearly trace the origins of the benefits given them. Examples of distributive policies include many that affect agriculture and food production such as direct cash payments for purchase of agricultural commodities, permits for grazing on public lands, and even grants for scientific research in land-grant universities.[18]

Redistributive policies are used to alter the allocation of wealth, property, or some other valued item among social classes or racial groups. The redistributive feature enters because for the most part benefits are distributed to the less advantaged at the expense of those who are better off. The policy-making process is often marked by high degrees of visibility and conflict. Such policies are often ideological; they raise basic issues about the proper role of government in societal and economic matters. Food assistance programs that require governmental intervention, such as food stamps and the National School Lunch Program, are examples of redistributive policies.

Regulatory policies seek to alter individual behavior directly by imposing standards on regulated industries or set the conditions under which various private activities can be undertaken. Conditions thought to be harmful (such as false advertising) are prohibited, while conditions thought to be helpful (such as nutrition information on food labels) are mandated. Such policies are likely to arouse controversy because private interests may be significantly constrained or have compliance costs imposed on them by regulatory actions. Powerful interest groups are likely to be organized around regulatory issues, and the interaction of these policy advocates plays an important role in determining the nature of the policy. Regulatory policies often involve complex, technical decisions for which appropriate policy actions cannot easily be determined. Because technical or scientific information is likely to be important in decision making, the role of experts in administrative agencies and interest groups is vital. In this book, regulatory policies are described as they influence the nature of information offered to consumers on the food label and the safety of food additives allowed in new food products.

If regulatory policies are considered the "sticks" of public policy, the fourth type of policy, *promotional techniques*, is the "carrots." The purpose of these policies is to encourage people to do something they might not otherwise do or to get people to do more of what they are already doing. Often such policies are not the product of enacted legislation or promulgated regulation but exist as "approved" documents that have the "force" of policy. Examples include the Dietary Guidelines for Americans, a document revised with the inputs of nutrition experts every five years to provide dietary guidance and advice to consumers. (This topic is the subject of a case study that follows chapter 7.)

Stage 4: *Policy Implementation*

Implementation refers to the process of putting a policy into action. Implementation may be defined as the carrying out of public policies, achieving the actions promised when policies are devised, or the forging of the required links in a causal chain that will accomplish the goals articulated for the policies.[19] The implementation process involves writing regulations, spending money, enforcing laws, hiring employees, and formulating plans of action. Implementing public policy is often a long, complicated procedure that includes interpreting congressional intent, balancing statutory and presidential priorities, creating administrative structures and processes, reviewing congressional debates on policy formulation as regulations are proposed, and building political support for enforcement of regulatory requirements.

The implementers of public policy in the United States are primarily those unelected employees of federal, state, and local governments who work with private organizations, interest groups, volunteers, and other parties to carry out government policy. Such a description closely depicts the "separation of powers" decreed by the Constitution—i.e., Congress makes the laws, and the executive branch implements them. In reality, the line between the creation and the implemention of public policy is often blurred; those charged with implementing laws are frequently the same individuals who helped to create them.

What happens at the implementation stage is affected by numerous other elements. Even seemingly simple programs can be difficult to implement if there are numerous participants with differing perspectives and if many specific decisions must be made before the policy is fully implemented. One example involves the wording of public laws or decisions: a law enacted by Congress and signed by the president is often vaguely worded as a result of the bargaining and negotiation needed to get a majority to support the bill. The resultant document may provide unclear implementation guidelines to the bureaucracy. Other problems may also exist. Insufficient resources may have been appropriated for adequate program implementation. Two or more agencies may have been given authority for implementation. An agency charged with implementing a given policy may even be hostile to it and can end up undermining and subverting the program in its implementation.

Policy Implementation and Regulation: Role of the Executive Branch

Implementation and enforcement of laws are the responsibility of the executive branch, headed, of course, by the president of the United States. The cabinet secretaries are political appointees, as are many of the administrators of subcabinet agencies; in Washington parlance, those who hold their positions as a result of a political appointment are referred to as "Schedule Cs." Others in the executive branch—tens of thousands in number—are civil service employees.

The Regulatory Process

Congress grants the fundamental authority to an administrative agency to engage in policy making through regulatory tools that include informal methods, rule making, and adjudication. The most important activity of these executive branch agencies is rule making, the mechanism by which agencies that are to implement the law actually spell out the particulars that are embodied by a piece of legislation.

Some executive branch agencies, but not all, are considered to be regulatory agencies—"a government body, other than a court or legislature, that exercises control or authority, subject to the rule of law, over certain private parties by establishing rules and/or making binding judgments that affect the rights of those parties."[20] Regulations are written by the agency to carry out the intent of Congress; these statements issued by agencies in the executive branch carry the power of law and can be legally enforced with fines for noncompliance. How closely the regulations carry out the legislative intent may depend on whether the philosophy and policies of Congress and the agency officials coincide. When the president and the majority of Congress are of the same political party, there is usually some degree of unanimity. When they are of opposing parties, some discrepancies may be noted between the legislation and the proposed rules and guidance materials.

Regulatory Tools

Regulatory tools include *rule making, adjudication*, and *informal methods*. The most important activity of agencies is rule making, a process of setting the rules or regulations that define the requirements for implementing the law.[21] In rule making, the agency issues a public statement of general or particular applicability and future effect. Public comment and input are encouraged before final rules are promulgated. The "final rule" must also undergo approval at both the agency and the administration level by the Office of Management and Budget (OMB).

There are also actions called "interim final rules," that fall somewhere between a "proposed rule" and a "final rule." An agency usually adopts interim final rules when it is rushed to issue a regulation but because of congressional time mandates, public crisis, and so forth it doesn't have time to go through the proposed-stage process. Interim final rules do provide the public with an opportunity to comment, but an agency is likely to make only minor changes.

Another process used when the regulations proposed are particularly contentious to all parties is called "negotiated rule making" or "neg-reg."[22] This procedure is growing in use and involves bringing all the parties together to hammer out a new rule with a "skilled neutral" such as the Federal Mediation and Conciliation Service. Unlike traditional rule making—in which the agency takes the lead, proposes the rule, and asks for written comment—neg-reg is done face-to-face. It is usually a short-term process and results in rules that seldom, if ever, are challenged in court. Proponents of the method say it avoids some of the biggest pitfalls of rule making in the more traditional manner—lengthy delay, impasse, vicious bickering, or endless proposals about which no one can agree.

The *Federal Register*, a daily publication that totals hundreds of thousands of pages a year, is an invaluable tool for monitoring regulation. It is the only publication that prints *all* notices and rules proposed and adopted by federal agencies. The companion document, the *Code of Federal Regulations* (CFR), is a compilation of *all* general and permanent agency rules; it consists of approximately 140 volumes under 50 titles. The CFR is updated annually to include all of the final rules that have been published in the *Federal Register* since the last edition of the CFR.

In addition to rule making, significant agency policy decisions also result from either "informal actions" or adjudication. *Informal actions* include inspections, meetings, recalls, and advisory opinions. (The term *informal* may be misleading because these actions are informal only in a legal sense. To the agency and to the regulated industry, they can have the same impact as any formal action.)

An *adjudication* is basically a decision issued by the judicial system determining how the law is to be carried out. The outcome of adjudication or the court decision is called an "order," similar to the "rule" that results from the rule-making process. In addition to these mechanisms of action, of course, administrative agencies use a variety of informal means to articulate policy under a statute; these may include press releases, speeches, statements, letters, advisory opinions, and other types of communications.

Results of Policy Implementation

Policy implementation results in outputs and impacts. *Policy outputs* are the tangible manifestations of policies, the observable and measurable results of policy adoption and implementation. Stated another way, outputs are what governments do in a particular policy area; the policy outputs of the food stamp program include the moneys spent, coupons printed, poor persons served, personnel hired. *Policy impacts* (also called policy outcomes) are the effects that policy outputs have on society. They are the policy's consequences in terms of the policy's stated goals as well as of the society's fundamental beliefs. For price supports or marketing orders on fluid milk, major impacts include the total amount of money paid to the dairy farmer or the price of milk to the consumer.

Stage 5: *Policy Evaluation*

The fifth stage focuses principally on the impact of policy, because we usually equate policy success or failure with the observed performance and consequences of that policy. Evaluation attempts to assess the outcomes of a policy—its effects on society—in order to compare them with the policy's intended goals. It asks whether the goals have or have not been met, with what costs, and with what unintended consequences. It considers whether policy is equitable and efficient (i.e., uses resources well) and whether it has satisfied the interests of those who demanded action in the first place.

Ideally, a policy should be evaluated only after it has been implemented. However, in the "real world," it rarely happens this way. Because evaluation is part of the policy-making cycle, it can be viewed both politically and technically. Evaluation is inherently political because those people who support a policy or program are likely to believe that it has succeeded, whereas those who are ideologically opposed are likely to conclude that the program has failed. Evaluation also has a technical component because it involves a formal, institutionalized process that draws on scientific principles and both qualitative and quantitative methods to help policy makers make good decisions about what has and hasn't worked. It is important, however, that understanding the facts derived empirically precede judgment about whether or not a program will continue. Policy evaluation must therefore be accompanied by empirical analysis of policy content. Such data (and the conclusions reached from such analyses) are often used by congressional committees as they perform program oversight and provide "feedback" for those who seek to change or modify existing policy. Another form of policy "evaluation" may occur in the courts; the judicial branch, including the Supreme Court and other federal court systems, has responsibility for legal oversight of the activities of both of the other branches of government. The judicial branch is infrequently involved in issues involving food and nutrition because most of the guidelines are governed by rules enforced by the regulatory agency in the executive branch. The judicial branch generally becomes involved only when there is evidence that legal authority has been violated and when legislative and executive branch (regulatory) options have been exhausted. In 1973 and 1974, class-action suits in the federal courts successfully forced the release of program funds for the Supplemental Nutrition Program for Women, Infants, and Children (more commonly referred to as "WIC") that had been impounded by the president.

Policy Subsystems

In addition to the "policy stages" heuristic to describe the public policy process, a second means developed to systematically examine and analyze the public policy process has been that of the *policy subsystem*. Policy issues are usually so vast and complex that only select groups, both from within as well as outside the government, act to influence the process and outcome.

A generation ago, political scientists were using the concept of the "iron triangle" as the vehicle for studying political subsystems; the three key components of this approach were: (1) the congressional committees or subcommittees dealing with a certain issue; (2) the executive agency that administered the program or performed a regulatory function by which the program operated; and (3) the lobbyists, who represented the executive branch agency's central clients. Employing the iron triangle model assumed that the policy areas were relatively "closed" and that there were stable relations among a limited number of participants.[23]

The iron triangle model soon became outdated for analysis of today's complex issues. The process for formulating public policy no longer is based on a predictable, closed, autonomous system. Rather, today's public policy issues rely on systems of disaggregated power, with a number of participants (both in and out of government) flowing in and out of the decision-making process for various lengths of time.

The "policy subsystem" approach to the study of public policy is preferred when analyzing today's public policy issues for several reasons. First, there has been a proliferation of interest groups, each vying for the attention of lawmakers and agency executives. Obviously, legislators do not wish to ignore representatives of constituents back home, no matter how outrageous their cause. Thus, as new groups push to become integrated into a subsystem, the process becomes more open to the public and less exclusive to Washington insiders.

A second reason for using policy subsystems as a tool for policy analysis is that the congressional structure has changed. In the past few years, the number of subcommittees has grown immeasurably. However, the increasing overlap of policy-making authority among subcommittees has opened the policy-making process to more interested parties. Since the November 1994 elections, legislators have reduced the number of congressional committees and subcommittees and have vowed to shrink the size of the legislative branch of government. It remains to be seen whether these actions will actually reduce the size and approach of interest groups and their strategies for lobbying.

Subsystems evolve because of a society's need to divide tasks and promote the development of knowledge. Subsystem actors develop policy expertise and continuing relationships with one another in areas of direct interest to themselves. Any major public policy arena consists of a complex set of semiautonomous subsystems that are organized around programs or even such narrow issues as titles within major legislative acts.

Policy subsystems can be characterized by networks of actors, their substantive policy domain, and various modes of decision making. Such subsystems are decentralized power structures, with close informal communications among their participants, organized to make focused demands on the political system and to influence specific programs—not to win elections or to form governments. Participants in these policy subsystems consist of representatives of interest groups, members and staff of congressional committees and subcommittees, bureau and agency personnel in the executive branch, and other policy specialists from universities, state and local governments, and the media.

Policy subsystems are characterized by their shared knowledge base directed toward a *specific* public policy issue. The boundaries identifying a policy subsystem may be fuzzy, but the glue that holds the group together is really the technical mastery of the subject matter that all parties possess.

Thurber[24] has described these subsystem participants as exerting a "cyclic" mode of influence. In their various roles, these participants move issues onto the public agenda, develop and pass legislation, make rules and regulations, prepare and pass budgets, and administer and implement programs, as well as evaluate and modify them. The specialized media, those professional journals and newsletters associated with specific interest groups or government programs, also frequently play a key role in subsystems and often are the only public windows to the subsystem's activities. In contrast, the generalized national news media are usually uninterested and unaware of these activities unless a crisis or scandal surrounding a subsystem's decisions arises. (Witness the national media attention focused on the topic of meat inspection that occurred in 1993 after several children had died from consuming hamburgers tainted with a particularly deadly strain of the E. coli bacterium)

Organized Interests

It has been said that politics is "the process of who gets what, when, and how."[25] If government is the entity that makes the rules determining who will get what is valued in a society,[26] then it is important to identify the groups that influence the policy process and the means they use to sway governmental action. Policy subsystems are dominated by organized interests that rally around specific focused public policy actions.

Subsystem actors are active in each phase of the public policy process that has previously been discussed in this chapter. Various organized interests (also commonly referred to as "interest groups") are active participants in the attempt to influence the development of food and nutrition policy in both the legislative and administrative arenas. Food and nutrition issues—especially those that deal with the dietary fat issue—are no stranger to interest groups. The number of such groups has proliferated in recent years, causing one to wonder if there will ever be enough monetary, logistical, and emotional support to sustain their existence for long.

Lobbying has long been regarded as the most direct means that organized interests use to gain access to lawmakers and regulators. Whether lobbying is primarily a response to emerging issues in the political environment or a reflection of the biases of activist elites remains a topic for debate. One view of lobbying is that it is a healthy influence within the political system that keeps Congress informed about issues, stimulates public debate, and encourages participation in the political process; others view lobbying as a far less benign activity. Indeed, lobbying activities are entirely legal and available to consumer groups as well as to food producers.

The Advocacy Coalition Framework

Sabatier and Jenkins–Smith are credited with conceptualizing the "advocacy coalition framework" (ACF) (Figure 2.3) as a means of understanding policy change, which they see taking place as the product of competition between several "advocacy coalitions."[27] An advocacy coalition is a grouping of policy actors from a variety of public and private institutions and from all levels of government who share a set of basic beliefs and who seek to change policy in order to achieve these goals over time. Further, the advocacy coalition approach aggregates actors within a policy subsystem into a manageable number of belief-based coalitions. According to the advocacy coalition framework, policy change over time is a function of three sets of processes. The first involves the interaction of competing *advocacy coalitions* within a policy subsystem. The second set of influences deals with *changes external to the subsystem*, such as changes in socioeconomic conditions, systemwide governing coalitions, or output from other subsystems that provide opportunities and obstacles to the competing coalitions. The third set of processes involves the effects of *stable system parameters*, such as social structure and constitutional rules, on the constraints and resources of the various subsystem actors.

The ACF assumes that coalitions are organized around common beliefs in core elements (such as the power of an unregulated marketplace or the role of government in influencing personal behavior), which change only as a result of factors external to the subsystem, such as macroeconomic conditions or the rise of a new systemic governing coalition. Coalitions seek to learn about policy making and the effects of various government interventions in order to realize their goals over time. This "policy-oriented learning," as Sabatier and Jenkins–Smith refer to it, is usually confined to more secondary aspects of the coalition's belief systems.

Several aspects of the ACF have been confirmed using several case studies

Figure 2.3 **The Advocacy Coalition Framework**

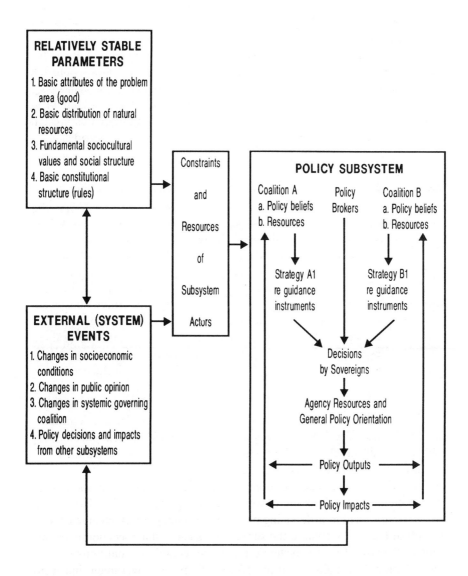

Source: P.A. Sabatier and H.C. Jenkins–Smith, *Policy Change and Learning: An Advocacy Coalition Approach*. Boulder, CO: Westview Press, 1993, p. 229.

as "real-world" data points to test the analytical framework. First, most policy subsystems, and the coalitions within them, include actors from multiple levels of government, and members of a specific coalition will use a variety of agencies at different levels of government in order to achieve their policy objectives.

Further, technical information (i.e., scientific evidence) and formal policy analysis play an important role in policy change. Such information is generally used in an advocacy fashion—that is, to buttress and support a predetermined position. Policy analysis (and the policy-oriented learning it creates) will not by itself lead to changes in the policy core of a coalition or public policy. Learning across coalitions is more likely when an intermediate level of conflict is involved, when the issues can be analyzed systematically, and when a professional forum is utilized. Policy-oriented learning can be subdivided into two components: first, fundamental normative precepts (which are nearly impossible to change); and second, precepts with a substantial empirical component, which, although still very difficult to change, can be altered over time through the accumulation of compelling evidence from a variety of sources.

Yet another attractive feature of the ACF is that it offers guidance about *how* coalition members seek to alter policy in specific situations. Sabatier and Jenkins–Smith argue that administrative agencies have the most direct impact on a coalition's ability to achieve its policy objectives because agencies are the institutions that actually deliver services or regulate target group behavior. Members of a coalition usually concentrate their efforts on agencies and officials that are relatively sympathetic to their point of view while seeking to minimize the authority of unsympathetic governmental units.

The advocacy coalition framework is used as the analytical framework of choice to examine the case studies presented in this book. The ACF model lends itself well to analyzing policy change in the food and nutrition arenas because it utilizes such ubiquitous features as scientific evidence, policy entrepreneurs, advocacy coalitions, and advisory boards or professional forums.

Summary

This chapter has introduced the reader to the nature and scope of public policy and the policy-making process. Further, two models were presented that can be used to describe and analyze policy making—the "policy stages" process and the "policy subsystems" model. The reader was introduced to the analytical model that will be used to examine the case studies presented in this book, the advocacy coalition framework. The next chapter will focus specifically on these processes as they apply to policy making in the food and nutrition arenas.

PART II

PUBLIC POLICY
IN THE FOOD SYSTEM

———— Chapter 3 ————

Public Policy and Bureaucracy in the Food System

At every step in the contemporary food chain, federal policy shapes the likelihood of what food producers will or will not do, and what people will or will not eat.

—N. Milio*

All of us are familiar with eating; *most* of us are familiar with shopping and preparing food; yet very *few* of us are familiar with food production, by gardening or farming. Further, what most of us don't realize is how government is involved at every step of the process—from food production to food consumption, even to the effects and impacts of what we eat. In this chapter, we consider more specifically the various stages of our food system and the nature of government's involvement at every point in the food chain. In addition, the chapter describes current food and nutrition policy and how it might be changed in the future to incorporate health and environmental concerns.

For decades, food and agricultural policy has been dominated by political and economic groups whose major concerns centered around producing food in quantities large enough that farmers would have a decent income and consumers could buy food cheaply. Other than harboring isolated concerns about adulterated or contaminated food, most consumers rarely made food choices on the basis of health concerns. In recent years, our abundant food supply—and the types of food choices now being made by Americans—combined to result in a situation in which many in our population now experience increased risk of certain chronic diseases, including those that are the leading causes of death in the United States. Agriculture's success story has become public health's nightmare. Nutrition has emerged as the link between agriculture and health concerns. This chapter will de-

---

*N. Milio, *Promoting Health through Public Policy*. Philadelphia: F.A. Davis, 1981, p. 150.

scribe food policy as it currently exists in the United States, positioning for a time when health concerns become linked with those of agriculture to form a true nutrition policy.

Overview of Current Food and Nutrition Policy

Although some may refer to food and nutrition policy synonymously for the purposes of simplicity of the argument, I submit that food policy is *not* nutrition policy. Food policy is designed to answer the question of what shall be produced and the related questions of how much, for whom, and at what price. Food policy is the outcome of legislation and government decisions aimed at providing food for the population, and it incorporates a wide range of measures for fiscal, trading, political, social, or consumer protection reasons. Many food policy questions focus on quantitative distinctions (i.e., producing *enough* food) versus qualitative distinctions (i.e., what *kinds* of food to produce). A food policy does not necessarily include any explicit consideration of health other than ensuring that sufficient food is available in a form that is safe, i.e., free from microbiological contamination or toxic effects.[1] In contrast, nutrition policy is the interface between food production—i.e., agricultural policy—and health concerns. It considers the impact of agricultural policy to include effects on human health as well as on the quality of the environment.

While agricultural policies directly affect the nature of the food supply, health/medical policy and environmental policy are both affected by and influence food consumption practices. Nutrition policy can no longer be considered synonymous with food policy or solely within the domain of agriculturalists. Health policy, especially that branch that addresses health promotion and disease prevention activities, has embraced nutrition as an essential element of chronic disease–prevention policy. Therefore, nutrition policy is an "intersectorial" type of policy, based on a paradigm of "food *plus* health" sector policies.

Nutrition policy is a prime example of linking scientific findings and consumer demand with government action. Nutrition policy has been defined by the World Health Organization (WHO) as "a concerted set of actions, often initiated by governments, to safeguard the health of the whole population through the provision of safe and healthy food."[2] Indeed, nutrition is an ideal area in which to demonstrate how the principles of health promotion can be incorporated into public policy. Food intake, in terms of its nutritional value as a major influence on health, involves issues of both individual choice and the social environment and certainly is susceptible to modification through changes in social and economic policy.

Nutrition policy includes a number of elements, ranging from the availability of safe, wholesome food to providing food security and services, such as education and health care. Identified as the most salient policy components in nutrition are the following six elements:

- Providing an adequate food supply at reasonable cost to consumers
- Ensuring the quality, safety, and wholesomeness of the food supply
- Ensuring food access and availability to those lacking resources or those unable to obtain sufficient food for themselves
- Providing research-based information and educational programs to encourage the public to make informed food choices
- Supporting an adequate science/technical research base in food and nutrition
- Improving access to and integrating nutrition services into preventive health care and medical services[3]

Despite calls in the late 1970s to develop and implement a comprehensive nutrition policy structure in the United States, no *single*, comprehensive policy yet exists.[4] In 1975, Senator George McGovern, then chairman of the Senate Select Committee on Nutrition and Human Needs, described his view of nutrition policy at that time as lacking focus, direction, and coordination, all factors that were contributing to growing conflicts within the administration over program priorities.[5] Nearly a quarter of a century later, nutrition policy remains fragmented.

One challenge faced by those who seek to centralize federal decisions in the areas of food and nutrition is the choice of agency that could serve as the "power base" responsible for final decisions. This task is both complex and politically sensitive because nutrition policy cuts across several policy areas, and no single federal agency can claim exclusive jurisdiction over these issues. In the United States, as in most developed countries, powerful economic interests are represented in the U.S. Department of Agriculture (USDA) and their allied constituents in major farm and food enterprises. Health interests, especially those supportive of preventive health services, in contrast, have a yet fledgling, but growing, "home" in the Department of Health and Human Services (DHHS), in agencies such as the Food and Drug Administration (FDA), the Centers for Disease Control and Prevention (CDCP), and the National Institutes of Health (NIH). Despite the fact that the U.S. Department of Agriculture was named the "lead agency" for nutrition in the 1977 Farm Bill, the Department of Health and Human Services has repeatedly disputed this claim because of its extensive array of research and educational programs in nutrition and health. Herein lies the dilemma of implementing effective intersectorial nutrition policy, thought by many to be the most effective means for implementing effective nutrition policy.[6]

Rather than a coordinated, comprehensive set of policy directives, nutrition policy currently exists as a mosaic of distinct, but related, health, social, and food-related programs, each with its own set of objectives and expected outcomes. Some policy scholars believe that such a mosaic of programs still serves as policy: "[W]e can assume that no matter what was intended by government action, what is accomplished *is* policy."[7] In sum, current domestic nutrition policy, in large measure, has emerged collectively as policy set in a number of separate—distinct, yet related—arenas, in response to environmental events, research findings, and consumer demands for particular foods and types of information.

Historically, government was directly involved with agriculture and food production through an elaborate system of direct assistance (in the form of price supports, subsidies, and the like) to farmers. In recent years, however, food and nutrition policy has become the focus of scrutiny from those concerned about the effects of long-standing food consumption practices on personal health and the impact of traditional agricultural practices on the environment.

In the United States, the primary policy approach currently used to influence food choices has been market-oriented, focused on the demand for food, viewing the outcome as consumers in a marketplace who need information to select certain goods and services. Educating the public about food and health is the public policy strategy preferred by most developed nations.[8] Providing information *alone*, however, is rarely sufficient to create widespread, substantive changes in food consumption patterns. In order for consumers to make healthful food choices that can be sustained over time, they must not only receive dietary advice but also have access to an adequate supply of affordable, healthful food. This book adopts a normative approach that the U.S. government must be committed to a strategy by which current food policy is modified to accommodate health concerns, focusing on prevention as a strategy and improved health of the American population as a desired outcome.

Historical Trends

Any discussion of governmental involvement in food and nutrition requires a basic understanding of the historical development of the evolution of food production, processing, and distribution; "lifestyle changes" among Americans; and significant developments in scientific and public health events. The nation's system of governmental policies—including food regulation, health legislation, and dietary guidance—has, in effect, resulted from changes in the food supply and changing concerns about public health and consumer protection.

The U.S. population in the early twentieth century was a geographically disperse, self-reliant people, dependent on the land for survival. (Agricultural policy was dominated by concerns of land settlement, primarily because there was plenty of land and few people to farm it.) Food was what you could grow, raise, or get at the local market. Choices were limited, and diets were what today we would describe as quite monotonous.

Upton Sinclair's exposé of the meatpacking industry, *The Jungle*, was credited as the impetus behind the passage of the first food safety laws, the Pure Food and Drugs Act of 1906 and the Federal Meat Inspection Act of 1907, which dealt with issues of adulterated food and fraud in the food-processing industry. More important, perhaps, is the fact that these laws acknowledged that the federal government had a responsibility and the legal authority to ensure a safe and wholesome food supply.[9]

In cities where concentrations of people created greater health hazards, public health activities were centered on issues dealing with sanitation and the control of acute, communicable diseases. At the turn of the century, government's role in the health arena began as an enforcer of quarantine rules and, fueled by medical advances, emerged in the 1920s as a proponent of vaccines and antibiotics as a means of reducing the prevalence of acute infectious diseases. The field of nutrition was born in the first years of the twentieth century, with the discovery of the first vitamin in 1908. For the next few decades, nutrition scientists were busy discovering many such compounds in food and elucidating their chemical structures and their metabolic roles. Home economists with the USDA's Cooperative Extension Service and nutritionists in public health agencies carried out educational programs to inform the public about how to choose foods and consume diets that would prevent nutrient deficiency diseases.

After World War I, with the help of government grants and sponsored research, agriculture began to incorporate new technologies, more capital investment, and more efficient farm management into its operation. The result of all these scientific developments and technological innovations was the creation of an efficient, integrated food production system, supplying the United States and the world with seemingly endless quantities of food.

The Great Depression of the 1930s created an economic disaster never before witnessed by U.S. citizens. Among the hardest hit were farmers. To compensate for their losses, the U.S. government developed a two-pronged approach—first, providing price supports and compensation for crops, and second, distributing excess food commodities directly to poor people.

From the mid-1930s to 1970, the index of aggregate food and farm output approximately doubled. The number of people employed in farming declined by two-thirds. The number of farm operations dropped by more than half. An increasingly large share of total agricultural output was being produced by a smaller number of farms. In addition, the marketing subsector and the farm service–farm supply subsector expanded and changed in economic structure, resulting in consolidation of individual units. The effect throughout the food system was further concentration of volume and service in fewer and fewer firms.[10]

As the food supply became more complex and new food products were developed, government assumed an increasingly important role in safeguarding the food supply. The passage of the Federal Food, Drug, and Cosmetic Act of 1938 was a milestone in providing the FDA with a broad array of legal authorities with regard to the nutrient content of food, such as establishing mandatory food standards, requiring a statement of ingredients, and prohibiting false and misleading labeling.[11] As nutrition scientists completed the identification of the structure of a number of the essential vitamins, the technology by which they could be synthesized in the laboratory was developed, and this new knowledge was applied directly to improve the food supply by means of enrichment and fortification programs.

As the food supply expanded and new markets were found, there was a need to develop better means of packaging and storing food for transport. This demand was most urgent during World War II, when the need to mass-produce and transport food to the American troops abroad was most urgent. After the war, the food industry boomed. New products were developed, new packaging and processing techniques perfected, and new marketing techniques employed. The result is that the American consumer today has more than twenty thousand different items available in the supermarket from which to choose.

As more scientific evidence accumulated about the nutrients—their structure, function, interactions, and human requirements—this information found its way to policy uses. Nutrition experts' efforts to establish quantities of nutrients needed to plan food supplies to feed military troops resulted in the publication of the "Recommended Dietary Allowances" in 1941, a report that describes the amounts of nutrients needed by groups of healthy people and is continuously revised to reflect the latest scientific findings. The National School Lunch Program was established in 1946 to feed schoolchildren a nourishing meal, an effort begun because so many young men had failed to pass their military induction physicals because of poor nutrition.

With most infectious diseases under control in the 1950s, medicine's attention turned to chronic disease, such as cardiovascular disease and cancers, and to conditions caused by genetic factors, such as congenital malformations and inborn errors of metabolism. Beginning in the 1960s and continuing through the present, there has been a surge of interest in the prevention of chronic disease and public health's interest in establishing programs to "promote health and prevent disease."

As science has discovered the links between diet and the risks of certain chronic diseases, the government has sought to provide research-based dietary advice to consumers, culminating in the first edition of the Dietary Guidelines for Americans in 1980. Further, the government has sought to provide information to consumers about the nutritional content of the food they are eating in the form of nutrition information on food labels. A voluntary program enacted by the FDA in 1973 was expanded by the passage of the Nutrition Labeling and Education Act (NLEA) in 1990.

The government's interest in nutrition and in providing dietary advice was motivated in part by the changing demographics of the population. With more of the population living longer, nutrition was seen as having a role in the quality of life of the aged and therefore could contribute to decreased health care costs.

This brief review of historical trends in agriculture, science, technology, and medicine has demonstrated that governmental interest in agriculture and food policy has tended to follow scientific developments and technological advances. As the general public awareness about health and fitness increased, it became inevitable that the government would become interested in nutrition. Unfortunately, governmental interventions have seriously lagged behind both new scientific findings and consumers' concerns about the links between food and health, causing many to voice concern over future policy directions in nutrition.

Stages of the Public Policy Process

One of the most prominent models used to describe the policy-making process is that of the "stages" heuristic, widely embraced by political scientists to describe the linear sequence of recognizing a problem, defining policy-based solutions, implementing that policy, and evaluating it. That general model was described in chapter 2. This section shows how the stages model can be applied to a description of changes in food and nutrition policy.

Stage 1: Problem Recognition and Definition

In the topical areas of food and nutrition, there are certainly many "problems." In the context of this book, however, we examine those problems that may exist and can best be addressed by using government policy mechanisms. Certainly, in a scientific field, the strength of the scientific evidence is key to defining the importance and the parameters of the problem. The second question that must be answered, of course, is, Can the government do anything about this problem?

In the late 1980s, nutrition emerged as a salient public policy issue with the publication of two landmark reports: *The Surgeon General's Report on Nutrition and Health,*[12] a 1988 publication, and the National Research Council's *Diet and Health: Implications for Reducing Chronic Disease Risk,*[13] which was published in 1989. While previous reports had acknowledged the relationship between diet and health, it was the scientific credibility of these two reports that legitimized the proposition that diet and nutrition were indeed linked to the leading causes of death in the United States. Spurred on by the power of these two reports, nutrition competed—successfully, this time—for governmental action, resulting in the passage of two major pieces of legislation in the 101st Congress in 1990: the Nutrition Monitoring and Related Research Act (Public Law 101-445) and the Nutrition Labeling and Education Act (Public Law 101-535), both of which had been under consideration in various forms by Congress for nearly a decade.

The strength of scientific evidence is certainly an important element in creating nutrition policy. But what if the evidence gathered is less than complete? When do we know *enough* to proceed? The criteria listed below have been suggested as a guide for making policy decisions. We should proceed when

- It can be demonstrated that the need is great
- An action produces the desired benefits
- The risks are not too high
- The intervention is economically feasible
- There are no viable, more scientifically certain alternatives[14]

Some have questioned whether we know "enough" to advise Americans to follow a low-fat diet to prevent the risks of certain chronic debilitating diseases. Most of the scientific evidence offered to date fits the above list of criteria quite well. Although some uncertainties exist, in view of what we know about dietary benefit and harm at this time, current dietary advice offers prudent policy. We must remember, however, that further research on dietary change and its effects on chronic disease is still warranted and encouraged.[15]

The issue of dietary fat as a public policy issue has passed the "litmus test" of the first stage. It clearly is a problem—Americans consume too much dietary fat, leading to increased risk of chronic disease, which costs the economy millions of dollars each year for treatment and lost wages. The second question that must be answered is, Can the problem be solved or alleviated by policy means? The answer again is clearly "yes" because a variety of policy instruments may be employed to assist Americans in making more healthful food choices.

Stage 2: Agenda Setting

After the problem has been debated and defined, it is necessary to capture the attention of policy makers so that they can place the problem on the "agenda," meaning that forum in which policy solutions can be debated and discussed. The political environment must be receptive to a cause before it can gain approval from policy makers. Further, it is helpful if the public is aware and supportive of the issue.

Nutrition rarely appears as a separate issue. Improved nutrition and other food issues are often linked with other political concerns—such as health care reform, welfare reform, economic security of farmers, or even national defense—in order to be acted upon. The voting public must view the issue as important to them, and politicians must perceive that sufficient public sentiment and "voter value" are associated with the cause before they will support it.

A good example of this dynamic occurred in January 1995 when the Republicans gained leadership in both houses of Congress for the first time in forty years. Pressure to cut the federal budget dominated the political agenda, reflecting the popular sentiment of the voting public. One of the first actions taken in the House of Representatives was the introduction of the Personal Responsibility Act, which targeted the food assistance programs for massive budget cuts to offset an enormous budget deficit. Consumer and nutrition organizations set to work to change political sentiment from one of budget cutting to one of government's taking responsibility for feeding vulnerable people. One influential group that represents a large portion of the voting public, the American Association of Retired Persons (AARP), convinced the House not to include feeding programs for the elderly as part of welfare reform. The AARP's sheer numbers and voting clout forced the House to maintain the Nutrition Program for Older Americans (NPOA) without change.

In March 1995, the House voted to "block-grant" a number of food assistance programs, including the school meals programs. The American School Food Service Association (ASFSA), however, fought back and challenged the prevailing political sentiment in the Senate. At first, the Senate, especially Senator Richard Lugar (R-Indiana), chair of the Agriculture Committee, favored the block grants for school meals programs. The ASFSA stepped up its lobbying efforts by sponsoring several media events to gain public support—inviting President Bill Clinton to a school cafeteria for lunch (to which the local press was also invited) and leading a march on Washington, which included young students, concerned adults, and several celebrities. As a result, the Senate changed its position on block-granting the National School Lunch and Breakfast Programs.

Stage 3: Policy Formulation

Once a decision has been made that the problem is amenable to policy solutions, then the process of choosing what policy to create is started. Regulations, executive orders, "memoranda of understanding," and the like are all considered to be forms of policy, but the most commonly encountered type of policy is that of a law.

Legislative Involvement

Given the crucial role played by congressional committees in initiating and modifying legislation, a review of those most germane to food and nutrition issues will be presented. Several House and Senate committees have direct legislative responsibility related to food and nutrition issues and often exert a "gatekeeper" function in the public policy process. After the 1994 elections, Republicans took control of the Congress and redesigned the House committee structure.[16] The Agriculture Committee has direct responsibility for various farm and commodity issues; food safety and inspection (the latter a newly added function); food assistance programs, notably food stamps; and oversight of USDA-managed education and research activities. The Commerce Committee provides oversight on industry and trade issues. The Technology and Competitiveness Committee is involved with oversight of the science and research base of nutrition and food issues, as well as with nutrition monitoring. The Education and Economic Opportunities Committee deals with food assistance programs, notably the National School Lunch and Breakfast Programs. In the Senate, the Agriculture, Nutrition, and Forestry; Labor and Human Resources; Government Affairs; and Finance Committees all deal with comparable nutrition and food-related issues.

Policy Instruments

In formulating public policy, the most appropriate policy instrument for the task must be decided. Those in policy-making positions can choose from among several specific techniques to alter individual and group behavior that can be employed at various points along the food system. The choice of policy instrument varies according to the policy objective sought, the constraints on the system and the capacity of the government to implement such policy instruments effectively, and the ability of the affected participant to utilize the designated policy tool and respond appropriately.

There are two basic types of policy instruments: (1) those that attempt to modify the food supply or (2) those that affect the demand for food. These two types of policy instruments are summarized in Table 3.1. Those policy instruments that affect the food supply are more direct, and, some say, more effective in actually changing consumer behavior. In effect, these strategies directly influence the types and amounts of food available for consumption; examples include actions such as product seizures, favorable pricing policies, direct distribution of food, or provision of meals. Food supply policy instruments also include price supports, production quotas, and marketing orders.

At the level of farm production, long-standing policies such as commodity price supports, crop subsidies, insurance against "acts of God," and even direct governmental purchase of certain commodities have been in place for decades. As the food supply has become more complex, governmental interventions—usually in the form of regulations to inspect, grade, standardize, and label foods—were enacted. These are direct controls with which the food industry must comply in order to offer its products for sale in interstate commerce. The marketing and distribution phase of the food chain is also governed by certain governmental operations in the form of marketing orders (primarily used for milk and dairy products) and pricing structures (tied in with production quotas and supply management techniques).

Examples of policy instruments that are intended to affect demand are market-driven. They include programs such as food labeling, price incentives, or informational campaigns, in an effort to persuade or entice the consumer to make particular food choices. Except for highly motivated consumers, these latter strategies have not been nearly as effective at changing behavior as they have been at creating awareness of nutrition. It is simply unreasonable to expect large numbers of the population to make individual behavior changes that are discouraged by the environment and existing social norms.[17] Tactics such as informational campaigns, however, are usually favored by policy makers, because they are viewed as a way to limit direct governmental interference and promote individual decision making.

Stage 4: Policy Implementation

After a policy instrument has been chosen and the standards for its use decided upon, the policy must be implemented. Usually, this task falls to an agency within the executive branch of government. In recent years, private-

Table 3.1

Types of Policy Instruments

Stage of the food system	Food supply policy instruments	Food demand (market) policy instruments
Production	Prohibit, limit or change production of certain crops, livestock; require production or provide price supports for lean meat or low-fat dairy products.	Encourage producers to produce only certain crops, lean meat, etc.
Distribution	Prohibit, limit distribution to certain food items; prohibit supermarkets from stocking certain products.	Encourage marketing of low-fat foods; allow unrestricted growth of new low-fat foods or food ingredients.
Promotion	Designate how foods should be promoted, e.g., labeling programs, warning statements, sales.	Competitively exploit certain markts and segments, e.g., low-fat foods.
Sale/consumption	Prohibit, limit sale of a product, e.g., ice cream with high fat content.	Reduce or increase costs by competitively using certain markets, mass production, price reductions; informational and educational campaigns.

Source: Adapted from R.A. Winett, A.C. King, and D.G Altman, "Legal/Regulatory and Free-Market Approaches to Modufy the Production, Distribution, Promotion, and Sale of Food". In "Steps to Make North American Diets Health Protective," *Health Psychology and Public Health—An Integrative Approach*, 1989, p. 273.

and public-sector "partnerships" have been favored as a mechanism for accountable policy implementation.

The Role of the Executive Branch

A number of administrative and regulatory agencies within the executive branch has direct responsibility for implementing of a variety of food and nutrition programs and for carrying out those regulatory activities mandated by Congress. Most of the laws enacted that affect nutrition, food, and health are passed to the U.S. Department of Agriculture or the Department of Health and Human Services for implementation.

The various agencies within the U.S. Department of Agriculture administer those programs related to food and nutrition "from the farm to the table" and beyond. For example, the Food Safety and Inspection Service (FSIS) and the Animal and Plant Health Inspection Service (APHIS) both deal with food safety issues, while Food and Consumer Services (FCS) administers the various food assistance programs. A new unit, the Center for Nutrition Policy and Promotion, has both a research arm, which analyzes data from food consumption surveys, and a "promotion" arm, which provides science-based educational materials for professionals and consumers based on the Dietary Guidelines for Americans. The Agricultural Research Service (ARS), the Economics Research Service, along with the Cooperative State Research, Education, and Extension Service (CSREES), has primary responsibility for conducting both extra- and intramural research and outreach programs in the department. Other activities of the USDA will be described in more detail throughout this book.

In the Department of Health and Human Services, the Food and Drug Administration, in particular, has direct responsibility in the area of food safety, food labeling, and approval for newly developed food ingredients, such as fat substitutes. Other agencies within the DHHS include the Administration on Aging (AOA) (with oversight responsibility for feeding programs for the elderly); the National Institutes of Health, which supports research and training programs in nutrition; and the National Center for Health Statistics (NCHS), which carries out surveys and other health data collection activities in conjunction with the National Nutrition Monitoring System.

The Regulatory Process

Executive branch agencies are given the authority by Congress to spell out how the law should be implemented; this process is called "rule making," and the instructions developed through this process are called "regulations" or "rules." An agency's "proposed rule" is published in the *Federal Register* and usually allows for a thirty-, sixty-, or ninety-day comment period. During this time, all interested parties are invited to submit reactions, analyses, or ideas about how the regulation should be modified. After the close of the comment period, the regulatory agency is obligated to review and record all comments and analyze them systematically. After a period of time for review and consultation with the Office of Management and Budget (OMB), the "final regulations" are published once again in the *Federal Register*. Those unhappy with the wording of the final regulations may appeal to the regulatory agency. Once published, the final regulations are then "codified" by being published in the *Code of Federal Regulations* (CFR), which is updated annually. Most regulations pertaining to foods can be found in Title 21 of the CFR.

The "negotiated rule making" ("neg-reg") procedure, which is invoked when proposed regulations are contentious and vigorously opposed by certain parties, was recently brought to the attention of the food and nutrition community. School food service administrators dissatisfied with the USDA's proposed rules for changing the school lunch program threatened in 1995 to invoke negotiated rule making in order to arrive at a mutually satisfactory agreement. Negotiations with the USDA were successful, however, and it was not necessary to invoke this approach.

Different agencies have different assigned responsibilities for regulation. Produce ingredient standards, labeling procedures, food additives, and the like are handled by the Food and Drug Administration, while the USDA's Food Safety and Inspection Service handles similar responsibilities for meat and poultry products. The Federal Trade Commission (FTC) is responsible for regulations pertaining to food advertising, while the Environmental Protection Agency (EPA) is responsible for regulations dealing with pesticide residues, standards for pure water (with the exception of bottled water, which is the FDA's responsibility), and the like.

Figure 3.1 is a visual representation of the various policy goals, instruments, participants, and strategies, according to the stages of the food system. The reader is challenged to think about how the current situation can be modified to accommodate concerns about production of more healthful food and protection of the environment.

Policy Subsystems

A second approach that had proved useful to policy scholars who seek to understand the public policy process is studying *policy subsystems*, those various groups and actors who focus attention on a particular part of the policy process or topic. Because the issues facing food and nutrition policy are so vast and complex, the concept of policy subsystems is a most useful one for examination and analysis.

Organized Interests

Interest groups that seek to influence issues of food and nutrition policy include trade associations, professional associations, and consumer advocacy groups. Trade associations may represent a particular phase of the food system, such as processing or marketing, or they may represent commodity-specific issues. For example, groups that represent farmers and focus their attention on issues dealing with production agriculture include the American Farm Bureau Federation, National Farmers Union, Farm Credit Coun-

Figure 3.1 Public Policy as Applied to the Food System

	Farmers	Food Industry	Food Distributors: Transportation Segments; Food Storage/Preservation	Retail food sales; Food service establishments; Vendors
PARTICIPANTS				
THE FOOD SYSTEM	INPUTS → Seeds, seedlings; fertilizer or feed equipment. FOOD PRODUCTION/ AGRICULTURE: FARMING. Farm commodities: e.g. grains (wheat, oats, corn), feed grains. animals for food, e.g. beef, dairy, produce, etc.	Commodities → FOOD PROCESSING & MANUFACTURING. Processed, Packaged Foods → Inspected, to Packer	Processed, Packaged Food → Wholesaler. MARKETING & DISTRIBUTION. 1. Foods sold at retail–food stores, supermarkets, etc. – for "at home" eating 2. Food Service Market ("away-from-home") – restaurants (incl. "fast food") – vending machines – work site cafeterias – institutional feeding– military, school lunch	Foods chosen, purchased; "grown at home," then consumed. FOOD CONSUMPTION. • Biological Effects • Satisfaction
POLICY GOALS	To create: 1. Stable incomes for farmers; 2. Cheap food for consumers	To produce: – safe, wholesome food for consumers	To deliver: – safe food to consumer – info about nutritional content of food to consumer	To provide: Science-based information about food to consumer – labeling – publications, programs
POLICY INSTRUMENTS	• direct subsidies to farmers • price supports • gov't. purchase (direct) of commodities • insurance (gov't. sponsored)	• regulations re: manuf. operations • regs on meat/food inspection - how, by whom • grading & food composition "standards of identity" for certain foods • direct gov't. purchases of certain foods for military, schools, etc.	• marketing orders (dairy) • pricing structures • food labeling	• consumer information • develop/endorsement of message (e.g. Dietary Guidelines) and tool (e.g. Food Guide Pyramid) • regs concerning advertising
"TYPE" OF STRATEGY	EVIRONMENTAL STRATEGIES/ (AFFECT SUPPLY) →			PERSONAL STRATEGIES/ (AFFECT DEMAND)

Research → EFFECTS; IMPACTS → Health effects; Impact on environment cil, National Grange, and the like. Agriculture has long enjoyed the reputation of having one of the oldest sets of organized interests influencing public policy. However, in recent years, as more and more people have left their farms and agricultural organizations have come to represent fewer and fewer constituents, the power of this sector's reputation has begun to wane.[18] Agricultural lobbyists must follow the issues being debated in the House and Senate agriculture committees. Today, these issues are just as likely to focus on pesticides, environmental problems, food safety, immigrant farm labor, or international trade as on rural, farm issues.[19] However, just as many were counting out the "agriculturalists" as power brokers on Capitol Hill, 1995 congressional action debating the future of food assistance programs and continuation of farm subsidies proved them wrong.[20] As the deliberations were reported, "The final results showed that well-organized, economically powerful special interests can still outweigh passionately committed ideologues when it comes to writing the fine print that is so important in determining who benefits from federal spending."[21]

Trade associations associated with the food industry are concerned about governmental activities such as the approval process for new food ingredients or products, grading systems, advertising, or food labeling. Among those groups representing the food-processing industry are the National Food Processors Association (NFPA), the Food Processors Institute (affiliated with the NFPA to provide training and educational programs for food industry personnel), and the Grocery Manufacturers of America (GMA). Associated with the marketing and distribution of food are the Food Marketing Institute (FMI), the Food Distribution Research Society, the American Institute of Food Distributors, and the American Wholesale Grocers Association.

Trade associations may also be commodity-specific. Those groups that closely monitor legislative and regulatory developments related to the meat/poultry industry include the National Cattlemen's Beef Association (formed as a merger between the National Cattlemen's Association and the National Livestock and Beef Association), the Pork Producers Council, the American Meat Institute, the National Broiler Council, and so forth. The National Dairy Council, the American Dairy Association, the International Dairy Foods Association, and the National Dairy Board, among others, are responsible for tracking policy-related issues involving milk and dairy products. The National Association of Oils and Edible Shortenings, the American Soybean Association, the National Association of Margarine Manufacturers, and the Malaysian Palm Oil Promotion Council, among others, attend to issues concerning food oils, margarine, and shortenings.

Professional associations often serve as the interface between the food industry, the food service delivery industry, and the food-consuming public. In the nutrition and foods area, these include the American Society for Nutritional Sciences (ASNS) (formerly the American Institute of Nutrition), the American Dietetic Association (ADA), the Society for Nutrition Education (SNE), the American Society for Parenteral and Enteral Nutrition (ASPEN), the American Society for Clinical Nutrition (ASCN), the American School Food Service Association, and the Institute of Food Technologists (IFT). Each of these professional associations is keenly aware of issues that affect its members; for example, the American School Food Service Association, the American Dietetic Association, and the Society for Nutrition Education would work together to influence funding for programs such as the National School Lunch Program, while groups like the American Society for Nutrition Sciences, the American Society for Clinical Nutrition, and the American Dietetic Association often band together for policy issues involving funding for nutrition research.

Consumer advocacy groups are important voices for keeping certain issues in the public eye and often serve as direct conduits for informing consumers about policy issues in food and nutrition. These include the Center for Science in the Public Interest (CSPI), Public Voice for Food and Health Policy, the Food Research and Action Center (FRAC), the Community Nutrition Institute (CNI), the Children's Defense Fund (CDF), the Center for Budget and Policy Priorities, Bread for the World (BFW), the National Consumers' League, the Consumers' Union, and the Consumer Federation of America (CFA). Throughout this book, these groups will be highlighted in the discussion of the specific issues in which they are involved.

Coalitions

In the subsystems dealing with various areas of food and nutrition policy, it is necessary to form coalitions of various organized interests in order to achieve action in any one specific area. Coalitions consisting of representatives of trade associations, consumer groups, and professional associations are frequently formed to address specific issues such as the role of medical nutrition therapy in health care reform, dietary guidance, food labeling, or food assistance programs. Further understanding of the role of coalitions can be provided by describing two such groups, both focused on the topic of nutrition labeling, but each with a very different purpose. The Food and Nutrition Labeling Group (FNLG) was initially formed in 1988 by Bruce Silverglade, the director of legal affairs for the Center for Science in the Public Interest, a consumer and health advocacy group. He then enlisted a "sign-on" from more than twenty health groups, professional associations, and consumer interest groups for the purpose of spearheading food-labeling reform. The efforts of this group have been credited by some as having made a substantial difference in the passage of the Nutrition Labeling and Education Act (NLEA) of 1990. After the law was passed, the coalition continued to work to influence the FDA's and USDA's writing of the regulations to implement the law.

A second coalition, formed *after* the passage of the NLEA, brought together several groups—both inside and outside government—to address emerging issues of educating consumers about the new food label and to share newly developed educational materials and resources. Members of the Food Labeling Education Dialogue Group (FLEDGE) included the Food and Drug Administration and the USDA's Food Safety and Inspection Service from government; trade associations such as the Food Marketing Institute and the Grocery Manufacturers' Association (GMA); professional associations such as the Society for Nutrition Education (SNE) and the American Dietetic Association (ADA); and consumer advocacy groups such as the Center for Science in the Public Interest, Public Voice for Food and Health Policy, the American Association of Retired Persons (AARP), the Consumers' League, and the Consumer Federation of America (CFA). After the food-labeling program was well established, FLEDGE was disbanded in 1995, but most of its former members continued to meet on a regular basis in conjunction with the FDA's Food Safety Task Force to monitor public- and private-sector educational efforts dealing with food products.

Lobbying

Those who seek to influence the course of food and nutrition policy are no strangers to lobbying efforts both by the food industry and by the public health and consumer interests community. The examination of these efforts on various issues brings to light the diverse tactics and resources used by these groups to influence the course of policy making.

In recent years, consumer advocates and public interest groups representing health interests (especially those advocating preventive measures and public health programs) have assumed an activist stance in the lobbying business. However, advocates complain that the playing field is still not level; food producers possess far greater resources for lobbying activities and usually have much more focused demands than do consumer and health groups. Many agree with Marion Nestle's statement that "[i]t is unfortunate that good advice about nutrition conflicts with the interests of many big [food] industries, each of which has more lobbying power than all the public-interest groups combined."[22]

Figure 3.2 **Systems Model of Nutrition Policy**

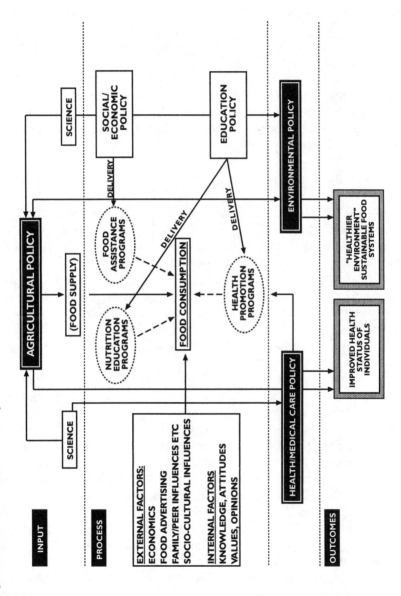

The Advocacy Coalition Framework

Sabatier and Jenkins–Smith's model of the "advocacy coalition framework" will be the analytical tool used to examine the activities described by the five case studies in this book.[23] This framework is useful as we attempt to understand the various forces, or coalitions, that seek to influence the course of policy making as it pertains to the National School Lunch Program; nutrition information on food labels; the regulatory approval process for a fat substitute, olestra; the issuance of dietary advice for the public; and the development and publication of a guide designed to influence the food choices of the general public.

Nutrition Policy: A Systems Approach

A systems model is helpful in showing the role of each component of the nutrition policy picture (Figure 3.2). This figure demonstrates both the simplicity and the complexity of nutrition policy. *Input* to the system takes the form of those sets of policies (mainly agricultural) that affect the quantity and the quality of the food available. *Process* is best conceptualized as all those events and situations that affect how the food supply will be used. The major process element in this scenario is food consumption, which, in turn, affects the *outputs* of the food system. The output of the system can be shown as a range of outcomes, including those related to health outcomes of individuals as well as "healthy," sustainable environments.

Agricultural policy sets the stage because it influences the quantity and quality of the food supply. We rely on the food production system to provide adequate quantities of food at reasonable prices for consumers, a basic tenet of agricultural policy. The types and amounts of food that are produced are directly affected by agricultural (i.e., farm) policy, which, in turn, affects the type, supply, and costs of food available from which the public can make food choices. Obviously, the specific types and amounts of food chosen by the public will affect their health and well-being. A related argument is that the quality of food choices made by individuals directly affects their use of the health/medical care system—that is, those who adopt health-promoting diets are less likely than those who consume unhealthful diets to use medical services. This observation has been the cornerstone associated with developing agricultural policies that are consistent with disease prevention policies, the major premise of this book. As pointed out in greater detail in later chapters, dietary fat has been shown to be the nutrient associated with more serious, deleterious health effects than almost any other single nutrient or food component.

Policy Issues in Nutrition

Governmental action to improve the health of the general public through dietary means has been a part of American policy for decades.[24] While compelling epidemiological evidence has convinced most "food-rich"[25] nations to support actions that will enable their population to have a more healthful diet, the United States faces some major policy issues. Among these policy issues are the goals and scope of national policy, especially concerning reductions in the consumption of animal fat; the choice of policy instruments (e.g., the weight of education and exhortation versus economics); and the development of an effective (i.e., results-producing) strategic apparatus to deploy national policy. This section describes in more detail several of the more cogent policy issues facing those in the United States who seek to establish nutrition policies that have the potential to improve public health.

Policy Issue 1: Is There a Public Imperative for the Development of National Nutrition Policy That Will Result in More Healthful Outcomes for the U.S. Population?

There is little doubt that there is support for government to promote healthful diets (assuming there is scientific evidence defining these) among those who are well-informed and willing to make dietary changes. This suggested role for governmental action is supported by a key assumption—since the impact on the health of the population and the productivity of the economy of faulty dietary habits is massive, the government is responsible for facilitating change and improvements for those who *want* to make dietary changes.[26] But what about those who do *not* wish to make such changes? What is the government's responsibility to and for them? Some would say that it is in the best national interest to force such changes on the public. Others insist that the government has no business meddling in its citizens' personal food choices regardless of the long-term economic consequences to the nation.

Policy Issue 2: What Is the Appropriate Scope of Public Policy in Nutrition?

Public policy in nutrition theoretically can be instrumental at each stage of the food system, from food production through food consumption, and including the health impacts of food consumption patterns. In the United States, policy makers have been more content to confine initiatives to the "demand" side of the equation—that is, influencing demand for healthful, low-fat foods by providing information and educational programs. "Supply"-side policy initiatives would include setting limits or targets for the types of food produced, mandating that the food industry produce more affordable lower-fat foods, or facilitating regulatory approval for safe fat replacers.

Policy Issue 3: With What Instruments and with What Force or Enthusiasm Should Public Policy in Nutrition Be Enacted and Enforced?

A number of options by which public policy can be implemented exist, all the way from government's role in providing science-based nutrition information and educating about the benefits to be gained from following dietary recommendations to subsidizing the production of certain crops and limiting or forbidding the production of others. The public policy debate centers on which of these options should be emphasized and enforced. Clearly, as noted above, the United States has long relied on educational and informational strategies to implement the nutrition portion of food and agricultural policy, types of policy instruments designed to further the food production goals of agriculture, and the market-based, economic incentives for the food industry. As Nancy Milio has noted, "The range of instruments with which policy goals may be reached includes the politically and economically less costly means: information, education, research, and evaluation. But these are also less powerful for effecting change compared to the more expensive—in political and economic risk—structural changes obtainable by altering such economic measures as subsidies and pricing, production controls, development and marketing support, direct services, and food composition and advertising regulation."[27]

Policy Issue 4: How Can the Current Dissonance between Agricultural/Food Policies and Consumer-Based Health Information Strategies Be Resolved?

Given the strength of the scientific evidence supporting the diet–health connection, the need for an "intersectorial" public policy to bring together agricultural interests and health concerns may now be warranted. Such a policy would indeed be challenging to create but would go a long way toward establishing an environment in which health-promoting food choices are easier to make.

It is these and other policy issues that will be presented and discussed throughout the remainder of this book. Inclusive, descriptive chapters are accompanied by case studies that present current issues and dilemmas in the food and nutrition public policy arenas. One need only be reminded that these are policy issues that affect *all* of us *daily*. Caught up in politics, consumer trends, emerging science, and expert opinions, the issue of dietary fat is clearly in the policy arena!

——————— *Case Study 1* ———————

Reinventing School Lunch: Attempts to Transform a Food Policy into a Nutrition Policy

This case study vividly describes policy making in the food system through the story of a "reinvention" of the fifty-year-old National School Lunch Program (NSLP). The narrative illustrates the power of history and the force of tradition in administering food assistance programs, the successful deployment of grassroots pressure channeled through powerful interest groups, and the dramatic role of "personality" politics. Further, the analysis examines the various forces that spring to life when long-standing regulatory policies are challenged and how the effects play out for the consumer—in this case, schoolchildren.

Description of the Key Issues

Overview of the National School Lunch Program

The largest and the oldest of all child nutrition and food assistance programs is the National School Lunch Program, permanently authorized in 1946 through the National School Lunch Act and created by Congress as "a measure of national security, to safeguard the health and well-being of the Nation's children and to encourage the domestic consumption of nutritious agricultural commodities and other food."[1] That same premise—feeding schoolchildren while supporting agriculture—remains a grounding principle for the National School Lunch Program today but also has served as the basis for rancorous disputes and conflicting policies regarding its operation.

Administered at the federal level by the U.S. Department of Agriculture's (USDA's) Food and Consumer Service (FCS) (formerly named the Food and Nutrition Service [FNS]), the National School Lunch Program is administered at the state level by the state department of education and usually at the local level by the school district administration.[2] All public schools are automatically eligible to participate in the program, and it is voluntary in private schools. Almost all public schools (99 percent) and the majority of private schools (83 percent) in the nation do participate in the National School Lunch Program—over 93,000 schools in fiscal year 1996, according to the USDA.

Even though the NSLP is available to about 92 percent of all students, only 56 percent actually participate, and participation is much greater in elementary schools than in secondary schools.[3] In 1992, 25 million children participated in the NSLP each day, at a cost to the government of $4.1 billion.[4]

Schools that elect to participate in the NSLP get both federal cash subsidies and donated agricultural commodities from the USDA for each meal served. The NSLP currently operates as an "entitlement," meaning that federal funds must be provided to all schools that apply and meet the program's eligibility criteria. A three-tiered reimbursement system is used to calculate benefits the school district receives, as follows: children from households with incomes at or below 130 percent of poverty receive free meals; those between 130 percent and 185 percent of poverty receive reduced-price meals; and those above 185 percent of poverty pay for a "full-price" meal. Federal subsidies to each school district are based on the number of children from each of the above groups (even those who are paying full price) who participate in the school feeding program. In 1993, free, reduced-price, and full-price meal subsidies to school districts were $1.695, $1.295, and $0.1625, respectively. Average full prices for lunches ranged from $1.11 in elementary schools to $1.22 in middle and high schools. Severe-need schools (defined as those providing at least 40 percent free meals, with higher costs than the regular rate) are eligible to receive additional assistance of $0.02 per meal served. Current estimates show that over half of all participating children receive either free or reduced-price lunches.[5]

The original 1946 legislation that created the National School Lunch Program set the standard for the kinds of foods that were to be offered to schoolchildren participating in the program. Until recently, these requirements were based on a standard "meal pattern" for all school lunches. The traditional school lunch, offered to children for half a century, was required to include the following foods:

1/2 pint fluid milk*
2 ounces protein (meat, fish, 2 eggs, 4 tablespoons peanut butter, or 1 cup dry beans or peas)

---

*It is interesting to note that, until recently, the School Lunch Program *was required to offer,* as one of its fluid-milk options, "whole milk," containing nearly 4 percent butterfat, compared with low-fat milk (1 percent or 2 percent), skim milk (0 percent fat), and chocolate milk (for which the percentage butterfat content varies). This fact is testimony to the power of the dairy lobby to resist changes in this meal pattern structure for half a century.

3/4-cup serving consisting of two or more vegetables or fruits or both (juice can meet half of this requirement)
8 servings of bread, pasta, or grain per week

This meal pattern reflects a goal that, over the period of one week, children will receive at least one-third of the recommended dietary allowances (RDA) (a standard set to meet the amounts of nutrients needed by groups of healthy people) for basic nutrients, such as protein, vitamins, and minerals. USDA studies show that low-income children depend upon the NSLP to provide up to one-third to one-half of their total daily nutrient intake.[6]

Policy Issues at Work in the National School Lunch Program

When the National School Lunch Program was established in the mid-1940s, the dietary concerns were not the same as they are today. Formulators of that original bill were worried about nutrient deficiencies and making sure that young people received *enough* food to be well nourished. Today, however, concerns are in the opposite direction: obesity among schoolchildren has reached an all-time high. The Dietary Guidelines for Americans, a document first released by both the U.S. Departments of Agriculture and Health and Human Services in 1980, serves as the basis for all nutrition policy. The third edition of that document (published in 1990) was the first to quantify the recommendation for dietary fat; its text suggested that healthy people (over the age of 2) should consume no more than 30 percent of their calories as fat. As explained in more depth later, studies had indicated that school lunches were failing to meet this criterion. Thus, a policy dilemma arises when a major USDA program—such as the NSLP—is not following policy guidelines issued by the same federal department!

Another major policy issue emanates from the initial two-pronged policy objectives for the National School Lunch Program—providing nutritious lunches for children while at the same time providing a ready outlet for agricultural commodities. Can the USDA be friend to both farmer and health professional? Can a food program also be a nutrition and health program? (Those who answer in the affirmative cite the phenomenal success of the "WIC" Program [the Supplemental Nutrition Program for *W*omen, *I*nfants, and Children], where targeted supplemental food has been shown to produce documented health benefits.)

This policy dilemma is captured directly in the controversy over using agricultural commodities in the National School Lunch Program. Those who favor their use cite economic reasons—that it is simply good business not to be wasteful but to use any surplus foods to feed hungry children. (In fact, according to one USDA estimate, if donated food commodities had not been used in 1987, the costs of the NSLP would have been $880 million higher than its actual cash costs.) Those who oppose the use of commodity products in school meals cite the fact that a number of these products (notably, processed cheese, peanut butter, processed meat, and the like) provide higher levels of dietary fat, cholesterol, sugar, and sodium than are suitable for children.[7]

To receive federal benefits for running the National School Lunch Program, the school district agrees to abide by the rules and follow the requirements for participation. This means that in order to accept cash subsidies to run the NSLP, the school district must also agree to accept various donated agricultural commodities, the value of which is estimated to be between 15 percent to 20 percent of the cash outlay for the NSLP. Both "entitlement commodities," valued at about 14 cents a meal, and "bonus" commodities are available to school food service managers. These donated foods are essentially "free" to the school food authority; the other 80 percent of the food must be purchased locally. Therein lies the dilemma—local school food service managers often feel that if they choose not to accept the donated commodities, they run the risk of pricing themselves out of an ability to provide free and reduced-price lunches to the children who need them.

Recognizing that some products are especially high in fat (and particularly saturated fat), the USDA has recently made a concerted effort to cut back on the amount of dietary fat in surplus commodities donated to schools. Low-fat beef patties are a good example of this initiative. In the early 1990s (the first years these alternative low-fat products were offered), they made up only 5 percent of the total ground beef used in the program. School lunch managers, already operating under tight financial constraints and recognizing that children will eat only those foods with which they are familiar, are reluctant to use the new lower-fat products for fear of operating at a deficit.[8] This aspect of running the NSLP was dramatically captured in the title of an article that appeared in the *Washington Post*, "Dissing the Salmon: Schools Can't Sell USDA's Delicacies," which described a situation in which the USDA had been able to purchase millions of pounds of flaked salmon and over a million pounds of frozen asparagus for distribution to schools, only to learn that the children refused to eat the food![9]

Advocacy Coalitions at Work in the National School Lunch Program

The policy subsystems at work in the National School Lunch Program are vast. The web of interest groups, consumer advocacy groups, and professional associations interested in the National School Lunch Program is as complex as it is dedicated. Those systems starting with the legislative and regulatory aspects of the program as well as those dealing with the implementation of the NSLP span the range from those who produce, process, and deliver the food to school administrators and school food service personnel, to cafeteria workers who prepare and serve the food, to advocacy groups and professional organizations that are interested in the delivery of government-sponsored food assistance programs, to parents and caregivers, and finally to the children who actually participate in the program. With a program that has existed for fifty years and is so prominently remembered by most adults in this country, it is no surprise that an entire industry has built up over the years to lobby for and to implement the NSLP.

The variety and array of agencies, legislative committees, media, interest groups, consumer advocacy groups, and professional associations that have built up around the issue of the National School Lunch Program are vast indeed. In the executive branch of government, the U.S. Department of Agriculture has had primary responsibility for the administration of this program since its creation in 1946. More recently, the School Lunch Program has been given a more prominent role as a key domestic policy area by the White House—i.e., the Executive Office of the President—both in welfare reform and in agriculture policy.

Within the Congress, two major types of committees exist that influence both the reauthorization of the program and its operation: the authorizing committees and the appropriations committees. The authorizing committee responsible for the NSLP in the House of Representatives was the Education and Labor Committee, reconfigured and renamed for the 104th Congress as the Economic and Educational Opportunities Committee. In addition, the House Committee on Agriculture—with its Subcommittee on Departmental Operations, Nutrition, and Foreign Agriculture—has played a key role in oversight of the operation of the NSLP. In the Senate, the Agriculture, Nutrition, and Forestry Committee has retained authorizing responsibility for the National School Lunch Program. Appropriations committees in each house of Congress—the Agriculture Appropriations Subcommittee in the House and the Agriculture, Rural Development, and Related Agencies Appropriations Subcommittee in the Senate—have final authority to approve the amount of money appropriated for the operation of the program. Thus, while an "education" committee in the House authorizes the program, an "agriculture" subcommittee actually approves the funding.

In November 1994, Republicans assumed control of both houses of Congress after a hiatus of forty years. The committee structure and leadership changed dramatically, resulting in changing roles and responsibilities for numerous legislators. A number of Republican legislators found themselves cast in the role of downsizing or even eliminating those very programs of which they were once personally very supportive. One example of this dilemma was William F. Goodling (R-Pennsylvania), whose personal story was chronicled in a detailed *Washington Post* article.[10] Representative Goodling, chairman of the House Economic and Educational Opportunities Committee, was quoted as saying, "I have long defended some of these programs, especially the school lunch program. But, that doesn't mean that school lunch or any of the other food and nutrition programs cannot be improved. And we are under the mandate from the Republican Caucus and in the Contract with America, to make some changes." Other GOP members in the House publicly described their ideological dilemma—while they remained supportive of nutrition programs, they were committed to giving state governments greater flexibility and less paperwork in the administration of the programs.[11]

A vast network of groups in the private sector exists to actively influence the operation of the NSLP. A group's interest in the program stems primarily from the base concern of the organization. If an organization mainly represents food or agricultural commodity interests, it will be far more concerned about commodity specifications, cost considerations, transportation, food storage and safety issues, and other matters related to the food offered to children in schools. These organizations range from agriculture production groups such as the Farmers Union to commodity-specific organizations, such as the National Cattlemen's Beef Association, the National Dairy Council, the United Fresh Fruit and Vegetable Association, and the National Wholesale Grocers' Association.

If the organization represents health and nutrition professionals, it will more likely be concerned with issues such as the nutritional quality of the meals served, whether the children are learning good nutritional and health practices, and personnel issues such as whether credentialed professionals are providing the needed services. Professional associations—such as the American Dietetic Association (ADA) (with nearly 70,000 members), the American Public Health Association (APHA), and smaller groups of professionals such as the Society for Nutrition Education (SNE) and the National Association of State Nutrition Education and Training Program Coordinators (NASNET)—are active in monitoring changes to the NSLP. Most active, however, in representing its members' vested interests regarding the administration of the NSLP is the American School Food Service Association (ASFSA), which has over 65,000 members.

Large organizations with specific targeted purposes such as the ASFSA have the resources to mount effective lobbying efforts, being able both to operate at the "grassroots" level and to hire well-trained, well-connected lobbyists in Washington. In this regard, the ASFSA has long retained the services of a well-known lobbyist in Washington circles, Marshall Matz, a lawyer who boasts a long record of key bipartisan accomplishments with various food and nutrition programs. In addition, the ASFSA has a "government relations" manager on its own staff to organize and coordinate the organization's lobbying efforts (incidentally, the person who most recently held this position was a key staff member for a member of Congress who was on the NSLP authorizing committee). The approaches and effectiveness of the American School Food Service Association's lobbying efforts as the organization has sought to influence key regulatory and legislative changes proposed for the National School Lunch Program are key to this case study.

Consumer advocacy organizations certainly are concerned about many similar issues, but their focus is usually on the recepients of program services—that is, whether entitled children are receiving access to the program and whether the program is meeting the needs of poor and disadvantaged groups. Other consumer groups have focused on the internal, "qualitative" aspects of the menus served in the NSLP, concerned primarily with the nutritional value of the food served. An example of the first type of organization is the Food Research and Action Center (FRAC), which has focused its efforts on the "access" issue for low-income children, while groups such as Public Voice for Food and Health Policy and the Center for Science in the Public Interest (CSPI) have mounted an extensive effort (primarily via the media) to inform the public about the nutritional quality of the meals offered in the School Lunch Program.

A number of coalitions has also been formed whose activities focus on the NSLP. The Child Nutrition Forum, organized and administered by the FRAC, consists of a number of child advocacy organizations, public interest groups, and professional associations; its focus is to bring these various groups together to draw legislative and media attention to access issues involving participation of low-income children in child nutrition programs, including school lunch, school breakfast, and other child care feeding programs. A more recently formed, but short-lived, coalition was Advocates for Better Children's Diets (A-B-C-D). Included among its members were many of the same organizations that are in the Child Nutrition Forum, but the group also included trade associations, such as the American Soy Association. Those unfamiliar with this issue may question why such a group would want to be involved in a coalition that seeks to influence the operation of the School Lunch Program. Texturized vegetable protein (made from soy) is a key ingredient of ground beef patties served to schoolchildren as

one measure to reduce the dietary fat in the School Lunch Program. Therefore, this product can be promoted in efforts to improve the "quality" (i.e.,
reduce the fat content) of the school lunch meals.

Specialized media also play a role in the web of groups that comprise the
School Lunch Program's policy subsystem by informing both the internal
and external groups about the activities going on in Washington related to
the program. For example, the American School Food Service Association
publishes two periodicals, the *School Lunch Journal* and the *School Food
Service Research Review*. Published twice annually, the latter publication,
which is designed primarily for the academic reader, contains articles that
feature evaluation and research conducted on the School Lunch Program.
Coalitions and advocacy groups also use publications as a means of dissem-
inating their message and often develop "media kits" to inform the public
via the print and visual media.

Documenting the Need for Policy Changes
in the National School Lunch Program

A substantive factual research base is often required to define the nature of
policy changes that may be needed. Older program evaluation reports, authorized and funded by the USDA, had focused on the nutritional content of
the school meals but had limited their analysis to those nutrients identified
in the original 1946 legislation. Times were much different at the close of
World War II, and the goals of the School Lunch Program were aimed
primarily at assuring that undernourished children would receive adequate
food with sufficient calories, vitamins, and minerals. Using data from the
Survey of Food Consumption in Low-Income Households, 1977–78, researchers in the early 1980s gave high grades to the NSLP.[12] Students
participating in the School Lunch Program had higher nutrient intakes than
nonparticipants, especially for protein and most vitamins and minerals, but
not for calories, iron, magnesium, and vitamin B-6.

Using data collected between 1979 and 1983, the USDA's Food and
Nutrition Service, under contract with the System Development Corporation in Santa Monica, California, conducted the National Evaluation of
School Nutrition Programs.[13] The study concluded that children who participated in the School Lunch Program received more of almost all nutrients
examined than nonparticipants. The positive impact of school lunch on
energy intakes as well as vitamins A and B-6 were noted, although the
program did not improve children's intakes of iron and vitamin C. It must
be noted that these evaluations focused mainly on assessing calories, vitamins, and minerals, according to the criterion for meeting one-third of the

RDA for those nutrients as specified in the 1946 legislation that established the program.

What was needed, of course, was a current analysis of the nutritional content of school meals reflective of the macronutrient content, such as fat. No longer were micronutrients, such as most vitamins and minerals, of major health concern, and the older evaluations did not provide much usable data on those nutrients shown to be associated with the development of debilitating chronic diseases, such as fat, cholesterol, and sodium. In the late 1980s and early 1990s, the only data available on the fat content of school lunches were those collected by consumer advocacy organizations as a result of conducting their own surveys. The Center for Science in the Public Interest in its "White Paper on School Lunch Nutrition" showcased the results of its analyses of lunches from three school programs.[14] In two of the programs, they found an average of 42 percent of calories from fat, and lunches from the third program contained 41 percent of calories from fat when whole milk was served and 35 percent when skim milk was served.

Another organization that was prominent in showcasing problems with the National School Lunch Program was Public Voice for Food and Health Policy, founded by Ellen Haas in 1983. In 1988, after reviewing menus from fifty school districts nationwide, Public Voice asserted that "many schools have pumped their menus with high-fat commodities contributed from farm surpluses, such as butter, cheese, eggs, and processed foods—[thus] cutting food costs but also cutting dietary value." At a press conference, Ellen Haas publicly went on record as suggesting that "the program is run more as an agricultural support program than a nutritional program."[15]

These first efforts to publicly expose the types of meals fed to schoolchildren as part of the National School Lunch Program were followed by a series of four reports issued by Public Voice—"What's for Lunch? A Progress Report on Reducing Fat in the School Lunch Program,"[16] in 1989; "What's for Lunch? II: A 1990 Survey of Options in the School Lunch Program";[17] "Heading for a Health Crisis: Eating Patterns of America's School Children,"[18] in 1991; and "Agriculture First: Nutrition, Commodities and the National School Lunch Program,"[19] in 1992. Most of these reports carried a common theme—that USDA administrators were placing higher priority on distributing agricultural commodities than on providing nutritious school lunches. Recommendations were usually targeted both to Congress to reform dairy policies and to the USDA to reform its commodity distribution practices to encourage the purchase of lower-fat dairy, meat, and poultry products and to expand the availability of fresh fruits and vegetables. The 1991 report, in particular, was notable because it was followed by a response from then USDA Secretary Edward Madigan, who publicly "pledged to take steps to reduce the fat content of meals provided by the National School Lunch Program, [thus] bringing their nutritive content into compliance with federal dietary guidelines by 1994."[20]

The data needed to reform the National School Lunch Program were actually collected as part of a study initiated during the George Bush administration by former USDA Secretary Madigan, who was also personally committed to improving the nutritional quality of the meals served in the School Lunch Program. This study, the School Nutrition Dietary Assessment Study, was conducted by Mathematica Policy Research, under contract with the USDA's Food and Nutrition Service.[21] The study collected meal information from a nationally representative sample of 545 schools and 3,350 students in May 1992. A most significant finding was that for the first time, the amount of dietary fat in school lunches was documented, and the results showed just how different the amounts of macronutrients were in school lunches compared to the amounts recommended in the Dietary Guidelines. School lunches provided much more dietary fat (38 percent, compared to the Dietary Guidelines' recommendation of 30 percent), saturated fat (15 percent, compared to 10 percent), and sodium (1,479 mg, compared to 800 mg). Further, less than 5 percent of the 515 schools sampled offered school lunches that were close to the Dietary Guidelines' recommendation for fat.[22] On the positive side, however, school lunches were providing one-third or more of the daily recommended dietary allowances for calories; protein; vitamins A, C, and B-6; and the minerals iron, zinc, and calcium. Thus, this study confirmed what many health professionals and nutritionists had long suspected—the NSLP does a good job of providing at least one-third of the RDA for many nutrients, but the meals contained far too much fat, saturated fat, cholesterol, and sodium.

One of the concerns reported was that those schools that offered low-fat (32 percent or less of calories) meals showed a 6 percent lower participation rate than other schools. The report noted, however, that NSLP participation rates in schools offering meals that were in the range of 32 to 35 percent of calories from fat were similar to participation rates in schools where the average meal's fat content was 35 percent or higher. According to the authors of the report, "these findings suggest that schools can make some modifications to reduce the fat content of lunches without adversely affecting participation; if, however, the fat content is reduced to levels below 32 percent of calories, participation falls substantially."[23]

Regulatory and Legislative Reform Efforts

In most traditional analyses, regulatory actions follow legislative changes. However, in the case of reform of the National School Lunch Program, this sequence of policy changes did not apply. The NSLP was permanently authorized, but related programs that were carried under the same legislation were due to expire in 1994. Thus, congressional action was needed to reauthorize these programs, and Congress used this forum as a vehicle to make changes in the NSLP as well. The changes proposed to the NSLP—both legislative and regulatory—will be discussed in chronological sequence in this section of the case study. (To highlight these various policy activities, accounts of the legislative endeavors will be in *italics*, while those initiatives taking place in the regulatory arena will be in "regular" font.)

Building on her success as a consumer activist and media specialist and fresh from her appointment as the USDA's assistant secretary (later, the position was elevated to the title of undersecretary) for Food, Nutrition, and Consumer Services, Ellen Haas decided to take her school lunch reform message directly to both the public and to the health professionals and consumer advocates who had supported her activities in the past. The School Nutrition Dietary Assessment Study had provided ample evidence for the kind of reforms in the quality of the school meals that she had long envisioned. This report, released in October 1993, was the first study of the school meals program in ten years and provided important documentation of the nutritional performance of the program. Disturbing—but a clear mandate for Haas—was the finding that virtually none of the schools offered meals that conformed to the Dietary Guidelines recommendations. The study had shown that school lunches exceeded dietary guidelines for fat by 25 percent, saturated fat by 50 percent, and sodium by nearly 100 percent. The report also stated that children who ate school lunch consumed significantly higher amounts of calories from fat than children who got their lunch elsewhere. Especially troubling was the finding that nearly half of the more than 25 million school meals served were to needy students, for whom this may be their only nourishing meal of the day.

This message was taken to the public in a series of public hearings focusing on "Nutrition Objectives for School Meals." These regional hearings were held in four cities—Atlanta; Los Angeles; Flint, Michigan; and Washington, D.C.—in late fall 1993. Originally announced in the *Federal Register* (58 FR 47853 September 13, 1993), the hearings were staged "to provide an opportunity for public dialogue before policy changes are proposed for the National School Lunch Program."[24] The response exceeded everyone's expectations. There were 350 witnesses at the four hearings—including children, parents, teachers, nutritionists and dietitians, school food service personnel, farmers, physicians, the food industry, and community leaders—and 2,500 additional comments were filed afterward by the public.

Over 90 percent of these comments supported changes in the National School Lunch Program and applauded the USDA's efforts to improve the nutritional quality of the meals served. In addition to these "public" hearings, Haas provided a forum for interested professionals by meeting regularly with a small group of representatives from consumer, health, and professional groups. In addition, she was a popular "keynote" speaker at meetings of these professional and consumer groups. She continued to court the media, especially those reporters with whom she had developed friendships from her days at Public Voice—Marian Burros from the *New York Times* and Laura Shapiro of *Newsweek*. Clearly, the objective of "creating a positive political climate" for reform of the National School Lunch Program had been initiated.

On November 2, 1993, Senator Patrick Leahy (D-Vermont), chair of the Senate Agriculture, Nutrition, and Forestry Committee, introduced S. 1614, the Better Nutrition and Health for Children Act.[25] Designed to add health-promotion aspects to current child nutrition programs that were up for congressional reauthorization in 1994, the bill was designed to improve child nutrition programs by making school meals conform to the Dietary Guidelines. It also provided for increased funding for nutrition education and increased access to meals for children during the summer.

Representative Kildee (D-Michigan) introduced a related bill in the House (H.R. 8) on January 5, 1993, and it was referred to the House Committee on Education and Labor (the name of the committee before it was changed by the 104th Congress). Hearings were held before the Subcommittee on Elementary, Secondary, and Vocational Education on April 12 and 14, 1994, some sixteen months after the bill was introduced.[26] The bill, known at this point as the Healthy Meals for Healthy Americans Act of 1994, received voice vote approval on May 18, 1994, from the full House Education and Labor Committee.[27]

During markup of the bill, several amendments were approved by voice vote, including one proposed by Representative George Miller (D-California) that would permit some schools to drop whole milk from their menus if it accounted for less than 1 percent of the total milk consumed at the school in the previous year. Miller's amendment initially was opposed by Representative Steven Gunderson (R-Wisconsin), whose dairy state had long supported the School Lunch Program's requirement that schools must offer whole milk along with other types. Gunderson offered a substitute that would have allowed milk purchases to be based on a survey of students' preferences. He later withdrew his amendment, saying that he thought the Miller amendment would have little effect in most school districts.

The action line of the story now shifts back to the regulatory arena.

Following on the heels of the widely publicized School Nutrition Dietary Assessment Study and personal stories gleaned from hearings and reported in popular media stories,[28] the USDA's Ellen Haas clearly had the tools she required—along with a formidable arsenal of departmental regulatory tools and legislative connections—to bring about changes to the National School Lunch Program. The approach used in making the announcement was Haas's trademark press announcement plus public relations effort, tied this time to regulatory reform.

On June 8, 1994, then Secretary of Agriculture Mike Espy and Undersecretary Ellen Haas announced the USDA's School Meals Initiative for Healthy Children.[29] In regulatory parlance, these changes were formulated as "proposed rules," a form of enforceable policy initiated by the executive branch that does not require congressional action. The complete text of the preamble and proposed rules appeared in the June 10, 1994, edition of the *Federal Register*, allowing for a ninety-day comment period, ending on September 8, 1994.[30]

The USDA's School Meals Initiative for Healthy Children was based on four strategies to update and improve the quality of school meals:

1. *Eating for health:* Using the power of regulatory reform to ensure that school meals would meet standards for fat and saturated fat content as well as for key nutrients and calories, thus meeting the 1990 Dietary Guidelines for Americans' recommendations
2. *Making food choices:* Launching a nutrition education initiative for children as well as working with professional chefs and other members of the food and agricultural community to offer training and technical assistance to local meal providers
3. *Maximizing resources:* Improving the nutritional profile of commodities by putting nutrition labels on commodities, working more closely with federal partners at the Department of Health and Human Services (DHHS) and the Department of Education (DOE), as well as establishing links to local farmers to enhance access to locally grown commodities
4. *Managing for the future:* Streamlining administration of the NSLP by using technology, reducing paperwork and procedures, and emphasizing flexibility

In order to ensure that schools met the Dietary Guidelines recommendations, a new plan was designed to replace the "meal pattern" system, which school lunch directors had followed since 1946 (i.e., planning meals by incorporating a USDA-specified number of servings of certain foods, such as meat/meat alternative, fruit and/or vegetables, bread, and milk), and use instead a "flexible system of menu planning" called "nutrient standard menu planning"[31] or NuMenus. The USDA-proposed rule mandated that schools use a "nutrient standard" to ensure that the meals offered to children complied with the Dietary Guidelines. The plan required school food services to determine the nutritional content of the school meals by using a computer analysis program, or alternatively, schools could use an "assisted" version of the nutrient analysis by receiving help from outside groups, like state agencies or consultants.

The American School Food Service Association, the major professional organization concerned with the administration of school lunch programs, initially applauded the USDA (at least in public statements) for the "high priority [it] has given to the National School Lunch . . . program" and for giving the 92,000 schools participating in the program four years to comply with the regulations.[32] But its campaign to overturn the regulations was just beginning. ASFSA members complained about the "paperwork burden" associated with compliance, the cost of the new foods in the program, and the level of technical competence required to use computers to determine the nutrient content of school meals. So the association took its cause—and its lobbyist—instead to the Congress, where program reauthorization debates were in progress.

On July 19, 1994, the House passed H.R. 8, and on August 25, 1994, the Senate passed S. 1614 by voice vote. Although the two bills had similar goals, a House–Senate conference committee was needed to work out differences between the measures. The amended legislation was finally approved by the House on October 5 by voice vote and agreed to by the Senate on October 6, 1994. The resulting bill, the Healthy Meals for Healthy Americans Act, was signed into law by President Bill Clinton on November 2, 1994, as Public Law 103–448.

The final legislation reauthorized child nutrition programs as expected but also contained some important policy changes. The USDA's proposed regulations had called for schools to adopt a "nutrient standard menu-planning" system by 1996, a method that would use computers to track the nutrient content of a meal offered in the School Lunch Program. This measure, in particular, was quite unpopular with many school food service directors, who voiced their opposition through the ASFSA's lobbying efforts. In response to this pressure, Congress offered a loophole—the final legislation included language that gave schools an additional option of using a "food-based menu-planning" system, which would allow school lunch directors to meet the Dietary Guidelines in their menus by tracking foods rather than nutrients—the way they were used to doing it.

After years of debate, Congress also settled the issue of whether schools

*must offer students whole milk as one of their beverage options. Nutrition-
ists have long argued that the requirement adds unnecessary fat to
children's diets. But under a carefully crafted provision in the law, the
whole-milk requirement was replaced with language that requires schools
to "offer students a variety of fluid milk [whole, chocolate, 1 percent, etc.]
consistent with prior year preferences." In other words, if students didn't
drink whole milk one year, it didn't have to be served the next. To placate
the dairy lobby, which strenuously fought the removal of the whole-milk
language, the bill required the USDA to provide schools with an amount of
low-fat cheese that is the "milkfat equivalent" of the "lost" whole milk.33*

The final bill also excluded a provision in the House version that would
have required the USDA to engage in a formal process known as "negotiated rule making," making it mandatory that the agency meet with interest
groups before it issued certain proposed regulations.34* This provision was
sought by groups such as the American School Food Service Association
that strenuously opposed the USDA's June 1994 proposed regulations and
wished to be able to change any contentious language before such regulations were issued. (Those close to the situation felt that "neg-reg," as it is
colloquially called, is just a way of letting a special-interest group write the
regulations it wants to implement.)*

The chapter on regulatory reform was not closed until June 13, 1995,
when the *final* rule on the Schools Meals Initiative for Healthy Children was
published as 7CFR Parts 210 and 220, "Child Nutrition Programs: School
Meal Initiatives for Healthy Children; Final Rule."** The USDA called this
final rule "the most comprehensive and integrated reform of school meals in
the 50 year history of these programs."35 (Much more than just new rules
for menu planning, the School Meals Initiative included support for innovative nutrition education, improved opportunities for technical assistance and
training for school lunch personnel, and reformulation of donated commodities.) The USDA's final rule was similar to that which the department had
proposed a year earlier, except that it included a new menu-planning approach: a food-based menu plan, which, while reminiscent of the plan cur-

---

*The USDA's official posture was that it would not agree to a period of "negotiated
rule making" in consultation with various constituent groups since these regulatory
proposals were made only after several months of public hearings and discussions
with special-interest groups. (Language requiring negotiated rule-making, a tactic
favored by the ASFSA, had been included in the House bill reauthorizing the Child
Nutrition Act.)

**The final regulations appear in the June 3, 1995, edition of the *Federal Register*.
Earlier versions of the proposed rules appear in the June 10, 1994, and January 27,
1995 editions of the *Federal Register*.

rently in use, suggested alternatives for reducing the fat content of the meal by adding foods such as grains, fruits, and vegetables. Thus, the final rules accepted three-menu planning approaches—the nutrient-based, the assisted nutrient-based, and the newly added food-based.[36]

In addition to these regulatory changes, the USDA initiated "Team Nutrition," a nationwide integrated program designed to help implement the School Meals Initiative for Healthy Children.[37] The mission of Team Nutrition was "to improve the health and education of children by creating innovative public and private partnerships that promote food choices for a healthful diet through the media, school, families and the community."

The Team Nutrition initiative was announced publicly on June 12, 1995, at a media extravaganza attended by first lady Hillary Rodham Clinton and USDA Secretary Dan Glickman.[38] In addition to the regulatory changes previously discussed, Team Nutrition included several other initiatives—a nutrition education initiative designed to motivate children to make food choices for a healthy diet; a training and technical assistance initiative to provide support to school food service personnel; and changes to reduce the fat content of agricultural commodities used in the NSLP.

Nutrition Education. This initiative clearly has received the lion's share of public attention and resources. Moving away from the "typical" sources of nutrition education materials and techniques, USDA Undersecretary Ellen Haas clearly wanted something different and reached out to popular media channels. In less than two years, partnership agreements were reached with the Walt Disney Company to use two characters, "Timon" and "Pumbaa," from its movie *The Lion King* as "spokestoons" to promote the importance of a healthy diet to children; with Scholastic, Inc., to develop nutrition education materials for use in schools; with the national PTA organization for distribution of materials promoting parent involvement in the effort; with the USDA's Cooperative State Research, Education, and Extension Service to develop and distribute a community action kit; and with the California Department of Education to serve as models and evaluation projects for Team Nutrition's community-based nutrition promotion efforts.

Technical Assistance and Training. The technical assistance component of Team Nutrition has included the development of "tasty, low-fat, low-cost" recipes with chefs working with local school food service directors (another source of great consternation for the ASFSA); the development of a training plan and standards; the participation of volunteer chefs at local school cafeterias; as well as the development of a national nutrient database and software to implement the NuMenus system in schools.

Commodity Improvement. As described earlier in this case study, the use of donated commodities has long been a source of frustration for those seeking to reduce the dietary fat content of School Lunch Program menus. One direct way of reducing the fat content of school lunches is to change the nature of the agricultural commodities offered free to school lunch administrators or to offer more "low-fat" commodities.

Staff at the USDA's Food and Consumer Service unit work with staff at other USDA agencies, the Agricultural Marketing Service (AMS) and the Farm Service Agency (FSA), in developing the specifications for commodities that are used in the NSLP. The AMS handles "Group A Commodities," such as livestock, poultry, dairy, and fruits and vegetables; while the FSA has its own dairy division and a domestic program that handles grains, peanuts, and other miscellaneous items. Unlike menu standards for the NSLP, commodity specifications are not published in the *Federal Register* or codified in the *Code of Federal Regulations* (CFR). Rather, they are distributed to the industries that bid to supply these foods. When specifications are developed, the requesting organization—in this case, the FCS—works with the AMS and the food industry to develop them. Issues that are considered in developing these specifications include technical feasibility of supplying the products, flavor and acceptability, body and texture, color, and nutrient quality.

To support the USDA's School Meals Initiative for Healthy Children and meet the concerns about agricultural commodities in the NSLP, the USDA established the Commodities Improvement Council in May 1994, early in the process of school lunch reform. Composed of USDA undersecretaries of Food, Nutrition, and Consumer Services and Farm and Foreign Agriculture Services and the assistant secretary for Marketing and Regulatory Programs, the council was charged with developing policy for improving the nutritional profile of USDA commodity offerings while maintaining the department's support for domestic agriculture markets.

The council established a Tri-Agency Task Force to conduct a comprehensive review of the specifications for all commodity products. The charge to the task force was to identify commodities that could be improved by modifying their fat, sodium, or sugar levels while making sure that the products were acceptable to schoolchildren. As a result of this review, more than two-thirds of the 142 distributed commodities (such as fruits, vegetables, grain products, and most unprocessed poultry products such as turkey and chicken) were excluded from further modification because they are typically purchased in their simplest, most natural or unprocessed form. Of the remaining 46 commodities considered for improvement, the council approved half for modification. Meat, cheese, and peanut butter were among the products targeted for fat reduction from their current levels.

Canned meat will be reduced from 22–25 percent fat to 19–22 percent, fresh ground beef and pork from 20–21 percent to 17–18 percent fat content, and frozen ground beef and pork from 17–19 percent to 15–17 percent fat content.[39] The task force also recommended that the USDA work with the food industry to develop some new products, including "lite" butter, low-fat macaroni and cheese, meatless spaghetti sauce, reduced-fat cheese, boneless turkey ham, and prune puree (to be used as a fat substitute).[40]

In addition to these low- or reduced-fat products, the USDA is also seeking to provide schools with additional quantities of fruits, vegetables, and grain products that contain virtually no fat. It is also pilot-testing a program in which fresh produce is purchased for the USDA by the Department of Defense and delivered directly to schools.[41] While the American School Food Service Association supported the commodity initiative, many school food service directors were skeptical of its effect, questioning whether children would accept the taste of reduced-fat, -sugar- and sodium products.[42]

The legislative story had not ended, however. Shortly after the final rules for the School Meals Initiative for Healthy Children were announced by the USDA, Representative William Goodling (R-Pennsylvania) introduced H.R. 2066, the Healthy Meals for Children Act. On July 19, 1995, the proposed bill was referred to the House Committee on Economic and Educational Opportunities, and on August 4, 1995, it was referred to the Subcommittee on Early Childhood, Youth, and Families. After languishing in legislative limbo for nine months, the bill was discharged from subcommittee action by the full committee on May 1, 1996, and on the same day, the committee considered H.R. 2066, amended it in markup, and passed it by voice vote, ordering it to be reported. After being reported to the House (as amended) by the full committee on May 7, it was called up by the House under suspension of the rules on May 14 and passed by voice vote. For many who were not following these developments closely, the bill is quite innocuous. It simply "amend[s] the National School Lunch Act to provide greater flexibility to schools to meet the Dietary Guidelines for Americans under the school lunch and school breakfast programs, as amended."[43]

On March 14, 1996, Senator Thad Cochran (R-Mississippi) introduced a similar bill (S. 1613) into the Senate. Described by Senator Cochran as "virtually the same as H.R. 2066," the bill passed the Senate on May 16, 1996, without amendment by unanimous consent. The bill, which passed by voice vote in both houses, met with bipartisan support in Congress.

Critics of the bill had argued that its wording was too vague and did not provide for accountability for schools to follow nutrient-based standards in the NSLP. Before the bill was signed by President Clinton, an important clause was added at the "eleventh hour" to alleviate administration con-

cerns. (A spokesperson for the ASFSA said that the decision apparently came directly from the Office of Management and Budget [OMB] in the White House, with Agriculture Secretary Dan Glickman's support.) The OMB's suggested amendment gave the secretary of agriculture the final decision-making authority to determine whether submitted menu plans met the nutrient standards for the NSLP; the official wording of the legislation now reads that schools can use any method "within guidelines established by the Secretary."[44] On May 29, 1996, President Clinton signed into law the enrolled version of the bill, which became Public Law 104-149.

Looking Back . . .

Why was such legislation needed when new regulations governing the implementation of the NSLP had just been promulgated? Several reasons may be offered. The first has to do with the larger political environment under which changes to the NSLP were made. The 104th Congress, which took office in January 1995, had originally attempted to "block-grant" the School Lunch Program as one of its first actions in the Contract with America legislative proposals. The rationale was to improve decision making and implementation at the local level and decrease the level of federal involvement. After vigorous lobbying by the ASFSA and others, the NSLP was not included in any "block-grant" legislation. However, it was appealing to Republicans to offer a bill later that appeared to decrease the level of federal involvement in the School Lunch Program.

Legislation that permits "maximum flexibility" in planning school lunch menus certainly sounds as though it would decrease federal involvement in how the program would be operated at the local level. As Representative William Goodling was quoted as saying, "The bottom line is that the basic responsibility for developing reasonable approaches to meeting the dietary guidelines is with the school food authorities, with Federal guidance and oversight, but not a panoply of prescriptive rules or preset options."[45]

Democrats and Republicans alike say this episode vividly "illustrates how a well-meaning federal agency carrying out a long-overdue change in nutritional standards barged into an area where local school districts know best."[46] Even the *Congressional Record* contains the following statement: "We are moving this bipartisan legislation because the USDA Food and Consumer Service under the direction of Ellen Haas is out of control. In the name of advancing good nutrition for children, the USDA is burying our schools in bureaucratic paperwork and regulatory micromanagement."[47]

The bill was backed by an intense lobbying effort by the American School Food Service Association, which used all its power—strong, effective lobbying coupled with an intensive grassroots letter-writing campaign from its 65,000 members—to ensure passage of the bill. It also enlisted the support of the American Association of School Administrators, the National School Boards Association, and the Association of School Business Officials by publishing estimates of increased costs associated with implementing the USDA regulations and by raising fears of increased "Washington involvement" in local affairs. Former House Speaker Tip O'Neill's maxim that "all politics is local" certainly held true in this case.

A second reason for the legislative activity is that school food service officials were quite unhappy with the new USDA regulations; in fact, after the proposed rules were announced in June 1994, the USDA received over 14,000 comments, 12,000 of those reportedly coming from disgruntled ASFSA members. Feeling that their comments had not been attended to in writing the regulations, fearing increased costs associated with implementing the new regulations, and desiring more flexibility in implementing them, the group sought the only way to offset regulations to which it was opposed—new legislation. This new act allowed school food service authorities to use "any reasonable approach" to meet the Dietary Guidelines for Americans under the National School Lunch Act. (Presumably this language also permits the very same meal pattern that the USDA, in the School Nutrition Dietary Assessment Study, had found to be high in fat and saturated fat, and had found not to meet Dietary Guidelines recommendations.) Further, the bill states, "The Secretary [of the USDA] may not *require* a school to conduct or use a nutrient analysis to meet the requirements," the clause to which school food service managers were most opposed.[48]

While the USDA and the ASFSA membership share many common goals and say they have never disagreed on the ultimate outcome of improving the nutritional quality of the NSLP, the "devil," as they say, "is in the details." The USDA regulations can specify the nutrient standards on which the NSLP is based, but the overriding legislation now stipulates how and when those nutrient standards can be met. The USDA's goals of having school meals meet the recommendations of the 1990 Dietary Guidelines for Americans can be met mainly by serving more grains and breads in school lunches and increasing the amount of fruits and vegetables offered, options that school food service managers maintain are too expensive. Further, in order to ensure that these requirements were met, the USDA wanted school food service administrators to keep track of the nutrient content of school meals by using computer-based nutrient analyses. School food service administrators balked, much preferring to continue using their current system and not wanting to implement new technology that was highly dependent on computers and personnel trained to use them.[49]

The third, and perhaps most telling, reason is the "feud" that developed between Ellen Haas and the American School Food Service Association, the primary professional organization supporting the lobbying effort behind the National School Lunch Program. Appointed as USDA assistant secretary in 1993 (over one of ASFSA's former presidents), Ellen Haas had one of the most powerful jobs in the federal bureaucracy and control over nearly 60 percent of the entire USDA budget (roughly $40 billion), the third largest nondefense department in the federal government.

During her professional rise in visibility and influence from local consumer activist to prominence at the national level, Ellen Haas became known as a clear, strong voice for consumers. She developed an enviable record of being able to court the media, policy makers, and "regular citizen advocates" with equal fervor and convince them of the validity of her views. In her role as executive director and founder of the consumer advocacy and research group Public Voice for Food and Health Policy, Haas demonstrated an ability to strongly and ardently advocate for changes in the quality of the foods served in the School Lunch Program. Since 1990, the series of reports issued by Public Voice had publicly—and personally—identified her with concerns about the quality of the food served in the School Lunch Program and had pitted her against the program's most powerful political ally, the American School Food Service Association. Now as the bureaucrat "in charge" of this vast and important program, how could she bring about the various changes that she had so long and so staunchly advocated?

The American Food Service Association was already piqued by the Haas appointment. Then, as one of her first public acts as assistant secretary at the USDA, the ASFSA was the target of criticism for participation figures in the NSLP and for the nutritional quality of the meals served to schoolchildren, criticisms it felt were unfair and undeserved. In announcing what needed to be done to improve school meals, the ASFSA felt Haas had overlooked the "good news" in the School Nutrition Dietary Assessment Study—that NSLP meals offered more than the recommended amounts of protein and selected vitamins and minerals, and that a statistically significant proportion of the schools surveyed were already meeting the Dietary Guidelines using the current meal plan.

Further insult came when the NSLP came under attack by the legislative proposals of the 104th Congress to block-grant the program. Many closely associated with the process felt that Haas had not been a true "advocate" for the NSLP when her personal dynamism and contacts were most needed on Capitol Hill. They felt she had taken personal ownership of the Team Nutrition project to such a degree that she had no time or interest in working with them to fend off the block-grant proposals.

The disaffection between the USDA's undersecretary and the primary professional organization for school food service managers was clearly a public embarrassment for the Clinton administration. The AFSFA accused Haas of writing "heavy-handed" regulations by proposing that criminal penalties would be imposed if school food service personnel refused to change the meal patterns that did not meet the Dietary Guidelines. Former officers of the ASFSA publicly criticized Haas's administration of the NSLP, saying, "Ever since Haas started in the administration, the Under Secretary has discredited the school lunch program . . . she has humiliated [school food service] people . . . maligned and discredited them."[50]

The "feud" between Haas and the ASFSA has manifested itself in a variety of rather subtle, but devastatingly personal ways; she was snubbed as a speaker at the ASFSA's annual meeting, a veritable "command performance" for the USDA undersecretary with responsibility for the NSLP. And when it came to Team Nutrition, the school food service group felt it had been insulted and bypassed. She was accused of snubbing old-timers at the ASFSA by bringing in executive chefs from high-class restaurants to "show them how to cook," and rather than reinforcing the efforts of local "experts," they felt that educational efforts had been turned over to Disney "spokestoons" and outside consultants. The relationship was never "healthy"—for either the undersecretary or the ASFSA—and probably irreparably harmed the effort to reform the NSLP.

Analysis and Comment

By Stages of the Public Policy-Making Process

Reform of the National School Lunch Program is a perfect example of the importance of the agenda-setting stage of the policy-making process. The reauthorization of the National School Lunch Program was due in 1994. This action was usually pro forma; no one seriously challenged the existence of the program after fifty years, and serious modifications to the content of the program were felt to be within the realm of USDA bureaucrats. Therefore, any major changes to the program would need to take place in the regulatory arena.

Nutrition and health professionals had clamored for change in the nutritional standards of the NSLP for years. All knew perfectly well that while school meals were meeting the recommended amounts of vitamins, minerals, and protein, they provided too much fat, saturated fat, sodium, and cholesterol. It took the power of a USDA-financed study, the School Nutrition Dietary Assessment Study, to bring this to the attention of policy makers who were in a position to remedy the problem.

The other key to putting reform of the NSLP on the public agenda was the appointment in 1993 of Ellen Haas as assistant secretary of Food, Nutrition, and Consumer Services. She served as a "policy entrepreneur" in this matter. Without her energy and attention focused on the matter of the *quality* of school meals offered to children in the NSLP, any reform efforts would certainly have been much milder and less riveting. In bringing the matter to the attention of professionals and the public (who usually are only mildly interested, at best, in these issues), the results might have been more successful in the long run and certainly would have exacted less personal cost to Haas.

By Applying the Advocacy Coalition Framework

Several factors articulated in the advocacy coalition framework (ACF) help to explain some of the workings in this policy reform effort. These include the efforts of the "policy entrepreneur" and the role of "personality politics," the force of mobilizing various interest groups around different facets of the problem, and the impact of changes external to the subsystem.

The "Policy Entrepreneur"

To her appointment as the USDA's undersecretary of Food, Nutrition, and Consumer Services, Ellen Haas brought the power of her personal agenda and the culmination of a consumer activist career—certainly a very different profile than that of most of her predecessors in the position. (In fact, after her appointment was announced, news reports almost prophetically called attention to the fact that Haas's advocacy background may not have prepared her well for the grind of policy making within so well entrenched a bureaucracy as the USDA.)[51]

Those who enter public life are often warned of the high personal cost that may be exacted. Ellen Haas is a case in point. Despite defendable accomplishments and notable progress in improving the nutritional quality of meals in the NSLP, Ellen Haas has been the victim of what many have termed "personality politics," pilloried by the media and publicly reprimanded by Congress, all without the support of powerful organized interests behind her.

Team Nutrition has been the USDA's highly visible effort to improve and update the nutrition component of the National School Lunch Program. It bears the marks of its creator, Ellen Haas. Such efforts, while notably creative and attention-getting, have not been immune to criticism. Haas has been criticized for using the power of her office for "showboating" and as a mechanism to focus attention on herself as a personality rather than on the programs and the citizens she serves. The campaign has been called "P.R. fluff" rather than a substantive educational effort. Others have questioned the sustainability of efforts such as Team Nutrition, noting that campaigns associated with a prominent "political appointee" personality are soon forgotten after that person leaves office. Two years after the initiative of Team Nutrition, about one-fifth of all NSLP schools are volunatarily using its program of curriculum guides and classroom materials.[52] In contrast, those who have known and worked with Haas for many years reject criticism of the program. "As with pudding," they say, "the proof is in the eating," meaning that the effectiveness of Team Nutrition will be borne out by subsequent evaluation studies.

The press, even those with whom she has worked closely over the years, has not shielded Haas from harsh criticism. Much of the nasty press has been played out on the Federal Page of the *Washington Post*, which published several articles criticizing Haas's expenditures, personnel appointments, and personal judgment in reference to the Team Nutrition program.[53]

During 1996, Haas was the target of a congressional investigation initiated by several Republican congressmen on the House Agriculture Committee. This investigation resulted in two General Accounting Office (GAO) reports and congressional hearings at which she was accused of mismanagement of the Team Nutrition program and violations of ethics standards and procurement law during her tenure of nearly four years.[54] The conservative press had a field day: "It should be clear by now that the taxpayer can no longer afford Ms. Haas' imbecilic 'allegories,' her dreadful incompetence, her expensive self-interest, her managerial ineptitude or her political crudeness."[55]

Ellen Haas announced her resignation as undersecretary for Food, Nutrition, and Consumer Services at the USDA in January 1997. In a letter to "Team Nutrition supporters" dated February 14, 1997, her last day in office, she thanked supporters, then listed what she considered to be her "legacy"—"updating nutrition standards in school meals for the first time in fifty years, providing unprecedented support for policy changes, improving the nutritional profile of commodities and moving away from command and control enforcement to support of local schools."

Haas's critics have suggested that the skills she honed as a consumer advocate simply were inappropriate for use as a government bureaucrat. Because, they maintain, she never learned to respect the system and the bureaucrats who worked there, her office was plagued with personnel problems and ethical controversies, which significantly weakened her policy goals for the School Lunch Program and caused her considerable personal embarrassment. Others have hinted that while she had some positive accomplishments, much more could have been done, if only she had been able to work with "grassroots" elements in a more positive way. Haas's admirers portray her as a visionary who, because of her passionate commitment to better nutrition for children, often failed to pay close enough attention to program details. Many public health and consumer groups have endorsed her efforts; spokespersons for groups such as the American Heart Association have gone on record saying that they believe that Ellen Haas was able to effect changes that will make this a healthier nation.[56]

Advocacy Coalitions

Health groups and consumer advocacy organizations clearly were supporters of the undersecretary and the tactics she employed to effect change. The large organized groups that had vested interests in keeping the program running the way it was, such as the American School Food Service Association and other groups related to local school administration, clearly opposed the USDA's regulations and were able to pass legislation that slowed down and changed the nature of the enforcement of those regulations.

In the process of "reinventing" the NSLP, Haas was able to accomplish regulatory change but failed to listen to and address the concerns of other policy players. Those actually running the school food services were influential policy players in their own right because they accomplished a parallel policy directive (in the form of Public Law 104-149), which redirected, if not derailed, Haas's initial policy agenda. Even those within government, the "lower-level" bureaucrats who were responsible for writing and enforcing the USDA regulations, were not enthusiastic about the new approaches being proposed; only those bureaucrats who were "political appointees" were supportive. Clearly, the political battles waged in Congress hurt the NSLP reform effort.

Changes External to the Subsystem

Several unforeseen changes altered the course of NSLP reform. The election of the Republican-dominated 104th Congress was a surprise. What would have been innocuous reauthorizations of the NSLP turned into nasty political battles. Further, President Clinton was described as becoming "less liberal" in his approach after the November 1994 elections in anticipation of his own re-election campaign in 1996. His signing of welfare reform legislation and his willingness to sign legislation that, in effect, weakened his own USDA regulations governing the NSLP were indications of this more "moderate" political climate.

Conclusion

Clearly, the National School Lunch Program is a microcosm of public policy in action. The support that farmers receive for raising certain crops through price supports and subsidies is an example of "distributive" policy. This food is then supplied to school food service managers, who serve meals either free or at reduced prices to needy children, an example of "redistributive" policy. The nutrition education component of the NSLP is clearly an example of a "promotional" or "exhortative" policy, giving government endorsement to a particular way of eating. Each of the first two types of policy mentioned is backed by powerful organized interests—the farm/agricultural lobby and the school food service lobby. On the other hand, the support from health and consumer groups that believe in the message of "better health through nutrition" is much less powerful in policy circles. Some have speculated that this is one reason why USDA efforts to reform the NSLP were not more successful or more easily accepted.

This case study of reforming the National School Lunch Program is also a vivid illustration of how difficult it is to take a "food policy" and transform it into a "nutrition policy" with a health focus. The system is simply not equipped to deal with those who maintain that more healthful lifestyles and improved eating habits will result in healthier children who are at decreased risk of chronic, debilitating disease. Promoters of such a nutrition policy approach must accept the challenge that a positive "payoff" may not be achieved until far in the future.

PART III

IMPLEMENTING PUBLIC POLICY IN THE FOOD SYSTEM

Politics enters the food chain at the point of food production, affecting nearly every subsequent component of our vast and complex food system, to the point of health effects and environmental impacts. Part III of this book describes the components of the food system, details governmental involvement at each point in the process, and reviews those public policy issues specifically related to the production of those foods that are the major sources of dietary fat.

Components of the Food System

The food system is a continuum of activities that range from food production to food consumption, or to use a more catchy phrase, "from the farm to the fork." The major components of the food system consist of a number of distinct, but interlocking phases: food production, food processing or manufacturing, food distribution/marketing, and food consumption. It is now time to add another, final, phase to the food system continuum—the effects of food consumption practices on human health and on the environment.

The food system serves as the link between agriculture and health. As noted in the schematic (Figure III.1), farmers are on one end of the continuum and consumers are at the other end. However, consumers are not just passive recipients of the food that comes to them. Consumer-driven demands work their way back through the food system, creating a dynamic in which food producers, processors, and sellers must be responsive to making those products available that consumers want. Coupled with emerging technology, these factors have created a food system that is revolutionizing the relationships between producer, processor, distributor, and consumer.

Food Production

The nation's largest industry is the food and fiber system. The scope and importance of U.S. agriculture extend far beyond the 3 million workers on the 2.1 million farms.[1] About one job out of six in the United States today is somehow related to farm/food production and processing. In 1994, U.S. food manufacturers, retailers, wholesalers, and food service firms employed 12.8 million people and contributed about 9.5 percent to our gross national product (GNP).[2] However, the proportion of the total U.S. economy and jobs tied to the farm/food sector has long been shrinking.

There are approximately 2.1 million farms in the United States, down from a peak of 6.8 million in 1935. However, the total area farmed remains essentially the same, about 1 billion acres. The distribution of farms is increasingly bimodal. Less than 20 percent of all U.S. farms are large operations that now account for 75 percent of all U.S. farm commodity sales. In recent years, production from about two out of five acres (that's 40 percent!) of U.S. crop land has moved into export markets. Farm exports make an important contribution to the U.S. balance of trade; in fiscal year 1996 alone, the volume of farm exports was 160 million metric tons, with a value of $60 billion.[3]

Food Processing

Farmers and ranchers supply the raw materials to the food industry for processing. Agricultural producers depend on food processors to help meet consumers' demands for fresh, safe, nutritious, convenient, and tasty, high-quality food products. Consumers are increasingly requesting that the industry convert those commodities not just into processed food products, but into actual meals and food combinations ready for *direct* consumption, (i.e., those requiring little, if any, cooking or preparation at the household level).

Food Distribution and Marketing

The food market is the elaborate system that moves food from producers and processors to consumers. Nearly 80 percent of the over $510 billion U.S. consumers spent for food in 1994 went to pay for marketing costs.[4]

Figure III.1 The U.S. Food System

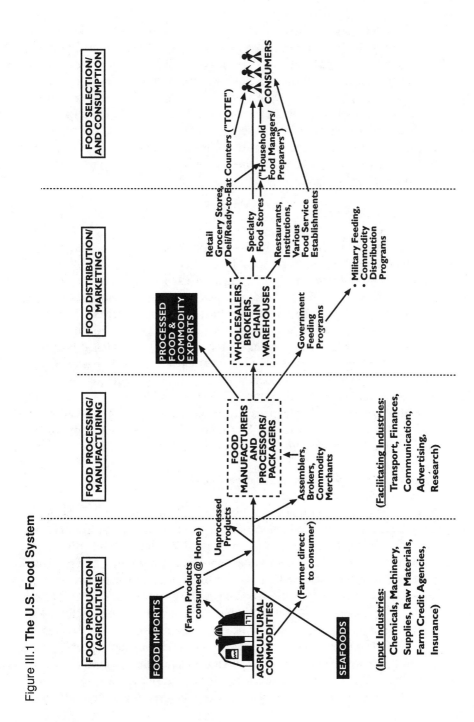

The farm value share of total consumer expenditures for domestic food has continued to decline as more of the costs of the final retail level products are added after the basic commodities leave the farm. This is in response to increasing consumer demand for more convenient and, hence, more highly processed and packaged food products. For an increasing number of farmers the key to higher profits lies not in more production but in more effective marketing. Many are finding that promotion activities, "niche markets," product differentiation, and specialty products, such as organic produce and "brand name" fresh products, are becoming increasingly important to their economic survival.

Food Consumption

Consumers are spending *more* money on food than ever before, but they are spending less of their total personal disposable income on food—just 11.2 percent compared with nearly 14 percent in 1970. Americans are also eating much more food, in the form of vegetables, bread, pasta cereals, fruit, sugars, and so forth. The most dramatic change, however, is not what is spent for food but where it is bought and consumed. In 1970, roughly 70 percent of food expenditures went for food prepared and eaten at home; by 1995, this figure had dwindled, as nearly half of all food consumed was "away-from-home" eating. Consumers have been clear in telling the market what they want—they want products that are easy to prepare, taste good, look good, are relatively inexpensive, and are safe to eat.[5] A growing number also say they want more healthful food, but many are not ready to give up convenience and taste to eat more healthfully.

Effects on Human Health and the Environment

Agriculture production now must meet two additional concerns regarding the *outcomes* of their production practices: (1) the nutritional quality, and indirectly the health effects, of the food produced, and (2) adopting practices that will protect the environment and natural resources. The producer is becoming more aware that the quality of the food produced will, in fact, affect human health. As Milio has eloquently stated, "Farm policy has far greater consequences for health, intended or not, than current food and nutrition policy. It affects people's health . . . more impressively through its direct effects on the types of foods available and their supply. Farm, rather than food, policy has the most important effect in the changes of cost of production. Production costs, in turn, have a greater impact . . . on what farmers produce and in what amounts than changes in consumer demand, whether that demand is induced by governmental food assistance programs or by market forces."[6]

Increasingly, there is great concern on the part of many about maintaining the integrity of the environment as a result of sound agricultural practices, the "greening" of agriculture, as some might say. Ensuring water quality, preventing soil erosion, and maintaining the quality of the soil (using principles of sustainable agriculture, including the application of a minimal amount of organic fertilizers or other chemicals, or adopting practices such as Integrated Pest Management, to give but a few examples) have become critical monitors of success of agricultural policy.

Policy Issues Related to the Food System

Although distinct components of the food system do exist (and will be used for purposes of discussion in this book), the distinctions are beginning to blur through production contracts and vertical integration. Traditionally, a food processor would purchase a commodity from a producer at a price determined at the time of purchase; today it is more common to operate through a price established long before purchase. This system is well suited to today's industrialized food markets. Vertical integration, where a single firm controls the flow of commodities across several stages of food production, is also becoming more commonplace.

Two policy issues have arisen out of these trends. The first is market power, whether manufacturing firms exert monopolistic power over firms in the farm sector. If market power is created by only one or two firms, the result may be that the consumer is offered a reduced variety of products at higher or more variable prices. The second concern regarding increased concentration of agricultural production is environmental protection, especially in areas near massive livestock operations. Failure to effectively manage waste products, ensure water quality, prevent soil erosion, and maintain soil quality may result in costly litigation and in reductions to consumer welfare. Thus, the choice between efficient production and environmental quality may well be made in the policy arena.[7]

———— Chapter 4 ————

The Production of Fat Down on the Farm: How Much Do Federal Agricultural Policies Really Matter?

More than 50 years of farm policy appear to support the pro-
duction of foods that health policy now recomends restricting.
                                                              —B. Carr*

This chapter will examine, in a primarily qualitative fashion, the major ways in which the federal government has intervened in farm commodity sectors responsible for the production of most of the dietary fat in this country. Although federal intervention in oilseed trade issues will be addressed, most of the discussion in this chapter will focus on federal policies affecting the meat and dairy sectors. These two sectors provide the bulk of the animal-based fat in the American diet and are the areas that nutrition policy audiences are most likely to equate with government interventions that favor dietary fat production. Government's role in food processing is discussed in chapter 5, in food marketing (chapter 6), and in food consumption (chapter 7.)

The stated goal of agricultural policy is laudatory—to "provide an economic environment which reduces income risk to producers and insures the long term capacity to supply the nation's consumers with adequate, high quality, reasonably priced food supplies."[1] To carry out this policy, a number of government interventions are in place, such as price supports or subsidies at the level of commodity production, marketing orders at the level of product marketing and distribution, and commodity promotion at the level of consumer selection.

Government's Role in Production Agriculture

Since the 1930s, policy makers have devised a variety of programs to assist agricultural producers in three general ways—supplement farmer incomes,

---

*B.A. Carr, "Living Off the Fat of the Land," *CRS Review*, March 1989, p. 18.

manage supplies, or support farm prices. Current law *requires* the secretary
of Agriculture to offer support for wheat, feed grains (corn, sorghum, barley, oats), cotton, rice, soybeans and other oilseeds (such as safflower,
canola, etc.), milk, peanuts, sugar, and tobacco. Such a small number of
commodities that must be supported greatly influences the economic health
of much of U.S. agriculture; they accounted for more than 40 percent of all
cash receipts from farm marketings in 1995. Other important commodities
receive no regular direct support; these include meats, poultry, fruits, nuts,
and vegetables, which together generated farm income of $120 billion in
1995. But even producers of these items can be affected by farm policy
decisions, either because such producers also raise some price-supported
commodities or because government intervention in one farm sector can
influence production and prices in another. Producers of all types of commodities—whether price-supported or not—are served by numerous other
USDA farm production and marketing programs, such as low-interest credit
programs, subsidized crop insurance, marketing orders, and research and
promotion activities.[2]

The first federally financed price support programs for commodities
were created as a "temporary" remedy for the devastated Depression-racked
agricultural economy. These policies (in conjunction with research and
technology advances coupled with a supportive budget and tax policy) have
produced impressive results.[3] These policies have indeed "worked"; no
other country has been able to provide its people with such security in food
production at so little cost to the end users themselves. There has, however,
been a "down side" to this success story. More than sixty years after those
"temporary" measures were put into place, many American farmers continue to rely on the U.S. government for financial security and have become
more and more dependent on the income protection afforded through an
elaborate system of agricultural farm subsidies and price support systems.

For years, critics have argued that U.S. commodity policies are outdated
and may be detrimental to the needs of modern agriculture and even to
society in general. A number of successive farm bills, particularly since the
1970s, have incrementally steered price and income support programs onto
a more "market-oriented" course, so that farmers would be less dependent
on the government for economic rewards from production agriculture.
Trends and recent legislative developments indicate that the government's
direct involvement in food production is diminishing, that government is
basically getting out of the farming business. The most recent "Farm Bill,"
passed in 1996 (the Federal Agriculture Improvement and Reform Act (P.L.
104-127, the FAIR Act)) called for phasing out price supports for a number
of agricultural commodities and set in motion the deregulation of many

long-standing means of governmental involvement, such as marketing orders for dairy products.[4]

Today, economic realities have become abundantly clear to the political process; no longer a developing sector of the economy, agriculture has matured to the point where it is in little need of federal support. Agriculture continues to shift from its past focus on farming, production, supply, and commodities to business, markets, budgets, and adding value to basic commodities. The environment created by the passage of Public Law 104-127 should accelerate that shift and alter both the focus and content of future agricultural policy.

Governmental Infrastructure Affecting Agriculture

Actors in the Agricultural Policy Process

From the earliest days of the United States, the legislative and executive branches of the government have established specific units devoted to the making and executing of laws related to agriculture. Both houses of Congress have an Agriculture Committee and several specific subcommittees devoted to the business of lawmaking in the field. The House's agriculture subcommittees are General Farm Commodities; Livestock, Dairy and Poultry; Risk Management and Specialty Crops; Department Operations, Nutrition and Foreign Agriculture; and Resource Conservation, Research and Forestry. In the Senate, the subcommittees of the Committee on Agriculture, Nutrition, and Forestry are Forestry, Conservation, and World Revitalization; Marketing, Inspection, and Product Promotion; Production and Price Competitiveness; and Research, Nutrition, and General Legislation.

The scope and range of agricultural policy making has evolved from its earliest beginnings when attention was focused mainly on supporting the individual farmer by assisting with credit issues and directly subsidizing crop production. Today, these committees are also faced with issues related to food safety and nutrition, environmental protection, and animal rights.

Add to this intragovernment mix of agriculture players a wide assortment of extra-government organized interests whose job it is to capture the attention of policy makers and keep agricultural and food issues at the front of the policy-making agenda. Despite an expanded agenda and an influx of congressmen who are no lcnger products of an agrarian society, the farm lobby has remained strong. Further, there are trade associations with registered lobbyists for nearly every imaginable commodity, food processing phase, or food product. Clearly agriculture vies for the attention of policy makers in a historically powerful manner unlike few other sectors or occupations.[5]

Support in the Executive Branch: The United States Department of Agriculture

Established by President Lincoln in 1862,[6] the U.S. Department of Agriculture (USDA) was one of the first departments formed in the executive branch. Today, the department has a budget of nearly $100 billion and thousands of employees, many of whom provide direct service to farmers and other clientele in each county of the nation. The department is active in the following areas (each headed by an undersecretary): Farm and Foreign Agricultural Services; Natural Resources and Environment; Rural Development; Food, Nutrition, and Consumer Services; Food Safety; Research, Education, and Economics.

Farm commodity programs are funded through the USDA's Commodity Credit Cooperation (CCC), which actually functions as a financing mechanism to farmers whose benefits are delivered by the Farm Service Agency (FSA) through a network of local ("county") offices overseen by committees of elected farmers. In a dramatic shift from the early days of the department, more than half of the USDA's budget outlay today is from the Food, Nutrition, and Consumer Services agency that has responsibility for administration of the large food assistance programs, such as food stamps and the National School Lunch Program (NLSP). This is the ultimate policy irony of the USDA, reinforced by structural arrangements in the Congress—the agency charged with implementation and regulatory authority over food production is the very same as the one with responsibility for nutrition education and dietary guidance.

Policy Issues Related to Dietary Fat

The major sources of dietary fat for American consumers are "red meat" (primarily beef), dairy products, and plant oils. Table 4.1 highlights the major governmental actions that affect the availability of each of these commodities. Key policy issues associated with the production of each of these primary sources of dietary fat in the American diet are (1) beef production, especially the controversial use of feedlots; (2) pricing policy of milk and dairy products; and (3) trade issues associated with various types of vegetable oils. These actions affect the *supply* and usually the availability of these products for the consumer. The consumer may not be directly familiar with the inner workings of such issues, but they do affect

Table 4.1 Policy Initiatives Affecting Production of Beef, Dairy, and Plant Oils

STAGES OF FOOD SYSTEM	BEEF	DAIRY	PLANT OIL
Agricultural Production	• Type of Bread • Type of Feed - **Subsidies for feedgrains** • Feeding/Fattening Procedure/Land Use • **Range - fed vs. feedlot**	• Type of Breed • **Price Supports for fluid milk**	Plant Source Processing from oilseeds **International Trade** issues for domestic oils - e.g. corn, soybean vs. "tropical" oils - e.g. palm, coconut
Distribution and Marketing	Suppliers - wholesale "boxed beef" **Meat inspection:** food safety issues associated with meat production during slaughter, processing **Grading Standards**	**Milk Marketing Orders -** ("Multiple Component Pricing")	Food Processing Industry - (use as food ingredient) Food Service Establishments - (use as cooking medium) Retail Market - consumer use
Consumer Level Issues	**Commodity Promotion Board**	**Commodity Promotion Board**	**Education/Promotion:** Healthfulness of vegatable oil vs. animal fat; issues re: "trans" fatty acids

the price and frequently the quality of the ultimate product that is available for consumption.

THE POLITICS OF DAIRY MARKETING:
THE MILKFAT CONUNDRUM

A complex set of social, economic, and political relationships affects the dairy industry in the United States. The dairy industry includes milk producers, dairy cooperatives, processors and manufacturers, and the firms that market milk and dairy products. The dairy industry is shaped by the production and market characteristics of fluid milk. Raw milk is a bulky (about 87 percent water), extremely perishable product with a high potential for disease transmittal. Sanitary production and handling conditions, rapid movement to market, refrigeration, and heat treatment are musts to ensure a safe product. Production (supply) and demand are seasonally unsynchronized, and small changes in supply and/or demand will cause large price fluctuations.

Dairying is an important part of the agricultural economy of the United States. In 1993, cash receipts from milk marketings totaled $19.3 billion, a figure equivalent to 10.3 percent of the total cash receipts (including government payments) from farming. (Only meat animals and feed crops had greater cash receipts for the year.) Further, consumers spend about 13 cents out of every food dollar on milk and dairy products.[7]

Milk production, assembly, processing and manufacturing, and distribution (marketing) are all coordinated by prices. During much of the history of the United States, fluid milk markets were local and largely isolated, with supplies and prices varying dramatically across markets and seasons. However, the fresh milk market is variable, with large demand at certain times and low demand at other. Because fluid milk cannot be "stored" per se, it is pulled from the market and used to manufacture products (such as cheese, butter, and nonfat dry milk) that can be stored without spoilage. Almost all fresh milk and milk product prices are thereby linked to the prices of the storable products.

Numerous public policies and regulations—at federal, state, and even local levels—create a complex regulatory system that greatly influences the operation of the dairy industry. Government policy has traditionally played a major role in the pricing and marketing of milk and dairy products in the United States. The two principal parts of federal dairy policy are the *price support* and *milk marketing order programs*, both of which have been under increasing pressure to change. The 1980s and the early 1990s were marked by attempts to reduce government program costs by adjusting dairy price supports and initiating voluntary supply control measures. As many characteristics of the dairy industry have changed since federal involvement first began in the 1930s, considerable debate among policy makers, analysis, industry leaders, and consumer groups has ensued as to the extent—and the nature—to which governmental involvement is still needed.

Americans' Love Affair with Butterfat

The importance of milkfat to the nation's dietary fat intake has taken on new meaning. The nation's dairy sector now provides nearly 30 percent of the total animal fat[8] and about 13 percent of the total fat consumed in the average American diet.[9] Since 1975, the annual consumption of milk in the United States, as a beverage or as processed dairy products, has increased from 116 billion pounds to 153 billion pounds in 1994, a 32 percent increase that far outstrips population growth for the same period.[10]

Some experts predict that for consumers to adhere more closely to the Dietary Guidelines for Americans recommendations, they will need to further increase their consumption of dairy products and, at the same time, shift to lower-fat products.[11] This move is already occurring in record numbers. Consumers are already switching to lower-fat dairy products, but only for beverage milk. For other dairy products, such as cheese and ice cream, high-fat varieties are still preferred.

Fluid milk consumption in the United States dropped steadily for two decades before finally stabilizing in the mid-1990s. The decline in milk consumption as a whole and the accompanying shift toward lower-fat versions has significantly reduced the fat intake of the nation's fluid milk consumers. Between 1975 and 1995, the milkfat consumed through beverage milk dropped from 47 percent to 37 percent of the total milkfat consumed by the U.S. population. During that period, the per capita milkfat intake from beverage milk consumption dropped from 7.26 pounds per year to 4.73 pounds per year.[12]

With beverage milk consumption steadily declining, most of the increase in dairy product consumption is accounted for by growth in cheese consumption. Total and per capita cheese consumption has risen rapidly over the past two decades. Per capita cheese consumption shot up nearly 100 percent between 1975 and 1994. Unfortunately, more cheese means more fat. Cheese is generally a high-fat product that requires a great deal of milk to manufacture. (As a rule of thumb, about ten pounds of milk are needed to produce a single pound of cheese.) As more milk is produced to manufacture high-fat cheeses and cheese products, the contribution of milk production to dietary fat intake increases accordingly.

The U.S. dairy sector is increasingly becoming a cheese-driven economy.

From 1972 to 1982, the sale of cheese nearly doubled.[13] Further, fat intake from cheese consumption increased from just over five pounds per capita in 1975 to nearly ten pounds per capita in 1994. Although some consumers have begun to shift from full-fat standardized cheese products to lower fat versions, standard, full-fat varieties still dominate the nation's grocery store dairy cases.

Other dairy favorites weigh in with their share of butterfat. Consumption of butter remains at near all-time high levels, with average annual per capita consumption in the mid-1990s virtually the same as in the mid-1970s. Since butter must contain at least 80 percent fat by law, reductions in butter consumption could offer great opportunities to reduce fat intake. "Lite" butters, permitted by the new general standard of identity in the federal nutrition labeling regulations, still represent too small a percentage of the butter market to make a dent in the foreseeable future. Although per capita consumption of frozen dairy desserts has dropped by nearly 10 percent between 1975 and 1974, data are unavailable to gauge the net impact of increases in consumption of high-fat premium ice cream on the one hand, and "low-fat," or "nonfat" versions, on the other.

The Milkfat Economy

If, in ten years, the production of dairy products were to increase by one-third and the consumption of lower-fat versions of dairy products were to skyrocket (the same scenario described earlier for meeting the Dietary Guidelines), would that really reduce Americans' consumption of milkfat? Most likely not without some major changes in the way milkfat is valued and utilized. The cruel irony about the nation's dairy economy and the supply of milkfat is that increases in milk production inevitably lead to increases in milkfat production and consumption.

For better or worse, the U.S. dairy sector is virtually a closed economy when it comes to milkfat. Even if a large proportion of American consumers increased their demand for lower fat dairy products in the coming years, the resultant reductions in fat intake from those products would inevitably be accompanied by increases in consumption of milkfat by other consumers. That is because the milkfat removed from the milk that is used in the production of lower fat foods, such as a "lite" cheddar cheese and skim milk, is destined to be sold for use in the manufacture of some other product, be it butter, ice cream, or high-fat cheese.

The nation's total (and per capita) intake of milkfat may be reduced by (1) producing less fluid milk, (2) destroying the milkfat skimmed from the production of lower-fat dairy products before it can be sold, (3) holding it in storage in the form of butter and cheese, or (4) selling it to consumers in other countries via the export market. None of these options seems particularly viable. Under the Dietary Guidelines scenario described earlier, milk production and consumption of dairy products must continue to increase. Outright destruction of milkfat is not economically feasible either as long as there is a still a market for it in the forms of cheese and ice cream. Storage is only a temporary solution. For decades, the federal government limited consumption of milkfat to some extent by storing hundreds of millions of pounds of surplus butter and cheese to help support milk prices. However, as butter prices, in particular, have been permitted to drop to near world-market levels in recent years, stored milkfat was released into market channels for consumption. Finally, dairy exports are growing but are still a relatively small part of the U.S. dairy economy.

To the extent that alternative outlets are limited, higher milkfat production will continue to be channeled to the American consumer. USDA data show that milkfat consumption, in terms of "commercial disappearance," has trended upward steadily over the past twenty years; it was 25 percent higher in 1994 than in 1975. Not surprisingly, milk production in the United States increased at the same rate during that period.[14]

Federal dairy programs enacted by Congress and administered by the USDA have the potential to exacerbate these tendencies. Since increases in milk production at the farm level automatically result in proportionate increases in the amount of milkfat available for consumption, any federal government program that stimulates increased milk production is likely to contribute to higher milkfat consumption as well. Two federal programs—dairy price supports and milk marketing orders—are prime suspects in that they affect how much farmers receive for their milk and thereby influence the amount of milk that farmers produce. In the following section, the basic mechanics of these complicated programs are described, and their historical and anticipated future impacts on milk production in the United States are discussed.

Government's Involvement in Pricing Dairy Products

Rewarding producers for the amount of fat in their milk is a historical artifact. The federal government's milk pricing system was based on butterfat content because this was one component that could not be adulterated. Thus, in order to protect against the watering down of fluid milk supplies or adding chalk to keep the milky, opaque appearance, fat became the component of choice by which dairymen could be compensated for the quality of their product.

Since the 1930s, the federal government has controlled the price of milk and other dairy products in the United States through two regulatory mechanisms: (1) the federal price support program, which establishes a minimum price farmers receive for milk through USDA purchases and storage of cheese, butter, and nonfat dry milk powder; and, (2) federal milk marketing orders, which govern the price farmers receive for milk earmarked for specific end uses.[15]

The Federal Dairy Price Support Program

Federal price support programs have dominated the pricing of milk in this country since the 1930s.* Because fluid milk is such a perishable commodity, the government has indirectly supported the price farmers received for it by actually buying dairy products. For nearly six decades, Congress has established a price floor (or minimum price) for milk used in the production of cheese, butter, and nonfat dry milk powder. When prices approached the price support level, the USDA, through its Commodity Credit Corporation (CCC), would purchase predetermined amounts of those processed dairy products and hold them off the market in storage. When prices rose again, the USDA was instructed by regulations to sell some of its stocks of those products to limit the upward movement of prices. As a result, prices paid to farmers for milk used to manufacture these products stayed relatively close to the price support level, which changed from time to time, according to various congressional actions.

Between 1975 and 1985, "net removals" of butter from the market by the federal government jumped from 63 million pounds to 334 million pounds a year, equal to more than one-fourth of the nation's butter production. Net removals of cheese leaped tenfold from 68 million pounds in 1975 to 629 million pounds in 1985, or about 12 percent of annual cheese output. Between 1980 and 1989, net USDA dairy price support expenditures totaled $17.6 billion, compared to $3.4 billion in the 1970–79 period.[16]

In recent years, the federal government's role in cheese and butter markets has been scaled back drastically. Throughout most of the 1990s, the price support level has been substantially lower than the market price. In part, this is due to the reductions in the price support level mandated in the

---

*Another federal program, "milk marketing orders," regulates the prices of Grade A (fluid) milk. However, since most fluid milk prices are based on those paid for Grade B (manufacturing) milk, the price support program essentially undergirds all dairy prices. About 90 percent of the nation's milk supply is Grade A, and about 45 percent of all Grade A milk sold is used for beverage products.

1990 and 1996 farm bills. From levels as high as $13.48 per hundred pounds of manufacturing milk in the early 1980s, the minimum price support level dropped to $10.10 for the 1990–95 period. The support price for manufacturing milk will fall to $9.90 for 1999 and be eliminated at the end of that year.

The widening spread between market prices and support levels, combined with steady growth in consumer demand for dairy products, meant it would be just a matter of time before USDA stockpiles were eroded. By 1996, total net cheese removals amounted to an insignificant four million pounds. Butter removals melted away altogether by the end of 1995. A string of years with minuscule government purchases drove federal dairy product stockpiles down from 17.7 *billion* pounds (on a milkfat basis) in 1984 to only 24 *million* pounds by October 1996. In fiscal year 1994–95, USDA's net expenditures on dairy price supports amounted to only $3.7 *million*.[17]

Two broad conclusions can be drawn from the data on dairy prices, production, and federal government stocks and purchases. First, federal price supports, particularly in the pre-1990s decade, likely created an incentive to produce more milk (and, therefore, more milkfat) than would otherwise have been produced in a free-market setting. Second, the primary effect of the federal storage of butter and cheese on milkfat consumption was to shift consumption from the 1980s, when USDA stocks were swollen, to the stocks-depletion period of the 1990s. Although a great deal of the butter was sent abroad, the domestic market was by far the primary avenue for depletion of federal butter stocks. The major exception to this shifting of consumption of dairy products from one time period to another is the federal food distribution programs, which provided hundreds of millions of pounds of surplus high fat dairy products annually to food assistance program recipients, including the National School Lunch Program. For years, the feeding programs represented a convenient "off-market" dumping ground to remove part of the surplus butterfat.

Ironically, despite the reduction and eventual phase-out of government price supports in the mid- to late 1990s, increases in milkfat production and consumption are expected, albeit for different reasons. Strong consumer demand for dairy products, especially cheeses, has kept prices well above minimum price support levels and enabled the USDA to liquidate its stocks despite growth in milk production averaging 1 percent per year during the 1991–95 period.

Federal Milk Marketing Orders

Milk marketing orders were first created through legislation passed in the 1930s to assure adequate supplies of good quality milk to consumers at reasonable prices, improve dairy farmers' incomes, and provide stability and orderliness in fluid milk markets.[18] Through federal milk marketing orders, the USDA directly regulates the price farmers are paid for milk in regions of the country where farmers have agreed, through referenda, to participate. The result is a "classified" pricing system that complements the price support program.

Under federal milk marketing orders, minimum prices are set that processors must pay for different uses of Grade A milk in markets covered by the orders. Federal milk marketing orders have two major characteristics: (1) classified pricing of milk according to use, such as beverage milk; "soft" (semiperishable) dairy products, such as cream, cottage cheese, and yogurt; and "hard" (storable) manufacturered products, such as cheese, butter, and nonfat dry milk; and (2) pooling or combining all revenue from the sale of milk in the geographic area covered by an order. These revenue pools provide all producers with a single uniform, or "blend," price for milk that is supplied to plants regulated under an order.

The first step in setting farmers' milk prices under federal milk marketing orders is the determination of the "basic formula price" (BFP), or Class III price, for milk destined to be made into manufactured products like cheese. Once the BFP is "discovered," a set of federal rules is applied to determine the premium above the BFP that farmers in each region will receive for Class II milk to be made into soft products like ice cream and Class I milk consumed as a beverage.

The price-enhancing character of the milk marketing orders is a subject of some controversy among analysts. Some believe that without milk marketing orders, the price for all milk, regardless of its use, would be much lower than the blend price that exists under the milk marketing orders. A 1995 study by the Food and Agricultural Policy Research Institute (FAPRI), for example, found that elimination of the federal milk marketing orders in 1996 would save consumers billions of dollars, in the form of lower prices, through the year 2002.[19] Under these circumstances, continuation of milk marketing orders can be expected to stimulate greater production of milk and milkfat than would occur in the absence of such a classified pricing scheme.

A number of dairy economists, however, believe that if the marketing orders were eliminated, the net consumer savings would be minimal.[20] They argue that elevated prices for milk used as a beverage allow for lower prices for milk used to manufacture processed products such as cheese. The result: more milk production but lower Class III prices charged to cheese processors. The increase in producer prices associated with marketing orders, according to this view, is "considerably less than 5 percent." It is worth noting, however, that at today's prices and production, each 1 percent increase means about $250 million in added revenue for the nation's dairy farmers.

By paying lower-than-free-market prices for milk, cheese manufacturers effectively have their product subsidized under federal milk marketing orders. Who pays the subsidy? The consumers of beverage milk, who pay Class I prices that are higher-than-free-market levels. To the extent that this hypothesis accurately reflects reality, subsidization of cheese manufacturing by beverage milk consumers would not have a favorable public health outcome. After all, under those circumstances, milk marketing orders force the production of high-fat products to be subsidized at the expense of beverage milk, which is being consumed increasingly in low-fat and nonfat forms.

Interaction of Dairy Pricing Programs

How do these two pricing programs interact? The price support program regulates manufactured dairy product prices paid to handlers, and the federal milk marketing order program regulates grade A fluid milk prices paid to dairy farmers by handlers. Each order contains two basic sets of provisions—one set fixes the minimum prices that milk processors must pay, while the other specifies how the returns for selling milk are to be distributed among producers. Figure 4.1 shows how the programs are interrelated; prices for all classes of milk within the federal marketing orders are based on the "Basic Formula Price" (originally called the "Minnesota–Wisconsin price," denoting its geographic base). Thus, as the prime mover of class prices in all federal order markets, this price provides a coordinating link between the federal milk marketing orders and the price support program. Further, it helps assure that minimum class prices will not rise when large government purchases might require a reduction in the support price. In sum, the federal price support program guarantees fluid milk producers an outlet for their product at a guaranteed minimum price and ultimately sets the minimum price for all dairy products through federal marketing orders.

What do these arcane regulations have to do with the production of milkfat? To the extent that they force upward the price of milk received by farmers and lower the price of milk used to produce manufactured products such as cheese and ice cream, they will stimulate milk and milkfat production and ultimately inject more milkfat into American consumers' diets.

Milkfat Pricing Paradoxes

The phaseout of the dairy price support program, as decreed in the 1996 Farm Bill, promises to remove part of the incentive for farmers to produce more milk and milkfat. On the other hand, as greater productivity stimulates increased milk output, the elimination of the price support program for

Figure 4.1 **Price Linkage Between Dairy Support System and Federal Orders**

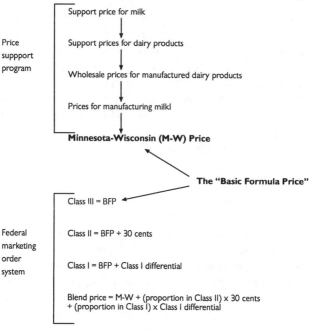

Source: Adapted from Blaney et al., "Dairy: Background for 1995 Farm Legislation," p. 19.

butter will make butter cheaper, and thus potentially a more attractive product for consumers. Ironically, then, in the market-oriented environment of the mid-1990s, American consumers appear to be doing no better than during the time when dairy pricing was heavily influenced by federal government purchases. Even as butter has become less desirable from a public health perspective, in a more market-oriented system it has also become more attractive from a retail consumer price perspective.

At the wholesale level, on the other hand, fat remains a valued component of milk despite the drop in the price of butter. Indeed, the federal milk pricing system places a premium on milk with a higher fat content. What is known as the "butterfat differential" is symbolic of that value. The butterfat differential signifies that the USDA, under the price support program, will support the price of milk with 3.67 percent milkfat at a higher level than milk with 3.50 percent milkfat. As the domestic price of butter has dropped, however, the butterfat differential has shrunk accordingly, from a high of about 30 cents per pound to its current level of 10 cents per pound.[21]

Nonetheless, the value of fat in the wholesale dairy pricing system is not likely to drop when the price support program is phased out in the year 2000. In today's dairy economy, with cheese production driving the whole-sale market for milk, the butterfat differential is still viewed as an economi-cally rational pricing mechanism. In fact, some analysts argue that the butterfat differential actually understates the value of high-fat milk to cheese production. This is because high-fat milk is usually higher in protein and therefore increases the productivity of cheese manufacturing.

It is no surprise, then, that the highest annual average fat content of milk used in the United States for beverage consumption during the 1970–94 period was 3.68 percent.[22] From the perspective of a cheese-driven dairy economy, it is more economical to make low-fat beverage milk by skim-ming the fat off of high-fat, high-protein milk, which is ideal for cheese production, than to take the water out of lower-fat cow's milk to make it more suitable for use in cheese manufacturing.

If anything, the value of high-fat milk could increase in the future. Many federal and state marketing orders have already adopted what is known as "multiple component pricing," in part to ensure that farmers are adequately compensated for high-protein and milk solids content by adding an addi-tional premium for those components to the price the farmer receives. Since high-protein milk is typically higher in fat, premiums paid for the protein component of milk would, in effect, be rewarding farmers for the high fat content of their milk.

It would appear, then, that as long as protein content is so highly valued in the dairy economy and high-protein and high-fat content remain inextri-cably linked, there will be little incentive for farmers to produce milk with a lower fat content. This is troubling, since one of the theoretical ways to reduce dietary intake of fat is to drive down the percentage of fat content in cow's milk through animal breeding. Indeed, in the early years, when the Jersey and Guernsey breeds were dominant among the nation's dairy cattle, the average fat content of milk was over 3.95 percent. By the early 1990s, however, Holsteins were the dominant breed, and the fat content of their milk has consistently averaged between 3.6 percent and 3.7 percent.

That genetically induced drop in the average fat content of the nation's milk supply presents a compelling challenge for the country's livestock breeders. At today's level of milk output, that kind of fat decrease means an 8 percent reduction in the country's milkfat supply. That is equivalent to nearly one-half billion pounds of fat removed from the milk supply per year, or nearly two pounds per person per year. Given that nearly all of the milkfat in the nation's milk supply tends to be consumed in one form or another, a similar genetically driven reduction in the future, combined with greater consumer preference for lower-fat dairy products, could generate important public health benefits.

Reducing Milkfat Production: A Difficult Challenge
With or Without Federal Intervention

In the absence of reductions in the fat content of the nation's milk supply, continued growth in milk production and dairy product consumption—even with a shift toward lower-fat products—may make it difficult
for Americans to meet the Dietary Guidelines recommendations. One
possible outcome is continued growth in dairy product consumption,
stable per capita milkfat intake, and a growing polarization in milkfat
intake between high-income consumers, who can most afford lower-fat
dairy options, and low-income consumers, who take the overflow of
milkfat off the market. If, however, export markets for high-fat dairy
products expanded and became a major vehicle for disposing of milkfat
created by a shift to lower-fat dairy products by U.S. consumers, per
capita milkfat consumption in the United States could decline. The
extent to which domestic milkfat consumption would actually drop depends on whether lower-fat dairy products become attractive to consumers in terms of price, taste, and performance characteristics. If export
markets expanded and lower-fat dairy products remained pricey and less
attractive, however, domestic dairy product consumption could well decline—especially if production growth does not keep pace with export
market expansion. In that case, the milkfat gap between high-income and
low-income dairy consumers could actually shrink as lower-income families purchase fewer dairy products as a result of higher domestic prices
even for high-fat items such as butter.

In summary, there is no easy way out of the nation's milkfat conun-
drum as long as milkfat is a valued commodity in the dairy product
economy with few uses outside of dairy product manufacturing. While
federal price support and milk marketing order programs have probably
contributed to greater milkfat production, elimination of those programs
is not a magic bullet for addressing the nation's milkfat dilemma. In a
market-oriented dairy economy, there is little reason to believe that it
will be easy to reduce per capita milkfat intake even if there is a substantial shift toward lower-fat dairy products. Expanded export market opportunities for high-fat dairy products in the future can help remove
some of the milkfat from the domestic market. However, if dairy products are to play an expanded role in helping Americans meet the Dietary
Guidelines recommendations, then it appears that much of the aggregate
dietary fat reductions, for the population as a whole, must come from
reductions in per capita consumption of the other high-fat food groups,
especially vegetable oils and meats.

BEEF PRODUCTION—THE FEEDLOT IS KEY

To many (especially those over the age of 50), beef is almost synonymous with "American," in a John Wayne-esque way. Americans have a love affair with beef; hamburgers are clearly identified worldwide as *the* American favorite. We're clearly a nation of red meat eaters.* Despite an overall decline during the 1980s, beef consumption rose to over 67 pounds per person in 1994.[23]

In spite of its popularity, the question of meat's proper place in our society is fraught with controversy. Proponents of the meat industry point to the nutritional benefits of lean meat as part of a balanced diet and encourage critics to keep the environmental impact of meat production in perspective as a contributor to a strong economy. Opponents passionately point out the health and environmental consequences of a meat-based diet, as well as the ethical issues of raising animals for slaughter. This section relates specifically to the topic of beef production and the dietary fat issue.

Cattle Production and the Dietary Fat Problem

What aspects of cattle production are related to the fat content of the beef product? These factors can be categorized as (a) cattle breed; (b) type of feed; and (c) "finishing" technique, before the beef is brought to market. The key factor related to dietary fat is the amount of marbling fat in the retail cut of beef; this measure is directly related to the issue of beef grading, a topic that is discussed in depth in chapter 6 of this book.

Cattle Breed

Different breeds of cattle have different percentages of total fat on the carcass, even at the same weight, and breed has a definite impact on marbling fat.[24] This fact alone makes a great difference to beef producers because sales are based at price per pound. It's quite beneficial to sell heavier carcasses; packers pay more because they must handle less material, an efficiency issue. Further, well-marbled meat will grade out at a higher level, producing another economic advantage to produce heavier, well-marbled carcasses. This, in itself, sends a strong signal to the calf producer, the one controlling the genetic makeup of the entire beef supply. The signal is clear—produce only big, healthy calves that will grow fat and convert feed efficiently.[25]

---

*Although the term, "red meat," technically refers to beef, pork, veal, and lamb, there are significantly more cattle raised than any other livestock, some 80 percent of which are beef cattle.

Cattle Feeding

In order to maximize profit, most cattlemen maximize production; in this way, for every unit of production, the relative cost of maintenance per animal is reduced. Most beef producers choose to feed their animals high-grain diets (containing a high proportion of corn* and sorghum) because the animals will reach desired market weight faster. The reasons for wanting animals to gain weight faster is that it will require less time and therefore lower the total nonfeed costs (i.e., labor, interest, depreciation on buildings, etc.) before the animal reaches the desired weight.

Some producers are increasingly choosing to feed forage instead of grain because it is less costly. At the same level of fatness, forage-fed animals will be worth slightly less per pound of live weight than grain-fed cattle because more weight is in the form of nondigested "roughage" in the rumen (or "gut") of the animal. These carcasses, in theory, should be more valuable because, overall, they contain less subcutaneous fat than their grain-fed counterparts. However, there is no price incentive for producers to produce carcasses with less subcutaneous fat. When the price of grain (primarily corn) is high, cattle producers have a choice; they can produce leaner carcasses and reduce production costs by increased forages.

Cattle are usually fed a specific amount, which enables them to gain weight at the level that muscle tissue will be interspersed with just enough "marbling" fat that the carcass can attain a "choice" quality grade. Producers frequently crossbreed smaller cattle with larger breeds so that the animals won't reach the choice grade until they attain heavier weights. The importance of using this technique is that the fatter the animal becomes, the less efficient it is, that is, it takes more feed and money to obtain each additional pound of weight gain.

Cattle Finishing

The end stage of cattle feeding before the animal is slaughtered is called "finishing"; this process can take place either on the range or at the "feed-lot." A calf is typically sold at a weaning weight of 500 to 600 pounds. The total life span of a beef animal is approximately 400 to 600 days, and producers aim for final weights of about 1,000 to 1,400 pounds, depending

---

*A federal price support system regulates the cost of corn, an important feed-grain in the production of beef. Whether or not this program contributes significantly to the "politics of fat" is a question outside the immediate scope of this book.

on the breed. On average, cattle remain in a feedlot for the last 90 to 120 days, which has become the "finishing" point of choice for most beef producers because animals lay down body fat so quickly in that situation.

Contained within the feedlots (which may cover larger areas of land) and physically separated from each other by raised banks or fences, the animals are fed a scientifically controlled diet of grain and processed feed (usually at a ratio of 80 percent grain, usually corn, and 20 percent roughage—hay, alfalfa, and other materials). On this ration, the cattle gain weight and fat rapidly. Further, the criterion used to determine the grade of beef, an acceptable amount of marbling fat (fat interspersed in the muscle of the animal), can only be produced by feedlot feeding.

Originally feedlots were a production "safety valve" for small beef production operations. Excess grain could be fed to cattle and other livestock to fatten them for market. The expansion of feedlots to their present massive scale was driven by several factors: cheap grain, cheap transportation, the development of antibiotics (which allowed previously impossible population densities of more cattle in less space), the USDA grading system (which will be discussed in greater detail in chapter 6), and the demand by national supermarket chains for a uniform product.[26]

Animals in the feedlot live in very crowded conditions and get little exercise. It is said that tenderness of the meat is affected more by the amount of connective tissue than inactivity of muscle use. Therefore, animals with less connective tissue are more tender than animals that have more of this type of tissue. A tender product is an attribute sought by most consumers of beef.

Perhaps the ultimate way to decrease the amount of fat in the animal carcass is to put the cattle on the range and simply permit them to feed from the grasses they find available on the land. These so-called "range fed" beef are usually quite lean because they must spend much more effort to obtain food and are continually moving in order to do so. It is also much more difficult to then retrieve the mature animals and transfer them to the stockyards for sale.

Today, almost *no* beef produced in the United States is finished on the range; the USDA estimates that approximately 95 percent of the beef that is produced in this country is finished at the feedlot. Grazing is used almost exclusively to maintain dairy herds and for raising the young cattle before they are sent off to the feedlot. The result is that less total land is needed for beef production; that is, more beef cattle can be raised on fewer acres of land.

There is movement to combine the range-fed with feedlot finishing methods by feeding calves at the feedlot for a specific period of time, then "finishing" on pasture. One study suggests that these pasture-finished cattle are leaner than feedlot-finished cattle.[27] While beef produced in this way may be suitable for the "niche" market, it probably will not qualify for the "Choice" beef grade because of its lack of marbling fat.

Marketing Concerns

Although government regulations govern the marketing of beef and are addressed in more detail in chapter 5 of this book, it is important to mention marketing concerns in this discussion of beef production. Consumers today usually demand a tender, tasty meat product; fat content (especially the degree of marbling fat) is the primary contributor to those product attributes. Today's lifestyles also dictate faster preparation methods, such as grilling and broiling, rather than long, moisture-based cooking methods, such as braising or stewing. A low-fat product, such as that produced as range-fed beef, must be cooked by these longer methods in order to produce a tasty, tender food.

Leaner beef has become a "niche" market for the beef producer. Certain "branded" products are increasingly available for the health-conscious consumer, although prices remain quite high.[28]

Advocacy Coalitions

A number of issues affect the cattle industry: low prices (profitability for the rancher and packer), fear of drug residues (quality assurance), and problems with waste disposal (environmental); of these, only one is health-related: concern over excess dietary fat contributed by beef. At least two very vocal perspectives affect policy decisions concerning beef production, and these different advocacy coalitions see the issue *very* differently. Those associated with the cattle industry want a plentiful beef supply produced at minimum cost so that an economically viable industry will be maintained. Opponents cite a number of health, safety, and environmental concerns.

Proponents of Beef Production

The cattle industry is well represented in Washington by over a dozen powerful trade associations. Some deal with production of beef cattle (such as the American Farm Bureau Federation, the Farmers Union); others deal with the processed product (e.g., the American Meat Institute, the American Association of Meat Processors). Still others seek to influence consumers' food choices.

By far, the largest beef trade association is the National Cattlemen's Beef Association, created in February 1996 by a consolidation of the National Cattlemen's Association and the National Live Stock and Meat Board/Beef Industry Council. The move was made to streamline the lobbying effort for the beef industry in response to a recommendation that the industry's association would need to merge if beef were to regain a more profitable share of the meat market.[29] The organization has approximately 230,000 members (cattle breeders, producers, and feeders) who contribute over $45 million in checkoff and membership dues.

In response to criticism levied on several fronts, meat industry representatives have dealt with health issues by sponsoring promotion programs that urge consumers to eat smaller portions of beef, with the environmental groups providing educational programs to feedlot operators and with those who oppose the use of hormones and antibiotics sponsoring public relations campaigns to refute the allegations. In 1989, several groups initiated "The Cattlemen's War on Fat." Initiatives included promoting research to help cattlemen producer leaner beef, as well as closer trimming of beef in packing plants.[30]

Opponents of Beef Production

Those who oppose large-scale beef production and consumption point to three definitive issues—food safety, environmental issues, and health and nutrition. Meat opponents point to food safety issues such as the role of residues from antibiotics, hormone implants (used to stimulate growth), and pesticides, which appear in retail cuts of meat, leading to health problems in some people who eat them.[31]

Critics of the meat industry say that beef production damages the environment by depleting natural resources and diverting vast quantities of grain to cattle that could otherwise go to feed hungry people. Use of the feedlot as an animal "finishing" point has several drawbacks. The sheer volume of waste products produced by keeping such large numbers of animals in such confined quarters is damaging to the environment because it is so difficult to avoid contamination of nearby water supplies. Many contend that current meat production techniques, with an emphasis on animal confinement, use of antibiotics, and food supplements, have provided the model for the conditions that generated the deadly "mad-cow disease" in Great Britian.[32]

Serious environmental damage can also result from using intensive cattle production practices. In California's naturally arid land, it takes 360 gallons of water to produce a pound of beef (irrigation for grain, trough-water for stock). The water and acreage required to raise beef for one person could feed up to 20 people if it were used to raise grains.

Jeremy Rifkin's 1992 book, *Beyond Beef*, blamed the meat industry for a whole host of societal problems, including environmental damage, ethical dilemmas, and health problems.[33] Based on the findings in the book, a $1 million "Beyond Beef Campaign" was launched with the support of thirty-five consumer, antihunger, public health, environmental, and animal rights groups in the United States and abroad. Using advertising, education, and lobbying tactics, the goal of the campaign was to reduce worldwide beef consumption by 50 percent. In response, groups such as the American Meat Institute, the American Farm Bureau Federation, and the National Cattlemen's Association formed the "Food Facts Coalition" to oppose Rifkin's arguments, which they described as an "extremist indictment that lacks scientific basis."[34]

Nutrition and health specialists have long warned against eating too much dietary fat, of which beef is a primary source. Recently, however, an economic argument has been added to the disease-prevention message. Groups such as the Physicians Committee for Responsible Medicine have estimated that over $60 million in health care costs are directly attributable to meat consumption.[35]

Governmental Positioning

Where has the USDA been on these issues? For the most part, the USDA has historically been supportive of the meat industry. The department administers the beef promotion program through the Agricultural Marketing Service; regulations have been issued on feedlot operation and the handling of the beef product at the stockyard and by packers. USDA publications promote the consumption of beef as part of a "balanced" diet.[36] Clearly, governmental involvement in the meat industry is not neutral, fueling continued criticism of the USDA's "schizophrenic mission"—supporting beef producers while issuing dietary guidance about meat consumption.

Conclusion: Beef Production Is Market Driven

The issue whether the dietary fat issue vis-à-vis beef production is one driven by government policies or the market is obvious: this is clearly a market-driven issue. Except for grading standards that relate directly to marbling fat content of beef, government policies have mainly dealt with safety rather than health issues. Consumers today continue to eat their steaks and hamburgers in record numbers, oblivious to the fat content of the product. Even the price does not seem to be a significant deterrent to meat consumption. A recent *Washington Post* article describing the current popularity of "steak houses" in the area listed costs of dinners in a sampling of chain restaurants; the prices ranged from $32 for a 24-ounce Porterhouse steak, U.S. Prime grade, to $17.95 for a 20-ounce T-bone steak, U.S. Choice grade.[37] Americans' love affair with fatty meat continues. . . .

OILS FROM PLANTS: A GROWING AWARENESS, A GLOBAL ISSUE

For the past twenty years, food supply data have confirmed that the amount of total fat available to the American consumer has increased. The source of this fat is nearly all from an increased use of polyunsaturated vegetable oils and using such oils as partial substitutes for fats from animal sources, such as lard.[38] To meet this increased demand for vegetable oils, production of U.S. sources has increased, and imports have escalated. Government and various interest groups have become involved in both production and trade issues for vegetable oils.

In the world of dietary fats, vegetable oils are the "good guys." Researchers have linked the consumption of fat, and especially saturated fat, with its ability to raise blood cholesterol, a major risk factor in the development of coronary heart disease (CHD). Thus, current dietary recommendations suggest limiting the overall amount of fat ingested, and especially reducing the amount of saturated fat consumed.

This is where vegetable oils come in. Most vegetable oils contain far more unsaturated fatty acids in proportion to the amount of saturated fatty acids. Thus, those who wish to monitor the amount of saturated fat they consume have long been advised to switch the source of the dietary fat they eat away from animal sources (which contain a much higher proportion of saturated fatty acids) to vegetable oils (which contain higher proportions of mono- and poly-unsaturated fatty acids). Monounsaturated fatty acids are supplied in the diet mainly by olive oil, and the principal polyunsaturated fatty acid is the linoleic acid, also known as an "essential" fatty acid because the body is not able to synthesize this exact structure. This section focuses on the types of vegetable oils in terms of their marketability and trade aspects.

Types of Vegetable Oil

Vegetable oils are clear liquid substances at room temperature, which can be classified as either cooking oils or salad oils.[39] Cooking oils are used in deep-fat or pan-frying operations, while salad oils have been refined, bleached, and deodorized so that they can be used in the production of bottled oils, mayonnaise, table spreads, and salad dressings. This discussion will focus on the following "more popular" vegetable oils used in food processing and cooking, those popular because of health implications, and the so-called "tropical oils." Government politics have affected the use—and the prescribed avoidance—of these food substances. The discussion that follows presents trade and political issues surrounding the use of vegetable oils. Table 4.2 describes the characteristics and uses of the most prominent plant oils.

Issues in Oilseed Production and Trade

Worldwide, oils of vegetable origin contribute a markedly higher percentage of visible fat than those of animal origin.[40] In 1990, vegetable sources supplied 24 grams of oil per capita per day, in comparison to 6 grams of fat from animal sources.[41]

Spurred by income and population growth in developing countries—as well as rapidly expanding food processing industries in Asia and other developing areas—the global growth in consumption of vegetable oils is outpacing that of most other agricultural products. Consumption of vegetable oils worldwide grew at an average annual rate of 4.2 percent over the past decade. This situation has stimulated a lively trade in oilseeds worldwide.

Since the 1950s, soybean oil has been the leading vegetable oil in production and in use worldwide. However, world supplies of other vegetable oils, notably palm and rapeseed, have been growing, gradually replacing the reliance on soybean oil. This growth can be attributed to the more competitive prices and health benefits of other oils but also to many countries' policies during the 1980s to promote domestic production of oilseeds and foster self-sufficiency in vegetable oils.

The U.S. soybean industry drives both the U.S. and the world oilseeds markets. Accounting for approximately one-quarter of the world oilseed production, U.S. soybean output leads prices and production prospects in other export-oriented oilseed producing countries.

Policies enacted by the European Community (EC) and the Indian government stimulated the production of oilseeds, particularly rapeseed, through a system of government supports that guarantee producers minimum prices for production. Competition from South American soybean growers and Asian palm oil producers also increased, severely curtailing soybean plantings in the United States. The 1990 Farm Act gave United States oilseed producers the incentive to plant the crop with the best market return. However, gains in production and export share have been modest.

With government policies stimulating large production of oilseeds and influencing trade patterns, the composition of world vegetable oil markets is

Table 4.2 Types of Vegetable Oils

NAME	SOURCE	USES	SPECIAL CHARACTERISTICS	UNIQUE FEATURES
Soybean Oil	Soybeans	Most widely used in salad and cooking oils; in >83% of all oils and 62% of all salad dressings.	Accounts for 40% of all intake of edible oils in U.S.	World's most plentiful vegetable oil; predominant oilseed grown in U.S.
Cottonseed Oil	Cotton	General purpose frying oil; ingredient in commercially baked and snack foods; used alone or in combination with other oils as general purpose salad oil, salad dressings, mayonnaise, sauces.	Preferred by restaurants because it rarely produces "off" flavors when frying.	Primary edible oil in U.S. until soybean oil became widely available.
Safflower Oil	Safflower	In making of premium margarines; as ingredient in infant formulas; and as highly "polyunsaturated" oils.	Contains approximately 75% polyunsaturated fatty acids.	Not suitable as frying oil because of high linoleic acid content, a polyunsaturated fatty acid.
Canola Oil	Genetically-engineered strain of rapeseed	Salad oil and as ingredient in formulated foods.	Favorable fatty acid profile; contains significant amount of mono-unsaturated fatty acids.	Extremely clear and light.
Olive Oil	Olive fruit	Salad oil.	Highest content of olive acid, a monounsaturated fatty acid, than other oils. More resistant to oxidative changes than other oils because of low acid content.	Can be used in low-temperature cooking.
"TROPICAL OILS" Coconut Oil	Coconut palm	Appealing creamy "mouthfeel" A key food ingredient in confectionery uses. Used in chocolate coating for ice cream bars because it stays hard.	Lower melting point than other oils; highest level of saturated fat of any vegetable oil.	Very stable against oxidative rancidity because it contains low levels of unsaturated fatty acids.
Palm/Palm Kernel Oil	Palm	Many of same uses; key ingredient in processed foods.	Melts easily, feels less greasy in mouth.	Very stable; less likely to oxidize.

changing. While soybean oil continues to dominate world consumption of vegetable oils, competing oils (such as palm oil and edible rapeseed oil) dominate the growth in vegetable oil trade.

On November 20, 1992, the United States and the European Community (EC) averted a potential trade war when they agreed to resolve an oilseed dispute over the EC's subsidies on oilseeds. The key feature of the agreement limits the EC's oilseed-growing areas.

Oils and Politics: An Unhealthy Mix

Americans' health concerns—coupled with increased availability of information about the fat content of foods—have fueled trade debates as well as changes made by the food industry in the labeling and composition of new foods. These concerns have substantially reduced U.S. imports of palm oil and have created a fertile environment for the agressive marketing of canola and olive oils, both of which contain *far* less saturated fat than palm oil. Consumption of canola oil in the United States grew more than 200 percent between 1987 and 1991, while that of olive oil grew by more than 300 percent between 1980 and 1991.

Trade Aspects of Oils

Hampered by foreign exchange constraints, developing countries continue to buy palm oil, which is less expensive than other types. Consequently, palm oil's market share has expanded from 26 percent of total world vegetable oil exports in 1975 to over 40 percent in 1992–93. With much of the growth in vegetable oil consumption occurring in developing countries, palm oil will likely continue to expand its market share throughout the 1990s.

Expanding oilseed production in South America, the EC, China, India, Malaysia, and Indonesia increased competition for U.S. oilseed and oilseed products in the 1980s. As a result, U.S. vegetable oil exports began to fall, prompting the U.S. government to launch a variety of programs in the mid-1980s to promote U.S. exports and challenge competitors who subsidize their exports. These programs included the Export Enhancement Program (EEP), which provides bonuses to U.S. exporters to help them sell U.S. vegetable oil at competitive prices on the world market. Similarly, the Cottonseed and Sunflowerseed Oil Assistance Programs (COAP and SOAP) stimulate exports of U.S. oils in designated countries. U.S. vegetable oil exports are also promoted through credit guarantee, food aid, and market development programs (including the Foreign Market Development Program and the Market Promotion Program). Bolstered by these programs,

U.S. vegetable oil exports rose again in the late 1980s and continued in the early 1990s.

While the United States and the EC continue to be the largest consumers of vegetable oils in the world, *growth* in demand is strongest in the newly industrialized countries in East Asia and in developing countries, such as China, India, and Pakistan. Developing countries are consuming more vegetable oils because of rapid growth in population and income. As income increases, preferences shift toward more processed foods and more food prepared away from home, both of which include vegetable oils as important ingredients. Growth of food processing industries in developing countries is anticipated to strengthen demand for vegetable oils even more.

Future increases in demand for vegetable oils may depend heavily on what happens in China—the world's second-largest vegetable oil importer. Until 1985, China was self-sufficient in vegetable oil production. Since 1986, however, consumption has substantially outpaced production, and vegetable oil imports—led by palm oil from Malaysia—have soared from 114,000 tons in 1980 to a forecasted 1.4 million tons in 1993–94. Chinese consumption of vegetable oils has expanded dramatically since the mid-1970s due to growth in population and per capita income. However, China's per capita consumption is still substantially below the world level so there is considerable potential to promote increased consumption of oils. The government of China is promoting food processing industries in areas close to crop growing areas in an effort to increase rural industrial development. The growing food processing sector, stimulated by market reforms and increased liberalization of imports (which lower prices for inputs), should trigger increasing demand for vegetable oils in the future.

Summary

Each of the three commodities discussed in this chapter—dairy products, beef, and vegetable oils—is a significant source of fat in the American diet. Equally intriguing are the policy dynamics affecting the production and subsequent supply of these products for the consumer. These "behind the scenes" efforts and actions of competing advocacy coalitions are usually invisible to the consumer who purchases such products. But their legacy in terms of effects on food availability and prices are quite real.

What about the supply side of the "politics of fat" equation, the *production* of dietary fat vis-à-vis the production of vegetable oil crops, "red meat," and milk? All of us have heard outrageous anecdotes and analyses pertaining to the federal government's extensive involvement in farm commodity production. There is little question that the federal government—mainly through price supports, income subsidy programs, marketing orders, and restrictions on imports of farm commodities from other countries—has played a heavy role in controlling farmers' agricultural output, prices, and incomes.

Given six decades of near "command-and-control" management over most of the U.S. farm economy by the federal government, it would seem natural to assume that the production of vegetable and animal fat in this country has been strongly influenced by federal agricultural laws and regulations. If the USDA supports the price of milk, making it higher than it would be in a free market, then is the department not encouraging the production of more milk, and accordingly, more milk fat, than would otherwise occur? Similarly, if the federal government limits the amount of beef that can be imported into the country from foreign competitors (who produce mostly leaner, range-fed cattle), then do the import quotas not raise the fat content of the U.S. beef supply? And the enormous income subsidies for U.S. producers of corn, sorghum, and barley—the primary grains fed to livestock in this country—do they not, in effect, subsidize confined feeding of cattle, which results in beef with a higher fat content?

The answer to each of these questions is a qualified "yes." Once again, however, as with any complicated set of federal programs and complex set of economic forces, the "devil is in the details." In these instances, the qualifiers are so strong that the end result is an inevitable conclusion that the federal government's impact on the production of fat in farm commodities has not been and is increasingly likely not to be a primary factor in the "politics of fat" in the twenty-first century.

Three factors have driven these general conclusions. First, even when federal government intervention in the farm economy has had an impact on the production of vegetable oils and animal fat, it has generally been grossly overshadowed or neutralized by other countervailing governmental forces or nongovernmental market forces. Second, over time, key agricultural production sectors have been moving toward substantially reduced, if not minimal, government involvement and greater market orientation. Finally, as the farm sector continues to evolve from a commodity-production, or "sales"-dominated, sector into a "marketing"-dominated sector, it will increasingly be pushed to participate in the consumer revolution regarding dietary fat intake.

The "politics of fat" has been conspicuously absent from debates over agricultural policy. At some point in the recent past, each of the policy vehicles used by the federal government to intervene in these farm sectors has been the subject of controversy. Whether it be feedgrain income subsidies, dairy price supports, milk marketing orders, or beef import quotas, farm policies have been highly politicized over the past two decades. On some occasions, such as the debates over highly visible farm subsidy programs, powerful advocacy coalitions have formed to support or eliminate the use of those policy instruments.

Rarely, if ever, however, have the politics of these issues been driven by the "politics of fat." Debates over fat in the American diet have, at best, been only at the periphery of the major public policy debates about federal intervention in the feedgrain, dairy, and meat-producing sectors. Questions about the impact of federal farm programs on the production of dietary fat have typically taken a back seat to equity, consumer pricing, or environmental arguments against federal intervention.

This absence of an overt "politics of fat" in the recent history of farm policy making is perhaps not that surprising. It indirectly supports the conclusion to be drawn in this chapter that the net impact of federal farm programs on fat production has been relatively small and is being reduced with current changes in farm programs. Clearly, other areas of government intervention, such as dietary advice, federal government purchases, food labeling, and food ingredient standards, have attracted far more of the attention of the key stakeholders involved in shaping the "politics of fat" in America. Collectively, these discussions are key to the debate about moving from a food policy to a true nutrition policy, where renewed emphasis is placed on both the healthfulness of diets and the sustainability of the environment as preferred policy outcomes.

FOR FURTHER CONSIDERATION:
THE TROPICAL OILS "WARS"

As consumers' awareness of the health benefits to be derived from the consumption of vegetable oils rather than animal fats has increased, so too has the demand for certain plant oils. The dilemma is that those oils that have been promoted because of their health benefits (i.e., due primarily to their high content of mono- or polyunsaturated fatty acids) are not the same as those oils prized by food manufacturers for their functional capabilities as a food ingredient.

These "wars between the oils" have provided a perfect example of the power of competing advocacy coalitions. U.S. governmental adjustments and promotions of world trade in food oils have been matched by an equally vigorous campaign between competing trade associations. The Malaysian Palm Oil Promotion Council hired a public relations firm, Edelman Public Relations (with offices worldwide), to represent their interests in the United States and promote their product primarily to health professionals who work with the public. Attractive, eye-catching materials (sanctioned by an Advisory Board composed of a number of "experts" in the field of lipid metabolism) have been distributed by the agency, including pieces titled, "Health, Nutrition and Palm Oil," "Answers to Consumer Questions on Palm Oil," and a quarterly newsletter, "Perspectives," subtitled, "A periodic report on new developments in fats and oils nutrition and health," containing abstracts and reports on recent research findings linking saturated fat to cardiovascular health.

Starting in about 1987, there was a rather nasty feud between these Malaysian palm oil producers and the American Soybean Association (ASA), which had mounted an extensive advertising campaign calling palm oil a "threat to consumer health." The country of Malaysia, which relies on palm oil exports to earn foreign exchange dollars, joined with the palm oil producers, who pointed out that soybean oil is most often sold in a hydrogenated form that makes it equivalent to a saturated fat, and jointly protested to the U.S. government and to the Congress. In 1989, ASA and the palm oil producers agreed to halt their reciprocal negative campaigns. ASA said it intended to "move on to an aggressive effort to promote the positive aspects of soybean oil. . . ."[42]

So what's happened to oil usage since the antitropical oil campaign, and did this changeover in product formulations really benefit consumers? Spokespersons for the Institute of Shortenings and Edible Oils, another trade association, emphasized that the percentage of market share of tropical oils as well as the percentage contribution of tropical oils to saturated fat consumption among Americans was very low to begin with in the mid-1980s. Palm oil and coconut oil consumption has gone down significantly; since 1986–87, palm oil usage declined 65 percent and coconut oil fell 47 percent while usage of most other vegetable oils increased. (The total usage of fats and oils had actually *increased* almost 15 percent in the same period.)

At about the same time that the advertising campaigns were heating up, Philip Sokolof, an Omaha industrialist turned nutrition advocate because of his recovery from a heart attack, self-funded an organization, the National Heartsavers Association. To call public attention to the dangers of high cholesterol, the group began taking out full-page ads in major newspapers charging that tropical oils were "poisoning" America. Whether or not such ads actually changed consumer behavior is anyone's guess. However, Mr. Sokolof firmly believes his campaign had an impact on dietary fat intake and consumers' avoidance of "tropical oils" in food. He has rated his greatest accomplishments as "getting people to read food labels and to think about saturated fat, regardless of its source."[43]

The food manufacturers played an important role in the "war" against tropical oils because many removed most of these oils from their products. In fact, in doing so, the amount of saturated fat usually dropped. For example, when Keebler replaced palm kernel and coconut oils with soybean oil, the saturated fat content of its Town House crackers declined 30 percent and that in Club crackers 15 percent. Why did the food industry take such steps? The power of consumer perception and demand again played an important role. According to Pepperidge Farm's Ann Davin, "Did we significantly change the products? No. It was much more a perception story than a true health advantage. . . . But it's what consumers told us they wanted."[44]

———— Chapter 5 ————

Government's Role in Food Processing: Regulating Fat as a Food Ingredient

*Changes in American eating habits will continue to have signifi-
cant consequences for farmers, [food processors, and marketing specialists] and [will necessitate changes in] public policy
[as well.]*

—B. Carr*

Food processors add utility and value to raw farm products. In this process,
the food manufacturers interface with both producers and consumers; they
buy commodities to be processed from farmers and typically sell their products, in turn, to food wholesalers and occasionally directly to retailers.
These activities collectively have been defined as "those that typically use
power-driven machines and materials, handling equipment, to mechanically
or chemically transform raw materials into foods and beverages for human
consumption."[1] Food processors also provide important marketing functions, such as new product and process development, packaging, labeling,
branding, storing, transporting, and financing.

Nearly fifty separate, distinct food processing and manufacturing industries in the United States add nearly $100 billion in value to raw food
products. These industries include the processors of meat products (e.g.,
meat packing, poultry, eggs), dairy products, preserved (i.e., canned or frozen) fruits and vegetables, grain milling products, bakery products, sugar
and confections, fats and oils, beverages, and miscellaneous foods such as
fishery products, coffee, and others. The food processing industry is becoming more and more concentrated, with mergers and acquisitions creating
fewer, larger, and highly diversified firms.

Sales in the U.S. food marketing system reached $825 billion in 1994, up
4.6 percent from 1993 sales.[2] In the international economy, the United States is

---

*B.A. Carr, "Living Off the Fat of the Land," *CRS Review*, March 1989, p. 18.

the largest importer as well as the largest exporter of processed foods. The value of processed food imports has generally exceeded that of exports.

In recent years, food processors have become more responsive to consumer demand, needs shaped by lifestyle, and new attitudes about health and diet. Consumers have asked for more "fresh" foods, which require processors to use new packaging technology and more rapid transport of products from farm to table. To fit in with consumers' busy lifestyles, food processors have developed "convenience foods," such as microwavable foods and refrigerated fresh foods, as well as prepackaged meals, entrées, and desserts that require virtually no cooking or clean-up.

The Role of Food Processing in the Food System

Responding to Consumer Demand

Most consumers love to eat fatty foods. Not only do such foods taste good, but they offer reminders of childhood "comfort foods," respites from the hurried, bustling lives most of us live. We want these foods but are admonished about the deleterious effects that come with their consumption. We are repeatedly reminded that second only to smoking, overeating (and the overeating mainly of these fatty delights) is the nation's leading cause of death.

We want to change our diets, but not too much. Consumers want to "change without changing." According to the NPD Group, which has been conducting surveys on eating trends in America since 1980, "Better for you" foods (e.g., lower-fat versions of products) now account for nearly one-third of all grocery purchases.[3] The public clearly wants (and will pay for) foods that "taste good" and also carry less fat. So, the demand has been created for products that are lower-fat versions of the ones with which one is familiar.

Food processors are responding to that demand by creating low-fat versions of long-time favorites. On average, more than 1,000 new low-fat and fat-free products have been introduced annually since 1990, according to the International Food Information Council. And most of these are designed to be identical to a full-fat counterpart.[4]

Clearly, advances in technology and new ingredients are a driving force behind the development of high-quality fat- and cholesterol-reduced foods. As the demand increases, food processors have a challenge to deliver well-rounded flavor and mouthfeel as well as reduced fat and calories in new products. This trend of "getting the fat out" has become a multibillion dollar phenomenon, and "fat replacers" have become the food industry's favorite means for delivering the taste, but not the calories of fat.[5]

Creating Replacements for Fat in Food

Although a number of terms have been coined to describe this diverse group of food ingredients, perhaps the most appropriate is "fat replacer," an ingredient that replaces some or all of the functions of fat and may or may not provide nutritional value.[6] Other commonly used synonyms include fat analogs, fat mimics (also called mimetics), and fat extenders or sparers.

Fat replacement occurs by any one of several technologies or combinations of ingredients, or both. The simplest technique for replacing fat is to add air or water to the product. To meet the challenge of stabilizing the air or binding the water, other ingredients are frequently added. The food industry's search for fat replacements has required a careful balance of ingredients and advanced processing technology to produce a reduced-fat product that replicates all the texture, mouthfeel, and flavor of the traditional product. In fact, achieving fat reduction is often the result of several ingredients and processing techniques used in combination, rather than a single ingredient used as a one-for-one substitution for fat.

Three basic techniques have been developed to produce ingredients that reduce the fat level of foods. The first two develop fat replacers using two other macronutrients, carbohydrates and proteins, that have fewer calories than fat. The earliest development and the most common approach has been to replace a portion of the fat in the product with carbohydrate-based substances, such as starches, dextrins, or gums. These plant substances soak up water and "plump up," creating tiny balls that simulate the slippery or slimy sensation in the mouth, which food technologists call "mouthfeel." The objective is to take water and "structure" it so that it produces a feeling in the mouth that mimics that of the high-fat food.

Simulating the slippery "mouthfeel" of fat is also the general principle behind the type of fat replacers based on "micro-particulated proteins." When heated at high temperatures, proteins from milk or whey (the watery portion of milk) or egg white coagulate into particles so small that the tongue perceives them as a fatlike smooth and creamy liquid. The practical food applications for these protein-based products are almost exclusively in nonheated foods, such as frozen desserts, yogurt, margarine, and the like, since the proteins are dispersed and denatured upon heating and lose their fatlike taste.[7]

When products that alter lipids are used as fat replacers, they taste like fat because they still are. These compounds have actually had their molecular structure as a fat modified so that they can't be digested by the body, and therefore no calories are available to wreck havoc in the body. This is the principle on which olestra was developed by Procter & Gamble nearly three decades ago.

Government's Role in Food Processing

The Regulatory Process

The major form of policy affecting processed foods are those regulations promulgated by the Food and Drug Administration and the U.S. Department of Agriculture (for food products containing meat and poultry). These regulations implement broad-based legislation (and any subsequent amendments to that legislation), such as the Federal Food, Drug, and Cosmetic Act of 1938 (FDCA), the Nutrition Labeling and Education Act (NLEA) of 1990, or laws governing the actions of the USDA, such as the Meat Inspection Act, the Poultry Products Inspection Act, or the Egg Product Inspection Act. In addition, a number of "memoranda of understanding," "executive orders," are used to govern both the *content* of food products as well as the techniques and actions that take place in the the processing of foods.

The Food and Drug Administration (FDA) has been the primary federal agency in charge of safeguarding the food supply. The FDA uses several strategies to fulfill this charge: (1) inspections of operations in food processing plants (particularly important in the matter of sanitation), (2) regulations imposed on processors about what can or what cannot be added to a food, and (3) an elaborate system of market surveillance programs.

For purposes of this book, we limit our discussion of government's involvement in the food processing system (a vast and complex array of laws, regulations, and other policy directives) to the monitoring of the *ingredients* in food. There are three main constituents of food, organized for purposes of discussion into three broad categories: natural components, unintended contaminants, and intentionally introduced food additives, the last of which serves as the subject of our discussion in this book.[8]

The 1938 FDCA had the effect of essentially dividing the food supply into *two* different regulatory categories. The first regulatory category included raw agricultural commodities, food itself, and functional substances added that were either approved by the USDA or by the FDA during 1938 to 1958, or that were "generally recognized as safe" (GRAS) for their intended use. The second category included all new food additives that did not fall within the first category and all color additives; manufacturers who wished to add ingredients that fell into this category were required to obtain approval from the FDA prior to putting the product on the market, a process now referred to as "premarket approval." According to Peter Barton Hutt, a preeminent attorney for the food industry and former chief counsel to the FDA, "the first part [dealing with GRAS substances as food ingredients] has been a complete success, and the other half [regulating new food additives using the premarket approach] a complete failure."[9]

Policy Implications of Fat Substitutes

Several fat replacers have been developed from natural ingredients (many of which are similar to substances already in food, such as amino acids, modified starch, and so forth) and therefore qualify to be recognized by the FDA as "GRAS" (*G*enerally *R*ecognized *A*s *S*afe). These substances do *not* need to undergo the same rigorous testing procedures as are required for food additives. Examples of GRAS substances used as fat replacers are Simplesse (a protein-based fat replacer made from egg white or whey milk protein), Oat Trim (a cellulose-based mimetic developed by the USDA); Avicel and Novagel (cellulose-based, contains guar gum), N-Oil (starch-based), Stellar (derived from cornstarch), Slendid (made out of pectin extracted from citrus peels), Salatrim (from modified soy and canola oils),[10] and the recently announced Z-Trim (developed by the USDA, made of fiber from hulls of oats, corn, or soybeans.[11])

The second category of food additives, including substances with no proven track record of safety, must be evaluated and approved by the FDA *before* they can be marketed to the public. Examples of this type of food additive are polydextrose, carrageenan, and olestra, which are all used as fat replacers. In order to obtain FDA approval, manufacturers of food additives must test their products, submit the results to the FDA for review, and await agency approval before using them in any food that is sold to the public. If the company fails to produce the type of evidence that is necessary to prove the product is safe, the approval will not be given and the product will never appear on the market. Thus, it is in the best (and only!) interest of the company to adhere closely to FDA regulatory requirements.

Other policy implications of the use of fat substitutes include the standardization of nutrient content claims mandated by the Nutrition Labeling and Education Act (NLEA) of 1990 and appropriate labeling of their inclusion and use on food labels. Another issue is how these substances can be identified and accounted for in tables of "food composition" published by the federal government.

Case Study #2, which follows this chapter, showcases the development and premarket regulatory approval process for one of the most revolutionary fat replacers ever formulated, olestra. This additive was developed by Procter & Gamble in a few years, but the regulatory approval process required over twenty years and twenty thousand pages of documents to document its safety to the satisfaction of the FDA.

———————— *Case Study 2* ————————

"Olestra": Regulatory Approval of the "Nonfat" Fat

This case study highlights "the politics of fat" in a way few others can. It vividly demonstrates the interplay of federal regulatory policy as it attempts to protect the public health by approving a safe "nonfat" food ingredient and, at the same time, allow the multibillion corporation that developed the product to aggressively market foods to that portion of general public that has the resources and inclination to purchase them. Thus, from a policy perspective, this case study vividly demonstrates the interplay between government regulatory agency personnel who "approve" the food products, the food processing industry that manufacture food products, and the consumer who eats them!

Never before has a single issue—or product—so captured the imagination, the energy, and the pocketbooks of so many players in the food policy arena. "Olestra," the "nonfat fat" developed by the Procter & Gamble (P&G) company decades ago, and approved in early 1996 as a food additive by the Food and Drug Administration (FDA), has been the controversial "poster child" symbolizing the interlocking nature of consumer demand, the science of food product development, and the influence of the regulatory environment. All the "players" in the public policy process have been involved—from the schizophrenic fat-phobic, but fat-loving, food-eating public to the alchemists in the food industry who have developed the techno-products to its three-piece-suit lobbyists who seek to influence the regulatory process to the academics paid to carry out the olestra research studies to the activists from consumer advocacy groups and the public health community who warn all who will listen about the product's possible deleterious health effects. The food industry's developmental process culminates with a regulatory decision—either approval or disapproval—made by the watchdogs at the FDA, the federal agency that must pore over mountains of scientific reports and the industry's legalistic petitions in order to issue "premarket approval" for this novel food ingredient before it can be offered for sale to the American public.

Figure CS2.1 **Visual Diagram of Olestra and How It Works**

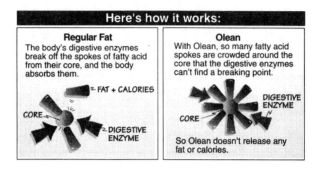

Source: Food Technology 50: 130, March 1996.

Introducing Olestra

Let us briefly review the science behind the development of the olestra compound (see Fig. CS2.1). Visualize a molecule of regular fat, called a triglyceride. It looks like a "Y"; the three spokes are fatty acids, joined to glycerol, an alcohol. In chemical terms, olestra is a "sucrose polyester." It looks like a spider with six or eight (rather than three) fatty acids attached to a center post that is a sugar compound, sucrose, rather than glycerol.[1] The digestive enzymes that break down fats in the gut do so by attacking the triglyceride at the central point where the fatty acids attach to the glycerol molecule. The junction point where olestra's fatty acids attach to the sucrose molecule is covered by so many arms of fatty acid that the enzymes can't get at it to break it down. So the molecule, having served its function in the mouth by making the food taste and "feel" like fat, sails on through the remainder of the intestines undigested and unabsorbed—and unable to contribute calories, either for energy or for depositing on the body.

The Product Development–Regulatory Approval "Two Step"

Olestra has been called "an example of the serendipitous nature of scientific research."[2] In the 1960s, Procter & Gamble scientists were conducting experiments to develop a more easily digested fat for premature infants. Instead of creating a fat that would be more easily digested and therefore a more readily available source of extra calories for these infants, they found, instead, that they had come up with a fat that couldn't be digested at all. Because of the manipulations done to the chemical structure of the fat, the product passed through the digestive system pretty much unscathed. The following section describes the legislative authority under which the Food and Drug Administration operates and the process P&G went through in securing the FDA's approval—noted as one of the longest and costliest in food additive approval history.[3]

Background: Statutory Language and Regulatory Environment

This section describes the "language of the law" and the environment in which the regulatory agency charged with implementing the law conducts its business. These factors basically determine the "hows" and the "whys" of the premarket approval process for the olestra product. The 1938 Federal Food, Drug, and Cosmetic Act (FFDCA) and its implementing regulations require that foods be inherently safe in order for them to be sold to the public. Further, this act prohibits companies from selling any food that is injurious to health and prohibits the addition of "poisons" to food.

The 1958 Food Additive Amendment to the FFDCA established a "premarket approval" system whereby any company seeking to market a food additive must first obtain approval from the FDA. Through this mechanism, Congress sought to shield the public from unsafe or potentially unsafe products. The amendment stipulates that a food is deemed to be adulterated if it contains any unsafe food additive and specifies that an unapproved food additive is unsafe. The amendment also broadly describes the type of data necessary to evaluate the safety of a food additive and provides general criteria for determining the safety and the suitability of the food additive for approval. The law decrees that the following factors must be considered:

1. The *probable level of consumption* of the additive and any substance formed in the food because of the use of the additive
2. The *cumulative effect of such an additive in the diet* . . . , taking into account any chemically or pharmacologically related substance or substances in such diet
3. *Safety factors* which in the opinion of experts qualified by scientific training and experience to evaluate the safety of food additives are generally recognized as appropriate for the use of animal experimentation data

The 1958 amendment also provides administrative procedures for premarket evaluation and approval of a food additive and for judicial review of agency decisions.

Thus, the language of the 1958 Food Additive Amendment established that a food additive must be shown to be safe before it can be added to food; it stipulated that a food additive must achieve some physical or functional effect in food; it set general criteria by which *relative safety* rather than absolute safety could be established; and it directed the FDA to set tolerance levels for use of a food additive. Notably *absent* from these criteria was any mention of a *potential health benefit* from an additive in food.

Approving new fat substitutes and meeting the requirements of the food additive amendment obviously involves complex decisions.[4] As Vanderveen and Glinsmann point out,

> ... often it is difficult to estimate the probable consumption and the cumulative effect on the diet that new fat substitutes and related substances may have. Application of a significant safety factor extrapolated from animal data may not be possible. Approaches used to prove the safety of fat substitutes may differ from those used for most food ingredients because such substances potentially may constitute a large portion of the diet of an individual. ... A large safety factor has been the standard for most new food additive approvals. Thus, to establish use with a lesser safety factor, one would need to establish safety with data from clinical trials in which human subjects consume levels of the fat substitute at and preferably above the highest expected exposure level to provide a margin of safety.[5]

Under provisions of the 1958 amendment to the FFDCA, the FDA is not to approve a food additive petition, "if a fair evaluation of the data before the . . . Commissioner [of the FDA] . . . fails to establish that the proposed use of the food additive, under the conditions of use to be specified in the regulation, *will be safe.*"

This provision is commonly referred to as the *general safety clause.* By requiring that the data for a new food additive "establish" *relative* safety, Congress squarely placed the burden of proving safety on the sponsor of a food additive petition, in this case, the Procter & Gamble company. It is not necessary for the FDA to prove that the additive is unsafe in order to deny approval. The term *safe* is not defined in the act itself. The legislative history of the amendment makes clear, however, that a demonstration of absolute harmlessness is not required to sustain the approval of a food additive,

> . . . Safety requires proof of a reasonable certainty that no harm will result from the proposed use of an additive. It does not—and cannot—require proof beyond any possible doubt that no harm will result under any conceivable circumstance. . . . The scientific panel which testified before the subcommittee . . . pointed out that it is impossible in the present state of scientific knowledge to establish with complete certainty the absolute harmlessness of any chemical substance.[6]

FDA regulations incorporate the concept of safety articulated in the amendment's legislative history. According to the *Code of Federal Regulations* (21 CFR 170.3[I])—" 'Safe' means that ... there is a reasonable certainty in the minds of competent scientists that the substance is not harmful under the intended conditions of use." Although the concept of "harm" is central to the act's safety standard, neither the statute, nor regulations implementing the food additive provisions, define harm. However, the legislative history supports the concept that an effect is *harmful if it affects health*, not if it is simply an undesirable or unexpected effect that has no adverse health consequences.

The Regulatory Challenge:
Assessing Safety, Not Benefit

The law leaves the methods and criteria for interpreting data up to the discretion and expertise of the regulatory agency. Congress did, however, in the legislative language of the 1958 Food Additive Amendment, direct the FDA to consider several factors in making its judgments regarding *safety*. The following discussion identifies these three factors and discusses the evidence that could be used to support each.[7]

(1) *"The probable consumption of the additive and of any substance formed in or on food because of the use of the additive. . . "*;

A fat substitute could become a significant portion of the diet, especially if people are consuming it at a level that directly replaces fat. Food additives that could be present in amounts above 10 percent by weight in relation to the overall food product are called "macroingredients"; olestra is considered to be such a substance. In most diets of Americans, 35–40 percent of the calories are from fat; therefore, fat makes up more than 20 percent of the weight of such diets. If half of the fat in these diets were to be replaced by a fat substitute, then the diet would consist of more than 10 percent of the fat substitute by weight. At such high consumption levels, traditional testing techniques, such as those currently used with animals, would be impossible to conduct.

(2) " ... *the cumulative effect of such additive in the diet of man or animals, taking into account any chemically or pharmacologically related substance or substances in such diet*";

If the ingested substance were poorly digested or not digested at all, the absorption of essential nutrients may be decreased through one of at least three mechanisms: (1) it absorbs the nutrients on its surface (in the case of a fiber or fiberlike substance); (2) it dissolves the nutrients (in the case of substances with lipidlike characteristics), or (3) it alters the function of the digestive tract (e.g., alters transit times or microbial ecology). Another nutritional concern with nondigestible fat substitutes is the effect on the total consumption of nutrients. Consideration must be given to how those nutrients associated with fats, such as essential fatty acids and fat-soluble vitamins, can be replaced in the diet. If nutrient interferences are found, the FDA must be provided with data to show that these effects are trivial in terms of public health or that they can be accurately estimated and safely corrected by "compensation"* in the new food product that contains the substitute. The potential effect of fat substitutes on the microflora in the gastrointestinal tract must also be considered. Some of these microflora are associated with the synthesis of nutrients, such as vitamin K, biotin, and volatile fatty acids, and their presence exerts long-term effects on bowel health.

(3) ". . . *safety factors which in the opinion of experts qualified by scientific training and experience to evaluate the safety of food additives are generally recognized as appropriate for the use of animal experimentation data.*"

General health concerns and populations with potentially increased risk must be considered in the approval process for new food ingredients when safety is predicated on nonabsorption. Consider, for example, a new ingredient that is not absorbed in healthy animals, does not affect the absorption or synthesis of essential nutrients by intestinal bacteria, does not have any toxic effect on the gastrointestinal tract, but does accumulate in body tissues or shows toxic effects when injected into animals. It may then be necessary to demonstrate that the ingredient would not cross the gastrointestinal tract wall in the event that the epithelial tissues were compromised by a disease or injury that is likely to occur in a subpopulation.

The laxative effects of ingredients *not* digested may also be of concern. The laxative effects of nondigested substances among individuals may vary. Some individuals have a low tolerance for nondigested substances, which results in frequent defecation or anal leakage. In either situation, a reduction in absorption of nutrients may occur. Generally, most adults can recognize an association between the occurrence of the laxation and the consumption of the nondigested ingredient, and, if the resulting effect is unacceptable to

---

*The FDA uses the term *compensation* rather than *fortification* to indicate the "adding back" of those nutrients that are present in a "natural" product but may have been removed or are not available for use in the new, substitute product.

them, they avoid such products. However, some adults and many children cannot make such an association. Under such circumstances, a limitation on the maximum exposure or special labeling may be necessary.

The safety evaluation of food additives is based on a projected effect on the general population. Specific effects in subpopulations are usually addressed through the provision of appropriate label information that can (but usually does not) consist of information statements or, if appropriate, actual warnings on the labels. As Vanderveen and Glinsmann warn, "In the case of novel fat substitutes, it may be difficult to predict the effect on subpopulations. Additional clinical trials may be necessary to define safety of use in subgroups at increased risk."[8]

In the case of olestra, the product's broad marketing potential and expected consumption by persons of all ages, including children, are aspects that have been considered in the safety evaluation. It is important for the reader to recall that the petitioner, in this case P&G, was not required to show, *nor is FDA permitted to consider*, that olestra had any benefits, health or otherwise, for consumers of the food additive. Again, the legislative history of the 1958 amendment is clear on this point: "The question of whether an additive produces such [a technical] effect (or how much of an additive is required for such an effect) is a factual one, and does not involve any judgement on the part of the Secretary of whether such effect results in any added 'value' to the consumer of such food or enhances the marketability from a merchandising point of view."

In summary, the general safety clause places on P&G the burden of proving that a fair evaluation of the data in the administrative record establishes that there is a reasonable certainty that olestra *will not be harmful* under the prescribed conditions of use. Only *if* Procter & Gamble can prove that it has met this requirement can the FDA approve olestra as a "food additive."

The Regulatory Approval Process for Olestra: "Out of the Lab and into the Regulatory Fryer"

The remainder of this case study will focus on the *olestra* product—how it came to be developed, the rigorous regulatory review process it has undergone in order to be approved by the Food and Drug Administration as an additive to food,[9] the media frenzy that has accompanied this announcement, and the marketing fervor that is beginning to result[10] (see Table CS2.1). The only mystery left is whether the fat-loving, but fat-phobic, public will accept this scientific breakthrough with their pocketbooks to the extent that it will justify Procter & Gamble's twenty-five-year and $200 million investment in olestra's development and testing.

Table CS2.1 **Chronology of the Regulatory Review Process for Olestra**

**1971   First patent granted on sucrose polyesters (SPEs), the
          class of non-digestible fats (which includes olestra) as
          fat replacers.**

          First meeting between P&G and FDA on SPEs.

**1975   P&G files Investigative New Drug Exemption (IND)
          on SPEs.**

**1979   P&G meets with FDA Food and Drug representatives
          together because of the unclear regulatory status of SPEs.**

1982   P&G meets with FDA (Foods) to review SPE testing program.

**1984   FDA (Foods) recognizes that SPE, as a food macroingredient,
          introduces a new dimension for low calorie ingredients.**

**1985   P&G meets with FDA (Foods) to review regulatory strategy
          in light of then current general interest in health claims for foods.**

**1986   P&G meets with FDA (Foods) to present all safety data and discuss
          products to be covered in a Food Additive Petition (FAP)**

**1987   P&G submits FAP; covers olestra/conventional oil blends to prepare
          savory snacks and for food service and home use in shortening and oils.**

1988   FDA defines additional absorption and toxicology data needed.

**1990   P&G narrows the petition to savory snacks only;
          FDA defines further nutrition testing needed to facilitate the review.**

1993   Last data requested by FDA submitted by P&G.

**1995   Majority of the FDA's Food Advisory Committee finds that olestra
          meets the safety standard of "reasonable certainty of no harm."**

**1996   FDA grants approval to P&G to use olestra as a food ingredient in
          savory snacks only.**

Source: For 1971–1992, General Accounting Office, "FDA Premarket Approval: Process
of Approving Olestra as a Food Additive," GAO/HRD-92-86, p. 5, 1992; for 1992–1996,
Food and Drug Administration records.

Separate units of the Food and Drug Administration (FDA) regulate foods (including food additives) and drugs. The formal approval process for food additives is initiated by the manufacturer filing a "food additive petition" (FAP); for drugs it is by the sponsor filing a new drug application (NDA). A FAP or an NDA can be filed at any time the petitioner (i.e., the company) believes it has the data necessary to satisfy FDA reviewers. A food additive manufacturer must show only that an additive is *safe*; a drug sponsor must show that the drug is both *safe* and *effective*. Although the Center for Food Safety and Nutrition (CFSAN), FDA's food center, operates independently from FDA's drug center, the two parts of the agency work cooperatively, and companies that are pursuing both approval paths can work with both centers concurrently. It is common for a manufacturer to interact informally with the FDA about the contents of anticipated submissions before filing a formal food additive petition or drug application.

The history of the relationship between the regulatory agency, the FDA, and a corporate giant, Procter & Gamble, is long and tortured, a rather sordid tale, with neither side able to claim "victory!" The company's first patent for olestra, obtained in 1971, marked the start of a twenty-five-year process of P&G's petitioning the FDA, getting advice, reformulating the product, and repetitioning. What follows is a more detailed accounting of that process.

Officials from P&G first met with the FDA's Bureau of Foods in May 1971 to discuss olestra. The same year, P&G obtained its first patent on the product. In this meeting, company representatives shared with the FDA the company's discovery and its plans to perform controlled human feeding studies. P&G hoped the studies would culminate in the FDA's approving olestra as a food additive. In 1973, P&G initiated human and animal studies to learn more about the biological and safety effects of this substance.

After concluding some of its human studies in June 1975, P&G's results demonstrated that the primary biological change attributable to olestra was a notable reduction in serum cholesterol. In its meetings with FDA, P&G discussed its intention to conduct more research to substantiate olestra's cholesterol-reducing effects. The FDA advised the company that it if planned to make claims that olestra lowered serum cholesterol, olestra would be regulated as a drug, not as a food additive. P&G filed an "investigational new drug" (IND)* application in November 1975. Documents

---

*"An IND application gives the FDA a vehicle for controlling drug manufacturers' human clinical testing of a new molecular entity prior to approval and marketing," according to the 1992 GAO report, "FDA Premarket Approval Process of Approving Olestra as a Food Additive," p. 5.

maintained by the FDA refer to the company's tests for safety and efficacy for the next ten years. P&G officials have stated that the company always sought the quickest and most expedient regulatory path to gain premarket approval for olestra and believed that since drug-approval testing protocols were already in place, they could follow them to prove that olestra was safe for use as a food ingredient that could be used to help lower cholesterol levels.

However, by the early 1980s, research data showed that olestra was not reducing the serum cholesterol levels of clinical trial participants by at least 15 percent, the FDA minimum requirement for approval as a drug. The IND application was consequently inactivated by P&G in August 1988.

In a meeting between FDA and P&G in late 1984, the agency explained that it had "liberalized" its policy on companies' making health claims on food additives. Probably because of this disclosure, P&G switched its focus to the food additive approval path in order to gain approval for olestra as a replacement for fat in certain foods. The company submitted an FAP on April 15, 1987, for the use of olestra as a calorie-free replacement in short-enings and oils. The petition (FAP 7A3997) was filed on May 7, 1987. In a notice in the *Federal Register* of June 23, 1987, FDA announced that the food additive petition had been filed by Procter & Gamble, proposing the issuance of a food additive regulation providing for the safe use of sucrose esterified with medium- and long-chain fatty acids as a replacement for fats and oils. The goal was to replace up to 35 percent of the fat in shortenings and cooking oils for home use, and up to 75 percent of fat used in shortening in commercial deep-fat frying and certain fried snack foods.

After this petition had been filed, the FDA's Center for Food Safety and Applied Nutrition (formerly the Bureau of Foods) began to critically study and respond to it in detail. (FDA cannot formally respond to a food additive manufacturer until the FAP is submitted.) After sorting through and reviewing the data submitted with the petition, the FDA concluded that additional safety and nutritional tests were needed and informed the company in 1989 that a carcinogenicity study in a second animal species, mice, would be necessary.

In July 1990, P&G notified the FDA that it was narrowing its petition on the intended use of olestra. The company then submitted a revised FAP to limit the intended use of olestra to a 100 percent replacement for conventional fats in the preparation of savory snacks (i.e., snacks that are salty or "piquant" but not sweet, such as potato chips, cheese puffs, and crackers). According to the FDA officials, the limiting of the petition substantially helped the company because it eliminated many of the reviewers' safety questions about the range of olestra's possible uses, a fact refuted by P&G officials who insisted that their 1987 FAP adequately supported olestra's potentially broad uses.

Given the FDA's estimate of consumption of the additive, data from the petition showed that olestra could reduce the uptake of fat-soluble vitamins from foods eaten together with olestra, and the agency stated that it could not yet assure safety of the additive. The FDA further stated that they needed to see the results from large animal testing to measure the effects of olestra consumption in large doses on fat-soluble vitamin absorption in pigs. P&G officials argued that the pig study was too costly, created delays, and was unnecessary to prove olestra's nutritional and safety effects. The company went on record as stating that its human clinical studies that had been conducted in the early 1980s already measured serum vitamin depletion levels, a measure they believed to be more accurate than that generated from a study of the effects of olestra in pigs.

The initial patent on olestra expired in 1988, and another three were slated to expire in 1994. In 1991, two bills (H.R. 2805 and S. 1506) were introduced in the House and the Senate to extend the terms of olestra's existing patents for ten years, starting on the date of FDA approval. At this time, the chairs of the House Subcommittee on Intellectual Property and Judicial Administration and the Senate Subcommittee on Patents, Copyrights, and Trademarks requested that the General Accounting Office clarify the circumstances related to FDA's and P&G's actions from 1971, when P&G filed the first FDA petition for market approval, to 1992. The GAO provided a document-based review of P&G's efforts to obtain approval to market olestra in 1992 but stopped short of recommending that the patent terms for olestra should be extended. A coalition of consumer advocacy groups wrote to the two subcommittee chairs urging them not to approve the legislation to extend the patent on olestra, saying that a ten-year extension after FDA approval may mean that P&G would end up enjoying patent protection for their product for twice the normal seventeen-year period.11 P&G successfully lobbied for special legislation that extended the lifetime of some of its patents, and legislation to this effect was passed in December 1993. One key patent was extended until January 25, 1996; if the FDA granted market approval prior to that date, the patent would be extended for two additional years.

In June 1995, the House Subcommittee on Human Resources and Intergovernmental Relations (under the Committee on Government Reform and Oversight) held hearings on FDA's review process for food additives. A number of industry witnesses used olestra as an example of a beneficial food additive to which the public had been denied access because its petition had languished on bureaucrats' desks for years. Representatives from consumer groups urged Congress to help revise the food additive review process, and FDA officials defended delays by attributing them to a lack of resources for expediting the review process.

By the fall of 1995, under industry pressure to take action and realizing that the patent on olestra was about to expire, the FDA focused attention on the olestra market approval decision. Two other factors converged to convey the urgency of the situation—P&G's increasingly negative public announcements about the FDA's treatment of their petition for the premarket approval of olestra,* coupled with public discourse from some health and consumer groups about the "dangers" associated with consuming olestra. The FDA did what it usually does when dealing with an unusually contentious situation—it called on the help of its advisory committees.**

Any public meeting held by a regulatory agency must be announced in advance in the daily government publication, the *Federal Register*. So, on October 17, 1995 (60 FR 53740), the FDA announced that a public meeting of the agency's Food Advisory Committee (the FAC) and a Working Group of the FAC would be held November 14–17, 1995. The *Federal Register* notice also called for public comment on P&G's request for market approval of olestra.

At the November 1995 meeting, members of the FAC Working Group on Olestra were charged to decide if (1) all the scientific questions had been identified, (2) the data were sufficient to address these questions, and (3) the data were sufficient to determine whether there was "a reasonable certainty of no harm from the use of olestra as contemplated."[12] Before approving olestra as a food additive, the FDA had to decide *not* whether the product's potential risks outweigh the potential benefits (i.e., offering the public tasty snack foods that save fat and calories), they simply had to determine whether there were enough scientific data to show "*reasonable certainty of no harm.*" The FDA pointed out to the group that approval of the petition "does not . . . require proof beyond doubt."

The November 1995 meeting was one of "high drama" for all parties involved—the FDA (and its Working Group on olestra), the petitioner—Procter & Gamble, and those opposing approval, led by Dr. Michael Jacobson of the Center for Science in the Public Interest (CSPI). A moment of diversion is needed at this point in the text to describe the work of Jacobson's group in its campaign to oppose market approval for olestra.

Never one to shy away from controversy with corporate America, Jacobson

---

*P&G officials note that they were not distressed about the *thoroughness* of the FDA review, but they were alarmed at the length of the entire process and the costs that had been incurred.

**It is interesting to note here that the case of olestra was the *first* time the FDA had used a Food Advisory Committee (FAC) to review the science presented in a food additive approval petition.

has headed the CSPI, a Washington-based consumer and health advocacy group, for over twenty years. The organization's campaigns have been media-driven for publicity, but the group has been successful in bringing public attention to "invisible" health and consumer issues. Over the years, the CSPI has clearly been in the lead advocating for food labeling reform and disclosure of the fat content of restaurant meals. The campaign against olestra is "vintage Jacobson," a textbook example of how to raise public consciousness and focus public attention on matters that had heretofore gone fairly unnoticed. It was not that Dr. Jacobson was a "Johnny-come-lately" in the olestra controversy. As early as 1988, he had written an op ed piece in the *New York Times* with the title, "Fake Food, Real Problems."[13]

The CSPI campaign against the market approval of olestra took place on a number of fronts—presentations to interested parties in Congress and the FDA, teaming with coalitions of other like-minded consumer groups, aligning one's work with that of prominent scientists who will speak to the veracity of the group's efforts, and taking the case directly to the public by means of direct mailings, as well as media accounts in newspapers, magazines, and talk show TV.

The first phase of the campaign was directed toward government entities, including both Congress and the FDA. In 1992, the CSPI led a coalition of consumer groups (including the Consumer Federation of America, the Consumers Union, and the National Consumers League) who urged the chairmen of two congressional subcommittees not to approve legislation to extend the patent on olestra. In June 1995, Dr. Jacobson appeared at hearings on the FDA's process for reviewing food additive petitions before the House Subcommittee on Human Resources and Intergovernmental Relations.

The second prong of the CSPI attack was to produce credible scientific evidence about the harmful effects of olestra. Jacobson and a CSPI senior scientist, Dr. Myra Karstadt, authored a ninety-page document, a "White Paper on Olestra," that reviewed the scientific evidence on the following issues: (1) consumption estimates, (2) effect of olestra on carotenoid absorption, (3) effect of supplementation of olestra with vitamin K on coumadin therapy, (4) effect of olestra on GI symptoms, and (5) animal carcinogenicity. This paper was submitted to the FDA in response to their request for comments on the olestra petition on October 25, 1995, with revised versions submitted on November 2 and 3, 1995. In addition, they solicited and obtained the support of two prominent scientists at the Harvard School of Public Health, Drs. Walter Willett and Meir Stampfer, who concurred that, "the probabilities of harm [from the consumption of olestra] appear substantial"

The third, and perhaps most astute, tactic was "taking the message to the people" in the form of direct solicitations and media appearances. The nearly one million "members" of the CSPI receive a monthly publication called *Nutrition Action*. In November 1995, the magazine appealed to its readers to either "sign and mail this coupon [printed on the page] or, better yet, write the FDA in your own words" to "reject Procter & Gamble's petition to approve the unsafe fat substitute, olestra." The periodical reported in its April 1996 issue that 2,450 out of a total 2,750 comments that the FDA received had come from *Nutrition Action* readers, and added that, "while that didn't stop the feds from approving olestra, it does put you in good company. Dozens of leading health experts and researchers also warned the FDA of the danger of unleashing the fake fat on the public. . . . We've appealed the approval, so stay tuned . . . and keep the cap off your pen."

After the FDA decision in January 1996 to approve olestra, Jacobson was no stranger to the media. He appeared on NBC *Nightly News* and the *Today* show calling olestra "a public health timebomb." His views were quoted widely in the major print media—newspapers including the *New York Times* and the *Washington Post*, as well as weekly news magazines, *Time* and *Newsweek*. When P&G opened a Web page about Olean (P&G's brand name for olestra) on the Internet in March 1996, the CSPI quickly followed suit, billing its site as "the truth about olestra" and including "David Letterman's Top Ten Olean Slogans."[14]

Do these tactics work? Many think they do. They certainly raise consumer awareness about issues to which they have never before been exposed . . . and in a manner they understand—fear. William Schultz, deputy commissioner for policy at FDA was quoted as saying that CSPI "has had a real impact on people's eating habits." Adding that CSPI could not "*prevent*" FDA's approval of olestra as a food ingredient, Schultz called Jacobson's opposition "laudable," adding, "they were very irritating, but they were the only ones there raising the right questions."[15]

CSPI was front and center representing the opposition to market approval for olestra at the November 1995 meeting of the FDA Food Advisory Committee's (FAC) Working Group on Olestra. At that time, the group also heard from the petitioner, P&G, and presentations by the FDA staff. Procter & Gamble maintained that their three decades of research, including more than one hundred laboratory studies and more than forty controlled clinical studies involving more than 4,300 men, women, and children, together with fifty-five additional human studies with an additional sixteen thousand people had shown conclusively that olestra was safe for use in savory snack foods.[16]

The FDA Working Group on Olestra held its meeting in November 1995, which was followed by a meeting of the Food Advisory Committee

(FAC). Of the twenty-two members of the FAC, seventeen concluded that there was "reasonable certainty of no harm," interpreted as a vote to approve olestra as a food additive. This recommendation was then communicated to FDA Commissioner Dr. David Kessler, who was responsible for making the final decision.

Henry Blackburn, a professor of medicine at the University of Minnesota, a member of both the FDA Working Group on Olestra and the FAC, commented on the presentations by the FDA staff at the November 1995 meeting in an article published in the *New England Journal of Medicine*:

> The presentations [by FDA staff] were thorough and thoughtful, covering all aspects of the findings, but virtually all the data were from studies carried out by the petitioner, Procter & Gamble. There were no relevant reports from disinterested investigators and no independent studies sponsored by the FDA. The FDA staff members had already concluded that olestra was safe and were acting as proponents of the petition for approval. This stance had a strong appearance of bias to those of us accustomed to the rigor and objectivity of reviews by study sections at the National Institutes of Health.
>
> What appeared to me to be collusion with industry is not only legal but also deliberate FDA policy—supportive and collaborative rather than adversarial—in considering petitions from industry. The FDA's expert staff and consultants make detailed recommendations intended to improve both the product and the quality of the petition, and these recommendations are documented in an administrative record. All the while, the agency tries to remain the guardian of the public health. But, in fact, the FDA does not have the research laboratories or staff, nor is it supported by the policies or funds it would need, to carry out extensive independent tests of food additives.[17]*

In the *Federal Register* of November 16, 1995 (60 FR 57586), the FDA announced that it would consider public comments on the petition, includ-

---

*Those familiar with the workings of the FDA food additive petition process point out that Dr. Blackburn's comments, while not totally inaccurate, reflect his lack of experience with the process. While he had been a reviewer for the clinical drug approval process, this was his first time serving on a committee reviewing petitions for food additive approval. Staff maintain that it is not the role of the FDA to conduct independent studies; the petitioner must conduct them, usually at the request of the FDA. This collaborative process between FDA and the petitioner, involving constant communication and interaction between the two parties, is the time-honored, traditional way of doing business. Rather than not granting approval, the usual procedure is for the FDA to go back to the company and request further studies, a process quite dissimilar to the grant and contract review process conducted by NIH study sections with which Dr. Blackburn is intimately familiar.

ing comments on the proceedings before the FAC, only if filed on or before December 1, 1995 (but later extended to December 21, 1995). This measure was felt to be necessary to facilitate the agency's decision-making process and to come to closure on the petition. Announcement of final approval came on January 24, 1996, one day short of the January 25, 1996, expiration of P&G's patent on olestra.

Approval was granted by the FDA in the form of a "final rule" published in the *Federal Register* on January 30, 1996. Taking up fifty-five pages of print, the notice that the "Food and Drug Administration (FDA) is amending the food additive regulations to provide for the safe use of sucrose esterified with medium and long chain fatty acids (olestra) as a replacement for fats and oils" provides extensive detail about the scientific evidence and process used in making the final decision. When FDA Commissioner Dr. David Kessler signed off on olestra, he did not grant Procter & Gamble a marketing "free-for-all." As a condition of approval, P&G will be required to conduct studies to monitor olestra consumption and its long-term effects. The FDA will formally review those studies at a meeting to be held within thirty months, which will be open to the public. Further, the FDA has stipulated that all foods made with olestra be labeled with the following statement: *This Product Contains Olestra. Olestra may cause abdominal cramping and loose stools. Olestra inhibits the absorption of some vitamins and other nutrients. Vitamins A, D, E, and K have been added.**

This current approval only covers olestra's use in savory snacks, such as chips and crackers. If the company ever wants to use olestra in other products or for other purposes, such as cooking french fries, P&G will have to go through a separate petitioning process.

Why Is Olestra Such a Special Case?

Olestra is probably the most studied of all food additives, and its market approval process was one of the costliest and the longest in history. But the case of olestra is also remarkably different from that of other food additives because the decision process also took twists and turns equally different from the approval path of other food additives. For one thing, olestra may replace a

---

*It is said that FDA Commissioner David Kessler did not want to approve olestra because of the evidence of health-related consequences from consuming the product that had been presented. However, the recommendation of his own agency and the vote of the FAC convinced him that approval could not be denied. This "information panel," interpreted by some as a "warning label," was presumably added directly at Dr. Kessler's request.

major portion of the fat in the diet, a "macroingredient" that typically furnishes about 35 percent of calories in the diets of American consumers. This is not a coloring agent or sweetener that substitutes for minor ingredients in food. Because olestra would be replacing such a large proportion of the fat in the diets of some people, the FDA recommended that P&G examine olestra's nutritional and gastrointestinal effects, not just toxicity.

What are these health issues that have so concerned scientists and sparked further controversy about whether the product is safe? Most of the issues have to do with the fact that olestra is no ordinary molecule. It has been synthesized in the laboratory, constructed by rearranging familiar molecules to create a brand new substance. From the standpoint of many food scientists, this structure is ideal; it passes through the gastrointestinal tract unaffected by digestive enzymes and therefore remains unabsorbed and unavailable to provide calories. However, because the fake fat's chemical structure so closely resembles that of real fat, it also has the potential to carry with it important substances—such as fat-soluble vitamins—which for public health reasons *should* be absorbed. To get around this problem, P&G will add the fat-soluble vitamins, A, D, E, and K, to olestra. That way, when olestra goes through the intestine, it is already so overloaded with these nutrients that it can't carry any more, and the fat-soluble vitamins carried in other fat-containing foods will be absorbed as they should be.

The remaining dilemma, however, is that olestra also attracts beta-carotene and other carotenoids, fat-soluble plant pigments that give fruits and vegetables their intense color. Although the evidence is not yet conclusive, many public health scientists believe that these substances may reduce the risk of cancer, heart disease, and macular degeneration, a common cause of blindness in the elderly. Procter & Gamble has said they do not intend to add carotenoids to olestra because they felt this action was not warranted at this time.* This action angered prominent Harvard epidemiologists who charged that olestra consumption may lead to subtle deficiencies of carotenoids over time, which, in turn, could increase the population's risks of certain chronic diseases. The evidence linking carotenoid consumption to lower risk of these chronic diseases is still, however, considered tenuous.

---

*P&G's data on the effect of olestra on carotenoid absorption was reviewed, at the FDA's request, by the National Cancer Institute and the National Eye Institute. Dr. Peter Greenwald, Director of the Division of Cancer Prevention at the National Cancer Institute, gave the following recommendation to the FDA: "I do not believe that a significant public health issue is raised by the reported effects of olestra on lipophilic [fat-binding] carotenoids, and I recommend against supplementing olestra with beta-carotene or other carotenoids at this time."

The majority of the FDA's Food Advisory Panel who voted to approve olestra apparently believed that the science wasn't there to show that eating foods (i.e., only savory snacks at this point) containing olestra at projected consumption levels could be harmful to the consumer.[18]

Another issue concerned the appearance of gastrointestinal problems associated with the consumption of olestra. Consumption of olestra-containing foods has been shown to cause diarrhea in some people, and the frequency of the problem increases with the amount of olestra eaten. The FDA is requiring, therefore, that all foods made with olestra bear an information statement describing possible effects of consuming the product.

The third major public health concern was an indelicate side effect known as "anal leakage." Apparently, the oily olestra separates from the rest of the contents of the bowel and, as one food scientist puts it, "dribbles out."[19] P&G says that it has increased the "stiffness" of the olestra product, and that after clinical testing in over 1,000 people, the problem no longer occurs, a conclusion disputed by the CSPI.

Media Frenzy and Marketing Fervor

Recognizing the colossal clamoring for the creation of food products that were almost "too good to be true"—those that carried all of the good attributes and none of the bad effects, the media jumped on the bandwagon to bring the news of olestra's approval to millions of unsuspecting and uninformed consumers. The full-color *Time* magazine cover of January 8, 1996, screams, "Fat-Free Fat?" while its weekly counterpart, *Newsweek*, took a more conservative stance with its article, "Fake Fat: Miracle or Menace?" that appeared that same week. The television show *Prime Time Live* even devoted a segment to presenting the pros and cons of olestra.

Procter & Gamble, in anticipation of a favorable conclusion to its twenty-five-year effort, took out *full page* ads in the January 26, 1996, issues of several newspapers, including the *Washington Post* and the *New York Times*, extolling the virtues of Olean with the tag line, "No Fat, No Compromises." The company also began a concerted effort to reach health professionals with their message. Full page "advertorials" were taken out in professional journals, such as the *Journal of Nutrition Education* and the *Journal of the American Dietetic Association*. Members of the latter organization, nearly 70,000 dietitians, received a glossy portfolio containing fact sheets about "Olean's Testing Program" and "References about Health Effects." The company has continued to court professionals by providing periodic updates on olestra and its market testing, funding key sessions at professional meetings, and funding research publications, such as the supplement to a nutrition science journal on the "assessment of the nutritional effects of olestra."[20]

CSPI also did not rest after the announcement of olestra's approval. On January 29, 1996, they filed a "Freedom of Information Act" request for biographical information on all consultants, members of the FDA's Working Group on Olestra and/or the FDA's Food Advisory Committee. Suggesting that persons who had significant food industry ties and research support could not make independent judgments regarding the effects of olestra, the CSPI sought information about committee members' research grants and contracts, any correspondence between the FDA and these individuals, and information related to the selection of members of these groups. Further, the CSPI filed a complaint with the Federal Trade Commission (FTC) to halt the P&G advertising campaign on Olean, citing their opposition to the wording, "No Fat, No Compromises."

In a measure ostensibly designed to get cash to support the construction of a new plant in Cincinnati, Ohio, where olestra will be made, P&G sold the exclusive rights to large quantities of olestra to Frito-Lay, the leader in the $15 billion snack food industry, essentially locking out Frito-Lay's competitors' efforts to use the product for more than a year.[21] Frito-Lay is using olestra as the key ingredient in Max fat-free potato chips, which were test-marketed in Cedar Rapids, Iowa, and two smaller cities starting in the spring of 1996. Thus, the war began . . . P&G sent over 1,100 health care professionals (including physicians, dietitians, and pharmacists) detailed brochures about the chips. Meanwhile, Frito-Lay hired five nutritionists from the three test cities as consultants. In an intensive three-day training program, a public relations firm coached the nutritionists on handling the media, and P&G scientists prepped them on Olean's development and the results of the scientific testing. Frito-Lay also created a separate group to handle all consumer calls on Max chips, transferring any caller who complained about health problems to P&G. (Only a handful called with complaints; many of the others called to find out where they could buy the chips.)[22]

The CSPI went on a counterattack. Within days of the Max launch, the center set up a toll-free hot line inviting consumers to lodge Max-related complaints. It also aired television ads that focus on a can of dog food as a voice-over asks whether viewers would feed their pets any food that carried the FDA label required on Max chips. The CSPI also organized news conferences in two of the test market cities in which various physicians and nutritionists warned about the risks of eating foods containing olestra, and several people described in graphic detail the severe gastrointestinal problems they had experienced after consuming olestra-containing chips.[23]

In further action that infuriated P&G, the CSPI hired a marketing research firm to conduct a telephone survey in the three test markets where olestra-containing chips were being sold by Frito-Lay, asking if anyone had experienced adverse effects after eating the chips. (The reason P&G says they are so opposed to this technique is because these are not scientifically controlled studies, but merely the collection of anecdotes and opinions.) The results of the telephone survey—20 percent of those who ate the chips reported experiencing gastrointestinal problems, 3 percent of them severe. These results again drew Dr. Michael Jacobson to publicly call for the removal of olestra from the marketplace.[24]

If taste is the reason why we prefer fatty foods—especially snacks—what do consumers say about eating olestra-containing chips? The media have covered several of these public "taste tests."[25] The verdict: Most consumers gave the chips good reviews; but nearly all tasters could recognize the new chip from its fat-laden original, and some complained that there was a chemical, "oily" aftertaste.

Analysis

By Stage of the Policymaking Process

The major impetus that pushed the regulatory approval process for olestra onto the policy agenda was the issue of patent expiration. In the early 1990s, P&G effectively lobbied Congress for extension of several of its key patents on olestra. One of these was extended until January 25, 1996. If the market approval was granted by the FDA before that date, the patent could be extended for two more years. Thus, timing was of the essence.

Relevance to the "Advocacy Coalition Framework"

This case study aptly demonstrates the viability of two major coalitions on almost diametrically opposite ends of the continuum in their approach to this topic—a prominent food manufacturer on one side, an outspoken consumer advocate on the other, both interacting with a federal regulatory agency. Procter & Gamble, with its $200 million investment over twenty-five years, together with its legions of lobbyists and support of many in the food science academic community, believed in the "marketplace" approach to product approval. If the consumer wants and will pay for the product, by all means, the consumer should have it. *Caveat emptor*—let the buyer beware. If consumers experience side effects from eating this product, the effect will be self-limiting—they just won't buy the product again.

At the other end of this continuum is the public health/consumer advocacy community—and, in this particular case, it was the Center for Science in the Public Interest, and its outspoken executive director, Michael Jacobson, who gave reason to believe that the product will produce deleterious side effects and have serious health consequences in the long run for many American consumers. It is noteworthy that, for the most part, the CSPI stood alone in the fight without the visible assistance of other consumer advocacy groups, several of which had supported the CSPI in public hearings against P&G patent extensions. It is said that several prominent consumer voices were on retainer as consultants to P&G and would not appear against the company.

Government employees occupied different positions in the advocacy coalitions. High-level appointees, in particular FDA Commissioner Kessler, were not happy with the decision to grant premarket approval of olestra and were instrumental in delimiting its effect, first by confining it as an additive to savory snacks only and second by inserting the "information panel" on the package label. Lower-level civil servants, on the hand, were most supportive of the P&G petition and felt that they had worked with the company for so long that approval should be granted without question. Academics—the "dueling scientists," again—lined up on both sides of the argument.

The ACF assumes that the legal structure behind a policy system's action tends to be stable over several decades.[26] In this case, the Food and Drug Administration has legislative authority to proffer regulations over new foods and ingredients in the food supply. When the capabilities of science force the FDA to exert juridiction over products that the existing structure is strained to regulate, problems ensue.

The Food and Drug Administration's premarket approval process is most assuredly in for an overhaul. The agency must—even in these times of budget austerity—have the expertise and the capability to use epidemiologic studies and clinical trials with adequate statistical power to detect effects and monitor human safety of these newly formulated foods.

Another issue—whose responsibility is it to monitor the results of consumer acceptance studies in anticipation of the FDA review in 1999? The FDA had requested P&G to conduct such surveys and report back to them in a quarterly postmarketing surveillance program. In early March 1997, P&G indicated that "follow-up testing indicates that some consumers are incorrectly attributing digestive effects to chips made with Olean" and that "the recent marketplace postmarket surveillance data continue to confirm that the vast majority of consumers eating snacks made with Olean notice no digestive changes."[26] Consumer groups warn that asking P&G to conduct these studies on their own controversial product is like putting the "wolf in charge of the hen house." Some have even called for P&G and CSPI to "bury the hatchet" and jointly conduct a double-blind, placebo-controlled trial to test the effects of eating olestra-containing products such a coordinated effort may be long in coming.[27]

The final decision will rest, of course, with the consumer. And, as we have repeatedly stated in this book—*taste* is everything! Initial taste trials seem to indicate that consumers are accepting this new product. But how many will continue to indulge in fat-free potato chips if the threat of gastrointestinal distress looms just around the corner?

Conclusion

After hearing predictions in the late 1980s that olestra products would produce a bonanza market of $1 billion annually, officials of Procter & Gamble probably never would have predicted that their "serendipitous" discovery would take twenty years and $200 million to gain FDA approval. With an FDA-mandated "information statement" on the label (for which P&G has petitioned to revise the wording) and all the media publicity about CSPI claims of alleged adverse health consequences, it will be interesting to see if olestra ever pays off as market analysts predicted.

Will the consumer benefit? Perhaps only a select few who consume great quantities of "savory snacks" and who wish to control their dietary fat intake in the process. A 1–ounce bag of regular chips, for example, containing 10 grams of fat and 150 calories drops to a fat-free 70 calories if made with olestra. For those who eat snacks only occasionally in small amounts, the savings are not that significant, especially given the potential risks to comfort and long-term health.[28]

Others argue that the olestra-containing snacks on supermarket shelves will provide a useful trial to see if such products improve Americans' diets. With a 5.5 billion pounds of salty snacks consumed per year (that's 22 pounds of potato chips, tortilla chips, and other such snacks per person), the impact from consuming olestra-containing snacks on dietary fat intake could be considerable. The problem, of course, is that no one can predict with certainty what will happen when free-living people make purchasing and eating decisions about fat-replacer-containing products in the "real world" where food choices are based on so many different factors.[27]

With warning labels and extensive media coverage of the health effects of olestra, the consumer has already been exposed to a great deal of information in advance of making the decision whether or not to consume foods containing this additive. It will be interesting to see whether the "information panel" about the potential for digestive disturbances remains a permanent fixture on products containing Olean. Questions about the efficacy of the use of the information panel approach abound. First, can the consumer understand this information on the package label and use it constructively to make an "informed" food choice? And, second, is this just one more example of placing further onus on the food consumer to be personally responsible for consuming a nutritionally adequate diet that also protects against chronic disease?

Policy issues surrounding this case abound. Can we continue to rely on the regulatory process as it is now conducted to protect the interests of the consumer, or are regulators too "close" to the industries they are charged to regulate to render an objective opinion? The olestra case will surely go down in history as a seminal study in regulatory policy, one with implications far into the next century.

Chapter 6

Government's Role in Food Marketing: Regulatory Approvals in the Food System

> *Some of the most profound policy influences that determine the fat content of foods are ones about which most consumers are entirely unaware.*

Have you ever wondered how food produced on the farm, on the ranch, or from the sea made its way to your plate? Wholesalers and retailers move fresh and processed food products from producers and processors to supermarkets and other food stores, as well as to restaurants and other food service establishments. The major functions of this segment of the food system are to purchase, transport, assemble, store, and distribute food to consumers.

Food retailing today refers to two main segments: food stores and food service establishments. The distinction between these two types of food outlets is diminishing, as many food stores include delis and restaurants, and many food service establishments offer take-out foods and home delivery. Convenience for the consumer, which includes both ease of purchase and ease of preparation, is a major goal of food retailers in the products and services they offer. The "take-out-to-eat" (TOTE) food is the fastest growing market segment in the food industry. The burgeoning trend toward "home eating, not home cooking" was responsible for nearly all of the growth in total consumer food expenditures last year.[1]

The trend toward fewer retail food sources results in greater average sales per store and substantial increases in the number of items stocked. New stores are getting larger, and they offer more food items to the consumer. It is estimated that the "average" supermarket today offers the consumer a choice of 20,000 to 30,000 different items. Further, studies show that a large proportion of all food-buying decisions are made in the grocery store. Such a situation offers an enormous challenge to those who seek to influence consumers' dietary behavior; what information—what kind and how much—is needed by consumers to enable them to make "informed" food choices from such an array of items in the supermarket?

Two examples are provided in this chapter that describe regulatory actions that affect the marketing and distribution of food. The first involves grading standards and definitions for beef, and the second analyzes food "standards of identity." For the most part, these food standards historically have been enforced by the FDA and the USDA to protect against economic adulteration of the food product, rather than used as a policy instrument to protect or enhance the public health of consumers. These two examples provide evidence that the role of the market, as it attempts to respond to consumer demands for more healthful foods, is emerging as a more potent influence on the types of products offered than are the protectionist devices of government.

ISSUE 1: "BEEF GRADING"

In general, laws provide broad policy or a statement of intent, while regulations are promulgated by executive branch agencies to provide the details of how that policy goal is to be met or intent is to be carried out. In certain cases, and particularly those involving food products, the regulations provide very specific information or guidelines designed to ensure safety and/or uniformity to the product. In a sense, such detailed regulations are written to "level the playing field" (i.e., specify to all the players *what* actions are to be performed, *how* they will be carried out, *what information* will be provided [both to manufacturers and to consumers], and so forth).

Regulations provide a historical record of government involvement. As such, they reflect the culture of the times, rewarding those qualities thought to be desirable at the time and reducing or making it more difficult to include other less desirable qualities. As time passes and science reveals new information and technology is improved, regulations developed at one time may not be suitable or appropriate for another. They become a "historical artifact," inappropriate as guidelines for government action with the current scientific and technology base. This is indeed what has occurred in the case of meat (especially beef) grading standards.

Grading Standards for Beef

Since higher fat content is equated with higher-quality grades, higher grades result in higher profits for the industry. The grading system for beef was developed at a time when fatty meat was prized by consumers primarily for its tenderness and palatability. The greater the fat content of the product, the higher the grade the product was assigned. Higher grades were sold at higher prices.

Early on, the grading system encouraged producers to fatten animals and deterred them from producing a leaner product. This fact, however, has been challenged by the prime trade association for the meat industry, the National Cattlemen's Beef Association, in its *Beef Handbook*, stating, "differences among grades of beef in terms of fat content and cholesterol are relatively small."[2] (There are actually separate grading systems for pork, lamb, veal, and poultry; but, because beef is the chief source of dietary fat, it will be the focus of discussion in this book.)

History and Overview of Beef Grading

The official beef grading standards were first formulated in 1916, published in 1924 as USDA Bulletin No. 1246, *Market Classes and Grades of Dressed Beef*, but did not become effective until 1926. The Federal Meat Grading Service was established on February 10, 1925. In 1927, the voluntary beef grading and stamping service was officially started.[3] Since that time, several changes have been made to the standards in terms of types, names, and grades.[4] Federal meat grading of products for sale through regular commercial channels is administered by the Livestock and Meat Standardization Branch of the Livestock and Seed Division of the USDA's Agricultural Marketing Service (AMS). In addition to this service, the division also has responsibilities for examination and certification for conformance with specifications for grade and other factors of meats offered for delivery to federal, state, county, and municipal institutions that purchase meats on the basis of contract awards.

The quality grade name is associated with a specific combination of carcass traits that indicates to producers, processors, retailers, and consumers the use for which the meat product is best suited. Theoretically, the consumer can learn what the grade names mean in terms of eating quality and as a guide to the most appropriate cooking techniques to produce a palatable, tender dish. (Beef cuts with less fat require different cooking procedures—such as moist heat methods, braising, or stewing—to ensure tenderness; higher fat cuts can be broiled or grilled without fear that they will be tough if overcooked.)

In addition to the quality grade name, yield grades are also assigned to the product. This grade indicates the quantity of edible meat in a carcass and is more meaningful to the retailer than to the ordinary consumer. The yield grade does not provide any guidelines for eating quality.

In order to be eligible for grading service, the meat must be inspected by a system acceptable to the U.S. Department of Agriculture. Inspection guarantees *wholesomeness* and is paid for with tax dollars. The meat grading system, however, is voluntary; those in the meat industry who use the grading system also pay for it. Grading must not be confused with inspection, or the grading stamp with the inspection stamp. By law, every animal that is slaughtered for meat sale must be inspected. Grading is not required by law.

Grading Procedures

The challenge, then, to those who perform the grading is to separate the large population of carcasses from meat-producing animals into classes and grades with similar meat characteristics. A USDA employee performs this task on the intact animal carcass before it is further broken into wholesale and retail cuts.

Grading is only permitted in carcass form at the plant of slaughter as a means of ensuring that grading is consistent. Lighting and the preparation and presentation of the carcasses are also carefully controlled. Typically, a grader may grade 250 to 275 carcasses per hour in a modern, high-speed facility.[5]

The federal meat grader weighs all the factors that affect the grade of the carcass, decides upon the grade, and makes an identifying mark with a stamp designating the grade: "xxx" for Prime, "xx" for Choice, and so on. Then a ribbon grade stamp (which includes the grader's initials) is applied over the entire length of the carcass with a roller; that is why federally graded beef is often referred to as "rolled." This procedure has been followed for many years. However, with the added emphasis on lean meat, subcutaneous fat is usually trimmed away before meat is sold to consumers. In such cases, the grade roll comes off with the fat unless special precautions are taken to leave the strip of fat displaying the grade roll.

Many question whether computers will ever replace human meat graders. Computers capable of receiving video, ultrasound, and infrared images and with the capability to digitize these images into a numerical grade is currently being researched. Although the process is likely to be much more consistent, it probably will be some time before computers are able to perform this task satisfactorily.

Criteria and Standards for Various Grades

The first step in beef carcass grading is to determine the *class*, one criterion of which is the apparent sex of the animal at the time of slaughter; carcasses from males differ from carcasses of females. The grade of a steer, bullock, heifer, or cow carcass is based on two general factors: (1) the palatability (indicating characteristics of the lean part of the meat) referred to as the *quality grade*; and (2) the *yield grade*, which is based on the percent of trimmed, boneless major retail cuts that can be obtained from the carcass.

After determining the class of beef to which the carcass belongs, the next step in quality grading is the determination of *maturity*. The maturity of the carcass is determined by the size, shape, and ossification of the bones and cartilages, and the color and texture of the lean. Usually, the Prime, Choice, Select, and Standard grades are restricted to beef from young cattle; the Commercial grade pertains to beef from cattle too mature for Select or Choice, and the Utility, Cutter, and Canner grades include beef from animals of all ages. Further, as carcass maturity increases, the texture of the lean will become progressively coarser, and the color of the lean will become progressively darker red.

A major indicator in quality grading is the amount of *marbling* (little flecks of fat dispersed throughout the muscle tissue or intramuscular fat) in relation to the age of the animal from which the carcass was produced. A certain level of marbling is necessary to assure optimum palatability, especially in terms of juiciness and flavor. Thus, marbling and maturity, together with the amount of time the animal was on feed, contribute significantly to the quality grade the carcass will receive. Marbling is a key criterion in grading because it can be readily observed by USDA meat graders, but other factors such as "time on feed" cannot be estimated by graders working in packing plants.[6] The specifications for official U.S. standards for quality grades and yield grades of carcass beef are shown in Figure 6.1.

The USDA beef grades have been revised periodically to make the taste and appearance of the various cuts more uniform within the grades. In 1976, in an effort to reduce the fat levels in each of the top grades, the old "Good" grade was made more uniform and restrictive in the cuts of beef that qualified for that grade. This change in grading standards enabled retailers to sell less-marbled, lower-fat cuts of beef that were still acceptable to consumers. However, because of concerns that consumers viewed the "Good" name as an indication of an inferior or mediocre product, the industry produced relatively little beef in this grading category.

That all changed in November 1987 when the USDA's Agricultural Marketing Service (AMS) supported the petition from several consumer and public health groups to rename the "Good" grade of beef to *Select*.[7] Designed to appeal to consumers who desired a lower-fat beef product with

Figure 6.1 **Relationship Between Marbling, Maturity, and Carcass Quality Grade**

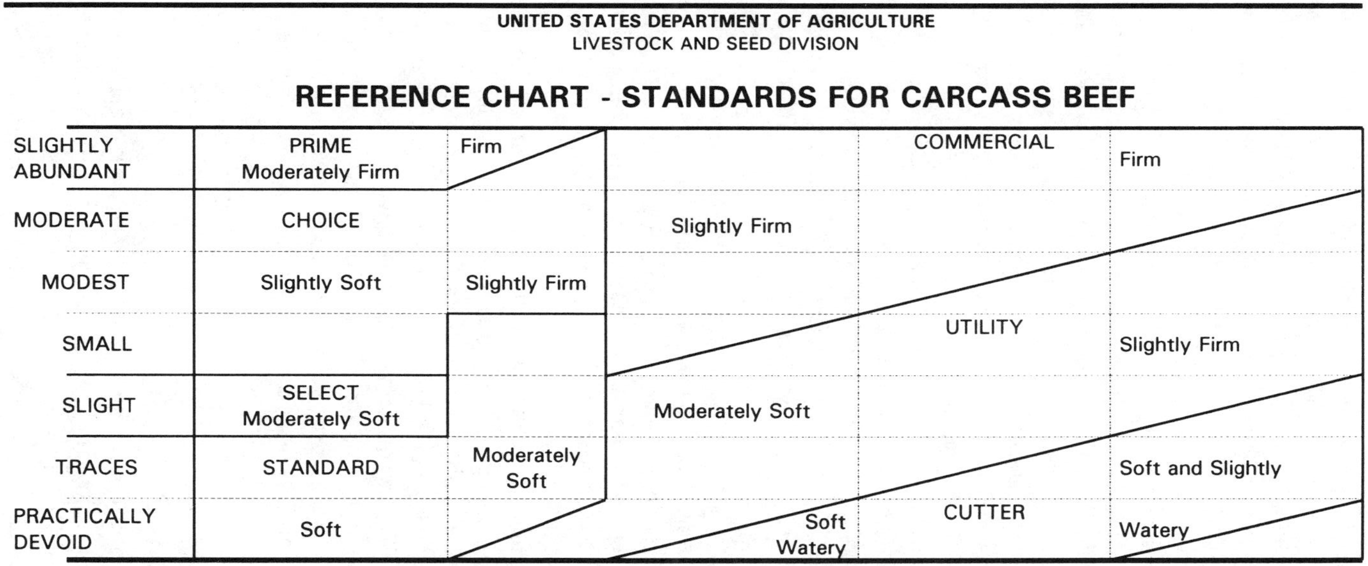

UNITED STATES DEPARTMENT OF AGRICULTURE
LIVESTOCK AND SEED DIVISION

REFERENCE CHART - STANDARDS FOR CARCASS BEEF

Source: U.S. Department of Agriculture, January 1997.

fewer calories, this was a change in name only, but with enormous ramifications. The meat industry supported the change because lower-fat beef costs less to produce—leaner cattle consume less feed before they are sold at market. Ideally, if more of this leaner beef is officially graded Select and provided through retail market outlets, consumers will be able to signal to the industry the quality, price, and trim level they prefer by the grades of beef they buy. The industry then could adjust production of a given type or grade of beef to meet that demand, resulting in a more accurate reflection of the difference in the value between grades of beef in the marketplace. In January 1997, the official standards were revised to restrict the select grade to A maturity only and to raise the marbling degree required for choice. These changes were made to improve the uniformity and consistency within the Choice and Select grades.[8]

According to the USDA *National Summary of Meats Graded*, nearly 80 percent of the total federally inspected beef slaughter was graded by the U.S. Department of Agriculture in 1990. Of the total weight of all carcasses quality graded, 2.2 percent graded Prime, 78.9 percent Choice, 18.8 percent Select, and 0.1 percent Utility.[9] It is interesting to note that in 1986, only 1.8 percent of the graded beef was Good; by 1989 (two years after the grade name had been changed), 9.3 percent had graded Select, showing a doubling of the amount of beef graded at this level from one year earlier. Figures for early 1997, issued by USDA's Agricultural Marketing Service, indicated further gains. For all geographic regions, nearly one-third of all beef graded at the "select" level for quality and yield; over half of all beef was graded as Choice.[10]

The *Beef Handbook* maintains that "there is a greater difference in fat content among cuts than among grades."[11] For example, Choice top round and top loin steaks likely contain less fat than the more heavily marbled Select rib steaks. Likewise, less expensive Select chuck roast may be lower in fat than its Choice counterpart, but still have more fat and calories than Choice top round and top loin. In fact, the *Handbook* goes on to point out that lean cuts of beef, particularly those from the round and some from the loin, are comparable in terms of fat content to some of the white meat chicken cuts.

Results and Outcomes

So, what difference does beef grading make to the consumer? Does the consumer really know the differences between grades of beef? Does this knowledge really influence purchase decisions? The top grades—USDA Prime, USDA Choice, and USDA Select—represent the types of beef that are the most familiar and widely available to consumers. It comes as no surprise that greater palatability and tenderness of beef cuts are equated with greater amounts of intramuscular fat, or marbling. If consumers purchase beef for its various attributes, such as taste, price, potential use, and/or cooking method (e.g., whether broiled or roasted), they should be informed about which grades provide which qualities. For example, consumers primarily concerned about taste would probably choose Choice or even Prime cuts. Consumers who prefer a leaner, lower calorie product and those who want a balance between price and taste would have the opportunity to purchase Select cuts.

It came as a surprise to some in 1987 when industry trade associations, like the American Meat Institute and the (then) National Cattlemen's Association, joined forces with consumer advocacy and public health groups, like Public Voice for Food and Health Policy, the American Cancer Society, and the American Heart Association, to petition the USDA to change the Good grade to the name Select. (Those familiar with the issues and the "policy climate" at the time say this move was hardly "surprising" when viewed in context; per capita beef consumption had declined over 20 percent between 1970 and 1987, and there was rapidly growing competition with chicken for consumers' food dollars.) The beef industry favored the change because it gave them a chance to sell a more uniform beef product than the "no roll" or "ungraded" beef that retailers had been using. Consumer groups felt the change provided consumers with a more consistent guide to leaner, lower-priced meat and made the product more attractive in their eyes.

A comment pertaining to the "advocacy coalitions" involved is of interest. While both the meat industry and public health/consumer groups promoted the change, it was initially resisted by the USDA. The reasons for the opposition from this key agency remain unclear. Was it because those responsible for the actual task of grading the meat products felt that there would be an economic disincentive to having more beef sold at a "lower" grade, or was it because beef producers, through their USDA contacts, felt they were being short-changed at the hands of their fellow meat processors?

Specifications for Meat Purchases

Since 1923, the federal Meat Grading and Inspection Service of USDA's Agricultural Marketing Service (AMS) has helped other organizations such as government agencies, private institutions, or not-for-profit food distribution programs in their meat procurement programs. The Meat Certification

Service is based on USDA-approved Institutional Meat Purchase Specifications, commonly called IMPS. The IMPS are voluntary guidelines for cut definitions and trimming practices used by the meat industry to help standardize quality control procedures.

Purchasers, be they hospitals, schools, hotels, or school food service personnel, may ask suppliers to submit bids on products based on the IMPS. When the purchaser requests delivery, the supplier asks the nearest USDA meat grading office to have a grader examine the product; this person is responsible for accepting the product and certifying that it is in compliance with specifications. The federal grader stamps each acceptable meat item with a shield-shaped stamp with the words, "USDA Accepted as Specified." This method of meat procurement assures the purchaser of a wholesome product of the grade, trim, weight, and other options requested. This system also encourages competitive bidding, which usually results in overall lower costs and eliminates controversies between buyer and seller over compliance of product.[12]

The IMPS now call for more fat to be trimmed from various cuts of beef than was designated in the past. The external fat on cuts of beef such as steak was reduced from one-half to one-quarter inch, and for the first time, the term "practically free of fat" was quantified as meaning that at least 75 percent of lean meat is exposed on the surface of the cut. This is indeed a step in the right direction for controlling the amount of fat on beef that is made available to consumers.

Grading and Labeling Standards for Ground Beef

Ground beef alone accounts for 45 percent of all beef sold in the United States and is the largest contributor of saturated fat in the diet. Unlike other fresh meat, ground beef sometimes carries nutrition claims, like "lean" or "extra lean." Unfortunately these claims are, at best, inconsistent from store to store, and at worst, outright deceptive.[13]

In order to ensure harmonization with FDA's implementing regulations for the Nutrition Labeling and Education Act of 1990 (NLEA), the USDA agreed to produce comparable regulations for the labeling of meat and poultry products (see Case Study 3, p. 179). Under these new regulations, terms like "low cholesterol," "very low fat" and "reduced calories" were defined for the first time. The labels for processed meat and poultry products were required to carry such information, but providing the same information for *fresh* meat and poultry products was voluntary. Producers could put it on the package labels, or the information could be presented on posters or in notebooks in grocery stores.

However, even before the USDA regulations even became effective on August 8, 1994, the Western States Meat Association in Oakland, California, asked for an exception to the part of the new regulations that pertained to the labeling of ground beef, the chief source of saturated fat in the American diet. Under the new regulations ground beef could be called "lean" only if it meets certain criteria—a 3.5-ounce serving must contain less than 10 grams of fat, less than 4.5 grams of saturated fat, and less than 95 milligrams of cholesterol. The product could be labeled "extra lean" only if one serving contains less than 5 grams of fat, less than 2 grams of saturated fat, and less than 95 milligrams of cholesterol. Ground beef seldom meets those criteria, so the meat association sought an exemption.

In response to that petition from the meat association, the USDA published a proposed regulation in the *Federal Register* on May 24, 1994, to allow ground beef to carry the same labeling that it always had with "percent lean, percent fat" (e.g., 70 percent lean, 30 percent fat, even though the ground meat did not meet any of the criteria being used for the descriptor "lean"). The proposal also stipulated that if the term *percent lean* is permitted on packages of the product, then nutrition labeling will be mandatory, but it can still be on a placard or in a notebook placed nearby the meat case in the supermarket.[14]

Trade associations and consumer groups lined up on both sides of this issue. The Center for Science in the Public Interest (CSPI), a forthright consumer advocacy group, vociferously opposed the proposed regulation saying, "consumers will continue to be misled and companies won't have any incentive to offer truly lean ground beef in order to use a valuable nutrient claim."[14] The CSPI, working through the Food and Nutrition Labeling Group (FNLG) to oppose this proposed rule, met with the then USDA Secretary Mike Espy to discuss the issue. The Society for Nutrition Education (SNE) endorsed the CSPI's comments, but the American Dietetic Association (ADA) in their comments chose to support the general concept of the proposal, thereby altering their previous comments on meat and poultry labeling. Other proponents of the proposed regulations included the Food Marketing Institute (FMI), the American Meat Institute (AMI), the National Cattlemen's Beef Association (NCBA), and other industry organizations. They maintained that their consumer surveys supported the notion of including the "percent lean" on meat packages rather than just listing the source of the product by cut of beef alone (as in "ground chuck.")[16] Although USDA had called for the comment period to close on August 22, 1994, no final rule had been been issued over three years later.

Clearly the issues of beef grading and labeling showcase the disputes—as well as some notable cases of cooperation—between the meat industry and consumer advocacy organizations. Whether the consumer has truly benefited from these initiatives remains an issue for discussion.

ISSUE 2: "STANDARDS OF IDENTITY"

From time to time, certain situations have demanded a "special look" by regulators because of the potentially confounding and confusing signals they are sending to consumers. One such issue pertains to food "standards of identity." The issue is directly related to food labeling reform, the subject of a case study in this book. The Standards of Identity were developed at a time when economic alteration of the *content* of processed foods was of primary concern, not providing nutritional information on food labels or striving to protect the public health through food. The NLEA, and its subsequently developed implementing regulations, developed nutrient-content- claim descriptors, like "low fat" or "light," to describe the fat content of particular food products. Without changes to the Standards of Identity, such definitions would have only limited application since the standards are based on the product having a certain defined set of ingredients, many of which are high in fat. Earlier we referred to the system of basing the beef grading system on the content and distribution of fat in the animal carcass as a "historical artifact"; likewise, too, are most food Standards of Identity.

Intended originally as a economic protectionist device, a Standard of Identity establishes the common or usual name under which a food product can be marketed, defines the product's composition, and specifies the ingredients it must contain.[17] As a policy instrument, Standards of Identity, in effect, serve as a "short cut" communication device between food manufacturer and consumer to ensure that the composition of processed food products remains the same from batch to batch. The problem occurs when the original composition of that food, as determined by its Standard of Identity, *should* change because it specifies a composition pattern that is no longer healthful.

The History of "Standards of Identity"

Enabling Legislation and Early Regulatory History

The Federal Food, Drug, and Cosmetic Act of 1938 (FDCA) prohibits the sale of adulterated and unwholesome foods.[18] A corollary to the prohibition of adulteration was the development of minimum specifications of ingredients for numerous processed foods. How can one determine if a product is adulterated unless there is a standard specification of the product's ingredients? Therefore, Section 401 of this act authorizes the Food and Drug Administration (FDA) to establish these standard specifications, or Standards of Identity, for individual processed food products.[19] This authority was conferred by Congress so that the FDA could, by prescribing the minimum composition of basic foods, prevent consumers from being deceived by products that resembled a familiar food, but failed to contain all the same ingredients and characteristics that consumers associated with, and thus expected from, that food product. This original legislation was not primarily concerned about the nutritional value of the food, but wanted to assure consumers that they were not being "cheated" by the omission or reduction in the amount of costly ingredients or the substitution of novel, usually cheaper, ingredients. Thus, Standards of Identity were originally developed to protect consumers from economic deception, to prevent cheapened products from being marketed as traditional foods.

Standards of Identity are, in effect, recipes—they prescribe the ingredients the food must contain.[20] For example, the Standard of Identity for peanut butter requires that any product marketed as "peanut butter" must contain at least 90 percent peanuts. Likewise, margarine must contain at least 80 percent vegetable oil. If, for example, a peanut butter–like substance does not contain 90 percent peanuts because other ingredients have been substituted for the peanuts, the product cannot be called the "common and usual" name, "peanut butter," but must be marketed and labeled under another name, such as "peanut spread."

Established by regulations passed mainly in the 1930s and 1940s, the standards were based mainly on "recipes" for the product as it existed at that time. The identities of most staple foods were codified to reflect required ingredients in traditional recipes, including minimum and maximum levels of some ingredients, such as fat or water.

The overall impact of Standards of Identity was that they gave food manufacturers virtually no flexibility to formulate novel processed foods if they were to be called by their "common or usual name." New substitutes for traditional food products—even substitutes that improved nutritional value by reducing the fat content—were difficult to market because the law forbade the sale of any product that "purport[ed] to be" a standardized food *unless* it complied with the standard of identity.[21] The only legal way that a food manufacturer of a new product could compete with a standardized food was by labeling it an "imitation" of the real thing.

For over thirty years after the enactment of the 1938 FDCA, FDA enforcement of the Standards of Identity effectively kept nonstandardized food products off the market. Foods that did not strictly comply with the standards, but closely resembled standardized products, simply could not use the familiar name of the product. Therefore, if a product did not meet the precise standards, the food manufacturer was required to market the product using the term *imitation* on the label. In and of itself, this legal requirement provided a potent incentive for manufacturers *not* to deviate from the standard recipe. They felt that consumers would regard the word *imitation* on the label as a sign of an inferior quality product or one loaded with artificial ingredients.

USDA's Authority for Standards of Identity

The U.S. Department of Agriculture derived its authority to set Standards of Identity for meat products from the Federal Meat Inspection Act (FMIA) and for poultry from the Poultry Products Inspection Act (PPIA) passed in the early 1900s. Standards of Identity for processed (rather than "fresh") meat and poultry products established specific requirements for a food's composition, including the kind and/or minimum amount of meat or poultry and maximum amount of fat (skin and moisture and any other permitted ingredients). Responsibility for Standards of Identity for both meat and poultry products belongs to the Food Safety and Inspection Service (FSIS) of the U.S. Department of Agriculture, which developed its standards by assembling information from cookbooks, recipes, and official agency files. Currently, the USDA's FSIS has approximately seventy-five standards for foods under its regulatory control.

General Principles Have Replaced Specific Recipes

During the 1970s, the FDA began changing Standards of Identity to permit more optional ingredients and to rely on general principles rather than specific recipes in establishing those standards. Key economic factors (such as the amount of peanuts in peanut butter or the amount of vegetable oil in margarine) remained, but a "safe and suitable" clause was added to many standards. This clause states that any "safe and suitable" additive may be used as long as it is functional and does not change the basic nature of the product or adversely affect its nutritional quality.[22] Today, most Standards of Identity state what ingredients must be present, may be used, or are prohibited. For example, in standardized whole wheat bread *all* whole wheat flour *must* be used, most other ingredients are optional and *may* be used (for example, shortening, emulsifiers, and so forth), but colorings *may not* be added unless in the form of a spice that imparts color (such as saffron or paprika). The FDA has established more than 280 standards for staple food items, including milk, peanut butter, jams and jellies, and milk chocolate.

During the 1970s, partly in recognition of advances in food technology, the FDA began to adopt a more flexible interpretation of Standards of Identity. For the first time, food processors were permitted to develop non-standardized food products without having to label them as "imitation" foods. The FDA promulgated regulations that permitted imitation foods to be marketed without being so labeled, as long as the label bore an appropriately descriptive name that was not false and misleading, and the food was not nutritionally inferior to the traditional product.

This new regulation stipulated that reducing the fat content in a food product was not to be considered the same as "inferior quality." However, terms like "reduced fat," "low fat," "reduced fat," or "fat free" were rarely used to describe a completely new version of a previously standardized product. Processors felt vulnerable in using such terms because there were no standardized definitions of these descriptors provided by the FDA.[23]

Standards of Identity for Low-Fat Foods

From a public health perspective, the most troublesome Standards of Identity were those that impeded processors from developing lower-fat products. Because most Standards of Identity were formulated before the hazards associated with consuming a high-fat diet were widely recognized, there are many who believe that these standards remain out of touch with the modern consumer's demand for healthier, low-fat food products.[24] Many standards require minimum fat levels in processed foods. Any product regulated by a standard that does not meet the minimum fat levels is prohibited from using the traditional, standardized product name on the label. It is easy to see how this requirement can cause serious marketing problems for an innovative food processor that has developed a new product identical in most ways to the original, except in fat content. The processor is forced to market the product with an unfamiliar name; consumers, in turn, are confused by this unfamiliar name and tend to view the new product as either of lesser quality or synthetic in comparison to the original, higher-fat product using the traditional name.

An example may be useful here. Until recently, it was not legal to name a product "Low-Fat Ice Cream" (even if it was technically feasible to make an ice cream with 3 percent butterfat) because the Standard of Identity for ice

Table 6.1 **FDA-Regulated Foods with Minimum Fat Standards**

Food Category	Number of Foods	Percent with Minimum Fat Standards
Cheese and related cheese products	73	90.4%
Milk and cream	31	77.4%
Frozen desserts	9	100.0%
Food dressings and flavorings	11	27.3%
Cocoa products	14	57.1%
Margarine	1	100.0%
Butter	1	100.0%

Source: Public Voice for Food and Health Policy, 1991.

cream mandates that the product must contain a minimum of 10 percent fat. A product with 3 grams of fat per serving did not meet the requirements of the ice cream standard and, therefore, could not be marketed under the common or usual name, *ice cream*. It could only be called *ice milk*, a name that signified a lower quality product in many consumers' eyes. The end result was that the standards placed lower-fat products at a competitive disadvantage, thereby reducing their availability in their marketplace and ultimately reducing consumer access to more healthful products.

The standard for butter is a classic example of a regulatory roadblock to the development and marketing of a lower-fat product. Federal law requires that a cream product contain at least 80 percent milkfat to be legally sold as "butter." Nevertheless, the technology does exist to produce butter using the same ingredients as the standardized product with as low as 39 percent milkfat content. As a consequence of the standard, however, this product, which has about half the milkfat content as the standardized butter product, cannot be sold labeled as "butter." It must be sold with another name, such as "dairy spread," one that often signifies an inferior quality product to uninformed consumers.

Other examples are of interest. The Standard of Identity for sour cream requires that it contain 18 percent fat and the Standard of Identity for mozzarella cheese requires it to be 45 percent fat. Thus, prior to 1993, under federal law, "reduced fat" mozzarella cheese or sour cream were required to have their own Standard of Identity or be called "imitation" or "substitute." The accompanying chart (see Table 6.1) shows minimum fat levels required in the standardized recipes of popular food items, all of which posed obstacles to the development and marketing of lower-fat versions.

Table 6.2. **Definitions of Nutrient Content Claims for Fat**

Fat Free:	Less than 0.5 gram of fat per serving.
Saturated Fat Free:	Less than 0.5 gram per serving and the level of trans fatty acids does not exceed 1 percent of total fat.
Low Fat:	3 grams or less per serving (If the serving is 30 grams or less or 2 tablespoons or less)
Low Saturated Fat:	1 gram or less per serving and not more than 15 percent of calories from saturated fatty acids.
Reduced or Less Fat:	At least 25 percent less per serving than reference food.
Reduced or Less Saturated Fat:	At least 25 percent less per serving than reference food.
"Light" or "Lite":	More than, or equal to, 50% less fat per reference amount or 1/3 fewer calories if less than 50% of calories from fat.
Lean:	*For meat and poultry products regulated by USDA only:* Less than 10 grams of fat, less than 4 grams of saturated fat, and less than 95 mg of cholesterol per reference amount and 100 grams for individual foods.
	FDA definition: On seafood or game meat that contains less than 10 grams total fat, 4.5 grams or less saturated fat, and less than 95 mg cholesterol per reference amount and per 100 grams.
Extra Lean:	*For meat and poultry products regulated by USDA only:* Less than 5 grams of fat, less than 2 grams of saturated fat, and less than 95 mg of cholesterol per reference amount and 100 grams for individual foods.
	FDA definition: On seafood or game meat that contains less than 5 grams total fat, less than 2 grams saturated fat and less than 95 mg cholesterol per reference amount and per 100 grams.

Source: Food and Drug Administration, "Focus on Food Labeling," *FDA Consumer*, May 1993, p. 32.

Recent Developments

To comply with the requirements of the Nutrition Labeling and Education Act of 1990 (NLEA), in 1993 the FDA established definitions for nutrient content claims (or descriptors) that may be used to describe a food or charactistics of a food. The regulations spelled out which nutrient content claims were allowed and under what circumstances they could be used on food labels. For the first time, food manufacturers were required to follow strict rules for using specific terms like *light* or *low fat* to describe the fat contents of their products. These definitions are given in Table 6.2.

The real breakthrough in nutrient content claim regulations came when the FDA adopted a "general standard of identity" that, in effect, supersedes minimum fat requirements or Standards of Identity for individual food products. The new "general standard" allowed manufacturers to reduce the fat content of such products and call them "low fat" or "light," as appropriate, as long as the food was still nutritionally and functionally equivalent to the regular version. For example, sour cream may be called "light" as long as its fat content is reduced to 9 percent, and it has vitamin A added to replace the amount lost when the fat was removed. Thus, if the company decides not to add the vitamin A, it must call the product "imitation light sour cream."[24] Similarly reduced fat or non-fat ice cream no longer has to be called "ice milk," even if it contains less than 10 percent butterfat.

One of the more interesting stories concerns the Standard of Identity for low-fat milks and yogurts. When a nutrient content claim (like "low fat") is part of the name of a food for which a Standard of Identity was established prior to enactment of NLEA, that food is exempt from the definition for the claim adopted under the NLEA.[26] According to the FDA's 1993 regulations, low-fat foods generally must have 3 grams or less fat per serving. However, the Standards of Identity for low-fat milks and yogurts, which were established prior to the passage of the act, allowed these foods to contain as much as 2 percent milkfat, which translates to 5 grams of fat per 8-ounce serving, or up to 60 percent more fat than is permitted under the definition for "low-fat"! Consequently, on November 9, 1995, the FDA published a proposal to revoke the Standards of Identity for certain dairy products whose names include a nutrient content claim, including low-fat and skim (nonfat) milks, low-fat and nonfat yogurt, and low-fat cottage cheese. In the absence of a Standard of Identity, low-fat milk must conform to the definition of "low-fat," i.e., no more than 3 grams of fat per serving, and not be nutritionally inferior to the food for which it substitutes, i.e., whole milk. The final rule, published in the November 20, 1996, *Federal Register*, clarifies for consumers the differences between 1 and 2 percent and skim milk. Under these new regulations, 2 percent low-fat milk will be renamed reduced-fat milk; 1 percent milk will qualify for the low-fat descriptor on the label, and skim milk can be called fat free or nonfat.[27]

The USDA's agency, the Food Safety and Inspection Service, is responsible for regulations pertaining to meat and poultry, and to any food products containing more than 2 percent (by weight) of meat or poultry. FSIS promulgated regulations for the descriptors, "lean" and "extra lean," which became effective in 1994. "Extra lean" bacon sounds like an oxymoron, but under current regulatory parlance, it does exist.

The USDA did not follow the FDA's lead and establish a "general" Standard of Identity for "low-fat" processed meat and poultry products. Further, they did not even examine the issue of Standards of Identity until pressured to do so by the Office of Management and Budget (OMB) in 1995. Instead, the USDA continues to rely on premarket approval of all labels placed on products they regulate. Therefore, each new lower-fat product must go through a separate USDA labeling review and be given its own standard before it can be sold or labeled as "reduced fat," "light," "low fat," or "nonfat." This is a cumbersome, expensive process that creates a disincentive for companies wishing to develop and market low-fat meat and poultry products.

In 1996, the USDA published an "advanced notice of proposed rulemaking" in the *Federal Register* calling for public comment to establish a general Standard of Identity for meat and poultry products. A number of food industry groups, notably the National Food Processors Association, suggested that FSIS proceed with issuing a final rule without making any changes to the current system. Several groups representing the meat industry, including the National Cattlemen's Beef Association and the Pork Producers Council, in a type of "delaying tactic," have offered to conduct consumer research on the subject, which then can be "entered into the comments" before any final rule is published.[28]

Included in the proposed USDA regulation were problematic issues such as defining "minimum meat requirements" in processed products and the use of "texturized vegetable protein" (TVP) to replace meat in processed products. Most of the food industry groups favored separating out such issues from the proposed rule. A number of industry groups, such as the NFPA, Nestle USA, and the American Council on Science and Health, as well as professional organizations, such as the American Dietetic Association, supported the use of TVP as a meat replacer ingredient, saying that "FSIS should not dictate ingredients to be used for specific functions if the ingredients to be used are safe."[29] However, in a strange departure, two consumer groups—the Center for Science in the Public Interest and Public Voice for Food and Health Policy—did not agree on their recommendations. Public Voice went on record as favoring a general Standard of Identity for meat and poultry products, but the CSPI did not, stating that "it opposed wholesale changes to meat and poultry standards of identity and composition."[30]

Role of Advocacy Coalitions

Since the late 1980s, a number of consumer, health, and even industry groups has called for both the FDA and the USDA to give immediate priority to overhauling the system of Standards of Identity, thus removing many barriers to the development of lower-fat, more healthful food products. In the late 1980s, for example, Public Voice for Food and Health Policy and the International Ice Cream Association formally petitioned the FDA to substitute low-fat ice cream's Standard of Identity for the "ice milk" Standard of Identity. The use of nutrient content claims, standardized by regulations that were effective in 1993 for the FDA (and in 1994 for the USDA), has helped this effort immeasurably, but progress has been slow.

The role of authoritative groups and advisory committees has also been helpful in urging a change in food standards. For example, the National Academy of Science "Committee on Technological Options to Improve the Nutritional Attributes of Animal Products" that prepared the 1988 report, *Designing Foods: Animal Product Options in the Marketplace,* called for a number of policy changes in reference to Standards of Identity. That committee recommended that all federally regulated Standards of Identity be made consistent and reduced in number.[30] Further, the report called for eliminating all specific ingredient and manufacturing process restrictions beyond those minimally necessary to maintain the recognized characteristics of each standardized food and to enhance the food industry's ability to produce and market new low-fat products.

Another example of food industry groups and consumer groups teaming up to address problems with Standards of Identity was the recent announcement of the revocation of standards of identity for low-fat dairy foods, such as milk, yogurt, and cottage cheese. The rule was proposed in response to a petition filed by two groups in 1995—one, the consumer advocacy group, the Center for Science in the Public Interest, and the other, a trade association for the dairy industry. For the CSPI, the change was seen as an opportunity to help consumers make more informed choices about buying low-fat products; for the Milk Industry Foundation, it was a chance to boost lagging milk sales by promoting low-fat and fat-free products. One must not forget, however, that the whole reason why a change to the standards of identity for low-fat milk was necessary in the first place was that a senator from a dairy state included an amendment to the legislative language of NLEA in 1990 that maintained standards of identity for dairy products. Years, many dollars, reams of paper, and hours of bureaucrats' time later—standards for milk were finally revoked and low-fat milk labels were truthful at last.

In the climate of "reinventing government" and budget constraints on regulatory agencies such as FDA and FSIS, an "advance notice of proposed rulemaking" was published in the December 29, 1995, issue of the *Federal Register*, requesting information about the utility of the system of standards of identity and how the system might be changed. Ninety-three comments were received at the end of the comment period, June 28, 1996. Most of the comments suggested keeping the Standards of Identity, but "fixing" the system to be more responsive to food product innovations; most food-related organizations who commented said they wanted standards limited to the name of the food and its essential characterizing properties. Opposition to changes in the current system were offered by several consumer advocacy groups (who wanted to maintain the system as a protection to consumers against potential economic fraud), the USDA's Food and Consumer Service (the agency that administers child nutrition programs, including the National School Lunch Program), and a few food-related groups with specific products, such as the Chocolate Manufacturers Association and the Florida Citrus Processors Association.[32] Michael Taylor, then USDA undersecretary for Food Safety, indicated that one approach would be to "offer full disclosure on ingredient labels that would show precisely the percent of fat in anything that's being marketed as a low-fat product." One wonders how this information could possibly be helpful to consumers when making food choice decisions. Clearly, the debate merits careful monitoring in the months ahead.

How the various "advocacy coalitions" line up is issue- and context-specific. When sales are down, the food industry is more likely to align themselves with consumer and health groups to seek win-win solutions. Examples of this phenomenon include the alliance of the meat processors with Public Voice for Food and Health Policy and several health organizations to change the name of the "Good" beef grade to "Select," the joint petition of the CSPI and the Milk Industry Foundation to repeal the Standard of Identity for low-fat milks and yogurt, and the teaming up of Public Voice and the International Ice Cream Association to repeal the Standard of Identity for ice milk.

Food manufacturers usually want more lenient, less rigid definitions of nutrient descriptors (i.e., which might be used to allow for more fat, saturated fat, and so forth, measures that the public health community regard as certainly less than optimum). Even within the food industry, challenges to current standards continue. For example, the meat processors and producers (particularly the National Cattlemen's Beef Association) are on the opposite side of other agricultural commodity groups, such as the American Soybean Association, on issues pertaining to the use of meat replacers. To achieve a lower-fat product, the ASA (and other industry groups, such as the National Food Processors Association, Nestle USA, Kraft Foods) would like to see the USDA approve the use of meat replacers, such as texturized vegetable protein (TVP) made from soybeans. This measure might allow the production of more healthful, less fatty meat, but begs the issue—"how much sausage must sausage have in order to be labeled as sausage?"

Dietary fat is "political," even when industry and consumer groups agree on a common position. The regulatory agency, as well, can often be an impediment to change if the traditional way of operation is challenged; the case of the USDA's opposition to changing the beef grade name to "Select" is a good example of this.

It is certainly the goal when modifying the general requirements for standardized foods to make it possible for food manufacturers to develop nutritionally modified products in response to consumer demand and label them using terms that consumers recognize. To do so in a nonmisleading and informative manner is a challenge.

Case Study 3

Food Labeling Reform: Dismantling the "Tower of Babel"

> *The tower of Babel in food labels has come down. . . .*
> —Dr. Louis Sullivan, former Secretary of DHHS, upon the release of final regulations on December 2, 1992, to implement the Nutrition Labeling and Education Act of 1990 (NLEA).

Food labeling has long been viewed by nutrition educators and consumer advocates—and, occasionally by regulatory agencies—as one of the most direct and efficient means of providing information about food contents to consumers. Whether or not it is an "effective" means of helping consumers make informed food choices depends in large measure on *what* information is provided and *whether* consumers understand and can use that information in making food choices. Because such a large proportion of the food supply is processed and packaged, attention on food labeling has largely been in the domain of the food industry, although recent efforts to expand nutrition labeling to fresh food items (such as produce, meat, poultry, seafood) and to claims made about food served in restaurants have taken place.

The passage of the Nutrition Education and Labeling Act of 1990 (NLEA) signified the end of a long journey for food labeling reform.[1] Never before had so many units—including congressional committees, executive branch agencies, public health and consumer groups, and professional and trade associations—focused their collective attention on a single nutrition issue.

This case study presents the background to the food labeling initiative, the legislative process resulting in the NLEA, and the outcomes of the subsequent regulatory processes by the FDA and the USDA. This discussion is presented in the context of the Advocacy Coalition Framework (ACF) approach, and concludes with an analysis of the outcomes and impacts of this significant policy event.

Description of the Key Issue

Food labeling is a *regulatory* issue involving government agencies, the food industry, and the consumer who purchases the final products. In particular, the passage of the Nutrition Labeling and Education Act in 1990 and the development of regulations to implement this far-reaching law is an intriguing story. It spans the spectrum of the policy-making sequence, from problem setting through agenda setting, policy formulation through legislation, and implementation through rule making; currently policy makers and scholars are in an evaluation phase of that process.

Presentation of nutrition information on the food label is a much more complex event than it might appear. First, there is the issue of content of the information—what information should be on the label? How much information should be there? How should it be presented—in numbers, adjectives, grams, or household measures? And, in what format? In particular, those who were promoting a reformed food labeling program had two main goals: (1) to provide useful information to consumers to help them make healthful food choices; and (2) to encourage the development and introduction of more healthful food products in the marketplace.

The Road to Food Labeling Reform

A History of Food Labeling through the 1980s— Creating a Climate for Reform

The initial legislation that authorized the federal government to regulate the safety and quality of food was the 1906 Food and Drugs Act, which prohibited interstate commerce in misbranded and adulterated foods. The original impetus for food labeling came from the 1938 Food, Drug, and Cosmetic Act, which had replaced the 1906 Food and Drugs Act. The FDCA corrected many weaknesses of the 1906 act and increased the economic regulation of foods; among other things, the 1938 act required the label of every processed, packaged food to contain the name of the food, its ingredients, its net weight, and the name and address of the manufacturer or distributor. The 1938 act gave the Food and Drug Administration (FDA) authority over food labeling, defined as a "display of written, printed, or graphic matter upon the immediate container of any article," as well as administrative controls to deal with such areas as standards of identity, the common or usual name requirement, and information disclosure for foods for special dietary uses.

In 1969, the White House Conference on Food, Nutrition and Health recommended that the federal government provide nutrient content information on labels of processed and packaged foods. To implement these recommendations, the Food and Drug Administration (FDA) established a voluntary food labeling program in 1973; this program was not mandated by legislation but evolved from the FDA's regulatory authority. The only foods that were required to carry a nutrition label were those that made a nutrient content claim or were fortified with various vitamins and minerals. Nutrition labeling was voluntary for almost all other foods, but the agency felt that nutrition labeling would give a "competitive advantage" to those food manufacturers who participated in the program. The regulations required that the label information be provided in a prescribed format, specified the nutrients that were required to be listed (eight vitamins and minerals, protein, fat, carbohydrate, and calories), and stipulated the standard value for expressing vitamin and mineral content of the product. Later, the USDA established a comparable program for meat and poultry products, based not on regulations but on a policy memorandum. By the time the food labeling reform effort had gained public attention in the late 1980s, approximately 60 percent of processed food, meat, and poultry carried nutrition labels.

The emphasis on vitamins and minerals in the 1973 regulations was due to widespread concern about hunger and malnutrition; macronutrients, such as fat, saturated fat, and complex carbohydrates, had not yet been linked conclusively to the prevention of chronic disease. The FDA established rules allowing cholesterol and fatty acid content labeling as an optional part of the 1973 nutrition labeling program. Reflecting the FDA's long-standing opposition to labeling claims regarding saturated fats and coronary heart disease, the regulations required that fatty acid or cholesterol information on a label must be accompanied by the following statement: "Information on fat and cholesterol content is provided for individuals who, on the advice of a physician, are modifying their dietary intake of fat and cholesterol." This disclosure statement reflected the agency's concern that such messages were not applicable to the entire population. By the time the NLEA was enacted in 1990, the FDA was no longer enforcing the requirement for this disclosure statement, and it rarely appeared on labels.

While the 1938 Federal Food, Drug, and Cosmetic Act (FFDCA) had given the FDA authority in both areas of food safety and labeling, the agency had been mainly preoccupied with issues dealing with food safety, such as monitoring of pesticide residues, food additives, and carcinogenic substances in food, from the 1950s through the early 1980s. As important as food labeling matters were in their own right, food safety issues clearly got the lion's share of FDA's attention and resources during that period. However, by the mid-1980s, food safety issues had subsided as the focal point of the agency's attention, and interest in food labeling was elevated to center stage.[2]

The 1980s was a decade in which scientific consensus was reached about the role of nutrition and the prevention of certain chronic diseases. This consensus-building effort began in 1980 when the USDA and the DHHS jointly released Dietary Guidelines for Americans, a set of generic dietary recommendations for the American public. Toward the end of the 1980s, two landmark reports were published—*The Surgeon General's Report on Nutrition and Health* in 1988, and the National Research Council's report, *Diet and Health: Implications for Reducing Chronic Disease Risk*. Just as the 1969 White House Conference on Food, Nutrition, and Health had provided an impetus for the initiation of the 1973 voluntary program on food labeling, it can be said that the publication of these two notable reports provided scientific support for those who wished to reform food labeling in the late 1980s. (At the very least, administration officials later credited *The Surgeon General's Report on Diet and Health* as the document that provided the scientific basis for the FDA's approval of health claims on food labels.)[3]

During the 1980s, the public's interest in nutrition clearly began to escalate. Many had begun to look to food labels for nutrition information, but at that time, only about 60 percent of processed foods carried nutritional labeling, and values for those nutrients most closely linked to health such as fat, cholesterol, and fiber were not listed. Those who wished to follow dietary recommendations grew increasingly frustrated in their quest for information on the food label that would indicate its nutritional content. The food industry had responded to consumers' interest in health by labeling many foods "light," "low fat," "no cholesterol," but in the absence of any federal standards for such wording, such claims were meaningless and often misleading. The media picked up on the issue, and people's attention was galvanized. Consumer complaints over misleading claims on foods made food labeling a "hot" issue.

The public also became concerned—and confused—over seeing misleading health claims on foods. Even a *Business Week* cover in 1989 brought public attention to the ridiculous nature of some health claims with its lead story, "Can Cornflakes Cure Cancer?"[4] Another factor that propelled the issue of "health claims" for foods into the public's consciousness was the marketing campaign developed by the Kellogg Company to promote the consumption of All Bran cereal. New scientific findings had shed light on epidemiological evidence showing that consumption of dietary fiber reduced the risk of certain cancers, notably colon cancer. Recognizing the FDA's traditional ban on disease-related food product claims, the company obtained endorsement from the National Cancer Institute and the Federal Trade Commission, all the while sidestepping the FDA. Congressional oversight hearings on the FDA's decision not to challenge the All Bran promotion provided a forum for officials to debate the broader subject of how to communicate information about diet and health to consumers. Thus, the health claims issue was easily expanded into a referendum on the federal food labeling system, drawing the food industry into the debate, and eventually sparking congressional interest in food labeling.[5]

At this point, states began to take action against individual companies. The Kellogg Company was sued by the state of Texas, not over All Bran, but over a breakfast cereal called "Heartwise" containing the compound psyllium. Under Texas law, no health claims on products were allowed; the Texas attorney general maintained that the product name was itself an "implied" health claim, and since the product was not an approved drug, it could not be sold. The state sued and won the case; Kellogg's subsequently changed the name of the cereal from "Heartwise" to "Fiberwise."

During this period, because federal enforcement of food label information by FDA and food advertisements by FTC was so lax on health claims, the states assumed ever-increasing levels of responsibility in this area. Large states such as Texas, California, and New York formed task forces to bring coordinated multistate litigations again food companies such as Kellogg's Quaker Oats, Kraft, and McDonald's between 1983 and 1990. Corporate attorneys were being forced to appear in any number of state capitals to deal with different state court litigations. Consumers were demanding more information, and the food industry was inconsistent in responding to that demand. It became apparent to the food industry that this fervor might only increase. What if all fifty states required different label information?

In the minds of many, national labeling uniformity was the linchpin that forced the food industry to agree to federal regulations for nutrition labeling and health claims.[6] (Uniformity occurs when a federal law preempts state laws or regulations; this phenomenon is usually called "preemption.") While the FDA clearly has federal authority over food labeling granted to it by the 1938 Federal Food, Drug, and Cosmetic Act, states also have considerable authority under their own laws, including in most cases a nearly identical local version of the federal FDCA. Thus, the FDA was not the only source of discipline in food labeling; potentially there were fifty-one sources (including the District of Columbia). When a company contemplates the prospect of having its products regulated by fifty-one different state bureaucracies, federal preemption becomes a much more desirable alternative.[7]

Finally, in the late 1980s, FDA began serious discussions to overhaul the food labeling system, in part to placate health professionals as well as to address demands from the food industry. In a letter to FDA Commissioner Frank Young in August 1988, a coalition of health and consumer groups asked him to make food labeling "a top priority in the coming year." This coalition, the Food and Nutrition Labeling Group (FNLG), consisted of over twenty public health and consumer groups, including the Center for Science in the Public Interest (CSPI), the American Public Health Association

(APHA), the American Dietetic Association (ADA), the Society for Nutrition Education (SNE), Public Voice for Food and Health Policy, and the American Association of Retired Persons (AARP), and was formed to publicly demonstrate that these organizations recognized nutrition labeling on foods as an issue with public health ramifications. The group also reminded the commissioner that the report of the Senate Appropriations Committee accompanying legislation providing funding for the FDA in fiscal year 1989 had contained language asking the FDA to initiate rule making to define "commonly used, vague, misleading nutrition and health claims such as lite, low fat, natural, and others."[8]

The election of George Bush to the presidency in November 1988 is noted as a key event in food labeling reform. During the Reagan administration, there was no action, if not strong opposition, to any food labeling changes or any attempt to restrain the food industry from using the food label to make health claims. In fact, then FDA Commissioner Frank Young is on record as having said, "No one ever died for lack of a food label." Oversight hearings held by Congressman Ted Weiss (D-New York) showed that the White House Office of Management and Budget (OMB) had actually prohibited the FDA from enforcing health claims regulations already on the books. After the Bush election, however, things changed. Commissioner Young invited public health and consumer groups to his office to discuss the food labeling issue. He informed them that he wanted to publish an "advanced notice of proposed rulemaking" in five areas—nutrition labeling, nutrition claims, health claims, ingredient labeling, and fruit juice labeling—exactly the same five issues that the Food and Nutrition Labeling Group (FNLG) had been pushing. If the coalition had not been visible with its efforts and the states not been actively suing food companies on a state-by-state basis, Frank Young probably would not have had a reason to change his mind. After the Bush election, he apparently felt more confident about moving ahead on the issue.[9]

During this period, interactions between the food industry and the FDA on the topic of food labeling were increased. Later in 1988, FDA officials told representatives of thirty-five companies at a meeting organized by the National Food Processors Association that it may be time for a new look at the information required on food labels.[10] The food industry, through remarks made at the annual meeting of the National Food Processors Association (NFPA) in January 1989, let it be known that they much preferred a voluntary food labeling program to any legislative action. About the same time, health professionals and consumer advocacy organizations were calling for new food labels with accurate information on the fat and cholesterol content of foods, substantiated health claims, and standardized terms for adjectival descriptors such as "lite" or "low."[11]

Calling food labeling the "dominant issue facing FDA," FDA officials announced that the agency was seeking a national consensus about what the food label should include.[12] Accordingly, the agency requested written comments and held public hearings across the country on the issues that it planned to address. Hearings were held between mid-October and mid-December 1989 in four cities across the nation—Chicago, San Antonio, Seattle, and Atlanta—each focusing on a different aspect of food labeling: nutrient label content; ingredient labeling, food standards, and descriptors; health messages; and label format. In all, approximately two hundred witnesses appeared. In addition, approximately 1,500 people participated in fifty "consumer exchange meetings" held with local FDA representatives.

In late October 1989, the FDA and the USDA jointly funded the Institute of Medicine of the National Academy of Sciences to conduct an independent study on the nutritional components of food labeling. This study was "designed to develop options for the FDA and the USDA to consider regarding regulatory compatibility and improved food labeling." Assistant Surgeon General James Mason later confirmed that "the study was initiated to help accelerate the food label reform process by having an independent scientific review available at the most strategic juncture in this process."[13] Having an impartial, scientifically rigorous advisory group serve as an "outside voice" for the analysis and debate of science-based issues with policy implications is frequently employed. Thus, contracting with such a prestigious group as the Institute of Medicine, a group within the National Academy of Sciences, was the tactic of choice by the two agencies within the executive branch to give them political cover and scientific credibility in their development of the content bases for food labeling. In March 1990, DHHS Secretary Louis Sullivan announced that the FDA was undertaking a comprehensive food labeling initiative. The FDA stated that it would be exercising its existing regulatory authority to cut down on unsubstantiated health claims for foods and would require more "useful" nutrition information on labels. One apparent motivation of the agency was to move quickly on their own in order to preempt any congressional initiative from the Democrats to reform food labeling.

By July 1990, the FDA proposed new regulations in what the agency termed "its first phase of food labeling reform." Three regulations were proposed: one on nutrition labeling, making labeling mandatory on most food products and revising the list of required nutrients; one on standardizing serving sizes; and the third on replacing and updating the nutrient standard used (the U.S. RDA) with new reference values.[14]

After only eleven months of accelerated study, the IOM committee released its report *Nutrition Labeling: Issues and Directions for the 1990s,*[15] in September 1990, between the release of the FDA regulations in July and the passage of the Nutrition Labeling and Education Act two months later. The IOM committee report made recommendations on the foods that should be covered by nutrition labeling, the nutrients that should appear on the label, the presentation and format of label information, and the legal authority under which labeling changes could be implemented. Also notable was that the report called for the nutritional labeling of foods sold in restaurants as well as fresh meat, fish, poultry, and produce. Joseph Levitt, FDA chief of staff, was quoted as saying that his agency felt "great satisfaction that the issues we are thinking about [were] ratified and enhanced by the report" and that it would be the "major scientific cornerstone" upon which the FDA's final regulations would be based.[16]

By the late 1980s, food labeling reform had become a "tug of war" between the DHHS and the USDA in the Bush administration, on the one hand, and Congress on the other, as to which group would have primary authority to establish the content and format of new food labels. These two competitors were aided by various private sector groups—lobbyists for the food industry, consumer advocates, educators, and public health specialists—each vying to see their particular viewpoint either written into legislative language or appearing in subsequent regulations. The story is complicated but intriguing, a perfect illustration of the intertwining roles among Congress and the executive branch agencies. The timing for the actual passage of legislation as well as promulgation of regulations was fraught with delays and "back room" dealings. To provide the reader with the clearest description of the food labeling reform process, each group's actions are discussed separately, but tied together in the accompanying diagrammatic timeline (see Figure CS3.1.)

Legislative Action: The Role of Congress

Virtually every Congress since the 1969 White House Conference on Food, Nutrition, and Health had introduced food labeling bills, and 1988 was no exception. The individual bills varied in scope—from outlining comprehensive modifications in food labeling regulations to single-item bills,[17] such as those addressing labeling of tropical oils as ingredients, health claims, and defining terms such as "lite" or "low fat." Throughout 1988, Congress began in earnest to consider comprehensive legislation to reform food labeling. Senator Howard Metzenbaum (D-Ohio), chair of the Senate Labor and Human Resources Committee, had long been interested in the food labeling issue and had held hearings on it in the mid-1980s. In 1988, he initiated substantive discussions with public health and consumer interest

Figure CS3.1 **Chronology of Legislative and Regulatory Events for NLEA**

The Nutrition Labeling and Education Act of 1990

A. Legislative Time-line

FDA	CONGRESS	OTHER
1988 Food label reform discussed; Discussions held with representatives of food industry and consumer groups.	Sen. Hatch and Metzenbaum consider proposing new legislation for food labels.	Food and Nutrition Labeling Group coalition formed.
1989 FDA holds hearings in 4 cities on food labeling issues from Oct.-Dec.; "Consumer Exchange Mtgs." held in four regions	7/27 H.R. 3028 introduced by Rep. Waxman (D-CA) and S. 1425 introduced by Sen. Metzenbaum (D-OH)	FDA and USDA fund IOM/NAS study on "Nutritional Components of "Food Labeling;" study initiated in October
	8/3 Hearings by House Sub-Comm. on Health and Environment	
	10/25 H.R. 3028 approved by House Subcommittee	
	10/31 "clean" bill reintroduced as H.R. 3562	
	11/13 Senate Comm. on Labor and Human Resources hold hearings on S. 1425	
1990 (Feb.-Mar.) FDA announces preparation of regulations.	4/25 S. 1425 reported out of Comm.	
7/19 FDA issues 3 proposed regulations published in *Federal Register*	7/30 H.R. 3562 passes House by voice vote	
	8/2 S. 1425 placed on Senate legislative calendar	9/26 IOM Report released
	10/24 S. 1425 passes Senate by voice vote	
	10/31 Enrolled bill presented to President Bush	
	11/8 Bill signed by President Bush	

P.L. 101-535: THE NUTRITION LABELING AND EDUCATION ACT OF 1990

A. Regulatory Time-line

FDA	USDA
1991 11/25, 26 proposed rules appear in *Federal Register*	11/25 FSIS issues parallel proposed regulations for meat and poultry
1992 Jan. FDA and FSIS hold joint public hearing on proposed rules.	
2/25 90-day comment period ends; FDA receives more than 40,000 comments	2/25 90-day comment period ends; FSIS receives 1,109 comments
1993 1/6 Final regulations published in *Federal Register*	1/6 Final rules published
1994 5/8 Final regulations become effective	7/8 Final regulations become effective

groups with the intention of developing a proposal for food labeling legislation. Senator Orrin Hatch (R-Utah), as the ranking minority member on the committee, was tapped as a spokesperson for the food industry and became actively involved in subsequent food labeling discussions. Leaders in a Congress controlled by the Democrats wanted nothing more than to take legislative action that would supersede any food labeling reform initiative that could be made by the Republican administration.

Throughout 1988 and early 1989, a variety of bills on different aspects of food labeling were floated among the various committees. Staff of the House Subcommittee on Health and the Environment of which Representative Henry Waxman (D-California) was chair, although mildly interested in the food labeling reform effort for some time, were so impressed by the membership and expertise represented by the Food Labeling and Nutrition Group (FNLG), a coalition formed to press for food labeling reform, that Representative Waxman was persuaded that this was the time—and the issue—on which the subcommittee should take a stand.[18]

On July 27, 1989, Representative Henry Waxman formally introduced H.R. 3028, the Nutrition Labeling and Education Act of 1989 (with twenty-five cosponsors); the intent of this bill was to amend the 1938 Federal Food, Drug, and Cosmetic Act to *require* nutrition labeling for *all* foods. This bill addressed a wide range of issues—foods covered by nutrition labeling, components of nutrient information, consumer education, allowed health claims, ingredient labeling, standards of identity, and state enforcement.

Hearings held by the House Subcommittee on Health and the Environment on August 3, 1989, showed how serious Congress was about food labeling reform and showcased the widely divergent views that had made food labeling such a contentious issue. Nineteen witnesses were called, ranging from the assistant secretary of Health and the FDA commissioner to several congressmen and representatives of voluntary health associations and trade associations. The leadoff witness, however, was Bruce Silverglade, legal director of the Center for Science in the Public Interest, who led the formation of the Food and Nutrition Labeling Group. Concerns voiced during the hearings about the bill included the following:

- Differing views of adequacy of existing FDA authority to require nutritional labeling of processed foods
- Problems of coordination and inconsistency in enforcing regulations among the FDA, USDA, and FTC
- Food industry objections to focusing on the potential harm of overconsumption of particular nutrients in foods rather than on their nutritional contribution to the "total diet"

- Food industry opposition to a mandatory, rather than voluntary, approach to nutrition labeling

The administration, fearing that they might be challenged in court about their enforcement authority, argued for broadly worded legislation that would not proscribe agency actions. Further, this hearing served to build a record to support a specific time line for implementation once legislation was enacted.

While House subcommittee members seemed generally sympathetic to the goals of the bill; however, the details proved so troublesome that Waxman was forced to recess an October 19 markup so that compromise language could be worked out on a variety of issues.[19] Republican members, who were sympathetic to the food industry, were particularly unhappy with a provision aimed at forbidding nutrition claims included in the brand name of a food that did not meet FDA standards. An amendment was ultimately adopted that would exempt claims within existing brand names from the new law, but only until regulations were issued pertaining to such claims.

Subcommittee members were also concerned about rules regarding the labeling of raw agricultural products, such as produce and fish. Waxman, supporting the view of a number of consumer groups, wanted to include the measure because he felt that it would help people compare the nutritional value of raw foods with that of processed foods. But even the bill's backers suggested that such a measure might prove more troublesome to retailers than it would be helpful to consumers.

On October 25, 1989, H.R. 3028 was approved—including provisions for labeling fresh fish and produce—by the House Energy and Commerce Subcommittee on Health and the Environment on a voice vote. However, some members who were unhappy about specific provisions of the bill (an example being Representative Michael Bilirakis from Florida who was opposed to the labeling of fresh fish) threatened to carry their concerns to full committee.[20] On October 31, 1989, a revised bill was reintroduced after markup as H.R. 3562 to the House Committee on Energy and Commerce, with twenty-four cosponsors.

On the same date (July 27, 1989) that Representative Waxman had initially introduced a food labeling bill in the House, a companion bill, S. 1425, was introduced in the Senate by Howard Metzenbaum, with seven cosponsors. Hearings were held before the Senate Committee on Labor and Human Resources on November 13, 1989, with many of the same witnesses who had been at the August House hearing testifying. The FDA commissioner raised some of the same issues that he had in the House hearing and also provided feedback on two of the four public hearings that had been held. Representatives from consumer groups, professional organizations, and voluntary health associations (such as the American Cancer Society and the American Heart Association) all supported the bill. This hearing appears to have been one place where a record was being built for establishing an appropriate standard for health claims and on setting a firm time schedule for issuance of regulations by the FDA once the legislation had passed.

S. 1425, which had been introduced the previous fall, was approved by the Senate Labor and Human Resources Committee by a vote of 10–5 on April 25, 1990.[21] Then, on May 16, 1990, H.R. 3562 was reported out of committee, and on June 13, 1990, the bill (as amended) was reported to the full House for vote and placed on the Union Calendar No. 331. Waxman's bill remained essentially intact as allegedly "nongermane" amendments to preempt state food labeling laws dealing with the labeling of pesticides and other cancer-causing contaminants were defeated.[22]

On July 30, 1990, H.R. 3562 was called up by the House under suspension of rules and passed the House (as amended) by voice vote, but only after a key compromise was reached with the food industry. In return for industry support for the final legislative package, Congressman Waxman agreed to language that would preempt a number of state food labeling laws dealing with health claims, ingredient labeling, standards of identity, and other similar requirements.

On August 2, 1990, S. 1425 was received in the Senate where it was read twice and placed on the Senate legislative calendar under General Orders, Calendar No. 784. On October 24, 1990, the Senate passed S. 1425, with amendments, by voice vote. One of these amendments was added by Senator James Jeffords (D-Vermont), exempting low-fat milk and yogurt from adhering to new definitions of low fat; the reason given was that the composition of milks was already defined by Standards of Identity, and the change would confuse consumers. (Actually, this action meant that 1 percent and 2 percent milks would have much higher butterfat content than would be allowed under NLEA; see discussion on Standards of Identity in this book for further explanation.) Finally, the bill was cleared for the White House on October 26, 1990, when the House agreed to the Senate amendments.

On October 31, 1990, the enrolled bill was sent to the White House, and President George Bush signed the Nutrition Labeling and Education Act into law on November 8, 1990, making it Public Law 101–535. In sum, the statute dealt with six separate matters:

- Section 403(q) was added to the FFDCA to require nutrition labeling for virtually all food products

- The FDA was required to define nutrient descriptors, such as "high fiber," "low fat," etc., which were commonly in use throughout the food industry
- The FDA was required to review specified disease prevention claims to determine whether they were appropriate for use on the food label
- The NLEA contained several new food standards provisions; among these were that vegetable and fruit juice beverages were required to state the percent of each juice on the information panel and all ingredients in standardized food products were required to be included in the statement of ingredients on the food label
- All of the labeling requirements under the FFDCA were explicitly made subject to national uniformity (federal preemption), thus removing state and local governments from establishing regulatory requirements related to the nutrient content of food
- In return for national uniformity, states were for the first time explicitly authorized to enforce the food labeling provisions of the FFDCA, with the same exceptions that apply to national uniformity, in federal courts, rather than state courts, after first informing the FDA and giving the FDA the opportunity to take action[23]

Regulatory Implementation of the NLEA

Even though the legislative battles had culminated with the passage of the Nutrition Labeling and Education Act of 1990, the real work for the regulatory agency charged with implementation of the law—the Food and Drug Administration—was just beginning. To ensure passage, legislation is frequently written in fairly general terms. It is then expected that the executive branch agency that implements the law will write the specific regulations to "execute" or carry out the intent of the law.

Although not written by Congress, regulations have the "force" of law and can be developed and adjudicated in much the same manner. In traditional rule making, the agency must follow a very specific course of action. First, the agency may issue an "advance notice of proposed rulemaking" by publishing it in the *Federal Register*. This step is not actually required by law, but is usually done by an agency to build political support for an issue or clarify issues that were particularly problematic during the legislative process. The advance notice can also ask for input and advice about troublesome issues the agency foresees in the wording of the regulation.

After allowing for a period of time for public comment and additional work by the agency, the "proposed regulation" is formally issued again by publishing it in the *Federal Register.* A period of time for public comment is allowed; this is usually thirty, sixty, or ninety days, the longer the time, usually the more complex the wording of the proposed regulation. After reviewing the comments and reworking the regulation (if needed), the "final rule" is published in the *Federal Register.* Before being "codified" in the *Code of Federal Regulation* (CFR), however, the regulation is sent to the White House Office of Management and Budget (OMB), the government arm that verifies that the costs of implementing new regulations are justified by the benefits. There are no "short-cuts" in this process, but the timing for each phase may be short, as it was in the case of writing NLEA regulations simply because deadlines for each stage of the process were specified in the language of the statute.

Wording of the NLEA required that proposed regulations be published by the FDA no later than November 8, 1991, one year after the bill became law. Final regulations were to be issued by November 8, 1992, and the effective date of implementation was specified—in the actual wording of the law—as November 8, 1993. If final regulations were not issued by that date, then the proposed regulations would become final automatically. It is unique to have such a procedure written into the legislation. Dates designated in the legislation were designed to "push" the agency to issue regulations in a timely manner, and this so-called "hammer provision" was included in the legislative language of the NLEA to ensure that regulations became final by the specified deadline.

In December 1990 (after the NLEA had been signed into law) Dr. David Kessler was sworn in as the FDA's commissioner. Dr. Kessler had written an article for the *New England Journal of Medicine* months before about the importance of food labeling reform. He proved to be a much more vocal and active proponent of food labeling reform than his predecessors had been.[24]

The deadlines specified by the NLEA obviously sped up the FDA's overall regulatory process, but the tight time line was described as "both a blessing and a curse" by Dr. Edward Scarbrough, then director of the FDA's newly created Office of Food Labeling, the group that coordinated the NLEA rule-making process. He further explained, "The timetable forced us to get the proposals out without a lot of over-review, re-drafting, and going back and forth, but staffers put in long hours, often working on weekends, to meet the one-year deadline."[25]

While many have claimed that the NLEA constrained the FDA in exercising its authority to release improved food labels, others think the FDA was relieved by having to comply with NLEA requirements. According to Thomas Scarlett, former chief counsel of the FDA:

> The FDA ... got a shortened rulemaking procedure for food standards. It got restrictions on health claims without having to out-maneuver OMB. It got a solution to one of the longest-standing impasses in food labeling history: FDA against the cranberry juice industry on the issue of percentage ingredient labeling of fruit beverages. [The NLEA required such labeling.] Finally, FDA was authorized to proceed with a project that would likely continue the favorable public relations engendered by the agency's crusade, kicked off with the "Citrus Hill" seizure, for honest (but not too complicated) labeling. . . . Had FDA started without the NLEA, the [rulemaking] process would have both substantially deferred labeling reform until the end of the decade and truncated its scope to a modest fraction of the NLEA's laundry list of changes.[26]

Not only was the time line for writing the implementing regulations tight, the language of the NLEA was specific in terms of what it wanted to achieve. The legislative language caused some problems for the technically trained bureaucrats at the FDA. Dr. Edward Scarbrough described one of the agency's dilemmas:

> For example, the law says "the label shall have" and named nutrients. One of the nutrients named was complex carbohydrates. But, there's no good definition for complex carbohydrates. Had we been working on nutrient list requirements without NLEA, we would not have included complex carbohydrates—we might have used a more general term, such as "carbohydrates other than sugar."[27]

The NLEA requirement for evaluating health claims as they related to certain nutrients was certainly one of the more troublesome issues faced by the FDA in writing enforcement regulations. The FDA received more than 7,000 public comments on the health claims issue alone, and each comment was considered in writing the proposed regulation. Only after reviewing more than 1,400 scientific studies and authoritative reports and making judgments about the scientific veracity of them relative to the health claim statement, did the FDA release its regulation permitting only seven of the ten diet-health relationships that Congress had specified that the FDA review.

The requirement to provide nutrient content "descriptors" (i.e., claims such as "lite" or "reduced") for certain food products also proved to be quite a challenge for the FDA regulators. Attempting to provide the consumer with information on the label that would be informative and not confusing and yet not wanting to limit food manufacturers' incentive to develop healthier (i.e., lower fat) products was a fine line the FDA staff walked. The regulations spell out which nutrient content claims were allowed and under what circumstances they could be used. The advantage to all is that "everyone now plays by the same rules."

Recognizing that each regulation presented its own set of challenges, compromises were necessary even when there were general principles that everyone accepted. The case for standardized serving sizes was one such regulation. Under the 1973 regulation, each food manufacturer could set whatever serving size they wanted; usually if you had a food product that was fortified or was nutrient dense, the serving size was set larger than if the product was relatively high in some more "undesirable" nutrient, such as fat. (This issue is important because the smaller the serving, the lower the fat, saturated fat, cholesterol, or sodium values on the Nutrition Facts panel and the easier to make a nutrient content claim.) The NLEA required that there be *standardization* of such serving sizes and that the food manufacturer no longer have discretion to decide on their own what that serving size would be. "No one seriously argued that the law shouldn't set serving sizes," Dr. Scarbrough explained, "but there were arguments with industry about numbers—is [a serving] one ounce or an ounce and a half?"[28] In the wording of the regulation, foods were grouped into 139 categories. The amount of food customarily eaten at each occasion, called the "reference amount," was established for each food category, and the FDA established rules that food manufacturers could use for converting the reference amounts into label serving sizes.

One of the last regulations to be issued was that pertaining to the *format* of the label.[29] In order to make a more informed recommendation, the FDA conducted two label format experiments. Results from the first indicated that consumers were better able to use labels with the least amount of information and consistently preferred those labels that had interpretational aids, such as adjectives and highlighted information. For the second study, the FDA added new format features and expanded the tests to measure other important label uses besides product comparisons. The FDA had hoped to find a label that combined the elements of consumer preference with performance (i.e., performing specific tasks correctly). Unfortunately, none of the seven label formats rated superior on all these aspects. The study also showed that the label format used most accurately by consumers was not necessarily the format that was most preferred. For example, consumers rated the adjective and the highlighted formats as the most desirable, though they were unable to use either format with a high degree of accuracy.

The FDA then requested assistance from industry and health professionals in determining the best nutrition label format. Several label formats were field tested on actual products by Kellogg and Frito-Lay. For the most part, consumer and public health groups advocated using those label formats most preferred by consumers. Several of the groups had already proposed specific label formats: the Center for Science in the Public Interest (CSPI) liked using the concept of a "stop light"—green for those nutrient values that should be increased in the diets of healthy Americans, yellow for which values were "neutral," and red for those nutrient values that should be consumed in lowered amounts. The American Heart Association suggested using bar graphs, while others proposed using some form of adjectives (e.g., "high," "medium," or "low"), grouping ("Choose a diet high in. . .," or, "Choose a diet low in. . ."), or highlighting. In discussions with the FDA, those representing the food industry, however, stressed that performance should outweigh consumer preference in the choice of format and strongly recommended that only those formats on which consumers scored best on the tasks the FDA presented should be used. Thus we now have a label designed by regulators to satisfy industry concerns rather than consumer preferences for nutrition information.

In the end—after after an expenditure of nearly $400,000—the FDA proposed using "the percent DV/with actual amount DV" format. While that format had helped consumers make correct decisions about levels of product consumption, it was among the worst performers on the communication and comparative product evaluation tasks. More than 60 percent of those surveyed did not know how to use the daily value (DV) information. The proposed rule on alternative label formats was published in the July 20 *Federal Register*, allowing for only a thirty-day comment period.

The FDA met the one-year deadline specified in the legislation to develop proposed rules for the implementation of the NLEA. Twenty-six proposed rules were published in the *Federal Register* by the FDA in November 1991 (after an exhausting year of tireless effort on the part of scores of the FDA staffers), allowing a ninety-day comment period.

At the same time, the USDA's Food Safety and Inspection Service (FSIS) published a parallel proposal for the nutrition labeling of meats and poultry. Although *not* bound to the same statutory mandate as the FDA, the USDA's Food Safety and Inspection Service (responding to pressure from health and consumer groups) agreed to reform its nutrition labeling on meat and poultry products and to work with the FDA to harmonize regulatory language for nutrition labeling and maintain a similar schedule for implementation of the law. This was done so that consumers could expect to see virtually identical food labels with the revised information in the new format appear on supermarket shelves at about the same time.

In late August 1991, USDA had issued two proposed regulations for its own label format. One proposal resembled the FDA's label format, but included the Dietary Guidelines recommendations at the bottom, such as "Eat a variety of foods." The other format proposed listing the amount of each nutrient in a product, as well as the Recommended Daily Intake range, reflecting nutrient needs across all population groups. For example, the Recommended Daily Intake for calories would be listed as "1,600 to 2,800."[30] The USDA did not like the FDA's use of a 2,000-calorie-a-day reference standard for calculating the %DV, preferring instead to use an average intake of 2,500 calories so the fat and saturated fat content of meat products would appear to be lower.

In January 1992, the FDA and USDA's Food Safety and Inspection Service called a public hearing on the labeling proposals. Ninety-two representatives from the food industry, the scientific community, and consumer groups presented their comments in person to a panel of FDA and FSIS officials. On February 25, 1992, the comment period ended. The FDA had received more than 40,000 comments in the ninety-day period, 8,000 on the last day alone! About 30,000 of these comments were form letters from organized campaigns.[31] The FDA then had the responsibility for compiling, sorting, and attending to all comments in revising the regulation so that final rules could be published by the statute-imposed deadline of November 8, 1992.

While both the FDA and USDA's FSIS were able to agree on virtually all of the language on the food label by the deadline, several issues—including the calorie level on which the %DV would be calculated, the listing of the percent fat content versus number of calories from fat, and restaurant food labeling— remained unresolved. By statute, final regulations were to have been published in the *Federal Register* by November 8, but internal wrangling between the two agencies delayed publication. Therefore, the "proposed" rules from a year earlier became "final" by default. The food industry was particularly upset. After all, it was they who were legally liable for complying to the law calling for new food labels. Food industry representatives were not sure whether they should print labels based on the proposed rules (which had become final by default), or whether they should wait on the "final" final regulations that had been in preparation for a November 1992 release. A lobbyist for Kraft–General Foods, who had formerly been a White House staffer in the Bush administration, called on the president to arbitrate the differences. Thus, final decisions about food labeling became the matter of discussion in a personal meeting with President Bush in December 1992.

Although none of us was in the room that day, those closest to the situation relay what happened this way. Only the highest officials were in attendance—the president (and probably his advisors), USDA Secretary Madigan, DHHS Secretary Sullivan, and FDA Commissioner Kessler. The main "sticking point" was the calorie level on which the percent DV would be calculated—2,000 (the FDA's proposal) or 2,500 (what the USDA preferred). Someone (speculations are that it was Commissioner Kessler) solved the impasse by relating that he had recently stopped at a McDonald's restaurant and the placemat listed the nutrient content of a "Big Mac" based on a 2000-calorie diet. The placemat was passed to Secretary Sullivan, who then shared it with the president. Although some think the president made the decision at that meeting, others who have close ties with the Bush administration insist that the actual decision came later.[32]

Whenever the actual decision was made, it resulted in a compromise: the %DV calculations on the label would be computed on a 2,000-calorie-diet basis, while the actual daily value quantities would be listed in a footnote at the bottom of the nutrition panel with columns for amounts based on *both* a 2,000- and a 2,500-calorie diet. It has been said that President Bush's concern over how he would look in the history books led him to chose the FDA label format (described by DHHS Secretary Sullivan as "the least intrusive while giving [consumers] maximum information") over the one preferred by the USDA.[33] The label format decision was Solomonesque—the top half was the FDA's, the bottom half the USDA's. Figure CS3.2 is a visual representation of the final food label format. It is noteworthy that the hundreds of thousands of dollars spent by the FDA to test consumers' preferences and performances on the new label format went for naught; the format of the new Nutrition Facts panel on the food label was decided by the president himself as part of a political compromise between feuding agencies in his administration. In any event, final regulations from both agencies were published in the *Federal Register* on January 6, 1993—all 700 pages worth!

Originally expected to implement the regulations by May 1993, the food industry petitioned the FDA for a one-year delay (until May 1994) claiming economic hardship in printing the new labels by the deadline. (The cost of printing new food labels was originally estimated to be about $4 billion; with the one-year delay, the industry estimated the cost to be less than $2 billion.)[34]

This request created a furor within the administration.[35] In March 1992, the USDA announced that it would delay until May 1994 the deadline for nutrition labeling for meat and poultry products. In May 1992, the FDA's Commissioner Kessler and DHHS Secretary Sullivan originally agreed to a nine-month delay. But, when the White House learned of the DHHS decision, it shut down the process to review the decision and referred it to the Competitiveness Council chaired by Vice President Dan Quayle to study the comparative cost savings to industry of a nine- versus twelve-month delay. The referral to these additional groups so angered Democrats on Capitol Hill that they charged that the delay was a political maneuver to garner the support of the food industry for President Bush in the 1992 election. Consumer groups were equally angry about the requested delay, and they mounted a media campaign, hoping to exert enough public pressure on the

Figure CS3.2 **The New Food Label**

The new food label will carry and up-to-date, easier-to-use nutrition information guide, to be required on almost all packaged foods (compared to about 60 percent of products up till now). The guide will serve as a key to help in planning a healthy diet.*

Serving sizes are now more consistent across product lines, stated in both household and metric measures, and reflect the amounts people actually eat.

New title signals that the label contains the newly required information.

Calories from fat are now shown on the label to help consumers meet dietary guidelines that recommend people get no more than 30 percent of their calories from fat.

% Daily Value shows how a food fits into the overall daily diet.

The **list of nutrients** covers those most important to the health of today's consumers, most of whom need to worry about getting too much of certain items (fat, for example), rather than too few vitamins or minerals, as in the past.

Daily Values are also something new. Some are maximums, as with fat (65 grams or less); others are minimums, as with carbohydrate (300 grams or more). The daily values for a 2,000- and 2,500-calorie diet must be listed on the label of larger packages. Individuals should adjust the values to fit their own calorie intake.

The label of larger packages must now tell the number of calories per gram of fat, carbohydrate, and protein.

Nutrition Facts

Serving Size ½ cup (114g)
Servings Per Container 4

Amount Per Serving

Calories 90   Calories from Fat 30

	% Daily Value*
Total Fat 3g	**5%**
Saturated Fat 0g	**0%**
Cholesterol 0mg	**0%**
Sodium 300mg	**13%**
Total Carbohydrate 13g	**4%**
Dietary Fiber 3g	**12%**
Sugars 3g	
Protein 3g	

Vitamin A	80%	•	Vitamin C	60%
Calcium	4%	•	Iron	4%

* Percent Daily Values are based on a 2,000 calorie diet. Your daily values may be higher or lower depending on your calorie needs:

	Calories	2,000	2,500
Total Fat	Less than	65g	80g
Sat Fat	Less than	20g	25g
Cholesterol	Less than	300mg	300mg
Sodium	Less than	2,400mg	2,400mg
Total Carbohydrate		300g	375g
Fiber		25g	30g

Calories per gram:
Fat 9 • Carbohydrate 4 • Protein 4

*This label is only a sample. Exact specifications are in the final rules.
Source: Food and Drug Administration 1993

Source: The Food and Drug Administration, 1993.

administration to hasten the release of the regulations.[36] In the end, the dates of the agreed-upon delays prevailed. Implementation of the final regulations became effective on May 8, 1994, for FDA-regulated foods and on July 8, 1994, for USDA-regulated meat and poultry products.

Contentious Issues in Food Labeling Reform

Food labeling reform brought to the fore several issues on which the "advocacy coalitions" differed. Certainly each group raised valid concerns and sought attention from policy makers about resolving each of these issues.

Preemption

While the House and Senate bills, as well as the administration proposals, all addressed the same basic concerns, there were some differences. Both bills would preempt state laws that had nutrition labeling requirements, although state laws regarding other aspects of labeling would not be affected. (The administration's proposed regulations would not have preempted state laws.)

Food manufacturers and grocer groups badly wanted the preemption language so they could avoid the expense and hassle of having to provide different information for the same products sold in different states. The preemption issue remained a key area of dispute throughout consideration of the food labeling bill, with the basic issue being how far the legislation should go in setting uniform food labeling regulations that preempt state laws. As a condition that they would support passage of the bill, the food industry demanded national uniformity of the food label through federal preemption of state food laws. On the other side, consumer groups opposed preemption altogether because they wanted states to have the option of imposing standards even more stringent than those proposed at the federal level.

The preemption issue was finally resolved by statements in the bill that state and local governments were prohibited from establishing conflicting labeling requirements related to nutrition, ingredients, food names, and related matters. The measure did not, however, preempt state or local authorities to require warnings about carcinogens or other substances that foods may contain. This language reflected the compromise made between manufacturers' groups, who wanted all state and local labeling requirements barred so labels could be uniform nationwide, and consumer groups, who wanted to leave state and local governments the option of putting into effect even more stringent requirements.[37]

The preemption issue did not go away, even after passage of the NLEA.

Subsequent to the passage of the law, a newly configured but related IOM/National Academy of Sciences committee was commissioned to examine this very issue. Their report, *Food Labeling: Toward National Uniformity*, published in 1993, stated that, in general, most of the federal provisions would accommodate virtually all state rules in six categories currently in effect.[38]

Scope of Coverage

One of the major differences between the voluntary program of 1973 and the NLEA was that nutrition labeling was now *required* on virtually all packaged foods. The only exceptions to this rule included small businesses with less than $500,000 annual gross sales, foods "for immediate consumption" in deli bars or restaurants, or foods with "no nutritional significance," such as coffee, tea, and chewing gum.

Writers of the law clearly wanted *all* food products to carry nutritional labeling. But problems existed with trying to label those items that were not packaged, such as fresh produce or seafood. Compromise language was written instructing the FDA to identify the twenty most commonly consumed fruits, vegetables, and seafood and to ensure a process whereby nutrient information could be provided nearby, such as on posters, signs, brochures, and the like. Although the program is "voluntary," the regulations do carry some teeth. Chief among them is the information that must be provided—name of the fruit, vegetable, or fish identified by the FDA as being one of the twenty most commonly eaten in the United States; serving size; calories per serving; amount of protein, total carbohydrates, total fat, and sodium per serving; and percent of the U.S. RDA for iron, calcium, and vitamins A and C per serving. In addition, 60 percent of the stores must carry such labeling. If this percentage of stores does not have the program, as determined by a biennial study based on unannounced store visits, the program becomes *mandatory*, a feature that most grocery stores do not want to have happen. Studies conducted in 1993 and again in 1995 found that approximately 75 percent of the stores were in compliance, based on the FDA surveillance study. It is important to note here that there is *no* USDA requirement that fresh meat and poultry products carry nutrition labeling.

Another provision that the NLEA originators wanted was to include was required nutritional labeling of foods served in restaurants. This provision was vociferously opposed by the National Restaurant Association (the trade association representing most food service establishments) and was not included in the legislation. Restaurants were required to meet FDA standards for nutrition and health claims, but the scope of this requirement later became another contentious issue between consumer groups and the industry.

It was not until August 2, 1996, that the FDA finalized extension of its regulations on health and nutrition claims to claims made on restaurant menus. The restaurant labeling action was especially problematic. While final rules for health and nutrition claims on processed food labels had been published by the FDA in January 6, 1993, restaurant menus were exempted from this regulation. (Only claims on restaurant posters, brochures, and table cards were covered by the original set of regulations.) In response to a lawsuit filed by the consumer advocacy groups Public Citizen and CSPI in March 1993, the FDA reversed its previous position and proposed to extend its health and nutrition claims rules to restaurant menus. The court case was then stayed. Although the comment period on the regulation ended in August 1993, no final regulation was issued by the FDA. This met with further legal action by the two groups who asked the federal court to resume proceedings in their lawsuit brought against the FDA. The court denied the motion to resume legal proceedings and continued the case until May 1995.

In the summer of 1995, the White House Office of Management and Budget (OMB) rejected publication of the FDA's final rule to extend health and nutrition claims to restaurant menus, reportedly because it was "too controversial." Because nutritional claims made on restaurant signs, placards, and table tents already were covered by FDA regulations (thus bringing most fast-food chains under FDA requirements), OMB did not feel that requiring the same of menus was necessary. In September 1995, the FDA issued "guidelines" to the restaurant industry regarding the use of nutrient content claims like "lite" or "low fat" on posters, brochures, and placements, but these guidelines did not apply to information appearing on restaurant menus.

In an effort to spur restaurants into compliance with the proposed menu-labeling regulation, the Center for Science in the Public Interest (CSPI) sent "legal demand letters" to six restaurant chains in early 1996 threatening legal action on the grounds that nutrition and health claims made on their menus were misleading and therefore violated state consumer protection laws.[39] This action is a good example of what happens when federal preemption is not in effect (as it would have been if restaurants had been included in the FDA regulation.) Because almost all states have misleading trade practice laws, the CSPI was unquestionably able to "sue" *each* restaurant under state law in order to get them to change their practices. Ultimately, the court found on July 6, 1996, that the FDA must, under the NLEA, finalize the restaurant menu claim rule. A final regulation was published in the *Federal Register* on August 2, 1996.

Specific Issues to be Addressed in Regulations

Unquestionably, the food industry had identified a market advantage in promoting foods that met consumer perceptions of a "healthy" diet. Not surprisingly, most of these promotions took the form of specific claims placed on the food label extolling the health effects of particular foods.[40] Formulators of the NLEA were adamant that the wording of the law provide for a mechanism by which the *validity* of health and nutrient content claims on foods could be established and ensure, by regulatory means, that these standards were then adherred to by the food industry.

Nutrient Content Claims

Before the passage of the NLEA, an increasing number of food companies had turned to marketing nonstandardized, lower-fat products bearing adjectival descriptors such as "lite," "low," "reduced," or "fat free" because of their perception that such descriptors would lure consumers who thought such terms meant the products were more healthful. For years, consumer advocacy groups had warned that the use of such descriptors created problems for consumers. For example, the use of the term, *lite*, for products such as butter and margarine was found to mislead consumers about the health effects of those products.[41]

An important part of the NLEA was the provision that no such term could be used on the label unless it had been defined by the FDA in regulations. The NLEA allowed those nutrient content claims that characterized the level of a nutrient, using terms defined in regulation, and were allowed to state the absence of a nutrient only if it was normally present in a food.[42] In its rule making, the FDA defined nutrient content claims for the terms *free, low, high, good source, reduced* or *less, light* or *lite, modified,* and *more.* Most claims were based on the amount of the nutrient in a reference amount of the food, not necessarily the serving size noted on the label. An example may prove helpful to the reader here. Rather than having the "light" vegetable oil that was just light in color or the "lite" cheesecake that was just light in texture, products bearing such terms now must show that the product contains "50 percent or more less fat per reference amount or one-third fewer calories if less than 50 percent of calories from fat," the definition given to "light" in the FDA regulations. Those who worked closely to finalize these descriptors claim that the food industry got what it wanted; several consumer groups preferred much more stringent standards.

Putting Nutrient Information into Context

Writers of the NLEA insisted that the specific nutrient information on the food label must be put into a context that consumers would understand. Those representing the Center for Science in the Public Interest (CSPI) wanted a code similar to a "stop light," with red, yellow, and green dots beside those nutrients that should be consumed in lesser, the same, or greater amounts. Told that such specificity in the legislative language would probably doom passage, writers set about to find an acceptable term to include in the law that would require the FDA to develop a regulation to state specific nutrient information in a meaningful way. The final language of the NLEA stated that nutrition information should be listed on the food label so that consumers can "understand its *relative significance in the context of the total daily diet*," the phrase agreed to by lawmakers that awaited further operationalization by FDA regulators.

To operationalize the phrase contained in the NLEA that nutrient information on the label should be presented "in the context of the total daily diet," FDA proposed that each nutrient listed would be accompanied by its daily value (DV), that is, the maximum amount that should be consumed daily for that nutrient, or, in the case of fiber, the minimum amount. Also included on the label would be the percentage of the DV that would be supplied by eating one serving of that specific food. Not everyone was pleased with the proposal; the food industry, for one, believed that the concept was too complicated for consumers to understand. But consumer advocates contended that the "DV concept" would be able to alert consumers to products that are high in fat, saturated fat, cholesterol, or sodium.[43]

Health Claims

A health claim is a food label message that describes the relationship between a food or food component, such as fat, calcium, or fiber, and a disease or health-related condition. To prevent consumers from being misled, the NLEA allowed only those claims that characterized the amount of a nutrient in a food or the relationship of a nutrient to a disease that was preapproved by the FDA. The act required the secretary to promulgate regulations authorizing disease claims that met the scientific evidence standard established in the law; the NLEA even went so far as to stipulate the actual wording of the standard for allowing disease prevention or health claims: ". . . based on the totality of publicly available scientific evidence (including evidence from well-designed studies conducted in a manner which is consistent with generally recognized scientific procedures and principles) that there is *significant scientific agreement*, among experts qualified by scientific training and experience to evaluate such claims, that the claim is supported by the evidence."[44]

The art of compromise is essential to good law making. Seeking a term that stood midway between "scientific consensus" (which was opposed by the food industry) and "substantial scientific evidence" (which, in the view of a number of consumer groups, was too weak to be meaningful), authors of the NLEA agreed to the term *significant scientific agreement* as the scientific evidence standard by which the validity of health claims would be judged. For example, if there are three scientifically valid studies saying that fat will decrease coronary heart disease and three studies saying that it will not, there is no "significant scientific agreement" to the claim; thus, the food manufacturer would not be permitted to use this health claim on its product.

FDA wrote regulations approving only seven of the ten health claims named in the NLEA because they felt that these were the only ones for which there was a preponderance of scientific evidence supporting the claim. These original seven were:

1. Calcium *and* osteoporosis
2. Fiber-containing grain products, fruits, and vegetables *and* cancer
3. Fruits and vegetables *and* cancer
4. Fruits, vegetables, and grain products that contain fiber *and* coronary heart disease
5. Fat *and* cancer
6. Saturated fat and cholesterol *and* coronary heart disease
7. Sodium *and* hypertension (high blood pressure)

In 1994, a health claim was approved for "folate *and* neural tube defects (birth defects involving brain or spinal cord)."

Model health claims are provided in the regulations to explain the complex relationship between a food component and a disease-related condition. Food companies do not have to follow the exact wording, but they must include *all* of the basic parts when making a health claim. A model health claim for the fruits and vegetables *and* cancer relationship follows:

> Low-fat diets rich in fruits and vegetables (foods that are low in fat and may contain dietary fiber, vitamin A, or vitamin C) may reduce the risk for some types of cancer, a disease associated with many factors. Broccoli is high in vitamins A and C, and it is a good source of dietary fiber.

FDA regulations also stipulate that a food must meet three basic rules to make a health claim, or to be labeled as "healthy" or "healthful," as follows:

1. *Disqualifying Nutrient Levels.* A food must not exceed set levels for nutrients such as total fat, saturated fat, cholesterol, or sodium to qualify for a health claim.

2. *Specific Nutrient Levels.* A food must meet specific nutrient require-ments for each of the eight health claims.

3. *10 Percent Daily Value Level.* A food must contain at least 10 percent of the daily value of one or more of the following nutrients: protein, dietary fiber, vitamin A, vitamin C, calcium, or iron. (This is the so-called "jelly bean" rule, a policy implemented to prohibit health claims on labels of foods that do not make a nutritional contribution to the diet beyond being a source of calories, such as jelly beans. Marian Burros, noteworthy food columnist for the *New York Times*, claims that this rule is named in "her honor." In her book, *Eating Well Is the Best Revenge*, she relates that "when the 'healthy' rule was announced at a news conference, she asked FDA Commissioner David Kessler if that meant jelly beans could be called healthy. It was back to the drawing board, and the current rule is the result.")[45]

In January 1996, a proposed regulation for "oats *and* coronary heart disease" was published in the *Federal Register,* the first "food-specific health claim," according to full-page ads taken out by the Quaker Oats Company in the *Washington Post* and the *New York Times.* As a side note explaining the degree of involvement of the food industry in such health claims, the summary accom-panying the proposed rule in the *Federal Register* states that, "FDA is propos-ing this action in response to a petition filed by the Quaker Oats Company."[46] On January 21, 1997, the final rule approving a health claim for oats was published by the FDA. Government scientists from the FDA, National Insti-tutes of Health (NIH), and Centers for Disease Control and Prevention (CDCP) had reviewed thirty-seven studies of oats consumption and coronary disease, one-third of which had been funded by the Quaker Oats company. The wording of an approved health claim would be as follows: *"Soluble fiber from foods such as oat bran, as part of a diet low in saturated fat and cholesterol, may reduce the risk of heart disease."* To meet the level of consumption at which statistically significant effects were produced, consumers would need to con-sume 3 grams of oat-based fiber, or nearly 1 cup of cooked oatmeal, or three packets of "instant" oatmeal.

Many in the public health community opposed the decision, saying that oat bran per se had no magical properties and that consuming soluble fiber from other food sources such as fruits and vegetable would have the same effect.[47] They saw this as an example of the food manufacturer manipulat-ing the regulatory process—from planning and financing scientific studies on which regulatory judgments are based, to putting political pressure on the agency to weaken wording of pending regulations, to advertising the fact that the product bears the desired health claim.[48]

Coordination of Food Advertising Activity with the FTC

In addition to the FDA and the FSIS, the Federal Trade Commission (FTC) is also involved in the food labeling issue.[49] The FTC regulates food advertising, where health or nutrient content claims are frequently made in advertising food. The FTC operates under the provisions of the Federal Trade Commission Act, which requires a significantly different degree of substantiation from that of the other food regulatory agencies. Although charged by law with ensuring that advertising is not "unfair," "deceptive," or "misleading," the nutritional claims that can made in advertising can be very different than those allowed on food labels. Concern about these differences and the potential for consumer confusion have brought about proposed legislation to require the FTC, in regulating food advertising, to hold to the same standards created under the NLEA for allowable health claims and nutrient content claims.

In 1994, the FTC issued a "policy statement" that food processors and retailers should use nutrient content claims (like "lite," "high fiber") in their advertisements only if they are consistent with FDA regulations for food labels. (Unfortunately, the FTC policy is not consistent with FDA regulations on the matter of health claims.) The policy statement cautions advertisers that claims not specifically allowed by the FDA will be carefully scrutinized for deception. As an example of this, the press reported that the FTC forced "Mrs. Fields Cookies" to change its advertising because the cookies advertised as "low fat" actually contained almost twice the amount of fat allowed under FDA regulations.[50]

A 1997 agreement between the makers of Promise margarine and the FTC is further illustration of the government's power to approve health claims before they can be used in food advertisements. In this case, the FTC reversed its previous position and maintained that health claims cannot be made for a high-fat food even if the food is low in saturated fat. Until recently, the FTC permitted advertising a food as cholesterol free even if it was high in fat. Now, in order to make a no-cholesterol claim, high-fat foods must also disclose their fat content.[51]

The FTC policy has been called "an appropriate harmonization between food advertising and labeling enforcement" by the Grocery Manufacturers of America (GMA), a trade association of food processors. However, consumer groups such as the Center for Science in the Public Interest (CSPI) maintain that the policy continues to confuse shoppers and asserts that "the FTC's policy permits food companies to circumvent the FDA's new food labeling regulations in advertising that are not permitted on the food label."[52]

Analysis and Further Comment

By "Stage" of the Public Policy Process

The *problem was identified* when consumers who were interested in obtaining accurate nutrient information for certain macronutrients were unable to do so. The issue came to the attention of policy makers who were able to put it on the *agenda* for official consideration. Several factors converged to focus policy makers' attention on the nutritional labeling issue—the public's increasing interest in health and nutrition, the emergence of major scientific documents linking diet and health, and the public perception that "the government" (in this case, the Food and Drug Administration) was not meeting the public's need for accurate nutrition information.

A *policy was formulated* with the passage of the Nutrition Labeling and Education Act in 1990. Because of this law, all foods will have nutritional labeling and consumers will have more information on the macronutrient content of foods. Further, national uniformity of food labels, an issue long sought by the food industry, assures that there will be consistent food labeling throughout the country. *Implementation of the policy* was accomplished by the writing of regulations by the FDA and the USDA's Food Safety and Inspection Service (FSIS). These regulations made a tremendous contribution in assisting consumer food choices by standardizing serving sizes, defining nutrient content claims, and establishing a standard for health claims on food labels. In sum, the goal of food labeling reform was to provide consistent, readable, understandable, and useful food labels that would enable consumers to make more healthful food choices. By and large, this goal was accomplished.

Recognizing that passing legislation and promulgating regulations does not lead to actual behavior change on the part of consumers, the NLEA judiciously called for activities that educate consumers about the availability of nutrition information on the food label and the importance of using that information to maintain healthful dietary practices—the "E" in NLEA! To implement this provision of the legislation, the DHHS's FDA and the USDA's FSIS initiated a multiyear education campaign called, "Read the Label, Set a Healthy Table," designed to promote consumer awareness of the changes on the food label and to motivate consumers to use the information on the food label in making food selections.[53] The "National Exchange for Food Labeling Education" (NEFLE), a coalition of professional, educational, food industry, trade association, and consumer groups, was created to network and coordinate efforts in developing label awareness and educational materials and informational campaigns. Unfortunately, this public education campaign was relatively weak, underfunded, and understaffed to do the job it needed to do.

At present we are in the *policy evaluation* stage. Already, several new petitions have been filed with the FDA for new health claims on food products as well as special exemptions for specific products. One year after implementation of the NLEA, a survey, "Shopping for Health '95," was conducted for the Food Marketing Institute (FMI) and *Prevention* magazine to determine the impact of the new label on consumers. Early results suggest that the Nutrition Facts panel has made a good impression—an increasing number of shoppers are aware of the label, say it's easy to understand, and are likely to use it in deciding what foods to buy. But the campaign is not reaching certain groups; awareness of the new food label is most limited among adults living in comparatively low-income households, those without a college education, and members of minority groups.[54] Moreover, the marketplace is responding; the FDA reports that market shares of products such as fat-modified cookies, cheese, and peanut butter have increased.[55]

However, the real test will come in a few years when we see if the new label has made any actual difference in consumers' food buying and selection decisions. Soon after the regulations to implement the NLEA were published in 1993, former DHHS Secretary Louis Sullivan optimistically predicted that the new food labels should show some measurable impact in the next five to ten years, but realistically noted that whether or not public health benefits are achieved is "not only a question of giving people information but motivating them to use the information [in making healthful food choices.]"[56] In the face of so many other variables affecting consumers' food choices, such as food advertising and social pressures, it is perhaps unrealistic to expect the food label in and of itself to result in more healthful diets. However, we do expect the food label to become a tool that consumers will use to make more informed food choices and an incentive for the food industry to create more healthful food products.

Food Labeling as Seen through the "Advocacy Coalition Framework"

The food labeling issue brings into play very distinct "advocacy coalitions" whose core belief systems and interactions are key to understanding policy change.[57] One advocacy coalition is the food industry, that combination of agribusiness interests that process and package raw commodities into a form for consumer use. The inherent value of providing nutritional labeling of food products is often questioned by those in the food industry, except when information about the nutritional content of their product will place it in the most favorable context possible. In the food industry, regulation often creates a situation where those more interested in product promotion or marketing are at odds with others who must be responsible for technical accuracy of nutrition information and product claims.

Throughout the 1980s, the food industry was fairly united behind the "less-information-is-better" approach as manufacturers of high-fat, high-cholesterol, high-sodium food products dominated industry politics and trade association activities. This approach shifted somewhat with the passage of the NLEA as food manufacturers tried to place their products in a more favorable light by selectively highlighting their more positive attributes.[58]

Another significant advocacy coalition that seeks to influence the food labeling issue is comprised of the consumer advocacy groups and the public health community. These groups espouse the need for nutritional informa-tion on food labels and more uniformity in the way the information is presented (i.e., terms and measurement standards should be consistent from product to product, company to company). Left on their own, it is unlikely that these groups can get all the information on the food label that they desire, so they favor government intervention to do the task.

This dynamic often results in a situation where more powerful economic interests are on one side, while health and consumer interests are on the other. One side is supported by politicians who may have a large food producer in their districts or states; other politicians, more likely those from urban regions, will support the labeling advocates. On one side, the coali-tion has core beliefs in the principles of laissez-faire capitalism and free, open markets, while on the other, the groups believe in the government's right to protect the health interests of the individual consumer against the economic power of the food conglomerates. (In the case of food labeling, however, the consumer/health groups were able to enlist the support of states' attorneys general who wielded considerable economic power with the food industry.)

These advocacy coalitions remained relatively stable throughout the course of the legislative and regulatory processes. However, the timing of specific events during this time altered the types of interactions among the various players. In the late 1980s through 1991, nutrition labeling became legitimate as a true public policy issue, creating a dialogue among affected groups resulting in passage of the NLEA in November 1990 and starting the regulatory process in the FDA. The process was outside the boundaries of Congress and the administration; discussions between policy makers, the food industry, and health groups, even the more rancorous ones, were open and productive. Early on, the consumer/public health advocates were aided in their efforts by others at the state and local levels of enforcement, such as state attorneys general who were willing to take on food manufacturers on "misbranding" charges. The food industry, led by lobbyists for the leading trade associations—in particular, those associated with the National Food Processors Association (NFPA) and the Grocery Manufacturers of America (GMA)—were able to obtain their primary objective: federal preemption to assure national uniformity of all food labels.

From 1992 to 1993, the force of the food labeling issue weakened as action turned "inside" to the regulatory agencies, the FDA and USDA's FSIS. Once the NLEA had passed, the food industry was relentless in presenting its preferences to FDA regulators. One of the industry's strongest arguments dealt with costs of the program, including nutrient analysis and printing new labels to meet a prescribed format; the National Food Processors Association (NFPA) estimated that the costs of label revisions would run over $2 billion.[59] The food industry also actively pushed their views about other aspects of the food label, particularly serving sizes, nutrition label format, and label claims. It seemed to many observers of the process that sympathetic FDA bureaucrats were able to craft regulations that were more favorable to the food industry's positions than those of the consumer groups on most issues.

The USDA, never a player in the legislative discussions, was persuaded to join in the regulatory process to "harmonize" the effort so that the final labels on meat and poultry products would be comparable to those developed by the FDA. After the FDA regulations were finalized in 1993 (and the USDA's in 1994), there was further weakening of the nutrition labeling issue. FDA opposed the dietary supplement industry, but lost. Commissioner David Kessler's attention was diverted by two other issues: (1) congressional efforts to weaken the FDA's regulatory authority and (2) the fights with the tobacco industry. Tobacco, rather than food labels, had become the FDA's main priority. During this period, the food industry petitioned the FDA on several occasions to weaken previous labeling regulations; one of these, the petition by Quaker Oats for a health claim on oat products, actually succeeded in a relatively brief period of time.

While divided on some issues, consumer and public health groups were held together both throughout the legislative and rule-making processes by their coalition, the Food and Nutrition Labeling Group (FNLG). Staffed by professionals at the Center for Science in the Public Interest (CSPI), there was a constancy of purpose and an attention to detail that few other coalitions have maintained over time.

As the process of policy making continued, each advocacy coalition gained some "policy-oriented learning." Certainly the use of authoritative advisory groups and scientific reports were instrumental in this regard. The consumer and public health community continued to rely on the substance of two landmark reports—*The Surgeon General's Report on Nutrition and Health* published by the Public Health Service, Department of Health and Human Services, in 1988 and the National Academy of Science/National Research Council's report, *Diet and Health: Implications for Reducing Chronic Disease Risk* published in 1989—for the scientific integrity of their efforts. The legitimacy of the food labeling reform efforts was also enhanced by two NAS/Institute of Medicine publications, *Nutrition Labeling: Issues and Directions for the 1990s,* published in 1990, and *Food Labeling, Toward National Uniformity* (on the issue of federal pre-emption of food labeling), published in 1992.

The food industry also employed the tactic of using advisory groups and authoritative reports. Initiated in 1993 and concluding in late 1995, the Keystone National Policy Dialogue on Food, Nutrition and Health was convened to discuss issues related to the implementation of the NLEA and to help the FDA set priorities on how to regulate claims in food labeling.[60] Authorized health claims were the focus of a substantial amount of discussion with this group because of "their potential to . . . sell healthful food products . . ." While important discussion certainly resulted from these debates, the report did acknowledge that "many questions remain unanswered, . . . [primarily] how public policy should be forged in areas where consensus has not been reached." The report has been criticized by academics and even some industry groups for its lack of specificity, but defended by others for the inclusivity of the process that was used in making its recommendations.[61]

In addition to the role of advisory groups, "policy entrepreneurs" were also important actors. The role of FDA commissioner is a difficult one indeed, spanning responsibilities and ethical decisions to the public health, the food industry, and the political environment. Dr. Frank Young, who was felt to be openly hostile to the notion of revamped food labeling during the Reagan administration, was observed to be much more open and friendly to the notion after Bush was elected. The most supportive actor, however, probably was Dr. David Kessler who became FDA commissioner in late 1990. Kessler was vocal, active, and supportive throughout the rule-making procedure, and undeniably enthusiastic about the results in his press conferences and publicity tours, a real "champion" of the food labeling reform effort.

Conclusions

As with any public policy effort, food labeling reform was the product of compromise and consensus. The expanse of the effort on the part of professionals (in particular, the public health and consumer advocacy community as well as representatives of the food industry), legislators, regulators, and even consumers, was monumental. Never before (and perhaps, never again) will a single food-related issue galvanize the efforts of so many disparate groups. Commissioned by the FDA to evaluate the potential health benefits of nutrition labeling changes, the Research Triangle Institute estimated that over twenty years, $3.5 to $105.6 billion in medical care costs would be saved.[62] With the food industry estimating an expenditure in the order of $2 billion to revamp food labels, this program (on paper, at least) appears to be quite cost efficient.

What issues remain? Probably the most potentially volatile issue is that of health claims on food products. The FDA must adhere to rigorous standards in judging which nutrients—and now, which foods—can be singled out for its association with disease prevention. The food manufacturer knows that a nutritionally literate consumer will purchase a product because of its association with health, but health claims cannot be permitted to be used simply for economic gain. We can only hope that the consumer will not be a pawn in this game of nutritional "one-upsmanship." We can take some solace in the results of an FDA-sponsored study. In this study, consumers were asked to respond to three different products, each carrying different health claims, nutrient content claims, and differing endorsements from government health agencies. The results are encouraging to public health professionals—consumers saw health claims used as an advertising tool rather than as a means to inform and educate about health.[63]

But the "$64,000 question" remains ... will the new food label truly help consumers make more healthful food choices? Consumers tell us they want *more* information and *say* they use the information on food labels. Certainly now, consumers have been given unprecedented access to accurate and detailed nutrient content information on nearly all of the foods they purchase. The new food label has been designed to give consumers a tool they can use to make healthier, more informed, food choices. We must realize, however, that availability of nutrition information can, in no way, produce change in dietary habits, but merely facilitate it. Individuals must now become aware of the label, comprehend its message, and incorporate this information into making actual food choices. Only then will the estimated billions of dollars in savings from medical care costs actually be translated into health benefits.

———— Chapter 7 ————

Government as a Provider of Dietary Advice

Political pressures on [federally dispensed] dietary advice have been unrelenting. . . Whether even the most unambiguous [dietary guidance] messages will [ever] overcome the impact of food advertising and lobbying efforts is uncertain.

—M. Nestle*

Everyone eats, so therefore everyone is an expert on food! Consumers today demand a lot from the food they eat; they desire a food supply that is safe and affordable, furnishes nourishment to sustain life and health, and provides satisfaction and pleasure when eaten. Just as consumers' expectations of the food they eat have changed, so too have their habits concerning where they buy their food, how much and what kinds of food they consume, and when they shop for that food.

The percentage of "take home" income that Americans spend on food continues to drop. This is not because food prices are dropping, but because incomes are rising faster than food prices.[1] Food spending in the United States rose to $647 billion in 1994, a 5.3 percent increase over 1993. However, after adjustments for inflation and population growth, total food spending per person fell about 1 percent in 1994. How we're spending our food dollar is also changing, and one of the major changes in recent years has been the amount of money spent on "away from home" eating. In 1994, spending for food consumed away from home increased more than for food eaten at home, accounting for nearly half of the food dollar.[2]

As Americans become more health-conscious and pressed for time, their food and shopping habits change.[3] They are concerned about various aspects of food—its cost, quality, and safety, but mainly they choose specific foods by a single criterion: *taste*. Different segments of the population look

---

*M. Nestle, "Dietary Guidance for the 21st Century: New Approaches," *Journal of Nutrition Educcation* 27(5): 273, 274, 1995.

for different products, services, and departments. Age-specific groups are characterized in the following way: the "mature market"—a growing economic force, with specific food concerns about cost and nutritional value; the "middle-aged shopper," deluged by family, money concerns, and pandemonium; "young adults," on the move with escalating career demands accompanied by demands for convenience and tasty food; "kids and teens," environmentally conscious but fascinated by new products. Ethnicity/race and regionality are also ways to identify segments of supermarket shoppers.

In the next decade, it is predicted that producer and processors will be even more closely linked and pushed by changing consumer demands for tasty, nutritious, *and* convenient products.[4] Thus, while the food industry seeks to ensure the quality and safety of the food it provides, it must also effectively respond to the ever-changing preferences and demands of individual consumers.

Slowly, but surely, Americans are changing their eating patterns toward more healthful diets. A considerable gap remains, however, between public health recommendations and consumers' practices. Data from the most recent report on Nutrition Monitoring in the United States indicate that Americans are doing better (but still not meeting recommendations) for nutrients such as total fat, cholesterol, saturated fat, and sodium, and are not getting nearly enough calcium and iron or eating enough fruits and vegetables.[5] And, what's worse, there's an increase in the prevalence of overweight individuals in the U.S. population; about one-third of adults and one-fifth of adolescents are now classified as being overweight.

Many consumers are attempting to follow dietary recommendations as they make food selections. Most are aware of the need to decrease dietary fat or to increase the amount of other nutrients like iron or vitamin C, but are often unsure how to do this. They turn to a variety of dietary advice givers—health professionals, the media, friends, family. The question to be answered in this chapter is—how much should the government be in the business of providing dietary guidance to Americans?

The Politics of Dietary Advice

For the many times that you have heard or read the phrases, "The government says . . ." or, alternately, "Government reports recommend . . . ," you may have wondered just who this "government" was and by what authority "they" were operating to offer such grandiose advice. This chapter describes how offering dietary advice to consumers often becomes a political issue. The content of the message, how it is delivered, and the effects it has on food consumption have long been matters of some interest—and some would say, concern—to the federal government.

A myriad of factors—some influenced by government actions, others not—affects which foods are offered for sale and how much food is available for consumers. These include: (1) the use of production and processing technology; (2) market prices of food; (3) government policies affecting food supply and prices; (4) government regulations regarding nutrition labeling of foods, food advertising, and food standards; (5) food product and nutrition information provided by the private sector, mainly through advertising; and (6) dietary advice provided by the government. The first four factors may conflict, to some degree with number six; a notable exception, however, are the newly revamped food labels that were designed to help consumers follow the government's dietary advice. Number five, the private sector's dietary advice, usually in the form of food advertising, may be in conflict with the advice the government is dispensing. Thus, it is all that much more important to ensure that dietary advice given out by the federal government is appropriate and correct; it is equally important to resist giving out dietary advice known to be ineffective and all that much more difficult to make nutrition education work to change American diets.

Policy Issues in Dietary Guidance

A number of policy issues in dietary guidance exist.[6] They are presented here as questions that underlie the fundamental discussion in this chapter and the case studies that accompany it.

- *To what extent is there a need for publicly funded nutrition education for the American people?* That is, should the government be involved in issuing dietary advice, and should tax dollars be spent on providing information to consumers about the foods they should or should not be consuming? Is this the responsibility of the public or the private sector—and, if the latter, who will ensure that the information they dispense is valid and unbiased given their interest in promoting their own, often less healthful, food products?
- *What are the decision rules that should be used by policy makers when deciding on the scope of intervention, message content, and so forth?* Should the government rely on external bodies, such as advisory committees, in making decisions about the content of the message? What criteria should be used in selecting persons to serve on advisory committees? Who decides "what" scientific evidence should be brought to the table for discussion? Who ensures that the "consen-

sus" messages are indeed valid and unbiased?

- *What is the appropriate scope of federal involvement?* How directly should representatives of the federal government be involved in writing the basic content of the dietary messages and deciding how that information should be disseminated? Or, should government enter into "public/private partnerships" to deliver the message? Does the public want the government to be actively involved in providing information about nutrition and dietary choices? (While consumers do recognize that other groups, such as voluntary health associations or the food industry, provide attractive, colorful materials on nutrition, research has shown that they usually believe that the information presented in nutrition materials produced by governmental sources is more reputable.)[7]

- *What should the content (both graphical and textual) of the nutrition messages be?* Consumer demand for certain foods reflects, to some degree, food production and agricultural policy. Should governmental advice be "Eat a lot of food," or "Eat a variety of many different kinds of foods," rather than advising consumers to make qualitative decisions about the kinds and amounts of foods they eat? (This argument is fundamental to whether we have a *food* or a *nutrition* policy. See chapter 3.)

- *What changes in other public policies are needed to ensure that people are able to act positively on the dietary advice they are given?* Can regulatory measures such as standards of identity and meat grading standards be changed to reflect the advice consumers are given? Should more "healthful" food choices be subsidized so they are available at cheaper prices, or, conversely, should "high-fat" foods be subject to additional taxes to dissuade their purchase?

- *What is the measure of success for government-supported dietary guidance efforts?* Is producing awareness of the health and diet links as a result of information exposure sufficient? Or must intervention efforts demonstrate sustained behavioral change before they are judged to be "successful?"

What are the most pertinent nutrition education policy issues as we prepare to enter the twenty-first century? That depends, in part, on what one believes is the appropriate role for government. Is it, as some believe, to preserve the integrity of individual decision making, or is it to modify the environment in such a way as to make health-promoting food choices easier? Many see these not as two separate questions but as the same question when the "individual" is the consumer. Modifying the environment is necessary to preserve the integrity of decisions made by individual shoppers in the grocery store because without some framework of nutrition education, consumers may not be well prepared to make health-promoting food choices. These two "different" roles for government are really a false dichotomy; government has a long-standing, traditional role in nutrition education and must play a strong role in any "free" society that provides science-based information to the public about making food choices.

In the past, nutrition education in the United States has focused on providing scientifically accurate "facts" about food and nutrition in order to assist consumers in making food choices. However, with the ever-increasing accumulation of epidemiological evidence linking diet with health outcomes, a public health perspective, that is, attention to modifying the environment, has begun to be employed.[8] The issue here is whether government should encourage individual independence in dietary choices (certainly the predominant view of recent Republican administrations) at the expense of collective action to make "healthful" food choices easier to make. Recognized as an outstanding example of healthful public policy,[9] the primary focus of the original Norwegian food and nutrition policy was to ensure that structural changes had been made that would support the desired dietary changes, and then to promote individual responsibility for dietary change.[10]

The epidemiological, or population-based model, assumes an equal risk of disease, given the identification of certain characteristics or "risk factors," such as age, gender, race, body weight, and behaviors such as smoking. The argument follows that if there is a common health risk (i.e., certain dietary patterns lead to increased risk for chronic diseases), the population as a whole should be urged to consume those foods that decrease that risk, with the result that the population will be "healthier" and more productive. Thus, strategies to promote the consumption of healthful diets, accompanied by environmental "manipulation" to allow healthful dietary choices to be made "easier," is what many have in mind when they suggest that the government should be more "proactive" in producing dietary change among Americans.

Others believe strongly that government should stay out of the business of giving advice to the public about what to eat. After all, these proponents point out, one's genetics has more to do with the risk of chronic disease than does one's short-term food choices. Further, a common argument from this contingent is that responsibility for behavior change lies with the individual, not with the government.

Even if one adheres to the "individual responsibility for behavior change" rubric, one certainly cannot dispute that the government has certain responsibilities regarding the transfer of information. First, if the research base that sets the foundation for certain dietary changes has been supported by public funds, the public has a right to know the research results and their implications. Further, it is the responsibility of government to disseminate clear, scientifically valid information on nutrition to both professionals and the public. And, finally, government must provide such information in a form that matches the information needs, literacy levels, delivery channel preferences, interest levels, and learning styles of Americans.

Accompanying this discussion are two case studies and one "sidebar," which showcase recent efforts by the federal government to issue dietary advice to the public through various mechanisms—advertising campaigns for agricultural commodities, development of an attractive nutrition graphic, and agreement on the content of the message to deliver to the public about nutrition. Each of these examples presents a "story" of various political influences on the process and on the content of the dietary advice provided to consumers.

An Advocacy Coalition Perspective on
Dietary Guidance for Consumers

In general, two advocacy coalitions predominate the discussion on dietary guidance for consumers—its content, its delivery, and evaluation of its effectiveness. These two coalitions are those representing the views and beliefs of the food industry and those representing the beliefs of the public health and consumer advocacy community. Depending on the context of the discussion, various government groups (high-level political appointees vs. lower-level government bureaucrats) may weigh in on one side of the debate or the other; this was particularly true in the case of the development of the Food Guide Pyramid where political appointees wished to revise or dismiss the project entirely versus those professional nutritionists working for the USDA, who had provided the scientific basis for the development of the graphic and did not wish to see the project rebuked. Another group that is less easily characterized as belonging to one "camp" or the other is the academic scientist who may view the case (and the scientific evidence on which it is built) quite differently; each of the case studies highlights the inputs of these "dueling scientists."

Perspectives on the Content of the Dietary Message

The federal government has a major responsibility in determining the *content* of any dietary guidance message. It has less control (or has chosen to exercise less control) over the distribution, dissemination, and delivery of this message to the American consumer. Basically, the content of the message has been written by groups of scientists, both in and outside government. Because of the nature of the deliberations, the input of coalitions representing agribusiness has been strong, and government has basically adopted these strategies to counter coalitions that advocate for aggressive "public-health-first" nutrition education initiatives and messages.

Impact on Food Production

Discussion of alternative healthier diets for Americans has been influenced by arguments that a movement away from animal protein-based diets would have an adverse effect on production agriculture. Objections to a "low fat" dietary message have often been voiced by producers who fear the economic implications of losing market share for certain commodities if consumers followed this dietary advice when making food choices. (Recall the results of the simulation presented in chapter 4, which indicated that advice to consume less fat and cholesterol by necessity translated into reduced intake of animal products and increased consumption of plant foods.)[11]

Need for Scientific Consensus

One of the most significant perspectives affecting most nutrition education messages that are dispensed by the federal government is that there must be scientific consensus about the content of the message. The problem is that there are different "sciences" on which such messages may be based. Nutrition scientists and others trained to gather evidence from animal model experiments and clinical trials often demand a degree of certainty that is not attainable using epidemiological or other population-based types of research designs. Thus, the argument of "whose" science should be used often becomes fodder for heated debate. Policy makers are frequently pleased to see basic disagreements over the science because these arguments can be used to delay or avoid any approach that is more proactive and more pro-consumer.

The No Bad Foods Restriction

Just as "science-based" becomes a mantra for the evolution of dietary guidance messages, so too does the "no bad foods" phrase. In an effort to appease food producers and processors, this phrase is usually expanded to promote the notion that "there are no good or bad foods, just good and poor diets." This perspective allows for consumers to include any high-fat foods that may have a poor nutrient profile, if, for the most part, they are making more "nutrient dense" (the ratio of nutrients, like vitamins and minerals, to calories) food choices. Thus, the rule of the game for dietary guidance messages is that if the federal government endorses the need for dietary change among the American public, it must be done in the "no good foods/ no bad foods" context.

The nutrition community continues to debate the use of the term *healthful* diet as it conjures up images of "good" and "bad" foods, terms that professionals abhor but the public seems to understand. Even the National Academy of Sciences' Committee for Dietary Guidelines Implementation adopted the terms, "health promoting" and "nutritionally desirable" to describe those foods whose consumption is encouraged to meet dietary recommendations. (Examples include fruits, vegetables, breads, and cereals.) In addition, the committee defined a "healthful" diet as one that meets dietary recommendations of the time (and is thereby composed largely of health-promoting foods) and one that meets nutrient needs.[12] To most consumer advocates and public health activists alike, such terminology is meaningless hyperbole.

Target the Genetically Predisposed

Recently, the approach has been adopted that if federally dispensed dietary advice encourages a change in diets, the message should target those subpopulations that are genetically predisposed to chronic illnesses caused by dietary excesses. This is an extrapolation of the "clinical/ high risk" approach where dietary guidance is provided only to those who "need it." The argument goes that as human beings, we are not alike, so our risks for chronic disease are probably dissimilar as well. Genetic information is seen as the next tool used to plan one's own personal, customized-for-health diet.[13] There certainly is nothing wrong with targeting especially at-risk population groups with specific messages as long as this approach does not result in a false sense of security for nongenetically disposed subgroups. Certainly adopting a "genetic profile" approach to nutrition education would portend great upheaval for policy makers charged with developing dietary guidance for the public. "The real challenge presented by *Genetic Nutrition* is to the muddle of making nutritional policy in the federal government, where the belief reigns still that the right plan, the right labeling strategy, or the right set of dietary practices is the key to health promotion and disease prevention. This ego-driven approach feeds on the lack of information, and has contributed to a pattern of policies and programs where the absence of science is filled with opinionated scientists and managers. . . . *Genetic Nutrition* provides a way for the family to identify what is the best diet and why, and now it is up to the policymakers to figure out how best to listen and to use this information."[14]

Dietary Messages Must Be "Balanced"

In this approach to dietary guidance policy making, there seems to be some unwritten rule that "responsible" nutrition messages require giving some attention to the public health advocacy coalition and some to the agribusiness-dominated coalition. Thus, it has become increasingly difficult, despite overwhelming scientific evidence and great public health need, to adopt aggressive pro-consumer nutrition policies. If public health objectives are placed first, nutrition messages must be developed that meet overall societal needs; this must not be a "hollow exercise" in creating "balanced" dietary messages that reflect the needs of both consumers and the agribusiness lobby.

Individual Nutrition Education
Has Not Been Successful

Despite the wealth of information that is available about healthy eating and living choices, many Americans are not heeding the advice they are getting. As one dismal indicator, there is a growing number of overweight and obese people in this country, creating a national epidemic. The problem is complex, and solving it is even tougher.

Before the last edition was published, the USDA sponsored focus groups to find out what consumers knew about the Dietary Guidelines.[15] The research uncovered that there was enormous confusion over what consumers knew about diet and what the Dietary Guidelines recommended. Dr. Eileen Kennedy, director of the USDA's Center for Nutrition Policy and Promotion, noted that "intellectually, consumers buy into the diet-disease relationship, but emotionally they don't."[16] Those who demand "effectiveness" in nutrition education efforts usually follow their cry with the rhetorical question of why should taxpayers' money be used for nutrition education if it is not effective. The problem with embracing this pessimistic outlook is that many policy makers may be tempted to dismiss all nutrition education activities conducted by the federal government altogether and push for other, less politically sensitive options, such as promoting the availability of lower-fat food products, a move that should complement, not supplant, nutrition education efforts.

Issues Remaining

Among the issues that remain regarding dietary guidance, and the government's role in providing that advice, are the following:

- The nature of the message. Will the dietary message continue to focus on "balance, variety, and moderation" in lieu of more specific, "less balanced," but perhaps more effective health-oriented dietary advice?
- How can dietary guidance be made more effective in actually changing dietary behavior?
- Although the validity of the dietary message is no longer in question, how can the government best implement these recommendations?
- How should the informational gaps left by the Dietary Guidelines and the Food Guide Pyramid be filled by state and local governments, health groups, and pro-consumer players in the private sector?

Effective implementation of the Dietary Guidelines recommendations was the topic of the Institute of Medicine's Food and Nutrition Board's 1991 report, "Improving America's Diet and Health: From Recommendations to Action."[17] Rather than relying solely on individual education strategies to change dietary habits (the mainstay of most government intervention efforts), the report recommended focusing on major sectors of society (such as government, the private sector [primarily the food industry], health care professionals, and educators) in order to increase the availability and accessibility of health-promoting foods and make such foods easily identifiable, economical, and appealing. While these approaches are certainly valid, consumers will continue to need some reasons for becoming interested in consuming these more healthful foods in the first place—hence, the continuing need for a federal role in dietary guidance.

Clearly the challenge is to educate the public so they can make more healthful food choices. Nutrition educators must provide the public not only with recommendations, but with practical knowledge and skills to help them change their diets to reduce the risk of chronic disease.[18] The debate no longer focuses on whether a public health approach is preferable to a screen-and-treat approach, but rather how the overall population can reduce their dietary fat intake to more desirable levels.[19] The strength of the evidence by which we can improve the health of the American people demands our best efforts and most effective actions.

FOR FURTHER CONSIDERATION:

COMMODITY PROMOTION PROGRAMS

Commodity research/promotion programs (also known as "checkoffs") are efforts authorized by federal legislation and funded by commodity producers that are designed to expand the market for selected agricultural products.[20] Generic promotion and research programs have existed at the local, state, and regional levels for more than fifty years. These programs are commonly known as "checkoff" programs because they are funded mainly by deductions or "checkoffs" from commodity transactions. Producers, handlers, processors, and importers paying the assessments control their checkoff programs by referenda voting, including the ability to terminate them by recall referenda.

In order to better coordinate promotional efforts for specific commodities across states, encourage equitable participation from all those who benefit from these programs, and create a larger funding base, agricultural industry groups sought federal legislative authority to establish mandatory national programs. The first federally authorized commodity promotion program was enacted in 1954, but the majority were created during the 1980s and 1990s. Of the nineteen programs that have been authorized, fifteen are currently active.[21]

Each checkoff program is commodity-specific and is based on separate federal enabling legislation. The enabling legislation for each program provides guidelines for the administration of the program and authorizes the secretary of Agriculture to issue an order based on proposals submitted by industry representatives. The legislation for each checkoff program authorizes a board of directors to run the program, specifies membership criteria for board members, and sets assessment procedures, including who will be assessed, the assessment rate, and how funds will be collected. Checkoff boards choose which promotional activities they will support and make the contracting decisions for carrying out the chosen activities subject to the secretary's approval. Agriculture policy makers favor these checkoff programs because these efforts are funded by assessments on the industries at minimal net cost to the federal government.

The USDA, through its Agricultural Marketing Service (AMS), is responsible for oversight of the commodity research and promotion boards. Specifically, the agency develops regulations to implement the check-off programs in consultation with the specific industry and ensures compliance with the authorizing legislation and the agency's related orders. AMS reviews each board's budgets, projects, and contracts to ensure that the board does not engage in prohibited activities, such as lobbying. Commodity-promotion boards reimburse AMS for any oversight costs incurred as a result of program administration.

Checkoff program activities used to expand domestic and export markets include advertising, promotion, nutrition education and research, market research, new product and process development, technical assistance, and effectiveness evaluation. Checkoff programs attempt to increase consumer demand through advertising by informing consumers about the attributes of the commodities. In this sidebar, specific advertising campaigns sponsored by commodity promotion programs are described for beef and dairy products.

Because these checkoff programs are designed to promote and market specific commodities, the enabling legislation expressly forbids the use of checkoff funds for lobbying purposes. Therefore, commodity trade associations generally use funds from their membership dues or other sources to represent the political interests of industry members.

Thirteen checkoff programs collected funds in 1993 (the most recent data available). If we also count a checkoff program for fluid milk, which started collections in 1994, the total collections from these fourteen active checkoff programs were nearly $550 million. The dairy program collected 41 percent of all funds collected, distantly followed by beef, which collected 15 percent of the total. The dairy program shared two-thirds of its checkoff funds with state programs, and the beef program shared 45 percent.

Generally, the USDA does not review the effectiveness of the programs. The only promotion programs that have mandated annual evaluations are for dairy products and fluid milk. The issue of whether program benefits exceed assessments and whether the money is optimally allocated to the various uses remains a constant point of debate. Those who monitor the expenditures of these boards believe that efforts to track performance of checkoff programs are inadequate. Even the producers, the funders of these programs, are now questioning the worth of the millions of dollars they pay in assessments. Consequently, the cost benefit of these programs—either to producers or to consumers—is unknown.[22]

Promotion of Beef: "The Beef Board"

Established in 1986 by a federal order (7 CFR Part 1260, July 18), the Cattlemen's Beef Promotion and Research Board (hereafter simply called the Beef Board) oversees the collection of funds, approves the annual budget for national checkoff-funded programs, and certifies "Qualified State Beef Councils" (QSBCs, of which there were forty-four in 1995). The function of this Board (according to the official "declaration of policy" in the U.S. Code) is to "finance . . . and carry out a coordinated program of promotion and research designed to strengthen the beef industry's position in the marketplace and to maintain and expand domestic and foreign markets and uses for beef and beef products."[23] Many question why the federal government should be in the business of facilitating a program that has the explicit goal of promoting agricultural products that are high in fat.

The Beef Board consists of 107 members, 101 of whom are domestic beef producers, each of whom was appointed by the secretary of Agriculture from nominations submitted by organizations that represent beef and dairy producers in each state or region. The Beef Board oversees the collection of $1 per head on all cattle sold in the United States and $1 equivalent on imported cattle, beef, and beef products. The QSBC may retain up to 50 cents of the money collected in their state, but at least 50 cents on the dollar must be sent to the Beef Board. In fiscal year 1994, the board had total revenue of nearly $45 million, 83 percent of which was from assessments on domestic sales.[35]

The Beef Board, through its twenty-member operating committee, is responsible for contracting with established national nonprofit industry-governed organizations—such as the National Cattlemen's Beef Association (created in 1996 by the consolidation of the National Cattlemen's Association and the National Live Stock and Meat Board/Beef Industry Council) to implement programs of promotion, research, consumer information, industry information, foreign marketing, and producer communications. Perhaps the most famous ad campaign—and, perhaps the most controversial, as well—initiated by this group was the "Beef—Real Food for Real People" campaign featuring actors James Garner and Cybill Shepherd.

To counteract consumer concern about the fat content of beef, the two major trade organizations of the beef industry—the National Cattlemen's Association and the Beef Industry Council of the National Live Stock and Meat Board—initiated the "War on Fat" campaign in 1989. Supported by funds from the "Beef Checkoff" program, the campaign involved several initiatives: support for computer software to measure the fat in wholesale cuts, closer trimming of beef carcasses, new packaging, consumer surveys, ultrasound technology for gauging fat content of the carcass, and genetics research.[25] In 1993, the group reported what they called "tremendous success," citing that trimmable fat was reduced by 27 percent, more than 40 percent of retail beef cuts have no external fat, and the fat content of ground beef was reduced by 10 percent.[26] Recent initiatives of the Beef Board have been a $72 million campaign to make red meat more convenient, consistent, and consumer-friendly by using branded, portioned products and "meal kits."[27]

Many have questioned whether these campaigns result in meaningful changes in food consumption or are just costly public relations efforts to improve the image of the beef industry. Couple these promotional activities—many created and endorsed by the federal government—with the American public's passion for "juicy" hamburgers and steaks. It is of no surprise, then, that beef remains the greatest source of dietary fat in the American diet.

The Promotion of Dairy Products:
"The Dairy Board"

From 1985 to 1995, per capita consumption of all dairy products dropped about 3 percent. However, during that same period of time, commercial disappearance of cow's milk (a measure of dairy product sales) increased by 9 percent. Since the U.S. population is growing at about half that rate, one can assume that consumers are using, on the average, about 4 to 5 percent more milk (and milk fat) in one form or another. Since fluid milk sales are dropping, consumers are getting more of their milkfat in the form of processed dairy products, such as cheese and ice cream.

What has been responsible for this increased consumption of high-fat processed dairy products? Several factors have contributed, including competitive prices, a strong economy, expanded exports, and the introduction of new products. Also contributing are those promotional efforts specifically designed to expand sales of dairy products, including those generic promotion programs sanctioned by the federal government. These farmer-financed promotion programs have received the most public attention and certainly the most dollar support in recent years.[28]

Government involvement in promotion programs has been limited to facilitating private efforts to increase dairy sales, that is, it helps by giving the dairy industry the legal authority to collect money for the purpose of product promotion. Although both federal and state governments have the authority to act, the federal role was greatly expanded under the 1983 Dairy Production Stabilization Act (DPSA), which mandated a new National Dairy Promotion and Research Board (NDB) funded by a nonrefundable 15 cents per hundredweight (cwt) assessment on the farmer/milk producer.

Although the National Dairy Promotion and Research Board (NDB) was initially mandated by legislation, the program was approved by 89 percent of those dairy farmers voting in a 1985 national referendum. The national assessment authority and the NDB will remain in effect unless or until either dairy farmers or the secretary of Agriculture determine that they have outlived their purpose and take steps to terminate them. There are thirty-six members of the NDB who serve three-year terms; each member represents one of thirteen regions in the forty-eight contiguous states. The United Dairy Industry Association (UDIA) and the NDB, along with the Dairy Export Council–organized Dairy Marketing Initiative (DMI), now coordinates dairy promotion research and export activities.

The farmer-based assessment of 15 cents per hundredweight (cwt) to generic milk promotion activities generates approximately $200 million per year. (The NDB gets slightly under $80 million of this annually, while the balance—about $120 million—goes to about eighty state and regional organizations.) With the increase in funding has come an increase in the creative energy devoted to promotional activities, resulting in bigger and better advertising of dairy products. Since the NDB was established in 1984, dairy product-consumption has increased dramatically. How effective have these expanded product-promotion efforts been? Fluid milk sales have been static, but 85 percent of the growth can be traced to increased cheese sales. With pizza the number one favorite food of children, the market for cheese remains secure.

A second promotion and research program was established by the Fluid Milk Promotion Act of 1990, which provides the authority for fluid milk processors to develop and finance generic advertising programs designed to maintain and expand markets and uses for fluid milk products produced in the United States. The Fluid Milk Promotion Order became effective in 1993, and it is administered by the National Fluid Milk Processor Promotion Board. USDA held a referendum in October 1993 on the proposed order; it was approved by 71.7 percent of the fluid milk processors voting in the referendum and represented 76.7 percent of all fluid milk products marketed. This program is financed by a 15-cents-per-hundredweight assessment on all milk marketed in the forty-eight contiguous states. The Fluid Milk Board is composed of twenty members appointed by the secretary of Agriculture, fifteen of whom represent geographic regions while five are at-large members. The act also mandates that there be an annual evaluation of the effectiveness of the Fluid Milk Promotion Program in conjunction with the National Dairy Promotion and Research Board report to Congress.

Through the various promotion organizations, dairy farmers support media advertising (national and local, television, radio, and print), consumer and retail promotion, food-service promotion, new-product development, nutrition research, nutrition education to schoolchildren and health professionals, industry communications, and public relations. The boards of farmer directors of the promotion organizations establish program policy and priorities and employ staff to implement programs. In March 1994, the NDB approved the creation of Dairy Management, Inc. (DMI), a joint undertaking with the United Dairy Industry Association (UDIA) and the Dairy Export Council. The purpose of the DMI is to provide better coordination of producer promotion funds by having a joint plan, joint budget, and joint execution. In December 1996, the National Milk Producers Federation became associated with the DMI.

One of the most recent advertising campaigns, sponsored by the national Fluid Milk Processor Promotion Board, is the "milk moustache" campaign targeted to young women. Appearing primarily as print ads in popular national magazines, the campaign is designed to promote the health, nutrition, and taste of fluid milk by featuring recognizable sports and media celebrities with "milk mustaches." In a move applauded by nutritionists, this campaign is the first ever by the dairy industry to include ads that are directed toward promoting the consumption of low-fat and skim milk.[29] The Milk Mustache campaign, call "the top print campaign in the U.S.," doubled its budget in 1997 to $110 million in an effort to reach teens, men, and college-age students.[30]

Other campaigns funded by the National Fluid Milk Processor Promotion Board in its $110 million budget for fiscal year 1997 include the "Drink 3" initiative, which urges Americans to drink three glasses of milk a day. This campaign stresses consumption of skim or low-fat milk as an easy, accessible, inexpensive way to get calcium in the diet. The success of the program will be measured by fluid milk sales, USDA consumption data, and survey results.[31]

Discussion

Producer-supported and government-administered commodity research and promotion boards are an anathema to most nutritionists and health professionals. When we already know of the dangers associated with high-fat diets, why should such funds be used to "promote" the consumption of *more* of these products, rather than directing increased spending on research to find ways to produce lower-fat, still tasty, beef or to promote consumption of skim and low-fat milks (the growth markets for fluid milk) and dairy products rather than cheese and premium ice cream?

The activities of commodity promotion boards are just one more example of USDA's dual responsibility, or, what some have termed, the agency's "schizophrenic mission." Here we have producer-financed advertising of high-fat commodities, beef and dairy, in direct competition with the department's very own dietary guidance policy as stated in the Dietary Guidelines for Americans. (See Case Study 4, p. 229) On the one hand, the department spends millions of dollars through sophisticated national media advertising campaigns to sell beef, ice cream, and cheese to consumers. (Included in the top fifty advertising accounts on network television, with a total advertising sales figure of nearly $1 billion in 1996, are those by the American Dairy Association for milk at $326 million, the Beef Industry Council at $113 million, and the American Dairy Association's cheese ads at slightly over $100 million.)[32] Compare the tone and force of these ads with the advice, "Consume a diet moderate in fat and saturated fat . . . " in government-produced pamphlets and educational programs. Which do you think is more compelling?

————— Case Study 4 —————

Dietary Guidelines

The comfortable alliance between the food industry, the health community, and the government as the primary dispenser of dietary advice, which had existed for half a century, came to an abrupt halt in the late 1960s when the link between food consumption and prevention of certain chronic, debilitating diseases was forged. Groups like the American Heart Association had advocated for years that the public should consume diets low in cholesterol and saturated fat to prevent heart disease. Soon to follow suit were statements from respected scientists at noteworthy events, such as the 1969 White House Conference on Food, Nutrition, and Health, which drew public attention to the links between diet and the risk of chronic disease. The climate for dietary guidance had changed forever, and the government was at the hub of the action.

The Significance of the "Dietary Goals"

The Senate Select Committee on Nutrition and Human Needs (under the chairmanship of George McGovern [D-South Dakota]) was established in 1968. The committee first focused its attention on problems associated with hunger and malnutrition in the United States, issues at the forefront of the political agenda in the late 1960s.[1] Soon after McGovern's resounding defeat in the 1972 presidential elections, however, the committee's staff began to shift its attention to the "overfed" in America. Its hearings in the mid-1970s served as a public forum for consumer advocates and health professionals to showcase the links between dietary excesses and chronic diseases, such as heart attack, stroke, and cancer, the leading causes of death in the United States at that time.

A new direction for dietary guidance was forever set in motion in February 1977 when the committee issued the first edition of the Dietary Goals for the United States.[2] This "revolutionary report," called "a central document in the history of dietary guidelines,"[3] was unique—notable because it was among the first to report several diet–disease hypotheses for which the scientific evidence has since continued to mount, such as the importance of dietary fiber, the possible relation of high-fat intake to breast and large bowel cancer, and the relationship between hypertension and salt intake. Further, it set *quantitative* target levels for reducing fat, saturated fat, and cholesterol in the American diet. The way in which the document was prepared was also unique; it was developed by political activists on the collective advice of outside experts and published as a congressional committee report, not a traditional document written by government-employed nutritionists and released by an agency such as the U.S. Department of Agriculture.

The Dietary Goals document set off strong and polarized reactions from nutrition scientists, the food industry, and various other professional and consumer groups in the United States. There have never again been so many published commentaries and criticisms (one of which runs to 889 pages!) as those following this first edition of the Dietary Goals.[4]

After receiving well over a thousand pages of printed rebuttal, the Committee released a revised report a few months later. In a dissenting foreword, ranking minority member Senator Charles Percy (R-Illinois) suggested that, given the "inadequacy of food data," the goals and recommendations were premature, and insisted on adding the following statement in bold type: "The value of dietary change remains controversial, and science cannot at this time insure that an altered diet will provide improved protection from certain killer diseases such as heart disease and cancer."

In the revised version, the committee attempted a compromise; it toned down the historical comparisons of diet, deemphasized food additives, added sections on obesity and alcohol consumption, hedged a bit on the cholesterol connection, and referred to the scientific controversies that existed with publishing such a report.[5] However, the Dietary Goals did retain its strong recommendations that the American public should increase or decrease their intake of certain foods in order to reduce their risk of certain chronic diseases.

The Dietary Goals drew public, as well as professional, attention to the need for guidance on diet and health. For the first time, the consumer was being called upon to make not only quantitative decisions (i.e., how many servings of a food to eat) but qualitative choices as well (i.e., eat less of some foods, eat more of others). Further, the consumer was asked to make choices *within* food groups, a never-before-heard-of practice.

The Dietary Goals document set in motion waves of controversy among professionals in the nutrition community. One controversy pitted those who favored using dietary approaches to promote health and prevent disease versus those who did not. Another controversy drew sides between those who favored setting quantitative targets for the intake of selected nutrients against those who believed that the public would benefit more from qualitative, food-based advice. The document also crystallized the arguments between two camps of scientists—those who believed in a "targeted" approach aimed at those who had been identified as being at "high risk" and then making appropriate dietary and other health recommendations versus those who believed in a "public health" approach, that is, having the general public adopt health-promoting behaviors, including changes in diet, that would do no harm but might be able to prevent the early onset of particular chronic diseases.

The Dietary Goals for the United States, the last accomplishment of the Senate Select Committee on Nutrition and Human Needs, was never withdrawn, nor was it ever declared an "official" U.S. government statement. Although the release of the Dietary Goals document created a tremendous furor in the scientific community and the food industry, its recommendations actually were quite comparable to those issued by authoritative groups a decade later. The concepts originally put forward in the Dietary Goals document have been modified and reissued in official or authoritative sets of recommendations in the United States and in many national sets of dietary guidelines around the world. In fact, in the six-year period from 1977 through 1982 alone, various groups and organizations issued six different versions of dietary guidance for the general public. Thus, the legacy of the Dietary Goals report was that it led to a number of other public and private efforts to publish dietary guidance information for the general public. One can only speculate whether Americans' eating habits would have been significantly improved by now if the government had taken a more aggressive stance and issued dietary advice that followed the recommendations of the Dietary Goals much earlier than it did.

In the face of opposition to the Dietary Goals from the meat, dairy, and egg industries, several leading health agencies, in particular the American Heart Association and the National Cancer Institute, as well as a leading professional association, the American Society for Clinical Nutrition (ASCN), issued statements reaffirming that researchers had reached consensus on the role of dietary fat, cholesterol, salt, sugar, and alcohol as influencing the development of specific chronic diseases. In addition, as one of his last official acts as secretary of Health, Education, and Welfare in 1979, Joseph Califano released a report titled, *Healthy People: The Surgeon General's Report on Health Promotion and Disease Prevention*.[6] In this report, public health officials announced goals for a ten-year plan to improve the health of the nation. It was notable because the nutrition section of the report suggested that people reduce their consumption of excess calories, fat and cholesterol, salt, and sugar to lower chronic disease rates.

Political History of the Dietary Guidelines

Language in the 1977 Farm Bill stated that the U.S. Department of Agriculture was to be the lead agency for human nutrition, a claim repeatedly questioned by those in the DHHS. In addition, that legislation authorized the creation of the Human Nutrition Center, a hub for human nutrition research, education, and outreach. Chosen to lead the Center was Harvard University's Dr. Mark Hegsted, one of the consultants who had contributed to the Dietary Goals report.

Development and Release of the 1980 Dietary Guidelines

The U.S. Departments of Agriculture and of (then) Health, Education, and Welfare institutionalized the public health approach to nutritional advice with the publication of "Nutrition and Your Health: Dietary Guidelines for Americans,"[7] which was released early in 1980. The document was written by an interagency task force, with little formal input from external scientists. Based on the most up-to-date scientific information available at the time, the Guidelines took the form of dietary recommendations directed to healthy Americans, not to individuals who were following special diets for medical reasons The language of these Guidelines, published in a pamphlet of twenty-four half-pages, was qualitative rather than quantitative and followed the approach of advising the reader to "eat more" of certain dietary components and "eat less" of others. The Dietary Guidelines consisted of seven statements, calling for Americans to eat a variety of foods; maintain ideal weight; eat foods with adequate starch and fiber; avoid too much sugar; avoid too much sodium; avoid too much fat, saturated fat, and cholesterol; and, if they were to drink alcohol, to do so in moderation.

Despite the fact that the USDA disclaimed that it used the Dietary Goals as the basis for its food plans and guides because "diets developed following these goals were so different from usual food patterns,"[8] the first set of Dietary Guidelines was remarkably similar to those recommendations contained in the Dietary Goals. There were notable exceptions, of course; the Dietary Guidelines offered no quantitative advice for specific nutrients such as fat or cholesterol, and two extra recommendations were added—one to "eat a variety of foods" and another urging that if one were to consume alcohol, consumption should be "moderate."

Considerable discussion among nutrition scientists, consumer groups, the food industry, and others accompanied the release of the first edition of the Dietary Guidelines document. One concern, voiced primarily by certain commodity and food industry groups, was that use of the term "avoid" in the language of the Dietary Guidelines pamphlet would be interpreted by consumers to mean that they should "eliminate" foods that contained fat, saturated fat, and cholesterol from their diets. Another concern, expressed at a much different level, was the contrast between the two sets of dietary recommendations issued by authoritative groups in the same year, 1980—the USDA/DHHS Dietary Guidelines recommendations versus those in the Food and Nutrition Board's "Toward Healthful Diets" report.[9]

The publication of these different documents sparked controversy among scientists, commodity groups, trade associations, professional associations, and other special interest groups with the agencies that had published the Guidelines. The controversy basically pitted the "public health" approach, issuing *uniform* dietary advice to the general public to make more "healthful" food choices based on evidence from epidemiological and other observational studies, against the "clinical" or "high-risk" strategy, where it was believed that information to change one's diet should be *targeted* only to individuals identified as being at risk for certain chronic diseases.

Despite the criticism that raged against the Guidelines, the report became accepted as official federal nutrition policy. Two key events helped to galvanize its position: publication of a "rather conservative" report from the National Academy of Sciences' National Research Council titled "Toward Healthful Diets," and the involvement of Congress, which, after holding hearings on the matter, issued a directive to develop a revised second edition of the Guidelines with the assistance of outside experts.[10]

Role of "Toward Healthful Diets"

Three months after the release of the Dietary Guidelines in 1980, the Food and Nutrition Board, a unit of the National Research Council/National Academy of Sciences, issued its own report, "Toward Healthful Diets." Advocating the clinical or "high risk" approach, the statement said that there was no reason for the average healthy person to restrict dietary intake of fat or cholesterol. This report emphasized programs to identify individuals in risk categories, such as family history of the disease, elevated blood pressure, diabetes, and specific blood lipid profiles, and expressed reservations about the adequacy of the scientific basis for *general* dietary guidelines for prevention of disease. Because this advice was counter to the mainstream of other dietary advice issued at the time, consumer advocacy groups, public health groups, and many nutrition scientists supported the recommendations of the Dietary Guidelines. Further, this support was solidified when it was learned that preparation of "Toward Healthful Diets" was wholly financed by the food industry and that at least two of the FNB scientists closely connected to the report also had strong ties to industry.[11] There was confusion in the media, controversy among various reputable scientists, and even Congress got into the act by holding separate hearings on each set of dietary recommendations.[12] There was no consensus or official judgment issued at the time, but it appeared that public criticisms levied against "Toward Healthful Diets" were stronger than those made against the Dietary Guidelines.[13]

Some of the commodity groups were particularly unhappy with the U.S. Department of Agriculture because their interpretation was that the dietary advice contained in the Dietary Guidelines for Americans could be achieved only by reducing the consumption of eggs, red meat, and milk products. They lobbied Congress to end funding for the Guidelines, and demanded and obtained hearings on the matter.[14] Later in 1980 (after the November elections but before the Reagan administration assumed office), the Demo-cratically-controlled Senate Agricultural Appropriations Committee di-rected that a committee be established to review scientific evidence and recommend revisions to the Dietary Guidelines.[15] At that point, no one was betting that the Dietary Guidelines would be continued.[16] During his confir-mation hearings, John Block, President Reagan's pick to be secretary of Agriculture, had made the statement that he was "not so sure government should get into telling people what they should or shouldn't eat."

The USDA took its responsibility as the "lead agency" for human nutri-tion (suggested by the legislative language in the 1977 Farm Bill) *very* seriously, and, as part of a 1980 departmental reorganization, acted to insti-tutionalize this responsibility by creating an agency to deal specifically with politically sensitive nutrition issues, the Human Nutrition Information Ser-vice (HNIS). This move had great appeal to the Reagan administration that had just assumed power for two reasons. First, it could abolish the Human Nutrition Center, headed by Harvard nutritionist Dr. Mark Hegsted, who was no favorite of the Republicans for his support of the Dietary Goals, and second, it would establish a "point place" where dietary guidance issues could be headed off directly.

At that time, two issues were at the heart of the USDA's political battles in nutrition—nutrition monitoring and Dietary Guidelines—both of which the USDA was on record as opposing. In creating HNIS, two groups of applied researchers were drawn from other units within the USDA to make up the agency's two divisions: the nutrition monitoring division, charged with collecting and analyzing data from USDA's periodic food consump-tion surveys; and the nutrition education division, whose mission it was to monitor and represent the USDA in all discussions related to Dietary Guidelines. This small agency, with a budget of less than $10 million, was dwarfed by its sister agency, the Food and Nutrition Service, which was responsible for the administration of food assistance programs and had a budget that ran into the tens of billions of dollars.

Despite its size, the political sensitivity of the tasks assigned to this new USDA agency was enormous. A "political appointee" was named as agency administrator so that any action related to nutrition monitoring or dietary guidance would be consistent with administration policy. Since the administration that had created the agency in 1980 did not support the Dietary Guidelines, HNIS often found itself opposing legislators and DHHS officials inside the government, and health professionals and consumer advocacy groups outside.

Dietary Guidelines for Americans, 1985 Edition

Following the congressional directive from 1980, a Federal Advisory Committee to review the Dietary Guidelines was finally appointed in 1983 by the secretaries of the USDA, the DHHS (formerly DHEW), and the National Academy of Sciences/National Research Council's Food and Nutrition Board. The group was charged to make recommendations to the DHHS and the USDA about the first edition of the Dietary Guidelines in anticipation of the next revision. Composed of nine nongovernment nutrition scientists, and chaired by a food scientist from the University of California–Davis, a majority of the committee had close ties to the food industry, as consumer groups pointed out.

In 1985, the DHHS and the USDA jointly issued a second edition of the Dietary Guidelines.[17] The group reaffirmed the principles of the first edition, making only minor changes to the 1980 text.[18] This revised edition was nearly identical to the first, differing from the original in only three words—"Maintain ideal weight" became "Maintain *desirable* weight," and "alcohol" became "*alcoholic beverages*." According to the USDA, the second edition received broad acceptance and was widely used as a framework for consumer education messages.[19]

The 1990 Edition of Dietary Guidelines for Americans

In 1987, a conference report of the House Committee on Appropriations directed the USDA, in conjunction with the DHHS, to "re-establish a Dietary Guidelines Advisory Group on a periodic basis."[20] In compliance with that directive, the USDA and the DHHS established a second advisory committee in 1989 that reviewed the 1985 Dietary Guidelines and made recommendations for revision in a report to the secretaries of Agriculture and HHS.[21]

The debate about the *content* of dietary guidance messages largely subsided with the publication of two authoritative reports in the late 1980s. Both *The Surgeon General's Report on Nutrition and Health*,[22] published in 1988, and the National Research Council's 1989 report, *Diet and Health*,[23] (prepared by a different Food and Nutrition Board Committee on Diet and Health than had prepared the 1980 report) reached similar conclusions and proposed similar modifications in the U.S. diet to reduce the risk of chronic disease. These two reports, along with the draft of a report by the Population Panel of the National Cholesterol Education Program,[24] were used as key resources by the Dietary Guidelines Advisory Committee in revising and issuing the 1990 education of the Dietary Guidelines.

In 1990, the DHHS and the USDA jointly released the third edition of the Dietary Guidelines.[25] The basic tenets of the previous documents were reaffirmed, with additional refinements made to reflect increased understanding of the science of nutrition and how best to communicate that science to consumers. To address concerns that the public increasingly perceived certain foods as "bad" and unfit for inclusion in healthy diets, the committee altered the phrasing of several of the guidelines to make their tone more positive. For example, for the phrase, "avoid too much . . .," the committee substituted, "choose a diet low in . . ." The 1990 edition of the Guidelines also validated the "total diet approach," (aka the "no bad foods" approach), saying that "any food that supplies calories and essential nutrients is recognized as potentially useful in a nutritious diet."[26]

One of the major issues in the 1990 revision was quantification of the fat and saturated fat guideline, that is, setting a numerical recommendation for the amount of these nutrients that should be consumed. In testimony received by the committee, producer groups, such as the American Meat Institute, American Cocoa Institute, National Cattlemen's Association, and United Egg Board, opposed the notion, while health groups, such as the American Heart Association, favored it. The committee believed that scientific consensus on this issue had been achieved, so for the first time in 1990, numerical recommendations appeared in the text of the Dietary Guidelines booklet for intakes of dietary fat and saturated fat, as 30 percent and 10 percent of calories, respectively, similar to the limits suggested by the Dietary Goals in 1977.

Criticism of the 1990 revision of the Dietary Guidelines was also directed to the wording of the guideline related to "maintaining a healthy weight." Throwing out separate tables for men and women on body weight ranges, the committee (reportedly at the urging of government officials who were staffing the committee) adopted a unisex table. Critics charged that this action allowed women 15 additional pounds, increasing their risk for some chronic diseases by as much as 50 percent.[27] For the first time, the 1990 edition of the Dietary Guidelines elicited no noticeable complaints from the food industry.

The Dietary Guidelines for Americans, 1995 Edition

After a decade of comparable attempts, the National Nutrition Monitoring and Related Research Act (Public Law 101-445) was finally passed in 1990. One important example of where Congress has taken action on dietary guidance issues is in the wording of Title III of this act. This "dietary guidance" clause requires the secretaries of Agriculture and Health and Human Services to jointly publish a report titled Dietary Guidelines for Americans at least every five years. This legislation also requires review by *both* secretaries of all federal publications containing dietary advice for the general public. Ostensibly, the purpose of this review is to ensure that any dietary information issued for the general public is consistent with the Dietary Guidelines for Americans or is based on new, valid medical or scientific knowledge.[28] In actuality, Title III gives either secretary "veto power" over any dietary advice issued by the other federal agency and was inserted there at the insistence of the USDA, which worried that dietary guidance issued by the DHHS might not be sensitive to agricultural perspectives.

In 1994, the USDA and the DHHS appointed an eleven-member Dietary Guidelines Advisory Committee to review the 1990 education of the Dietary Guidelines and determine if, on the basis of current scientific knowledge, revisions were warranted. In addition to a thorough review of scientific papers published since the last Dietary Guidelines revision, the committee held three public meetings from September 1994 through March 1995 and solicited both oral and written comments from the public.

The fourth edition of the Dietary Guidelines for Americans, issued in 1995, was the first to be issued under the 1990 Nutrition Monitoring statute.[29] The Dietary Guidelines Advisory Committee concluded that the central messages of the seven Dietary Guidelines remained sound and of major importance in choosing food for a healthful diet. Although the thrust of the guidelines remained on helping individuals make appropriate food choices, the benefits of healthful diets and the importance of dietary patterns were emphasized in an attempt to place less significance on specific foods. There was less emphasis on weight loss and more emphasis on weight maintenance in relation to energy balance, including the role of exercise. Two changes in the text of the Dietary Guidelines booklet captured the attention of the media—vegetarian diets were recognized as being consistent with the

Guidelines, and the health benefits of alcohol were recognized when consumed in moderation. Some who had been critical of the wording of the Guidelines in the past went so far as to praise this edition as a "triumph of science and reason over politics."[30]

Table CS4.1 shows the changes in the wording of the text of the Dietary Guidelines throughout its four editions. Although the titles of some of the guidelines have changed, there have been few changes in the overall theme of the Dietary Guidelines over their fifteen-year existence. There are seven guidelines in each edition. The target audience has remained unchanged; they are directed to all healthy Americans two years of age or older.

The Dietary Guidelines for Americans currently serves as the official statement of federal policy on dietary guidance. The Guidelines, as a policy instrument, forms the basis of federal food, nutrition education, and information programs. In addition to serving as the focal point for federal nutrition policy, the Dietary Guidelines messages have also been adopted by numerous food and nutrition organizations as the basis for their own dietary policy.

In terms of nutrition education, the Dietary Guidelines' messages serve as the content base for a number of ongoing educational activities, such as the National Cholesterol Education Program, the National Cancer Institute's "5–a-Day for Better Health" Program, and food labeling education activities. In terms of nutrition programs and food assistance, the DHHS uses the Dietary Guidelines as the educational component of service delivery programs of the Health Resources and Services Administration, the Administration on Aging, the Indian Health Service, and the Administration for Children and Families in the Head Start program. The USDA used the recommendations from the 1990 edition of the Guidelines to develop the nutrient standards for meals served as part of the National School Lunch Program, a part of the Healthy School Meals Initiative program (see Case Study 1, p. 67).

Analysis

By "Stage" of the Policy Process

Although the link between diet and the risk of chronic disease had been publicized for decades, it was the power of certain epidemiological evidence that provided an incentive for government policy. The initial publication of the Dietary Guidelines for Americans in 1980 was undoubtedly bolstered by scientist-advocates on the "inside" of government who knew the issues and how to use the power of government influence to bring this evidence to the attention of the American public. Once, of course, the "agenda" was set by executive branch bureaucrats, others who opposed this

Table CS4.1 **Language of Four Editions of Dietary Guidelines**

Dietary Guidelines for Americans
1980–1995

1980	1985	1990	1995
Eat a variety of foods	Eat a variety of foods	Eat a variety of foods	Eat a variety of foods
Maintain ideal weight	Maintain desirable weight	Maintain healthy weight	Balance the food you eat with physical activity—maintain or improve your weight
Avoid too much fat, saturated fat, and cholesterol	Avoid too much fat, saturated fat, and cholesterol	Choose a diet low in fat, saturated fat, and cholesterol	Choose a diet with plenty of grain products, vegetables, and fruits*
Eat foods with adequate starch and fiber	Eat foods with adequate starch and fiber	Choose a diet with plenty of vegetables, fruits, and grain products	Choose a diet low in fat, saturated fat, and cholesterol*
Avoid too much sugar	Avoid too much sugar	Use sugars only in moderation	Choose a diet moderate in sugars
Avoid too much sodium	Avoid too much sodium	Use salt and sodium only in moderation	Choose a diet moderate in salt and sodium
If you drink alcohol, do so in moderation	If you drink alcoholic beverages, do so in moderation	If you drink alcoholic beverages, do so in moderation	If you drink alcoholic beverages, do so in moderation

Source: Food Economics and Nutrition Review 9:9, 1996.
*In the 1995 edition, the order of the third and fourth guidelines has been reversed.

action (i.e., mainly representatives of the agribusiness industry) sought relief from the legislative branch to mollify these efforts. The persuasiveness of the health lobby to a Democratic Congress (during a Republican administration) was sufficient to prolong the effort rather than "kill" it (as had been expected) so that a couple of editions of the Dietary Guidelines were published even before irrefutable scientific evidence "caught up" with the process. Those in the federal government also did not want to seem as "laggards" in this process. Between 1977 and 1989, at least ten authoritative bodies within and outside the government proposed dietary recommendations to promote good health and to reduce the risk of specific chronic diseases such as heart disease, cancer, osteoporosis, and obesity.[31]

A Perspective from the View of the "Advocacy Coalition Framework"

Coalition Orientation and Stability

Predictably, the initial coalitions that influenced the dietary guidance process broke down into two groups—those representing the public health and consumer advocacy community and those representing the interests of the food industry. Government bureaucrats, for the most part, were aligned with the first group since it was they who were charged with the preparation of the documents. However, those in the U.S. Department of Agriculture surely experienced great dissonance in promoting Dietary Guidelines during the Reagan administration, when the Secretary of Agriculture had publicly claimed that "government should not be in the business of telling people what to eat."

Development of subsequent editions of the Dietary Guidelines utilized a number of external advisory groups and committees. As the reader will recall, the first edition of the Dietary Guidelines was prepared internally by staff from the USDA and the DHHS. Upon recommendation of Congress, the 1985 and the 1990 editions used an outside advisory committee, with members chosen by the secretaries of the USDA and the DHHS. This action took the responsibility for the advice from "within" the government and made it seem as though the government was being responsive to outside scientific authorities.

Policy-Oriented Learning

Each advocacy coalition "bent" a little from their original positions. Perhaps those who moved the farthest from their initial belief systems were those in the food industry who accommodated their messages to the compelling scientific evidence that demonstrated a clear relationship between diet and disease. Agribusiness sought ways to be part of this movement by actions as direct as calling attention to a food's healthier components to altering the product to make it less problematic. As Bruce Silverglade, director of legal affairs for the Center for Science in the Public Interest, has said, "In the mid-1980s, the [food industry] shifted their strategy and stopped trying to dispute the science and instead began to place their products in a 'favorable' light by selectively highlighting the positive." This approach was reaffirmed by James Cleeman, coordinator of the National Heart, Blood and Lung Institute's National Cholesterol Education Program (NCEP) (clearly a bureaucratic insider), who is quoted as saying, "[The food industry] is acting in their enlightened self-interest, and they've seen a demand from the public for healthier products."[32]

The public health and consumer advocacy community never got as much as they wanted in the Dietary Guidelines documents, feeling that the government and their external scientific advisors had "given in" too much to the pressures from the food industry. They believed that stronger messages (to decrease fat consumption to 15 or 20 percent, rather than the current recommendation of 30 percent) were more in keeping with a policy that would probably produce more dramatic, demonstrable results. The U.S. Department of Agriculture is a particular target because of its dual responsibility to serve farmers and food producers as well as consumers; consider the following quote from a notable *Washington Post* columnist: ". . . the department remains politically compromised by not rebuking the meat and poultry industries that promote their sick foods as health foods."[33]

Impact of Changes External to the Subsystem

Indeed, politics played a strong role in the development and continuation of the four Dietary Guidelines documents. The first edition, released in early 1980, was published long before the November 1980 elections when the Democrats, those who had written and paved the way for the publication of the document, were defeated. The release of an accompanying document, called simply "Food," designed to help consumers follow the Dietary Guidelines with specifically designed menus and recipes, clearly was a much narrower call, being released just days before Reagan took office in January 1981.

When Republicans called "foul," it took its fight directly to Congress in an effort to suppress publication of the Dietary Guidelines document. A Congress led by the Democrats did not take such action, but in a typical "political" manner decreed that future revisions should be reviewed and released under advisement of scientific experts. In the end, the battle of "dueling scientists" favored the public health arguments, and subsequent revisions of the Dietary Guidelines only served to reinforce the "diet-disease" message.

Summary

Several explanations may be offered as the reasons why the dietary advice issued by government for consumers changed so dramatically after the mid-

1970s. First, the scientific evidence was stronger, more consistent, and more coherent than it was a decade earlier, thus calming the fears of those who took issue with the science base. Second, dietary recommendations to reduce the risk of chronic diseases, such as heart disease and cancer, are consistent, thus alleviating the need for "different" sets of advice for "different" diseases. Third, consumer advocacy groups became more effective in reaching the public and influencing certain policy makers, thus shifting the balance in favor of consensus. And, last, food producers and processors, who had initially seen the dietary recommendations as economically damaging, now realize the potential economic benefits of touting certain products for their health benefits.[34]

Others believe that the "revolution" in America's health and food habits can be attributed mainly to the involvement of the mass media.[35] Many consumers have sought out more healthful food products, certainly advertised with great enthusiasm. Exercise programs, medical and wellness "talk shows," and even infomercials have certainly contributed to bringing good health and dietary practices to the attention of the American public. We believe that government can be an effective player in this "revolution" by creating environments in which health-promoting food choices are easier to make.

———— Case Study 5 ————

The Politics of the Pyramid

The federal government has been in the business of giving dietary advice to consumers for nearly a century. The U.S. Department of Agriculture issued its first food guide* that translated recommendations on nutrient intake into recommendations on food intake for young children in 1916. This initial publication was followed a year later by dietary recommendations for the general population, a guide based on five food groups—milk and meat, cereals, vegetables and fruits, fats and fat-containing foods, and sugars and sugary foods.

The depression of the 1930s led to economically based family food plans, developed by USDA home economists to help people shop for food. These family food plans defined the amounts of foods (in twelve major food groups) to buy and use in a week at four cost levels to meet the nutritional needs of men, women, and children of different ages. Similar food plans are still in use today. For example, one of the lower-cost plans—the Thrifty Food Plan—is still used as the basis for the Food Stamp program allotment.

During World War II when the public was coping with the exigencies of wartime food restrictions, the demand for simple and practical nutrition education materials was established. Availability of nourishing food was an obvious issue during the war, so alternate food choices were suggested as part of the dietary plan, a practice still followed by dietitians and nutritionists today. As a result, a number of private groups and government agencies developed several daily food guides, most based on seven to ten food groups. In 1943, the "Basic Seven" food guide was issued by the USDA as the leaflet "National Wartime Nutrition Guide."

---

*A distinction must be made between *food guides* and *nutrient guides* or *standards*. An example of a nutrient standard is the recommended dietary allowances (RDA). First formulated by experts in 1941 to guide decisions about food supplies for the military, they are amounts of nutrients recommended to be consumed daily by groups of healthy people. Their uses are widespread—from guides for food assistance programs, to standards for food product development, guides for food selection, and descriptive research—and they exist mainly to serve the needs of professionals, rather than the general public for whom the "food guides" have been designed.

All of these materials stressed a common theme—that the major dietary problems of the U.S. population could be resolved by balancing the proportion of "protective," or nutrient-dense foods, with foods that contribute primarily to the energy value of diets. This theme of *balance* in components of the total diet prevailed as a basis for food guides until the development of the Four Food Groups guide.

"Food for Fitness—A Daily Food Guide," which became well known as the "Basic Four" food guide or the Four Food Groups, was developed by USDA nutritionists in the mid-1950s. This guide recommended a minimum number of servings to be consumed from four food groups—two servings of milk and milk products; two servings of meat, fish, poultry, eggs, dry beans, and nuts; four servings of fruits and vegetables; and four servings of grain products. The premise under which this food guide was developed was different from its predecessors in that it was not a guide for the *total* diet. Rather, the "Basic Four" was developed as a guide to a *foundation* diet, that is, it was designed to meet only a portion of the calorie needs and the major portion of the recommended dietary allowances for nutrients. It was assumed that individuals would eat more food than the guide stated in order to satisfy their full calorie and nutrient needs. The "Basic Four" provided little guidance on the selection of fat and sugars in the diet or on appropriate calorie intake.

In addition to its uniqueness as the first food guide to specify the number and size of servings, the "Basic Four" was also the first to be sent out by the USDA nutritionists to food industry and commodity groups for review in order to reach consensus on the food categories.[1] As long as the guide encouraged consumers to purchase more foods from a variety of groups, agricultural producers and food processors raised no serious objections. As such, the "Basic Four" remained the basis of the USDA's nutrition education policy for the next two decades.

This food group–related advice was comfortable, common ground for both nutritionists and the agricultural/food industry alike. It was not until the mid-1970s when dietary recommendations began to focus on nutrients, rather than foods, that food industry and producer groups began to voice their displeasure with certain dietary recommendations issued by the federal government.

In the past two and a half decades, the type of dietary guidance provided to consumers has shifted in focus. Early food guides had advised consuming a particular number of servings from specific food "groups," the goal being to eat enough of specifically identified foods to provide the nutrients and energy required for "good health." The emphasis had been on the quantity of foods to be selected, not on the quality of those food choices.

The USDA produced several colorful, glossy magazines in the early

1980s in order to reach consumers with dietary advice. *Food*, containing the "Hassle-Free Guide to a Better Diet," was published by the USDA in 1980, just days before President Reagan was sworn in. The "Hassle-Free Guide" added a fifth food group—fats, oils, and alcohol—to the Basic Four and also advised, "Cut down on fatty meats." This was the first USDA-produced food guide to highlight the need to moderate the use of fats, sugars, and alcohol and to give special attention to calories and dietary fiber. It also became the *last* federal publication to use the phrase "cut down" in reference to meat.[2] After the Reagan administration took office and a Republican-dominated USDA advisory committee suggested that there was no longer a need for federally produced nutrition education materials,[3] *Food 2* (composed of the original material on fat and cholesterol that had been deleted from *Food* because it was too politically sensitive for a USDA publication) and *Food 3* were published by the American Dietetic Association in 1982.

Food Guides—Post–Dietary Guidelines

By 1980, it had become apparent that dietary guidance could no longer be relegated to simple "eat more" food guides. The public was becoming more "nutritionally literate," and the scientific evidence linking diet to health outcomes was becoming more and more convincing.

In the early 1980s, nutritionists at the USDA's Human Nutrition Information Service (HNIS) identified the need to replace the Basic Four with a well-researched food guide that would "operationalize" the Dietary Guidelines by specifying the numbers and sizes of servings of foods to eat on a daily basis. For the next several years, HNIS nutritionists developed and documented the research basis for a new food guide, and published this information in a peer-reviewed journal article in 1987.[4]

About the same time, nutritionists with the USDA's Human Nutrition Information Service (HNIS) and the American Red Cross collaborated on the development of a nutrition course for consumers that could be taught by volunteer lay leaders.[5] The basis of the "dietary guidance" aspects of that course was depicted as a "Food Wheel," a graphic that presented various food groups and the recommended number of servings to be chosen from each in a circular format, a variation of a pie chart. The USDA also used the food guide in several of its consumer publications in the mid-1980s, showing it in a table format with the generic, government-ized name, "A Pattern for Daily Food Choices." In these classes, the "Food Wheel" (see Fig. CS5.1) failed to generate much public enthusiasm; consumers felt it was too confusing to communicate desired messages about diet and chronic-disease prevention.

Clearly, what was needed was a new symbol, another graphic, to communicate the basic messages of the Dietary Guidelines—balance and variety in food choices, moderation (of fats, oils, and sugar intake), and proportionality (the relative amount of food from each major food group). The result of these efforts was the "Food Guide Pyramid"; its development is the subject of this case study.

The First Phase: Development and Withdrawal of the Pyramid

In early 1988, HNIS contracted with Porter–Novelli, a social marketing research firm in Washington, DC, to develop the graphic design for this new food guide.[6] The mandated mission of the agency administering the project (USDA's Human Nutrition Information Service) was "to collect, disseminate and consult on technical, educational, and nonprint material and information on food use, food management, and human nutrition problems, . . . thereby improving the general health of the American public."[7] However, educational material must be targeted more specifically than to just the generic "American public" to be effective. Therefore, the first audience that the staff chose to address was the same as those chosen for the booklet presenting the Dietary Guidelines for Americans in 1990—adults with at least a high school education who had eating patterns typical of the U.S. population as a whole. The new booklet and graphic were not to be developed specifically for or tested with adults who were recepients of food assistance programs, such as Food Stamps or WIC (even though these programs were administered by another agency within the USDA and accounted for over half of the entire USDA budget at that time), adults with low literacy skills, different ethnic groups, individuals on special diets, or young children. It was assumed that materials would be adapted or developed later specifically for these target audiences.

During 1988 and 1989, HNIS nutritionists drafted the text for the new food guide. The marketing research firm then matched this text with several different graphic designs that they had drawn up before submitting this material for consumer reactions. Five different designs were tested—a circle (a.k.a. "The Food Wheel"); blocks in a row; blocks in a circle; an inverted pyramid (the "funnel"); and a pyramid. The two block designs were eliminated because it was felt that they conveyed less information. The inverted pyramid was rejected because its shape was distracting; and the circle (similar to "The Food Wheel") did not appear new or interesting. This left the pyramid, which was perceived to be novel and presented the information in such a way as to have the desired result. As one focus group participant put it, "One thing the pyramid idea gives you . . . you know you

Figure CS5.1 **The "Food Wheel" Diagram**

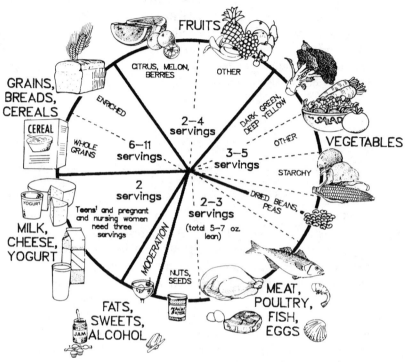

[1] Teens under 19 who are pregnant or nursing need 4 servings a day.

Source: The U.S. Department of Agriculture and the American Red Cross, 1982.

are supposed to eat more of the bread and cereal and less of the things near the top."

During the next few years, the "Eating Right Pyramid" (as it was then called) was further developed and reviewed, and received agency clearance.[8] In 1990 and 1991, drafts were sent for review to thirty-six leading nutrition experts outside of government. The Pyramid was also presented at twenty professional conferences and a number of media meetings. The graphic had already been included in a National Dairy Council publication and was scheduled for printing in several textbooks. The manuscript was also subjected to standard USDA review and clearance procedures. It passed review by a committee representing ten USDA agencies and the Department of Health and Human Services (DHHS); it went on to clear six levels of USDA policy review (including that at the level of the assistant secretary) and three USDA divisional reviews. The fully approved Pyramid page boards were sent to the printer in February 1991 and assigned a March publication date. The Consumer Information Center in Pueblo, Colorado, the main distributor of government publications for consumers, advertised its availability, and orders began to arrive. Color adjustments delayed the printing, but the Pyramid graphic, and an accompanying booklet, was expected to be issued in a press run of a million copies by late April 1991.

"As luck would have it . . ." goes an old saying. It aptly describes the events of the next few weeks. While the Pyramid was at the printer, a series of coincidental events led to its untimely withdrawal. In early April 1991, a health and animal rights advocacy group, the Physicians Committee for Responsible Medicine, asked the USDA to replace the "Basic Four" food guide with a new guide that was based only on plant foods. Hearing rumors that the "Eating Right Pyramid" was about to be released, reporters called and urged the USDA developers to briefly describe their graphic so that they could use this information in their story as a point of contrast with what the physicians group was suggesting. Because release of the Pyramid graphic was imminent, the USDA staff were pleased to talk with the reporters about their work, an early public relations effort, they thought. The original story in the *Orange County Register* (in California) comparing the two guides was picked up and expanded by a *Washington Post* reporter. The *Post* story appeared in print on a Saturday morning. (The timing of this article was somewhat unusual in and of itself because most food-related articles appear in the *Post* in Wednesday's "Food" section.)

The National Cattlemen's Association, a meat producer lobbying group, had been meeting in Washington that Saturday and read the *Post* story. Coincidentally, they had scheduled a Monday morning meeting with then USDA Secretary Edward Madigan who had held office only a few weeks. Whatever the agenda had been for that Monday morning meeting, one can be sure that it was quickly changed to include the Cattlemen's great displeasure about the Saturday *Post* story, which they vociferously relayed to the newly appointed secretary. (Reportedly, the group did not like the smaller space devoted to meat products, compared with the old "Basic Four" graphic, and objected to the placement of their products near the fats, oils, and sweetners group at the top of the Pyramid.) Madigan reportedly replied, "If many of you were surprised [by that story], I'm the secretary of Agriculture, and I was surprised too." Those close to the secretary have said that they had never seen Secretary Madigan so angry; in fact, he was reported to be "livid."

Over the next ten days, other trade associations (such as the National Milk Producers Federation and the American Meat Institute) joined the protest and called for the rejection of the graphic. The atmosphere within the USDA was electric and tension-charged. USDA nutritionists who had worked on the text for the food guide were asked to provide answers to a myriad of questions about the Pyramid's development. Staff were questioned about peer review (which the document had undergone), about "clearance" (which it had passed at all levels), and how they dealt with criticisms from the peer reviews of the draft document. All contracts related to the Pyramid's development and testing were thoroughly and painstakingly reviewed to detect errors or violations. The staff were able to answer all questions and left the meetings with the administration thinking that all was well and that publication of the Pyramid was imminent. They report being "stunned" by the events of the ensuing several weeks.

Less than two weeks after its original story, the *Washington Post* reported that USDA Secretary Madigan had announced that he was withdrawing the Pyramid from publication in order to have the graphic tested with schoolchildren and low-income adults. However laudatory the reasons Madigan gave for the withdrawal of the Pyramid, the explanation for his decision, however, was widely disbelieved. Most were convinced that he had simply cowered under the demands of the powerful meat and dairy lobby.

Behind the Scenes

What we have in this case is a classic clash of two cultures. One was represented by the political appointees—Secretary Madigan, his assistant secretary and deputy assistant secretary of Food and Consumer Services (to which HNIS reported), and the administrator and associate administrator of HNIS, the agency whose staff had developed the text of the Pyramid and had awarded the contract to Porter–Novelli for the development and testing of the graphic to accompany the text. The other culture was represented by civil service employees, professional nutritionists, and staff in the USDA's Human Nutrition Information Service. Each culture has different loyalties; political appointees are loyal to those who have given them their positions, civil servants are loyal to their profession, the base of their expertise. Political appointees are committed to the process, to seeing that it goes smoothly, without political embarrassments, and that all constituencies are satisfied. Civil servants are committed to the content of the project, to seeing that all technical details are correct and will pass the test of professional scrutiny.

It is also important to explain the reasoning behind the withdrawal of the

Pyramid within the context of a man, newly appointed USDA Secretary Edward Madigan. Madigan came to the USDA after nine terms as a congressman from the farm belt of Illinois, and reportedly had been encouraged to seek the position of USDA secretary by commodity and farm groups. As ranking Republican on the House Agriculture Committee, Madigan was no stranger to nutrition issues and had supported both food assistance programs and the NLEA during his term in office. Described as a "fiery Irishman," Madigan was furious that he had been publically embarrassed because he had not been fully briefed about the release of the Pyramid before it appeared in the press. He wanted the staff at the USDA to know "who was boss" and wanted to impose his own brand of discipline on the department. Even though he could understand their professional expertise, he regarded the professional staff at the HNIS (the group who had developed the Pyramid) as "out of control" and filled with hubris.

It is no wonder then that the details of the meeting in which the staff who developed the Pyramid were informed of the decision to cancel it are remembered so differently by the two groups. Recall that the staff had been in the process of developing this document for over three years, nearly a decade if all of the basic research was considered. They had followed usual protocol in awarding the contract, putting the document through peer review and USDA clearance procedures. They thought they had done everything "right," yet here was a man they hardly knew, the newly appointed secretary of Agriculture, who had undone years of painstaking work in a matter of weeks. Outraged and emotionally distraught in a meeting with the deputy assistant secretary (who had been assigned to "take care" of the matter), HNIS staff said, "no one will believe the reason given for cancellation [i.e., to gather additional data from children and from recipients of food assistance programs] because 'everyone knew' that the real reason was that the meat and dairy groups were so displeased over the Pyramid graphic". To this, the administration representative replied, "If you [the staff] keep repeating the official reason for cancellation, it will be believed." The staff brought up the fact that their counterparts, the professional community, would be outraged over this capricious action. To this the political appointee responded, "the nutrition community is so small and without political clout; therefore, whether or not they are 'outraged' is not really a serious concern." The third, and final, point made by the staff at that meeting was that the media coverage would be bad for all—the USDA, the commodity groups, and nutrition and health groups. To this point, the USDA official stated, "Even if the media does pick up the story [which he thought most unlikely], it will be forgotten in days."

"Silence is Golden ... "

In the ensuing weeks, the HNIS nutrition staff were silenced. They were criticized for not being "team players," were told that they were never permitted to talk with Secretary Madigan, and were essentially ostracized from further involvement in the project. Presentations to professional audiences about the consumer research performed on the Pyramid publication were canceled, and Cooperative Extension Service personnel were instructed not to use the Pyramid in any of their educational programs.[9]

The staff, however, could not be silenced from speaking with their professional colleagues—nor with the media. In the following months, hundreds of letters protesting the secretary's actions were received by the USDA from health and consumer groups, professional organizations, and "common citizens." The national press also provided constant public attention on the issue. In the six months after publication of the Pyramid was canceled, the suppressed graphic was published in the *Washington Post*, the *New York Times*, *USA Today*, *Science*, *Fortune*, *Newsweek*, *Time*, and *Consumer Reports*.

The volume of media attention had several important effects—for one, it educated the public. Marian Burros, of the *New York Times*, said, "Had it not been for the ham-handed manner in which the pyramid was withdrawn, it might have glided into relative obscurity. Now everyone who follows nutrition politics knows about it."[10] The media pressure also forced the administration step-by-step down a path that eventually led to the release of the Pyramid.

Testing of a "New" Pyramid ...
Back to the Drawing Board

Very quickly after publication of the Pyramid had been recalled from the printer, the word "canceled" was replaced by "on hold," which then became "on hold for future research." Initially, the USDA staff were told that if they wanted the Pyramid released, they would have to conduct additional research to prove that the graphic was useful and understood by "vulnerable groups" that were important to the secretary. The problem with this directive (in the staff's eyes) was that definitions of these "vulnerable groups" were not to be publically announced in advance, and no budget was to be provided with which to do this additional research. As media attention on the process continued, the administration considered various political research firms to do this research, but it did not want to consider the usual routes, such as open competition for a grant or cooperative agreement, because these procedures required too much time.

In July 1991, four months after the withdrawal of the Pyramid, the USDA announced that it had awarded a six-month $400,000 contract to a Cambridge, Massachusetts–based consulting firm for the purpose of testing the value of the Pyramid against other graphic designs. The test group was to be adults and children participating in federal food assistance programs. Because Bell Associates was a minority-owned firm, the USDA was able to quickly award the contract without a competitive bid.

It was at this point that nutritionists at the Department of Health and Human Services became involved. Never close allies with the USDA when it came to nutrition policy, the DHHS reportedly also contributed some funding (reportedly in the neighborhood of $200,000) "to keep the USDA honest." Continued questions about the legitimacy of the research forced Bell to form an advisory group of qualified nongovernmental nutritionists, educators, and evaluation specialists.

The other group that became involved at this point was Congress. Democrats in the House were gleeful that a scandal had arisen at the USDA to which they could call public attention. In early May 1991, Congressman Ted Weiss (D-New York) announced that the Committee on Government Operations would hold a hearing on the matter. (The hearings were never held, but key political appointments at the USDA were held up.) The Pyramid was also discussed at House Agricultural Subcommittee hearings on October 16, 1991, during which George Brown (D-California)—no friend of Republicans at the USDA—noted that the past USDA actions indicated to him that "it is time to assess the pros and cons of moving nutrition, research, education, and monitoring responsibilities to another department."[11]

The selected contractor, Bell Associates, conducted its research in two distinct phases. The first set of results was submitted in a report to the USDA in December 1991.When its focus group research produced ambiguous results confirming that the Pyramid design was at least as effective as any other at conveying the intended messages, the USDA requested further testing. Thus, back to the drawing board it was. (When the final results were finally accepted by the USDA, Bell was paid at least $850,000 for its work, more than double the original amount in the contract and far more than the $160,000 paid to Porter–Novelli for its original design of the Pyramid.)[12]

After conducting countless more interviews and focus groups with numerous groups using a variety of graphic designs, the contractor narrowed the field to two design options—the Pyramid and the "bowl." (In general, bowls and pie charts were preferred by most industry representatives, while the pyramids were preferred by nutrition professionals.) After a quantitative phase of testing, Bell sent a draft report to the USDA saying the two designs were virtually indistinguishable in their impact. (Those familiar with the research maintain that the data clearly showed that the Pyramid was superior, but the contractor wrote the results differently to satisfy what it thought the USDA wanted.) At that point, USDA officials were faced with an uncomfortable dilemma. With little research basis for deciding between the two designs, they could choose the original Pyramid and risk embarrassment over the delay and additional costs (as well as continued opposition from food producers), or they could choose the bowl design for what might be interpreted as political rather than scientific reasons.[13]

The USDA then appointed an internal review group, composed of both USDA and DHHS nutritionists, to respond to the draft report that had been submitted by the contractor. The committee recommended that Bell reanalyze the data using a weighted scoring system that would compare the bowl against the Pyramid for communicating the basic dietary guidelines concepts of variety, moderation, and proportionality. This reanalysis indicated that both designs effectively conveyed the need for variety in food intake, but that the pyramid was significantly better at conveying the concepts of moderation and proportionality.

While this distinction was very clear to the nutritionists who examined the reanalyzed data, USDA officials maintained that the choice of graphic was a "policy decision." On March 23, 1992, seven nutritionists at both the USDA and the DHHS signed a memorandum to the USDA administration, stating that, in their professional view, the research results supported only the selection of the Pyramid. One of the nutritionists also called a representative of a meat-industry trade association indicating that this internal memo would be released to the press if the secretary did not choose the Pyramid. Further, the group informed congressional staff about the situation. Public release of that memo would almost certainly have meant additional "bad press" for meat interests and the USDA, and it probably would have triggered congressional hearings. Timing also favored a "cutting your losses" type of decision by the administration in that the presidential election was only months away—not a good time for an administration standing for reelection to experience further "bad press."

Re-Release of the New "Food Guide Pyramid"

One year, one day, and slightly less than $1 million later—on April 28, 1992, Secretary Madigan held a press conference to announce the release of the "Food Guide Pyramid." The new Pyramid differed from its former version in thirty-three rather minor ways, most notably its title—"Food Guide Pyramid," rather than "Eating Right Pyramid" (mainly to avoid undergoing copyright infringement action with Kraft, which had a product line with a similar name); further, pictures of foods were redrafted (e.g., the picture of the milk carton was changed to a glass of milk), and the serving numbers were moved outside the graphic (see Figure CS5.2).

In the end, the hardest task may have been to convince Secretary Madigan himself. The secretary of the USDA was reported to have preferred the bowl design and was unhappy with the decision to release the Pyramid, but he publicly denied having been pressured. It may have been that it simply was no longer "worth the fight." Feeling vindicated, USDA staff announced that "the political people [at the USDA] were forced into this decision by the internal staffers, the Department of Health and Human Services, and the professional community."[14]

The Role of Advocacy Coalitions

To what do we attribute this review and release of an important dietary guidance tool when, under most circumstances, its withdrawal would have caused hardly a ripple of attention? After all, the Food Guide Pyramid was simply a document, a graphic designed for the public to impart some information about eating more healthfully. This was *not* a law, nor even an official regulation, merely a document that had been sanctioned by two departments of the executive branch.

The question must be asked: Can the public depend on government for dietary guidance in the best interests of their health? When the Pyramid was released it was billed as 'the triumph of science over politics." However, the battle lines were blurred—the politicians tried to use the research methods of scientists to control the outcome but were not successful. On the other hand, the nutrition community banded together, more in support of the principles involved than for the release of the graphic itself, and successfully worked with the media, usually the domain of expounding politicians.

Reporters characterized the Pyramid conflict as the result of a classic dilemma in American government: the constitutional right of food companies to lobby in their own self-interest—even when, as in this case, that right conflicted with the right of the American public to be presented with scientifically valid information that, when followed, could protect their health.[15] To most in the professional community (including the nutritionists inside the USDA), the release of the Pyramid was seen as a symbol of a strong professional community that fought for science over politics as the basis of dietary guidance for the general public. To them the one-year delay in the release of the graphic and the expenditure of almost $1 million serve only as disgraceful signs of political games being played with taxpayers' dollars.

What has happened to the Pyramid since its release in April 1992? In

Figure CS5.2 **The "Two Pyramids"**

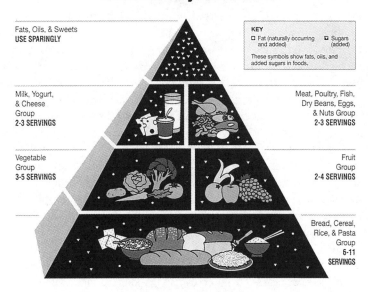

Food Guide Pyramid
A Guide to Daily Food Choices

Fats, Oils, & Sweets
USE SPARINGLY

KEY
▢ Fat (naturally occurring and added)   ◩ Sugars (added)
These symbols show fats, oils, and added sugars in foods.

Milk, Yogurt, & Cheese Group
2-3 SERVINGS

Meat, Poultry, Fish, Dry Beans, Eggs, & Nuts Group
2-3 SERVINGS

Vegetable Group
3-5 SERVINGS

Fruit Group
2-4 SERVINGS

Bread, Cereal, Rice, & Pasta Group
6-11 SERVINGS

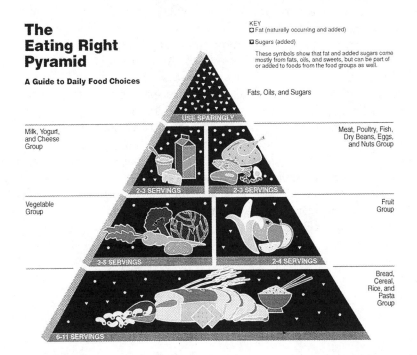

The Eating Right Pyramid
A Guide to Daily Food Choices

KEY
▢ Fat (naturally occurring and added)
◩ Sugars (added)
These symbols show that fat and added sugars come mostly from fats, oils, and sweets, but can be part of or added to foods from the food groups as well.

Fats, Oils, and Sugars
USE SPARINGLY

Milk, Yogurt, and Cheese Group
2-3 SERVINGS

Meat, Poultry, Fish, Dry Beans, Eggs, and Nuts Group
2-3 SERVINGS

Vegetable Group
3-5 SERVINGS

Fruit Group
2-4 SERVINGS

Bread, Cereal, Rice, and Pasta Group
6-11 SERVINGS

many respects, the Food Guide Pyramid has become the nutritional icon of the 1990s. Its use has become so commonplace that the controversy surrounding its release is hardly remembered. There are those, however, who feel that this tale should never be forgotten because it raises the question of the appropriate role of government in providing nutrition and health guidance to the public.

The Food Guide Pyramid is only a tool, a scientifically valid graphic that can be used to educate the public about the advice contained in the Dietary Guidelines for Americans. The Pyramid stands as the basis for the content of nutrition education programs, and the hope was that it could guide Americans in making healthful food choices in a food supply that is constantly changing and constantly tempting.[16] However, no graphic can communicate all things to all people and, the Pyramid notwithstanding, must be accompanied by printed information and complete explanations to communicate its message. The "Food Guide Pyramid" is a "complex illustration in which many different food and nutrition messages are embedded . . . [further,] it is a complex operation that requires a series of sequential, meaningful, educational and motivational experiences to understand and implement."[17]

If, as they say, "imitation is the sincerest form of flattery," then the Food Guide Pyramid should feel honored indeed! The Pyramid is now printed on a variety of food packages—from cereals to TV dinners, and even on dog food! It is even being used in certain restaurants to promote healthful eating.[18]

The most famous imitator is the pyramid designed to present the dietary recommendations found in the "Mediterranean" diet.[19] This guide differs from the Food Guide Pyramid in two important ways: (1) it recommends no more than 12 to 16 ounces of meat a month, in comparison to USDA's up to 6 ounces a day; and (2) it suggests that fat, mostly in the form of olive oil, can range in the diet from less than 25 percent to more than 35 percent of total calories. It also promotes physical exercise as an important component to good health and recommends moderation in alcohol consumption.

Despite the controversy over its initial release, promoters feel the Food Guide Pyramid has emerged stronger and received more media attention than it otherwise would have. The Food Guide Pyramid was developed as an educational tool for its time—developed from a sound research base in the health, epidemiological, and communication fields and to meet the needs of a public desiring health advice in an appealing, understandable form.

—— PART IV ——

SUMMARY AND CONCLUSIONS

Chapter 8

The Politics of Fat:
What Have We Learned and
Where Should We Be Headed?

The main issues now are whether or not a comprehensive national nutrition policy is imperative, and whether it is feasible to develop a coordinated, action-oriented policy in a pluralistic society that must satisfy competing pressures from agricultural, health, economic, medical and industrial sectors.

—S. Palmer*

This book has described the myriad ways in which the government through various public policy instruments has influenced the American food supply and the demand for that food by consumers. In this final chapter, we review what each of the chapters and case studies (devoted to a particular section of the food system) has revealed as well as the cross-cutting themes that have emerged through this analysis. Finally, we offer some conclusions about the effectiveness of current policies and propose means by which a more health-focused food policy can be developed in this country.

What Have We Learned?

As described throughout this book, the federal government has employed an impressive arsenal of powerful policy tools that can and do influence behavior throughout the food and agriculture system. Some of these tools affect the production of farm commodities that bring dietary fat into the food chain, some determine the extent to which fat is used as an ingredient in processed food products, and still others are designed to influence the amount of fat consumed in the daily diets of the American people.

One of the inescapable conclusions to be drawn from the case studies and

---

*S. Palmer, "Food and Nutrition Policy: Challenges for the 1990s," *Health Affairs*, Summer, 1990, p. 106.

analyses in the preceding chapters, however, is that surprisingly few of those federal policy instruments have either the suspected effect or the hoped-for impact. Indeed, some of the federal policies that may have the clearest impact on American dietary fat intake, all too often, are those with decidedly negative consequences; a good example of this policy irony (of which most consumers and many professionals are quite unaware) is food standards of identity.

On the positive side of the ledger, mandatory nutrition labeling will undoubtedly lay the groundwork for potential future shifts in consumer behavior. However, other overt nutrition policy initiatives to decrease dietary fat consumption may have been so compromised by the intervention of anticonsumer advocacy coalitions that their impact on fat consumption is likely to fall far short of expectations. A potentially troubling initiative that demonstrates this phenomenon is the new school lunch regulations that held so much early promise but were attenuated by the efforts of an advocacy coalition composed mainly of school food service workers and even some government insiders. The 1993 regulations developed by the FDA to implement the NLEA were not as strong as they might have been, from a consumer and public health perspective, because of the influence exerted by advocacy coalitions dominated by industry representatives that also included federal agency career employees and political appointees.

Both federal dietary advice and nutrition labeling initiatives remain externally overshadowed by private sector food advertising and internally compromised by the "no bad foods" admonition. Food advertising expenditures—some of which are, ironically, facilitated by federally sanctioned check-off programs—are hundreds of times larger than budgets for federal nutrition education programs. Which are the more powerful and persuasive set of influences on dietary behavior?

Many of the federal programs that affect production of farm commodities either have had little impact on the production of dietary fat and/or are being phased out or redesigned. While dairy programs have arguably contributed the most to enhanced animal fat production and consumption, they are mandated to become more market-oriented by the year 2000.

Given the array of actions that affect policy in food and nutrition, it should perhaps come as little surprise that the composition of the advocacy coalitions working on those policies often shifted to fit the policy initiative. On most occasions, particularly when the substance of federal nutrition information and dietary advice was the focus of discussion, food and agricultural industry interests found themselves positioned against coalitions dominated by consumer and public health groups. In point of fact, federal agency personnel have ended up more frequently promoting compromises that aligned them more with the food industry's voices than with public health needs or outcries from consumer groups.

However, when federal regulation of industry is viewed as a hindrance to the supply of lower-fat foods, it is likely that pro-reform advocacy coalitions composed of consumer and industry groups will emerge. In that case, the opposition advocacy coalition is often made up of federal agency personnel and small segments of agribusiness that have a perceived stake in protecting the old ways of doing business. The recent attempts to reform the USDA's Standards of Identity provide a key example. The beef grading example offers an extreme case, in which the primary opposition to federal reform came mainly from those within the federal bureaucracy itself.

After at least two full decades of these battles and shifting advocacy coalition alignments, dietary fat remains plentiful in the food supply—in forms that Americans like and prefer. Many consumers wish to cut down on the amount of fat in their diets, but find it increasingly difficult to do so as they fight a massive case of collective dissonance between intentions and behavior. Where has the federal government been throughout this struggle? Certainly, in the "thick" of it all, but as a marginal player rather than as a forceful advocate when it comes to promoting public health through food policy.

Ultimately, questions about the "politics of fat" come down to whether the federal government is going to be a decisive part of the solution or a part of the problem. Based on the major case histories of the past decade, it is difficult not to conclude that the federal government, particularly the heavily conflicted USDA, has rarely, if ever, demonstrated a strong political commitment to rebalancing the dietary fat equation in this country. Too often, Congress and federal agencies have lined up in advocacy coalitions that are designed to protect interests of the food industry, maintain the bureaucratic status quo, or even continue to withhold valuable information from or mislead consumers. Not surprisingly, the federal government policies examined in this book tend to have lagged behind science, consumer concerns, and even the food marketplace. Worse yet, in some cases they have likely interfered with consumers' ability to make more healthful, lower-fat food choices.

A View of Federal Policy Performance in Nutrition

After reading through this book, one can only conclude that federal nutrition policy (if one can even call it that) is on the brink of failure. From a food policy perspective, however, we have been somewhat more successful. Americans enjoy one of the cheapest food policies in the world. Most

Americans have plenty of food, and most can afford to purchase what they "want" in addition to what they need. In many ways, however, that policy—when considered in relation to health outcomes—can only be described by the phrase "too little, too late." Americans eat a *lot* of food, as evidenced by our ever-climbing obesity rate, but the healthfulness of those food choices leaves much room for improvement.

Federal policy can—and should—create an environment in which health-promoting food choices are easier to make, and health-damaging food choices are more difficult. Unfortunately, just the reverse situation has been true. In many ways, consumers are "way ahead" of the federal government in their awareness of food choices that will promote health and their desire to have healthful food choices widely available at favorable prices. Federal food policies simply have not kept pace with consumers' concerns about food and health, and, in some cases, have actually hindered consumers' attempts to adopt more healthful diets.

In what areas has federal food policy failed the consumer? The few millions of dollars spent by the federal government to provide dietary advice to the consumer (much of the message compromised by attenuated, qualified statements designed to mollify the food industry) are completely engulfed by the billions of dollars spent on food advertising for high-fat food favorites. Even the government has been a player in this duplicity as it promotes high-fat dairy and meat commodities in its commodity promotion programs. Food labels now carry a Nutrition Facts panel to give the consumer accurate information about the nutrient content of that packaged food. However, many of the terms used on that panel are not well understood by consumers and may even allow for some misinterpretation of factual information. Despite agreement on common nutrient content claims and health claims on the food label, the Food and Drug Administration has been compromised in its efforts because of a recent barrage of attempts to weaken nutrition labeling regulations even further.

What consumers can't see or understand about the food product further undermines their efforts to make healthful food choices. Among the prime examples discussed in this book are the beef grading standards and Standards of Identity for processed food products. Despite recent efforts to revamp both systems, the true fat content of many products is still hidden under the cover of economic protection from adulteration by food "standards of identity." When it is in the economic interest of the food industry to push for more healthful, lower-fat food standards, action usually occurs. It is quite a costly challenge for the public health/consumer advocacy community to become aware of the "opportune" moment in which to build successful coalitions to push for reform. And even when the industry and consumer groups agree and push for change, it is often personnel in the federal regulatory agency who become the "road block" to effective action.

It is disappointing that federal policy makers often line up in advocacy coalitions either opposing outright consumer-friendly reforms or join with industry in minimizing the damage to the status quo, despite a strong public health mandate for change. Such opposition can often be traced to political motives for elected officials. But, all too often, it is a "knee-jerk" reaction of the career public servant that "nothing can be done" or "we've tried that before, and it didn't work." The slow, incrementalist approach to nutrition policy making is surely "alive and well." What would embolden policy makers to push for more meaningful change in current food policy?

It is often said that without the food industry as a "full partner" in any food and nutrition policy efforts, it is doomed to failure. Certainly, recent developments in dealing with the tobacco industry offer hope for those interested in revolutionizing food policy. Indeed, even state governments are willing to take on tobacco advertisements with counter messages;[1] could we in nutrition possibly adopt a similar approach to temper the powerful sway of food advertising? We must adopt federal nutrition policies that are not compromised or weakened in the name of dietary "balance" or "moderation." If change is to be made, it must happen soon in order to effect positive health outcomes.

Major Cross-Cutting Themes of the Book

Policy Ironies

This book has repeatedly demonstrated ironies that exist in various government policies, some an artifact of history and tradition, others newly created. Federally supported marketing orders and pricing structures reward the promotion and sale of high-fat foods to consumers. These policies, in many cases, are in direct contradiction to those health-oriented policies that admonish consumers to make lower-fat food choices. The result is consumer confusion and a reluctance to undertake further positive, health-promoting behaviors.

Certainly there are differences between legislative policies enacted by Congress and regulatory policies promulgated by executive branch agencies. (While legislation takes precedence over regulation, it is clear that regulations to implement legislation can often be written in such a way as to favor one group over another. Thus, consumer groups have long charged that many food regulatory policies have been written that favor agribusiness interests at the expense of consumer benefits.)

Further, there are differences in policies promoted by different agencies within the executive branch. For example, an agency within the Department of Health and Human Services/National Institutes of Health, the National Heart, Lung, and Blood Institute, has sponsored for a number of years a National Cholesterol Education Program, while the U.S. Department of Agriculture administers commodity promotion programs for beef, pork, dairy products, and eggs, the major sources of fat and cholesterol in the diet. Further, even within a single federal department—the U.S. Department of Agriculture—a number of agencies are charged with responsibility for commodity promotion, while others, such as the Center for Nutrition Policy and Promotion, develop and promote the Dietary Guidelines and perform research on how well consumers are following these recommendations.

Tensions Between Government Regulation and the Marketplace

In today's public policy arena, the distinctions between government regulation and marketplace competition are not as distinct and disparate as some would believe. Rather, we see a continuum between the two extremes. In some cases, such as nutrition information on food labels, we see that government regulation enhances the marketplace and "levels the playing field" for food industry competitors. In other areas, government regulation is seen as interfering with an open marketplace; one example of this is the "information panel" on packages of olestra-containing food products "warning" that consumption of the product has caused gastric distress in some people. While some have charged that this label information is unfair to the manufacturer of the fat replacer, others see this action as one that protects unwary, uninformed consumers about a potential health problem associated with consumption of that product.

Disparate Interests, Disparate Influence: Advocacy Coalitions

The Advocacy Coalition Framework (ACF)[2] espouses that various advocacy coalitions, through their belief systems, influence the direction of public policy. Currently in this country, there are groups, mainly represented by those in the food industry, whose belief system centers on the power of the marketplace, while other groups, such as those representing public health and consumer interests, have long depended on protection provided by government regulation.

It is said in some circles that current food policies favor agribusiness interests. In supporting subsidies for the production of high-fat items and developing regulations that support the approval of fat replacers, such policies often lag behind scientific findings and consumers' needs for better and more meaningful product information. However, some public policy scholars, such as Nancy Milio, assert that the United States' consumer-focused, educational approach geared to affect demand for healthful foods is designed to avoid conflict with the economic and commercial interests of the farm-food industry.[3]

Moving from a Food Policy to a Nutrition Policy

Certainly, a variety of mechanisms must be employed to move from a food/agriculture policy to a nutrition/health policy in the United States. Three categories of government initiatives stand out as being the primary means for influencing food policy to incorporate health outcomes. These are (1) easing or accelerating agricultural adjustments by changing the mix and/or volume of agricultural commodities produced, thus changing what food is available to the consumer; (2) measures that improve the nutritional characteristics of popular foods; and (3) measures that promote desirable changes in consumers' food choices.[4]

Earlier in this book, we made a distinction between food policy and nutrition policy. Nutrition policy explicitly incorporates health considerations into food policy decisions. By changing legislation, levying taxes, or employing other fiscal or trade measures, a food policy may be transformed into actually being a nutrition policy that will contribute to positive health outcomes. One of the *few* countries to adopt a comprehensive food and nutrition policy is Norway. This complex policy is truly "intersectorial"; it encompasses health and diet, agricultural self-sufficiency, rural development, and environmental conservation, as well as world food security goals.[5] Straightforward, forceful policies, such as those directly affecting food production by offering economic incentives for more "healthful" foods (as is done in some of the Scandinavian countries), probably would never be accepted in the United States in an era of "moderate" policies.

A simulation was conducted to determine the impact if American consumers had adopted diets consistent with the dietary recommendations put forth in the 1977 staff report from the Senate Select Committee on Nutrition and Human Needs, titled Dietary Goals for the U.S.[6] The simulation study found that if such dietary recommendations had been followed, the effect on farmers would vary greatly, depending on the commodity they produced. Crop farmers, in general, would have been the winners, benefiting from higher farm prices and incomes. Livestock and egg producers would have faced declines in the demand for their products as well as a drop in farm prices and income. Poultry, wheat, and rice farmers would have benefited from increased demand for their products. Corn growers would have been adversely affected, mainly because of a drop in the demand for pork and beef, and indirectly for feed corn as well as for corn-based sweeteners. Overall, net farm income would have fallen slightly, and the cost of government-farm programs would have been increased, mainly due to dairy price supports. Consumers' food costs would have declined, primarily because crop foods are generally cheaper than animal foods, and a shift away from animal foods generally makes for a lower-cost diet.

Significant changes in American agricultural practices would be required if most Americans followed healthier dietary patterns. Without question, the volume, mix, production, and marketing of agricultural commodities would need to be modified.[7] In order to lower dietary fat consumption, the following agricultural shifts would need to take place: (1) significant increase in fruit and vegetable production; (2) smaller increases in cereal production; (3) moderate increases and marked shifts in the mix of dairy products, away from high-fat to low-fat items; (4) shifts in the mix and characteristics of meat products, resulting in production of more poultry and fish and less fatty red meat, and continuing trends to restructure the meat industry to produce animals with lower fat content; and (5) lower fat intake from all sources and a shift in product mix from saturated fats to unsaturated oils.

It is interesting to speculate about such shifts in agricultural production and marketing. To even mention setting such targets implies a shift away from merely regulating the supply side of the food market toward the manipulation of demand. This is a tactic that tends to conflict with the principle of individual freedom of choice and with the free operation of the market, principles that American policy makers have been reluctant and unwilling to tamper with since the first tenets of agricultural policy in this country were established.[8]

A number of countries, particularly the Scandinavian nations of Norway and Sweden, have demonstrated successful ways to promote health by integrating farm, economic, and health policy. Such programs have attempted to improve a country's (or region's) diet through policies that include educational campaigns, increasing the availability of low-fat foods (e.g., fresh fruits, vegetables, breads, pasta), subsidizing production of more "healthful" products (e.g., low-fat milk), limiting conditions of sale (that is, determining when and where certain products may be sold; e.g., not making certain foods available to children at school meals), and shifting demand through pricing policies (e.g., taxing snacks or high-fat foods).

How would these approaches work in this country? Some now think that actions used to control alcohol and tobacco consumption should be generalized and applied to other products, such as high-fat foods. Needless to say, using such policy instruments may meet with a great deal of controversy, especially when they affect individuals' rights to make personal food choices. Many regard these types of policy instruments as an example of using the "heavy hand of government" to influence individual and social behavior.

If the United States were to move to a more health-oriented food policy, what types of policy approaches should be considered in order to encourage more healthful food choices? One option would directly *control the conditions of sale* for foods high in fat, especially in food service operations under direct control of the federal government. For example, this option could be implemented in school feeding programs by requiring school cafeterias to offer tasty and attractive lower-fat alternatives to familiar high-fat foods or prohibiting the sale of high-fat snacks in school-based vending machines.

A second policy alternative would be to use *pricing structures* to influence individual purchasing decisions. Taxation by federal, state, and local governments (the so-called "sin taxes") is currently used to control the sale of potentially harmful products, such as tobacco. Comparing food to tobacco, some experts have already called for taxing "unhealthy" foods, such as those high in fat, then funneling the proceeds into nutrition education and public exercise programs.[9] Further, tax subsidies could be used to encourage production of leaner commodities rather than those with a high dietary fat content. Tax incentives could also be used to encourage restaurants and other food service establishments to offer healthy alternatives to high-fat food items. Obviously, any approaches involving taxation of food would be very controversial!

A third policy option would be to *control advertising and the information* given to consumers about certain food products. This strategy has been used to limit promotion of some products among populations for whom they constitute a health risk. The newly revised Nutrition Facts panel on the food label is an example of this type of policy instrument. Going a step further, advertising could be limited (or made more costly) for foods high in fat, or some type of warning label on these products could be required, such as those now appearing for pregnant women on alcoholic beverage containers.

The fourth type of policy instrument—a frequently used, popular public health strategy—is that of *education*. Educational programs, rather than more direct limitations on behavior or food choices, are preferred by many. The reason many support using educational approaches is that personal freedom to make informed choices is retained, whether or not it actually results in any health-promoting behavior change. However, we must recognize the powerful effect of environmental forces that control personal behavior, ones that using more indirect educational approaches can never remove. In other words, if only high-fat foods are available when people want to consume them, they should recognize the consequences and the probable outcomes associated with those food choices.

This set of policy alternatives was presented to consumers in Minnesota as part of the Minnesota Heart Health Project.[10] The policy instrument ranked highest by respondents (as being the most feasible to implement) were those policies by which the school cafeteria would limit the offering of high-fat foods as well as prohibiting the sale of high-fat foods in school vending machines. Education was also well accepted as a legitimate policy instrument that may be effective to limit high-fat food choices. In general, these consumers preferred policy proposals in which changes in food choices were *offered* to the individual. These respondents certainly did not endorse any limitations or sanctions on food choices that would have occurred by changing the nature of the food supply or other environmental policy strategies, such as taxes. Therefore, the range of federal policies that may be acceptable to the general public may be the most limiting factor of all in implementing a food policy that is based on health outcomes.

Just as providing dietary information alone will not result in changes in dietary behavior, making dietary changes alone will not produce favorable health outcomes in the population. Healthful eating must be a component of total health promotion efforts. Dietary changes are adjuncts to, not substitutes for, a comprehensive system of health promotion, disease prevention, disease treatment, nutrition support, and economic and food assistance measures. Merging agricultural and food production policy concerns with health policy concerns seems to be the most viable approach to ensure success.

Ensuring a Viable Food and Nutrition Policy for the Twenty-first Century

In chapter 1, we introduced four policy issues for the consideration of those who sought to establish nutrition policy. In that discussion, we agreed that there was support for the development and implementation of national nutrition policy that would result in more healthful outcomes for the U.S. population; that the scope of public policy should include both public and private sectors; that policy should be influenced by both "supply side" and "demand" policy instruments; and that an "intersectorial" nutrition policy offered the best chance of success.

Options Worth Pursuing

Several options may be pursued to ensure a viable nutrition (not food!) policy in the years ahead. The basic premise of the book—public policy should ensure that health-promoting food choices are easier to make for consumers—suggests a "macro" approach, a focus on the environment rather than on the individual. These options will be discussed in terms of changing the *structure*, the *products*, and the *process* to take on policy change and ensure its success.

In discussing the development of "options," one is really articulating *how* policy should function. The proper role of government is to allow the market to function effectively and to protect consumers from the vagaries of the marketplace. In the regulatory arena, the playing field should be "leveled" (i.e., while they will probably never have equal resources, those representing public health and consumer concerns must have the same access to policy makers and information as do those representing the food industry.

Structural Changes

Some have suggested making significant *structural changes* to the "machinery" of government. The concept would be to put all congressional authority for food and nutrition issues into only one or two committees in the House and in the Senate. Unfortunately, this proposal probably would never be acceptable to all parties. Advocates now know that they have several committees with authority in the food and health arena; the committee to which legislative initiatives are assigned may be key in ensuring passage.

Likewise, all food and nutrition activities could be consolidated into one agency in the executive branch. Executive branch agencies are known by reputation as entrenched bureaucracies. Despite the political party in power, very little changes at "lower levels" of government by civil service employees (i.e., nonpolitical appointees). Their allegiances are to their peer groups and to the system, not to a political party or to an individual who will be their titular supervisor for only a few years at best. Many have advocated for a single federal agency devoted to *food safety* issues; perhaps it is now time to revisit whether all other federal food and nutrition activities could be consolidated as well.

Focus on Product

Another approach is to focus on the *product* of government policies (e.g., provide incentives to change the food supply, provide information to consumers, and so forth). The government, theoretically, could provide incentives so the food industry could create tasty, low-fat analogs of high-fat food favorites. However, such government intervention no longer is needed; the market already has well compensated the food industry for its efforts in this area. The consumer knows the "low-fat" message well, and when the product is tasty, it will sell. One problem already found is that while such products may be low in fat, they are not "low calorie." Thus, excess calories continue to be a problem for many people in this country as surveys document an increase in obesity.

Another problem is that regulatory agencies are already overwhelmed trying to keep up with the approval process for such foods and novel food ingredients. Certainly, a "let the buyer beware" approach smacks of corporate irresponsibility. Fixing up our food supply with sophisticated new ingredients fits into our national preference for solving problems technologically. But "fixing up" the food supply by adding or subtracting nutrients and food ingredients to guarantee that consumers "cannot go wrong" in their food choices would require a level of regulation that neither producers nor consumers are prepared to accept.[11]

Another "product" that government has the capacity to deliver is providing tasty, low-fat food in their own food services to the military, to workers in "federal" buildings, and of course in programs such as the National School Lunch Program. As our case study on "Reinventing School Lunch" has shown, even this approach is not without built-in problems.

It has been suggested that government should sponsor enhanced informational campaigns or attractive educational materials for consumers, featuring direct, convincing messages about making healthful food choices. Again, beyond consumer awareness of the dangers of high-fat diets, which already seems to be well established, the viability and effectiveness of this approach resulting in sustained behavioral change for *all* consumers—not just the affluent and well-motivated—is questionable.

While I have been disparaging of the results produced by government's recent broad-based, "one-size-fits-all" approach to nutrition education in this discussion, I submit that education is perhaps the only truly feasible, widely acceptable choice to prepare the populace to make well-informed, healthful food choices. Applying new technological fixes in the form of novel new foods is not a strategy that will improve the American diet. If, in fact, education is the only way that American eating habits can be improved, can we afford to ignore this as a policy strategy that must be strongly supported with an eye on demonstrating the efficacy of such efforts? If we're going to rely on nutrition education efforts as the only viable policy option, let's ensure that those efforts are successful!

Process Approaches

The *process* used to move from food-based to nutrition/health-based policies is also important. All voices must be included, not just the powerful or the "loudest." Advocacy coalitions, including public health and consumer groups, have been shown to be articulate, convincing participants in the discussion.

The nature of the content of the policy discussions should also be considered. Newly proposed policies affecting agribusiness, the producers and processors of food (whether by legislation, regulation, or in other forms), should include a "nutritional impact statement" (similar to required "environmental impact statements"). Regulatory policy should require efficacy studies for newly proposed food additives as well as study results that examine product or ingredient safety.

Satisfactory collaborative efforts are likely to be most successful when many different people support the change and believe that their efforts will turn out favorably for them. Coordinated efforts—involving both public and private sectors—are essential. In order to ensure that the American public consumes a more healthful diet, there needs to be a commitment to formulate a coordinated approach to action. Plans should be developed in cooperation with all who are influenced by, or have a special interest in, the outcomes. Development of such a plan will require patience, political skills, and good will on the part of public officials and others involved in the political process. Examples of recent successful efforts are the report "Healthy People 2000: National Health Promotion and Disease Prevention Objectives," and the multisectorial program the National Partnership to Improve the American Diet. Objectives for these comprehensive programs were formulated through a public process that involved federal, state, and local governments, as well as private and voluntary groups, and draft documents were also made available for public comment. Such open and inclusive processes are needed to develop nutrition policy that has the support of all sectors.[12] The problem here, however, is once the document is produced, what then . . . ? Document writers are often frustrated when successful collaborations are thwarted by a lack of sustained interest, funding . . . , and substantive action.

Examples of "Success"

In categorizing the case studies presented in this book as "successes" or "failures," a more useful description, perhaps, might be to see each of these examples along a continuum from "most successful" to "least successful." Among the more "successful" is the revamping of the entire food labeling system. For the first time, through massive legislative and regulatory reform, consumers have straightforward information about nutrient content of the food on the food label as well as this information expressed in the context of standardized serving sizes to make product comparisons easier, and a standardized set of nutrient content descriptor claims so the consumer can "believe" the veracity of such terms. The next hurdle is to focus on improving the process for approving health claims so consumers can get truthful information rather than "product hype."

Moving on down the continuum to cases that exemplify "quasi" successes or failures are the FDA approval of olestra and the development and dissemination of dietary guidance tools, such as the Dietary Guidelines and the Food Guide Pyramid. Consumers are now given information about a food additive that may cause gastric distress on the label of an Olean-containing snack food product; such action would never have taken place if it had not been for the efforts and vigilance of a single consumer advocacy organization.

The Dietary Guidelines and the Food Guide Pyramid are probably a step in the right direction in terms of giving consumers information for making healthful food choices. However, it has been pointed out that the content of nutrition messages may have been compromised so much by input from various organized interests that the messages are too generic and nondirective to consumers to help them make health-promoting food choices. Researchers have examined changes in the types of food contributing fat, saturated fat, and cholesterol between 1977 and 1985 and between 1985 and 1989–90.[13] During the 1977 to 1985 period, the amount of fat, saturated fat, and cholesterol derived from meat products fell substantially, a decline the authors attribute to the effectiveness of government and general information sources.

It is safe to say that the "jury is still out" when judging whether the efforts to "reinvent" the National School Lunch Program have been more or less successful. Although accomplishing nutrient standards limiting the amount of dietary fat in school meals is perhaps more a goal than a reality at this point, regulations (the "machinery of government") have been promulgated by the USDA and are in place. One hopes that current administrators of the NSLP will be forceful advocates in enforcing the existing regulations without delay so that more healthful meals will be served to schoolchildren.

Those who have observed federal policy making for some time remind us that nothing ever "just happens." There is usually a crisis, a long-standing unresolved situation, an individual, or even, a presidential "whim" that starts the policy-making process. In nearly all of the cases that were discussed in this book, the scientific basis for reform was established—the link between dietary fat consumption and the increased risk of certain chronic diseases. What did differ was the role of "policy entrepreneurs" and the various advocacy coalitions that espoused different sides of the issues. Two cases, that of food labeling reform and NSLP reform, had policy entrepreneurs who were "within" the government—FDA Commissioner Kessler for the former, and USDA Undersecretary Haas for the latter. Problems in what the food manufacturer, P&G, thought would be "routine, but delayed" approval for the fat replacer olestra turned out to be a major referendum on the FDA's regulatory process; responsibility (and perhaps the credit) for this can be attributed to a policy entrepreneur outside the government, Dr. Michael Jacobson of the Center for Science in the Public Interest, a consumer advocacy group.

Advocacy coalitions that included experts from the public health community were helpful in articulating the case for reform in nearly all cases discussed, but their effectiveness seemed to depend on the strength of the "opposition" from entrenched bureaucratic interests and from the powerful agribusiness industry. Clearly, a movement has begun in which economic interests of these groups are beginning to be challenged by those in health and consumer groups who espouse views based on "health promotion" and "disease prevention" arguments. In several of the cases discussed, the advocacy coalitions included government bureaucrats. Indeed, the Food Guide Pyramid would never have been released had it not been for health professionals—both in and outside of government—who used the media to reach the general public with their message. In the cases of olestra and school lunch reform, however, one suspects that government bureaucrats were more closely aligned with those groups that were resisting change.

In Summary

Even if all the "desirable" policies that have been promoted throughout the course of this book were to be implemented, which would be most viable in creating an environment in which health-promoting food choices would be easier to make? Which approaches should be adopted when moving from a food-based policy to a nutrition policy that is based on health outcomes? Government policies *can* make it so that health-promoting choices are easier, tastier, more convenient, and no more costly than health-damaging food choices. This is not only possible, it is essential. As Americans we must demand no less!

Notes

Notes to Chapter 1

1. P.A. Sabatier and H.C. Jenkins-Smith, *Policy Change and Learning: An Advocacy Coalition Approach.* Boulder, CO: Westview Press, 1993.

2. The information for this section was obtained from various sources, including: Institute of Food Technologists' Expert Panel on Food Safety and Nutrition, "Fats in the Diet: Why and Where?" *Food Technology*, pp. 115–120, 1986; J.E. Kinsella, "Food Lipids and Fatty Acids: Importance in Food Quality, Nutrition, and Health," *Food Technology*, pp. 124–145, 1988.

3. A. Drewnowski, D.D. Krahn, M.A. Demitrack, K. Nairn, and B.A. Gosnell, "Taste Responses and Preferences for Sweet High-Fat Foods: Evidence for Opiod Involvement," *Physiology & Behavior* 51: 371–379, 1992.

4. A. Drewnowski, "Fats and Food Acceptance," in *Nutrition in the 90s: Current Controversies and Analysis*, ed. G.E. Gaull, F.N. Kotsonis, and M.A. Mackey. New York: Marcel Dekker, 1991, pp. 25–39.

5. Food Marketing Institute, *Trends in the United States: Consumer Attitudes and the Supermarket.* Washington, DC: Food Marketing Institute, 1995.

6. Research reported at the American Association for the Advancement of Science, February 16, 1997, in Seattle, by Dr. Linda Bartoshuk, and reported by S. Blakeslee in "Chocolate Lover or Broccoli Hater? Answer's on the Tip of Your Tongue," *New York Times*, February 18, 1997, p. C2.

7. Food Marketing Institute, *Trends in the United States: Consumer Attitudes and the Supermarket*; Food Marketing Institute and *Prevention* magazine, *Shopping for Health: New Food Labels, Same Eating Habits?* Washington, DC: Food Marketing Institute, 1995; N.M. Childs, "Consumer Attitudes, Concerns, and Confusions Regarding Fats in Their Diet." Presented at the Annual Meeting of the Society for Nutrition Education, St. Louis, July 1996.

8. The Gallup Organization, *How Are Americans Making Food Choices?—1994 Update.* Conducted for American Dietetic Association, Chicago, and International Food Information Council, Washington, DC, 1994.

9. P.R. Thomas, ed., Institute of Medicine, Committee on Dietary Guidelines Implementation, *Improving America's Diet and Health: From Recommendations to Action.* Washington, DC: National Academy Press, 1991, p. 41.

10. M.F. Kuczmarski, A. Moshfegh, and R. Briefel, "Update on Nutrition Monitoring Activities in the U.S.," *Journal of the American Dietetic Association* 94: 753–760, 1994.

11. M. Nestle and C. Woteki, "Trends in American Dietary Patterns: Re-

search Issues and Policy Implications," in *Nutrition and Health: Topics and Controversies*, ed. F. Bronner. Boca Raton, FL: CRC Press, 1995, pp. 16–23.

12. "Results from the 1994 Continuing Survey of Food Intakes by Individuals (CSFII)," *What We Eat in America, 1994–96*. Washington, DC: USDA/Agricultural Research Service, 1996.

13. A.M. Stephen and N.J. Wald, "Trends in Individual Consumption of Dietary Fat in the United States, 1920–1984," *American Journal of Clinical Nutrition* 52: 457, 1990.

14. R.D. Mattes, "Fat Preference and Adherence to a Reduced-Fat Diet," *American Journal of Clinical Nutrition* 57: 373–381, 1993.

15. D.P. Keenan, C. Achterberg, P.M. Kris-Etherton, R. Abu-Sabha, and A. Von Eye, "Use of Qualitative and Quantitative Methods to Define Behavioral Fat-Reduction Strategies and Their Relationship to Dietary Fat Reduction in the Patterns of Dietary Change Study," *Journal of the American Dietetic Association* 96: 1245–1250, 1996.

16. D. St. George, "Fattening of America: Less Is No More," *New York Times*, November 20, 1996, pp. B1, B6; and H. Balzer, "NPD Group's *10th Annual Report on Eating Patterns in America*," presented at Georgetown University, Washington, DC, July 9, 1996.

17. P. Hollingsworth, "The Leaning of the American Diet," *Food Technology*, April 1996, pp. 86–90.

18. B.R. Stillings, "Trends in Foods," *Nutrition Today* 29(5): 6–13, 1994.

19. *Surgeon General's Report on Nutrition and Health*, U.S. Department of Health and Human Services, Public Health Service. Washington, DC: U.S. Government Printing Office, 1988, p. 22.

20. J.M. McGinnis and W.H. Foege, "Actual Causes of Death in the United States," *Journal of the American Medical Association* 270(18): 2207–2212, 1993.

21. *Surgeon General's Report on Nutrition and Health*, p. iii.

22. C.E. Woteki and P.R. Thomas, eds., *Eat for Life*. Washington, DC: National Academy Press, 1992, p. 87.

23. G. Oster and D. Thompson, "Estimated Effects of Reducing Dietary Saturated Fat Intake on the Incidence and Costs of Coronary Heart Disease in the United States," *Journal of the American Dietetic Association* 96(2): 127–131, 1996, and reported in *Tufts University Diet and Nutrition Letter* 14: 3, 1996.

24. Coalition for Nutrition in Health Care Reform, White Paper, "*Rx: Good Nutrition: Putting 'Health' into Health Care Reform*," 1994, p. 3.

25. N. Milio, "A Framework for Prevention: Changing Health-Damaging to Health-Generating Life Patterns," *American Journal of Public Health* 66: 435–439, 1976.

26. N. Milio, *Nutrition Policy for Food-Rich Countries: A Strategic Analysis*. Baltimore: Johns Hopkins University Press, 1990. (See especially chapter 7, "An Assessment of Strategic Effectiveness," pp. 121–130.)

Notes to Chapter 2

1. T.J. Lowi and B. Ginsberg, *American Government: Freedom and Power*, 2nd ed. New York: Norton, 1992, pp. 308–344.

2. C.E. Lindblom, *The Policy-Making Process*. Englewood Cliffs, NJ: Prentice Hall, 1968, p. 4.

3. N. Milio, *Nutrition Policy for Food-Rich Countries*. Baltimore: Johns Hopkins University Press, 1990, p. 1.

4. H.G. Halcrow, *Food Policy for America*. New York: McGraw-Hill, 1977, pp. vii-17.

5. C.A. Lindblom, as quoted in C.O. Jones, *An Introduction to the Study of Public Policy*, 2nd ed. North Scituate, MA: Duxbury Press, 1977, p. 7.

6. C.A. Lindblom, "The Science of 'Muddling Through,' " *Public Administration Review*, spring 1959, p. 86.

7. Lowi and Ginsberg, *American Government*, p. 38.

8. D.M. Welborn, "Conjoint Federalism and Environmental Regulation in the United States," *Publius* 18: 27–43, 1988.

9. The discussion of the public policy process as presented here is drawn from a variety of scholarly sources. Among them are: J.E. Anderson, *Public Policymaking: An Introduction*, 3rd ed. Boston: Houghton Mifflin, 1997; C.E. Cochran, L.C. Mayer, T.R. Carr, and N.J. Cayer, *American Public Policy*. New York: St. Martin's Press, 1990; C.O. Jones, *An Introduction to the Study of Public Policy*, 3rd ed. Monterey, CA: Brooks/Cole, 1984; D.J. Palumbo, *Public Policy in America—Government in Action*. San Diego: Harcourt Brace Jovanovich, 1988.

10. Jones, *Introduction to the Study of Public Policy*.

11. Anderson, *Public Policymaking*.

12. Jones, *Introduction to the Study of Public Policy*, ch. 2.

13. J.W. Kingdon, *Agendas, Alternatives, and Public Policies*, 2nd ed. New York: HarperCollins, 1995.

14. L.S. Sims, "The Ebb and Flow of Nutrition as a Public Policy Issue," *Journal of Nutrition Education* 15(4): 132–136, 1983; A. Downs, "Up and Down with Ecology—The "Issue-Attention Cycle," *Public Interest* 28: 38, 1972.

15. N. Chapman, "Consensus and Coalitions: Key to Nutrition Policy Development," *Nutrition Today* 22: 22, 1987.

16. Cochran et al., *American Public Policy*.

17. Various permutations of these policy types have been described, first by Theodore Lowi in the paper "Four Systems of Policy Politics and Choice," *Public Administration Review* 33: 298–310, 1972 (July–August). Randall Ripley and Grace Franklin describe four types of domestic policy: (1) distributive, (2) competitive regulatory, (3) protective regulatory, and (4) redistributive, in their 1991 book *Congress, the Bureaucracy, and Public Policy*, 5th ed. Belmont, CA: Wadsworth. In a more recent text, Lowi includes a description of "promotional techniques" that have relevance to our discussion of food and nutrition policy. (Lowi and Ginsberg, 1992. *American Government*, pp. 309–312.)

18. Ripley and Franklin, *Congress, Bureaucracy, and Public Policy*, pp. 17, 20.

19. J. Pressman and A. Wildavsky, *Implementation*, 3rd ed. Berkeley: University of California Press, 1984, pp. xii-xiii.

20. P.M. Hyman, "The Regulators," *Food Technology* 31: 43, 1977.

21. B.W. Mintz and N.G. Miller, *A Guide to Federal Agency Rulemaking*, 2nd ed. Washington, DC: Administrative Conference of the United States, 1991.

22. C. Skrzycki, "The Rise of 'Neg-Reg': Finding Common Ground in the Middle of the Table," *Washington Post*, February 23, 1996, pp. B1, 2.

23. M.A. Peterson, "Congress in the 1990s: From Iron Triangles to Policy Networks," in *The Politics of Health Care Reform: Lessons from the Past, Prospects*

for the Future, ed. J.A. Morone and G.S. Belkin. Durham, NC: Duke University Press, 1994, pp. 103–147.

24. J.A. Thurber, "Dynamics of Policy Subsystems in American Politics," in *Interest Group Politics*, 3rd ed., ed. A.J. Cigler and B.A. Loomis. Washington, DC: Congressional Quarterly Press, 1991.

25. H.D. Lasswell, *Politics: Who Gets What, When, and How*. New York: McGraw-Hill, 1936.

26. G. Wasserman, *The Basics of American Politics*, 2nd ed. Boston: Little, Brown, 1976, pp. 3–11.

27. P.A. Sabatier and H.C. Jenkins–Smith, eds., *Policy Change and Learning: An Advocacy Coalition Approach*. Boulder, CO: Westview Press, 1993.

Notes to Chapter 3

1. W.P.T. James, *Healthy Nutrition: Preventing Nutrition-Related Diseases in Europe*. Copenhagen: World Health Organization, Regional Office for Europe. WHO Regional Publications, European Series, no. 24, 1988.

2. E. Helsing, "Nutrition Policies in Europe—The State of the Art," *European Journal of Clinical Nutrition* 43: 57–66, 1989.

3. L.S. Sims, "Public Policy in Nutrition: A Framework for Action," *Nutrition Today* 28(2): 10–20, 1993.

4. L.S. Sims, "Nutrition Policy through the Reagan Era: Feast or Famine?" Presented at the Pew/Cornell Lecture Series on Food and Nutrition Policy. Ithaca, NY: Cornell University, November 1, 1988.

5. J.E. Austin and C. Hitt, *Nutrition Intervention in the United States*. Cambridge, MA: Ballinger Books, 1979, p. 356.

6. N. Milio, *Nutrition Policy for Food-Rich Countries: A Strategic Analysis*. Baltimore: Johns Hopkins University Press, 1990, pp. 155–172.

7. D.J. Palumbo, *Public Policy in America—Government in Action*. San Diego: Harcourt Brace Jovanovich, 1988, p. 17.

8. M. Lipton and E. deKadt, *Agriculture–Health Linkages*. Geneva: World Health Organization, 1988.

9. P.B. Hutt, "National Nutrition Policy and the Role of the Food and Drug Administration," *Currents* 2: 2, 1988.

10. H.G. Halcrow, *Food Policy for America*. New York: McGraw-Hill, 1977, pp. 2–5.

11. P.B. Hutt, "A Brief History of FDA Regulation Relating to the Nutrient Content of Food," in *Nutrition Labeling Handbook*, ed. R. Shapiro. New York: Marcel Dekker, 1995.

12. U.S. Department of Health and Human Services, *The Surgeon General's Report on Nutrition and Health*. U.S. Public Health Service Pub. no. 88–50210. Washington, DC: U.S. Government Printing Office, 1988.

13. National Research Council, National Academy of Sciences, *Diet and Health: Implications for Reducing Chronic Disease Risk*. Washington, DC: National Academy Press, 1989.

14. APHA Technical Report, "Public Health Policy-Making in the Presence of Incomplete Evidence," *American Journal of Public Health* 80(6): 746–750, 1990.

15. J.R. Marshall, "Editorial: Improving Americans' Diets—Setting Public Policy

with Limited Knowledge," *American Journal of Public Health* 85: 1609–1611, 1995.

16. "New Names, New Sizes for Panels," *Congressional Quarterly*, December 17, 1994.

17. T.L. Schmid, M. Pratt, and E. Howze, "Policy as Intervention: Environmental and Policy Approaches to the Prevention of Cardiovascular Disease," *American Journal of Public Health* 85(9): 1207–1211, 1995.

18. J.M. Hansen, *Gaining Access: Congress and the Farm Lobby, 1919–1981*. Chicago: University of Chicago Press, 1991, pp. 1–8.

19. G. Browning, "Sagging Aggies," *National Journal* 24(8): 452–455, 1992.

20. "Milking the Government," (editorial) *Washington Post*, December 14, 1995, p. A22.

21. G. Gugliotta and B. Vobejda, "Hill Action on Food Programs Reflects Disparity of Influence," *Washington Post*, November 29, 1995, p. A4.

22. M. Nestle, "Food Lobbies, the Food Pyramid, and U.S. Nutrition Policy," *International Journal of Health Services* 23(3): 483–496, 1993.

23. Sabatier and Jenkins–Smith, *Policy Change and Learning: An Advocacy Coalition Approach.*

24. W.H. Stewart, "The Use of Government to Protect and Promote the Health of the Public through Nutrition," *Federation Proceedings* 38(12): 2557–2559, 1979.

25. A term coined to describe "those nations with sufficient resources to provide their entire population with a healthy diet." From Milio, *Nutrition Policy*, p. 3.

26. J. Schmandt, R.A. Shorey, and L. Kinch, *Nutrition Policy in Transition*. Lexington, MA: Lexington Books, D.C. Heath, 1980, pp. 3–22.

27. Milio, *Nutrition Policy*, p. 16.

Notes to Case Study 1

1. Excerpted portions of the law as cited in J.E. Austin and C. Hitt, *Nutrition Intervention in the United States*. Cambridge, MA: Ballinger, 1979, p. 93.

2. Food Research and Action Center (FRAC), *Fact Sheets on the Federal Food Programs*. Washington, DC: FRAC, 1991.

3. "The ABCs of Federally Funded Programs for Kids," *Health Care Food & Nutrition Focus* 13(4): 1996, reprinted in *The Digest*, Chicago, IL: The American Dietetic Association, winter 1997, pp. 1, 6.

4. P.L. Splett, "Federal Food Assistance Programs: A Step to Food Security for Many," *Nutrition Today*, March–April 1994, pp. 6–13.

5. Statistics provided by the U.S. Department of Agriculture, Food and Consumer Service, 1996.

6. L.S. Sims, chapter 12, "Public Policy and Legislation," pp. 286–327. In *Nutrition in the Community: The Art of Delivering Services*, ed. R.T. Frankle and A.L. Owen, 3rd ed. St. Louis: Mosby–Year Book, 1993, p. 311.

7. *Empty Calories: The Reagan Record on Food Policy*. Washington, DC: Public Voice for Food and Health Policy, 1988.

8. *Eating Less Fat: A Progress Report on Improving America's Diet*. Washington, DC: Institute for Science in Society, February 1992.

9. E.L. Wee, "Dissing the Salmon: Schools Can't Sell USDA's Delicacies," *Washington Post*, October 30, 1994, pp. B1, 3.

10. D. Maraniss and M. Weisskopf, "Food Program Defender Becomes a Dis-

mantler: Nutrition Program's Champion Accepts a New Direction," *Washington Post*, April 4, 1995, pp. A1, 8.

11. "House Panel Approves GOP Plan Eliminating National Nutrition Programs," *CNI Nutrition Week* 25(8): 1–2, February 24, 1995.

12. R.L. Kerr, "The National School Lunch Program and Diets of Participants from Low-Income Households," CNC(ADM.)359, USDA/Consumer Nutrition Center, 1981.

13. S. Hanes, J. Vermeersch, and S. Gale, "The National Evaluation of School Nutrition Programs: Program Impact on Dietary Intake," *American Journal of Clinical Nutrition* 40: 390–413, 1984.

14. Citizens' Commission on School Nutrition, "White Paper on School Lunch Nutrition." Washington, DC: Center for Science in the Public Interest, December 1990.

15. L.M. Grossman, "Surplus Food Said to Lower School Lunch Nutritional Value," *Washington Post*, August 26, 1988, p. A13.

16. J. Shotland, "What's for Lunch? A Progress Report on Reducing Fat in the School Lunch Program." Washington, DC: Public Voice for Food and Health Policy, September 1989.

17. P.M. Morris, "What's for Lunch? II: A 1990 Survey of Options in the School Lunch Program." Washington, DC: Public Voice for Food and Health Policy, September 1990.

18. P.M. Morris, "Heading for a Health Crisis: Eating Patterns of America's School Children." Washington, DC: Public Voice for Food and Health Policy, September 1991.

19. P.M. Morris, "Agriculture First: Nutrition, Commodities and the National School Lunch Program." Washington, DC: Public Voice for Food and Health Policy, September 1992.

20. S. Rich and M. Gladwell, "USDA Targets Fat in School Lunches," *Washington Post*, September 12, 1991, p. A8.

21. J. Burghardt and B. Devaney, "The School Nutrition Dietary Assessment Study: Summary of Findings." Princeton, NJ: Mathematica Policy Research, October 1993.

22. N. Chapman, A.R. Gordon, and J.A. Burghardt, "Factors Affecting the Fat Content of National School Lunch Program Lunches," *American Journal of Clinical Nutrition* 61 (Suppl): 1995–2045, 1995.

23. "School Lunches Found High in Sodium, Fat in USDA Study," *Food Chemical News*, November 1, 1993, p. 41.

24. Letter written by Ellen Haas to prospective hearings participants, U.S. Department of Agriculture, September 1993.

25. "Bill Encourages Child Health & Nutrition," *CNI Nutrition Week*, October 22, 1993, p. 2; L. Michaelis, "Nutrition Programs OK'd by Panel," *CQ Weekly Report* 52(5): 1723, June 25, 1994.

26. R.M. Wells, "Panel Reauthorizes Lunch Program," *CQ Weekly Report* 52(18): 1130, May 7, 1994.

27. J.L. Katz, "School Lunch Program Boosted in Committee Vote," *CQ Weekly Report* 52(20): 1310, May 21, 1994.

28. L. Shapiro with T. Namuth, "Fat Times at Ridgemont High," *Newsweek*, November 8, 1993, p. 75.

29. U.S. Department of Agriculture/Food and Consumer Services, "USDA Announces Proposed Health Standards for School Meal Programs," press release, June 8, 1994.

30. "Proposal Limits Fat in School Lunches," *CQ Weekly Report* 52(23): 1533, June 11, 1994.

31. USDA, press release, June 8, 1994.

32. "USDA Proposes National Overhaul of School Meal Nutrition Requirements," *CNI Nutrition Week* 24(2): 1–2, June 10, 1994.

33. "Access and Nutrition Key Parts of New Bill," *CNI Nutrition Week*, October 14, 1994, pp. 4–5.

34. "Child Nutrition Renewals Address New Guidelines," *CQ Weekly Report* 52(39): 2893, October 8, 1994.

35. "USDA Proposes," *CNI Nutrition Week*.

36. "USDA Finalizes School Food Dietary Guidelines," *CNI Nutrition Week*, June 16, 1995, p. 3.

37. U.S. Department of Agriculture/Food and Consumer Service, "Team Nutrition," press announcement, June 15, 1995.

38. "USDA Launches School Meal Initiative with Fanfare," *CNI Nutrition Week*, June 16, 1995, p. 3.

39. U.S. Department of Agriculture, "Tri-Agency Commodity Specification Review Report: Improving USDA Commodities." Washington, DC: USDA, October 1995.

40. C. Sugarman, "Building a Better School Lunch: USDA Orders Less Fat, Salt in Program Foods," *Washington Post*, Health section, October 24, 1995, p. 16.

41. U.S. Department of Agriculture, Food and Consumer Service, Food Distribution Division, "Commodity Close-Up" and "Spotlight on Commodities" brochures, 1995.

42. "Department of Agriculture Cuts the Fat Out of More Foods in School Lunches," *CNI Nutrition Week*, October 27, 1995, pp. 1, 6.

43. *Congressional Record*, H.R. 2066, May 14, 1996, pp. H4910–4913.

44. "Congress Allows Schools 'Any Reasonable Approach' to Meet Dietary Guidelines," *CNI Nutrition Week*, May 17, 1996, pp. 1, 6; "School Lunch Amendment Gives Secretary Final Word," *CNI Nutrition Week*, May 24, 1996, p. 3.

45. "School Lunch Amendment," p. 3.

46. E. Schmitt, "Agriculture Dept. Rebuffed on School Lunches," *New York Times*, May 15, 1996, p. A17.

47. *Congressional Record*, May 14, 1996, p. H4912.

48. Ibid.

49. "School Food Officials to Implement New Standards," *CNI Nutrition Week*, March 8, 1996, p. 2.

50. "Former ASFSA Head May Vote Dole Because of Haas," *CNI Nutrition Week*, June 7, 1996, p. 8.

51. Several news columns discussed comparable issues; these included: M. Burros, "A Critic of Federal Food Policy Is on the Inside," "Eating Well" column, *New York Times*, June 23, 1993, p. C4; C. Sugarman, "From Adversary to Appointee at Agriculture; Nutrition Advocate Now Heads Programs She Often Criticized," *Washington Post*, October 4, 1993, p. A17; S. Pratt and W. Rice, "It's a Long Road toward Better Menus, Though Some Schools Have Caught On," *Chicago Tribune*, November 18, 1993, p. C1.

52. K. Baar, "School Lunches: When They Love Even the Greens," *New York Times*, September 3, 1997, pp. C1, 5.

53. First, an article appeared condemning Team Nutrition for the purchase of im-

printed polo shirts, which had been distributed with stringent guidelines about their use. Haas was called to task for "wholly inappropriate expenditure of taxpayer dollars and a serious error in judgment on the part of the persons responsible for Team Nutrition." (B. McAllister, "USDA's Clothes Call: Ensuring 'Team Nutrition' Doesn't Lose Its Shirts," *Washington Post*, October 6, 1995, p. A23.) Less than a week later, the same reporter was back with another article, this time supporting the criticism levied by Congressman Bill Emerson (R-Missouri), who chastised Haas for approving an expenditure of $400,000 for the use of two "spokestoons" from the Disney film *The Lion King* to promote school lunches. (B. McAllister, "Disney School Lunch 'Spokestoons' Leave Lawmaker with Sour Taste," *Washington Post*, October 9, 1995, p. A25.) To make matters worse, this article was then editorialized in the paper several days later. ("Cartoon Meals," editorial, *Washington Post*, October 12, 1995.) Haas defended the department's use of the "spokestoons," saying, "[T]hey speak to children in a language they understand and in a medium they understand, television." (A. Kamen, "$400,000 Talks, in Any Language," "In the Loop" column, *Washington Post*, October 15, 1995, p. A19.)

54. Haas was called to testify before the House Agriculture Committee (with Republican Pat Roberts of Kansas as chair) on the matter of authorizing focus groups run by a Democratic pollster, a questioning that lasted more than five hours. (Using taxpayer money for political purposes is definitely prohibited for federal bureaucrats.) In addition to questioning Haas's administration of the major food assistance programs, Representative Roberts raised questions about the letting of USDA subcontracts and personnel decisions. All of the following reports carried basically the same information: B. McAllister, "GAO Faults Pollster's Contract," *Washington Post*, May 9, 1996, P. A21; A. Kamen, "Having the Nutrition Chief for Lunch," "In the Loop" column, *Washington Post*, May 10, 1996, p. A25; "GAO: Haas' Agency Used 'Questionable Judgment,' and Haas Intimidated Staff," *CNI Nutrition Week*, May 10, 1996, pp. 1–2. Also, the *New York Times* published a particularly onerous editorial criticizing Haas's style: "How to Harm Food Stamps," *New York Times*, May 17, 1996, p. A23.

55. " . . . and now," editorial, *Washington Times*, September 29, 1996, p. B-2.

56. S. Fritz, "Controversies Crop Up around Agriculture Official," *Los Angeles Times*, October 5, 1996, p. 14; C. Sugarman and S. Squires, "Embattled Agriculture Official to Announce Her Resignation," *Washington Post*, January 16, 1997, p. A19.

Notes to Part III

1. Unless otherwise noted, all statistics are from: U.S. Department of Agriculture/National Agricultural and Statistics Service. *Agricultural Statistics, 1995–96*. Washington, DC: U.S. Government Printing Office, 1995.

2. "Spotlight on the U.S. Food System," *FoodReview*, May/August 1995, p. 1.

3. Geoffrey Becker, Congressional Research Service. Personal Communication, October 29, 1996.

4. H. Elitzak, "Food Marketing Costs Increased in 1994." *FoodReview*, May/August 1995, pp. 20–23.

5. *Kiplinger Agriculture Letter*, Washington, DC: The Kiplinger Washington Editors, Inc., February 3, 1995; September 15, 1995; October 27, 1995.

6. N. Milio, *Promoting Health through Public Policy*, p. 147.

7. S.W. Martinez and A. Reed, "Expansion of Concentration in the Food Industry Raises Policy Concerns," *CNI Nutrition Week*, September 27, 1996, pp. 4–5;

A. Barkema, M. Drabenstott, and K. Welch, "The Quiet Revolution in the U.S. Food Market," *Economic Review*, May/June 1991, pp. 25–37.

Notes to Chapter 4

1. L. Myers, "Food Consumption Data Needs for Food and Agricultural Policy," *Journal of Nutrition*, 1994, pp. 1853S-1859S.
2. G.S. Becker, "An Introduction to Farm Commodity Programs," *CRS Report for Congress*, No. 96–782 ENR, September 20, 1996.
3. R.L. Thompson, "The Impact of Budget and Tax Policy on Agriculture and Agribusiness: The American Experience," Presented at the Conference on Food and Agrarian Policy, Moscow, March 13–14, 1996.
4. J. Ben-Joseph, "Examining the New Farm Bill," *Nutrition Notes*, June 1996, pp. 3–4; E. Schmitt, "House Approves Biggest Change in Farm Policy Since New Deal," *New York Times*, March 1, 1996, pp. A1, A25; J.B. Penn, "End of the 'Agriculture Era,'" *Choices*, First Quarter, 1996, p. 1; G. Gigliotta, "Senate Passes $46 Billion Farm Bill," *Washington Post*, February 8, 1996, pp. A1, A7; G. Gugliotta, "House, 270–255, Passes $46 Billion Farm Bill," *Washington Post*, March 1, 1996, p. A6; "Conservation Initiatives in the Farm Bill: The Ambivalent Agriculture Committees," *Ag Committee Watch* 1(1): 1, 4, June 1996. Washington, DC: Public Voice for Food and Health Policy.
5. See, for example, D. Rapp, *How the U.S. Got into Agriculture . . . And Why It Can't Get Out*. Washington, DC: Congressional Quarterly, 1988.
6. J.L. Vetter, *Food Laws and Regulations*. Manhattan, KS: American Institute of Baking, 1996, pp. 1–23.
7. D.P. Blaney, J.J. Miller, and R.P. Stillman, *Dairy: Background for 1995 Farm Legislation* (AER-705). Washington, DC: U.S. Department of Agriculture/Economic Research Service, 1995.
8. National Research Council, Committee on Technological Options to Improve the Nutritional Attributes of Animal Products, *Designing Foods: Animal Product Options in the Marketplace*. Washington, DC: National Academy Press, 1988.
9. M. Nestle and C. Woteki, "Trends in American Dietary Patterns: Research Issues and Policy Implications," in *Nutrition and Health: Topics and Controversies*, ed. F. Bronner. Boca Raton, FL: CRC Press, 1995, pp. 1–44.
10. U.S. Department of Agriculture, Economic Research Service, *1995 Dairy Yearbook*. Washington, DC: U.S. Department of Agriculture, December 1995.
11. P. O'Brien, "Diet, Health and Agriculture," *U.S. Public Policy and the American Diet*. Washington, DC: National Planning Association, September 1995.
12. USDA, *1995 Dairy Yearbook*.
13. D.L. Pelletier, A. Kendall, and A. Mathios, *Lowfat Milk Promotion: Opportunities Created by a New Policy Environment*. Ithaca, NY: Cornell University, January 1996.
14. USDA, *1995 Dairy Yearbook*.
15. This discussion is based on several references, including: Blaney et al. ,*Dairy: Background for 1995 Farm Legislation*, p. 20; A.C. Manchester, *The Public Role in the Dairy Economy: Why and How Governments Intervene in the Milk Business*. Boulder, CO: Westview Press, 1983; R. Fallert and D. Blaney, "U.S. Dairy Programs," *National Food Review*. 13(1): 41, 1990.

16. U.S. Department of Agriculture, Farm Service Agency, *Commodity Fact Sheet*, Washington, DC: USDA, August 1996.

17. USDA, *1995 Dairy Yearbook*.

18. This discussion is based on a number of references, including the following: R. Fallert and D. Blaney, "U.S. Dairy Programs," *National Food Review*, 13(1): 41, 1990; A.C. Manchester, *The Public Role in the Dairy Economy: Why and How Governments Intervene in the Milk Business*. Boulder, CO: Westview Press, 1983; M.A. Marchant, *Political Economic Analysis of U.S. Dairy Policies and European Community Dairy Policy Comparisons*. New York: Garland Publishing, 1993.

19. Food and Agricultural Policy Research Institute, *Impacts of Commodity Program Elimination on the U.S. Dairy Sector*. Working Paper 5–95. Washington, DC, April 1995.

20. Blaney, et al., *Dairy: Background for 1995 Farm Legislation*. Washington, DC: USDA, 1994.

21. D.L. Pelletier et al., *Low Fat Milk Promotion*, 1996.

22. USDA, *1995 Dairy Yearbook*, pp. 10–11.

23. "U.S. Appetite for Meat Continues to Grow: USDA," *CNI Nutrition Week*. March 17, 1995, p. 6.

24. "Genetics Impact Marbling," *National Cattlemen*, September 1989, p. 16.

25. K. Bost, "Are Consumers Getting What They Want?" *Agricultural Outlook Forum*, February 25, 1997.

26. B. Browning, *The Trail of Two Burgers*. Snowmass, CO: Rocky Mountain Institute Agriculture Program, 1990.

27. F. Martz, J. Gerrish, K. Moore, and V. Tate, *Pasture-based Beef Finishing*. Columbia, MO: Forage Systems Research Center, n.d.

28. B. Liebman, "Brand-Name Lean Beef: Is It Worth It?" *Nutrition Action Healthletter*, October 1986, pp. 6–7; M. Burros, "Brand-Name Lean Beef: Is It Really Better?" *New York Times*, January 31, 1990, p. C1; "Laura's Lean Beef: Ten Years of Growing a Branded Beef Product Dedicated to All Natural Beef," *Feed-Lot*, June/July/August 1996, pp. 6–7.

29. "Four Major Beef Industry Associations May Merge," *CNI Nutrition Week*, March 17, 1995, p. 6.

30. "The Cattlemen's War on Fat," promotional sheet distributed by the National Cattlemen's Association, November 1993.

31. A. Forman, "Meat Debate Sizzles as Opponents Face Off Over Role in Diet," *Environmental Nutrition* 18(1): 1, 6, January 1995.

32. A. Cockburn, "On Meat Street: The Dark Side of Our Fetish for Flesh," *Washington Post*, April 21, 1996, p. C3.

33. J. Rifkin, *Beyond Beef: The Rise and Fall of the Cattle Culture*. New York: Dutton, 1992.

34. "Beyond Beef Targets Unsustainable Practices," *CNI Nutrition Week*, March 20, 1992, pp. 4–5; E.N. Carney and P. Starobin, "From the K Street Corridor," *National Journal* 24(16): 948, April 18, 1992.

35. N.D. Barnard, A. Nicholson, and J.L. Howard, "The Medical Costs Attributable to Meat Consumption," *Preventive Medicine* 24: 646–655, 1995.

36. J.F. Guthrie and N. Raper, "Animal Products: Their Contribution to a Balanced Diet," *FoodReview* 15(1): 29–34, 1992.

37. C. Sagon, "Chain Reaction," *Washington Post*, April 30, 1997, p. E1.

38. Nestle and Woteki, "Trends in American Dietary Patterns," 1995.

39. This section is based on the following references: J. Giese, "Fats, Oils, and Fat Replacers," *Food Technology* 50(4): 78–83, 1996; C. Martinsen-Brannon, "Good Chemistry: How Form Shapes Function in Food Oils," *Journal of the American Dietetic Association* 91: 777–778, 1991; S. Schmidt, "Just the Oil Facts," *Nutrition Action* 21(2): 12–13, 1994; "Sorting Out the Facts about Fat," *IFIC Review*, March 1993; C. Sugarman, "So You've Given Up Palm and Coconut Oil?" *Washington Post*, Health section, June 9, 1992, p. 20.

40. This section is based largely on information contained in the following references: N. Morgan, "World Vegetable Oil Consumption Expands and Diversifies," *FoodReview* 16(2): 26–30, 1993; M. Ash, G. Douvelis, J. Castaneda, and N. Morgan, *Oilseeds: Background for 1995 Farm Legislation*. (AER-715), Washington, DC: U.S. Department of Agriculture, Economic Research Service, 1995.

41. "Global Trends in the Availability of Edible Fats and Oils," in *Fats and Oils in Human Nutrition: Report of a FAO/WHO Joint Expert Consultation*, chapter 4. Rome: Food and Agriculture Organization, 1993, pp. 25–32.

For Further Consideration

42. "Fat and Oil Groups Agree to Bury Hatchet," *CNI Nutrition Week* 21(3): 7, August 24, 1989.

43. L. Jaroff, "A Crusader from the Heartland," *Time*, March 25, 1991, pp. 56–58. Sugarman, "So You've Given Up."

44. Sugarman, "So You've Given Up."

Notes to Chapter 5

1. B. Senauer, E. Asp, and J. Kinsey, *Food Trends and the Changing Consumer*. St. Paul, MN: Eagan Press, 1991, p. 285.

2. A.E. Gallo, "Food Marketing Sales, Mergers, and New Product Introductions Rose in 1994," *FoodReview*, May/August 1995, pp. 24–25.

3. H. Balzer, *NPD Group's 10th Annual Report on Eating Patterns in America*. Presented in Washington, DC, at Georgetown University, July 9, 1996.

4. P. Hollingsworth, "The Leaning of the American Diet," *Food Technology*, 50(4): 86, 88, 90, 1996.

5. B.R. Stillings, "Trends in Foods," *Nutrition Today* 29(5): 6–13, 1994.

6. Background information for this section was drawn from the following references: J. Giese, "Fats, Oils, and Fat Replacers," *Food Technology* 50(4): 78–84, 1996; Position of the American Dietetic Association, "Fat Replacements," *Journal of the American Dietetic Association* 91(10): 1285–1288, 1991; R. Kosmark, "Calatrim: Properties and Applications," *Food Technology* 50(4): 98–101, 1996; P. Kurtzweil, "Taking the Fat Out of Food," *FDA Consumer* 30(6): 7–13, 1996; "Fats and Fat Replacers," *Food Insight*, September/October 1995, pp. 1, 4–5; A.M. Miraglio, "Nutrient Substitutes and Their Energy Values in Fat Substitutes and Replacers," *American Journal of Clinical Nutrition* 62(suppl): 1175S–1179S, 1995.

7. F.M. Clydesdale, "Meeting the Needs of the Elderly with the Foods of Today and Tomorrow," *Nutrition Today* 26(5): 13–20, 1991.

8. Further discussion of this topic may be found in: J.V. Rodricks, "Safety

Assessment of New Food Ingredients," *Food Technology* 50(3): 114–117, 1996; P.B. Hutt, "Approval of Food Additives in the United States: A Bankrupt System," *Food Technology* 50(3): 118–122, 1996; J.L. Vetter, *Food Laws and Regulations*. Manhattan, KS: American Institute of Baking (see especially Chapter 6, "Food Additives and Other Substances Used in Foods," pp. 115–149), 1996.

9. Hutt, "Approval of Food Additives."

10. Stillings, "Trends in Foods," p. 12.

11. "New Fat Replacer Promises No Unpleasant Side Effects," *Washington Post*, August 26, 1996, p. A6; "USDA Develops Fat Replacer," *Nutrition and the M.D.*, November 1996, p. 7.

Notes to Case Study 2

1. C. Sugarman, "Food Scientists Fake the Flavor and Feel of Fat," *Washington Post*, January 11, 1995, p. H8.

2. S. Squires, "FDA Decision Nears on Fat Substitute," *Washington Post*, Health section, January 23, 1996, pp. 8–9.

3. This discussion is based on a number of sources, including the following: Final rule: Food additives permitted for direct addition to food for human consumption; olestra. [Docket No. 87F-0179], 21CFR Part 172, *Federal Register* 61(20): 3118–3173; J.E. Vanderveen and W.H. Glinsmann, "Fat Substitutes: A Regulatory Perspective," *Annual Review of Nutrition* 12: 473–487, 1992; General Accounting Office, *FDA Premarket Approval. Process of Approving Olestra as a Food Additive*. GAO/HRD-92–86, Washington, DC: General Accounting Office, 1992, pp. 1–10; H. Blackburn, "Olestra and the FDA," *New England Journal of Medicine* 334(15): 984–986, 1996.

4. This discussion basically follows the points made in the following paper: J.E. Vanderveen and W.H. Glinsmann, "Fat Substitutes: A Regulatory Perspective," *Annual Review of Nutrition* 12: 473–487, 1992.

5. Vanderveen and Glinsmann, "Fat Substitutes," p. 477.

6. H. Rept. No. 2284, 85th Congress, 2nd sess. 4–5 (1958). Accord: S. Rept. No. 2422, 85th Congress, 2nd session. 2 (1958).

7. Vanderveen and Glinsmann, "Fat Substitutes," p. 481.

8. Ibid.

9. The discussion for this section, which covers the time period from 1971 to 1992, largely follows the account described in the following report: General Accounting Office, *FDA Premarket Approval. Process of Approving Olestra as a Food Additive*, GAO/HRD-92–86, Washington, DC: General Accounting Office, 1992, pp. 1–10.

10. "Letting the Chips Fall Where They May," *Tufts University Diet and Nutrition Letter* 14(1): 2–3, 1996.

11. "Congress Urged Not to Approve Olestra Patent Extension," *Food Chemical News*, January 6, 1992, p. 42.

12. Blackburn, "Olestra and the FDA," p. 984.

13. M.F. Jacobson, "Fake Food, Real Problems," *New York Times*, February 19, 1988.

14. R. Narisetti, "Anatomy of a Food Fight: The Olestra Debate," *Wall Street Journal*, 1996, pp. B1, B8; "Uh-oh-Olestra," *CNI Nutrition Week*, May 17, 1996, p. 1.

15. M. Burros, "Food Heroes or Zealots?" *New York Times*, May 29, 1996, pp. C1, C6.

16. C. Sugarman, "FDA Begins Review of Oily Calorie Cutter," *Washington Post*, November 13, 1995, p. A3.

17. Blackburn, "Olestra and the FDA," pp. 984–985.

18. "Letting the Chips Fall Where They May."

19. Sugarman, "Food Scientists."

20. J.W. Suttie and A.C. Ross, eds., "Assessment of the Nutritional Effects of Olestra," *Journal of Nutrition* 127(85): 1539S–1728S, 1997.

21. R. Frank, "Frito Lay and Olestra," *Wall Street Journal*, May 31, 1996, pp. A3, 4.

22. Narisetti, "Anatomy of a Food Fight."

23. Ibid.

24. M. Burros, "Consumer Group Cites Illnesses in Urging Ban of Fat Substitute," *New York Times*, July 2, 1996, p. C6; "Group Wants Fat Substitute Off Shelves." *The Washington Post*, July 2, 1996, p. A13.

25. M. Burros, "An Olestra Chip Taste Test: 7 Who Dared," *New York Times*, January 31, 1996, p. C2; J.B. Klis, "FDA Approves Fat Substitute, Olestra," *Food Technology*, February 1996, p. 124; "Olestra Taste-Test," *New Woman*, May 1996, p. 84; N. Hellmich, "Taste-Testing Olestra Chips," *USA Today*, July 12, 1996, p. A12.

26. P.A. Sabatier and H.C. Jenkins-Smith, eds., *Policy Change and Learning. An Advocacy Coalition Approach*. Boulder, CO: Westview Press, 1993.

27. C. Hassall, Procter & Gamble, personal communication, March 7, 1997.

28. K. McNutt, "Letter to the Editor," *Nutrition Today* 32(3): 137, May/June 1997.

29. P.R. Thomas, "Olestra: Another Technological Fix for the Food Supply," *Journal of Nutrition Education* 28: 193–194, 1996.

30. K. McNutt, "What's Bothering Olestra Opponents?" *Nutrition Today* 32(1): 41–45, 1997.

Notes to Chapter 6

1. *The Kiplinger Agriculture Newsletter*. Washington, DC: The Kiplinger Washington Editors, Inc., September 1994.

2. *The Beef Handbook—Nutrition and Health*. Washington, DC: The National Cattlemen's Beef Association, 1996.

3. J.R. Romans, W.J. Costello, C.W. Carlson, M.L. Greaser, and K.W. Jones, *The Meat We Eat*, 13th ed. Danville IL: Interstate Publishers, 1994. (See chapter 12, "Federal Meat Grading and Its Interpretations," pp. 359–463.)

4. U.S. Department of Agriculture, Agricultural Marketing Service, "Official United States Standards for Grades of Carcass Beef," Title 7, Chapter 1, Pt. 54, Sec. 54.102–54.107, *Code of Federal Regulations*; amendments effective January 31, 1997.

5. Romans et al., *The Meat We Eat*, pp. 461–463.

6. *The Beef Handbook*.

7. G. Clarke and J.W. Wise, "USDA Adopts "Select" Beef Grade Name," *National Food Review*, January–March 1988, pp. 26–27.

8. Romans et al., *The Meat We Eat*, p. 408.

9. U.S. Department of Agriculture, Agriculture Marketing Service, "Official United States Standards for Grades of Carcass Beef," Title 7, Chapter 1, pt. 54 sec. 54.102–54.107, Code of Federal Regulations; amendments effective January 31, 1997.

10. USDA National Steer and Heifer Estimated Grading Percent Report, for week ending February 8, 1997.

11. *The Beef Handbook.*

12. Romans et al., *The Meat We Eat*, pp. 459–460.

13. B. Liebman, "Where's the Beef Labeling?" *Nutrition Action Healthletter* 24(5): 8–10, 1997.

14. M. Burros, "So How Should the Labels Read on Ground Beef?" *New York Times*, June 1, 1994, p. C4; *Federal Register*, May 24, 1994, p. 26916, Docket 93–030P.

15. As quoted in *CNI Nutrition Week*, July 8, 1994, p. 7.

16. Personal correspondence with the American Dietetic Association regarding "USDA proposed rule on 'percent lean' labeling of ground beef and hamburger," August 15, 1994.

17. J.L. Vetter, *Food Laws and Regulations*. Manhattan, KS: American Institute of Baking, 1996. (See chapter 5, "Standards of Identity for Food Products," pp. 109–114.)

18. A. Rosenfeld, *No License to Label*. Washington, DC: Public Voice for Food and Health Policy, 1991.

19. V.J. Rhodes, *The Agricultural Marketing System*. 3rd ed., New York: John Wiley & Sons, 1987. (See especially part 3, chapter 18, "Public Policy Issues in Marketing-Procurement.")

20. D.A. Kessler, "The Federal Regulation of Food Labeling: Promoting Foods to Prevent Disease," *The New England Journal of Medicine* 321(11): 717–725, 1989.

21. R. Merrill, "History of FDA Regulation of Food Labeling," unpublished. 1990.

22. Vetter, *Food Laws and Regulations*, p. 111.

23. Kessler, "The Federal Regulation of Food Labeling."

24. Rosenfeld, *No License to Label.*

25. D. Stehlin, "A Little 'Lite' Reading: Special Situations," *FDA Consumer*, May 1993, p. 31.

26. J.T. Tanner, "Ask the Regulators," *Food Testing and Analysis*, August/September 1996, pp. 7–8.

27. M. Burros, "What is 'Low Fat' Milk? A New Label Is Proposed," *New York Times*, May 31, 1995, p. C5; "Food and Drug Administration Revokes Standards of Identity for Certain Low-Fat Dairy Products," *Food Chemical News*, November 25, 1996, p. 28; "Dairies Ready to Roll Out a New 'Fat Free' Milk Label," *CNI Nutrition Week*, November 29, 1996, p. 3; "Low-Fat Milk, By Any Other Name . . . ," *Tufts University Diet and Nutrition Letter*, January 1997, p. 6.

28. *Federal Register*, p. 47453, No. 95–051A, September 9, 1996; also "Regulatory Update" from the National Cattlemen's Beef Association, January 1997.

29. "FSIS Should Adopt General Standard of Identity for Meat and Poultry Products, Food Groups Say," *Food Chemical News*, January 6, 1997, pp. 12–13.

30. "CSPI Opposes Wholesale Changes to Meat and Poultry Standards," *Food Chemical News*, January 20, 1997, pp. 19–20; and letter to FSIS docket clerk from Art Jaeger, on behalf of Public Voice for Food and Health Policy, dated November 15, 1996.

31. Committee on Technological Options to Improve the Nutritional Attributes of Animal Products, Board on Agriculture, National Research Council, *Designing Foods: Animal Product Options in the Marketplace*. Washington, DC: National Academy Press, 1988, p. 106.

32. "Comment Deadline Brings Many Requests that Standards of Identity be

Retained, But Modernized," *Food Labeling and Nutrition News*, July 18, 1996, pp. 5–7; C. Skrzycki, "At USDA, the Meat of the Matter Is a Recipe for Change," *Washington Post*, September 13, 1996, pp. D1, 2.

Notes to Case Study 3

1. D.V. Porter, "Food Labeling Reform: The Journey from Science to Policy," *Nutrition Today* 28(5): 7–12, 1993.

2. T. Scarlett, "The Politics of Food Labeling," *Food Technology* 46: 58–63, July 1992.

3. "CSPI Launches Legislative Campaign against Saturated Fat," *Food Chemical News*, April 25, 1988, pp. 35–36; "Surgeon General Report Puts Priority on Dietary Fat Reducation," *Food Chemical News*, August 1, 1988, pp. 41–47.

4. "Can Cornflakes Cure Cancer?" *Business Week*, October 9, 1989, cover.

5. Scarlett, "The Politics of Food Labeling."

6. B. Silverglade, Center for Science in the Public Interest, Washington, DC, personal communication, March 8, 1996.

7. Scarlett, "The Politics of Food Labeling."

8. "Health Professional, Consumer Coalition Asks FDA to Make Labeling a Priority," *Food Chemical News*, August 22, 1988, p. 18.

9. B. Silverglade, personal communication, March 8, 1996.

10. "Food Label Revisions . . . ," *Food Chemical News*, October 3, 1988, pp. 2, 25.

11. As reported in *Food Chemical News*, January 16 and February 13, 1989.

12. "Food Labeling Is the 'Dominant Issue' Facing FDA, Commissioner Young Says," *Food Chemical News*, December 5, 1988, p. 2.

13. As reported in *Food Chemical News*, June 4, 1990, pp. 41 and 42.

14. *Federal Register*, Docket #90N-0135C, #90N-0165C, and #90N-0134C, July 19, 1990.

15. D.V. Porter and R. Earl, eds., *Nutrition Labeling: Issues and Directions for the 1990s*. Washington, DC: Institute of Medicine/National Academy of Sciences, 1990.

16. As reported in *Food Chemical News*, October 1, 1990, p. 49.

17. D.V. Porter, *Food Labeling*, CRS Issue Brief, Order Code IB80055. Washington, DC: Congressional Research Service, Library of Congress, August 7, 1989, p. 10.

18. B. Silverglade, personal communication, March 8, 1996.

19. J. Rovner, "Uniform Nutrition Labeling Endorsed by House Panel," *CQ Weekly Report*, 47(43): 2878, October 28, 1989.

20. Ibid.

21. J. Rovner, "Senate Committee Approves Nutrition-Labeling Bill," *CQ Weekly Report* 48(7): 1274, April 28, 1990.

22. D. Wisenberg, "House Committee Approves Food Labeling Measure," *CQ Weekly Report* 48(20): 1569, May 19, 1990.

23. P.B. Hutt, "A Brief History of FDA Regulation Relating to the Nutrient Content of Food," pp. 1–27. In *Nutrition Labeling Handbook*, ed. R. Shapiro. New York: Marcel Dekker, 1995.

24. D.A. Kessler, "The Federal Regulation of Food Labeling. Promoting Foods to Prevent Disease," *The New England Journal of Medicine* 321(11): 717–723, 1989; also see J. Kosterlitz, "High-Wire Act," *National Journal* 24(22): 1289–1294, May 30, 1992.

25. J.E. Foulke, "Cooking Up the New Food Label," *FDA Consumer*, Special Issue on Food Labeling, May 1993, pp. 14–19.

26. Scarlett, "The Politics of Food Labeling."

27. Foulke, "Cooking Up the New Food Label," p. 16.

28. Ibid.

29. This discussion is based on the following references: B.M. Derby and S.B. Fein, "Meeting the NLEA Education Challenge: A Consumer Research Perspective," in *The Nutrition Labeling Handbook*, ed. R. Shapiro. New York: Marcel Dekker Food Science and Technology Series, March 1994; "Deciding the Look of Tomorrow's Food Labels," *Food Insight*, September/October 1992, pp. 2–3; "Performance, Not Preference, Stressed in Format Comments," *Food Chemical News*, August 12, 1991, pp. 7–8.

30. C. Sugarman, "Fighting the Food Label Wars: Two Government Agencies Fail to Agree on What the Packaging Should Say," *Washington Post,* Health section, September 15, 1991.

31. Foulke, "Cooking Up the Food Label," p. 15.

32. Personal communication with Peter Barton Hutt, September 10, 1996.

33. D. Madigan, "Nutrition Label Choice Is 'a Great Legacy,' Bush Decides in Showdown," *CNI Nutrition Week*, 22(47): 1–2, December 11, 1992.

34. R. Hildwine, "The Challenges of 'Nutrition Facts': The Food Industry Implements Mandatory Nutrition Labeling," *Nutrition Today* 28(5): 26–29, September/October 1993.

35. C. Sugarman, "The Politics of a Quarter-Million Labels," *Washington Post*, June 17, 1992, p. A23.

36. E. Carlson, "Critics See FDA Flip-Flop," *AARP Bulletin*, May 1992, pp. 1, 6–7.

37. J. Rovner, "House Gives Stamp of Approval to Food Nutrition Labeling," *CQ Weekly Report* 48(31): 2523, August 4, 1990.

38. D. Porter and R. Earl, eds., *Food Labeling: Toward National Uniformity*, Washington, DC: National Academy Press, 1992.

39. R.L. Allen, "Latest CSPI Attack Sparks Menu Changes, Debate," *Nation's Restaurant News*, February 5, 1996, pp. 3, 66.

40. B.A. Silverglade, "Regulatory Policies for Communicating Health Information," pp. 88–95. In *Mass Communication and Public Health*, ed. C. Atkin and L. Wallack. Newbury Park CA: Sage Publications, 1990.

41. P.M. Morris and R. Lucas, *Blinded by "Lite": How Consumers View Food Labeling Claims*. Washington, DC: Public Voice for Food and Health Policy, 1992.

42. D.V. Porter, "Health Claims on Food Products: NLEA," *Nutrition Today* 31(1): 35–38, 1996.

43. C. Sugarman, "The FDA Tries Some New Math: Which Nutritional Label Adds Up?" *Washington Post*, July 22, 1992, pp. E1, 10.

44. D.V. Porter, "Health Claims on Food Products: NLEA."

45. M. Burros, *Eating Well Is the Best Revenge*. New York: Simon & Schuster, 1995, p. 332.

46. "Food Labeling: Health Claims; Oats and Coronary Heart Disease." Docket No. 95P-0197, *Federal Register*, January 4, 1996.

47. D. Brown, "Oat Bran Product Makers Win Right to Label Health Claims," *Washington Post*, January 22, 1997, p. A2; M. Burros, "Oat Bran and Soluble Fiber: the Debate Continues," *New York Times*, February 26, 1997, p. C3; C. Sugarman, "Feeling Your Oats. Getting the Grain's Newly Touted Heart Benefits Will

Require Lots of Servings," *Washington Post* Health section, February 18, 1997, p. 20; "Oats in the Offing," *Tufts University Health and Nutrition Letter*, March 1997, p. 7.

48. K. Day, "The Power of Institutional Endorsement. Cereal Firms Cheered as FDA Allows Use of Its Name in Touting Health Benefits of Oats," *Washington Post*, February 1, 1997, pp. K1, 2.

49. Porter, "Health Claims on Food Products: NLEA."

50. "Mrs. Fields Cookies in 'Low Fat' Settlement," *New York Times*, March 2, 1996.

51. M. Burros, "A Margarine Maker Agrees to Alter Its Health Claims," *New York Times*, February 12, 1997, p. C3.

52. "Food Ads and Labels Take Step Toward Conformity," *CNI Nutrition Week*, 1995, pp. 6–7.

53. "Putting the 'E' into NLEA!" *Nutrition Today* 28(5): 37–40, September/October 1993.

54. "First Steps: The Nutrition Facts Label at One Year," *Food Insight* (published by the International Food Information Council), July/August, 1995, pp. 1, 4–5.

55. A.S. Levy and B.M. Darby, *The Impact of the NLEA on Consumers: Recent Findings from FDA's Food Label and Nutrition Tracking System*. Washington, DC: Food and Drug Administration, January 23, 1996.

56. Madigan, "Nutrition Label Choice Is 'a Great Legacy,' Bush Decides in Showdown."

57. P.A. Sabatier and H.C. Jenkins-Smith, eds., *Policy Change and Learning: An Advocacy Coalition Approach*.

58. J. Kosterlitz, "The Food Lobby's Menu," *National Journal* 22(39): 2334–2338, September 29, 1990.

59. Hildwine, "The Challeges of 'Nutrition Facts': The Food Industry Implements Mandatory Nutrition Labeling."

60. *The Keystone National Policy Dialogue on Food, Nutrition, and Health*. Final Report. Washington, DC: The Keystone Center, 1996.

61. "FDA Food Advisory Committee Studying Keystone Recommendations," *Food Labeling & Nutrition News* 4(44): 14–15, August 1, 1996.

62. G.A. Zarkin, N. Dean, J.A. Mauskopf, and R. Williams, "Potential Health Benefits of Nutrition Label Changes," *American Journal of Public Health*, 83(5): 717–724, 1993.

63. "Americans Have Little Faith in Health Claims on Foods," *CNI Nutrition Week* February 7, 1997, p. 8.

Notes to Chapter 7

1. D.M. Smallwood, J.R. Blaylock, S. Lutz, and N. Blisard, "Americans Spending a Smaller Share of Income on Food," *FoodReview*, May/August 1995, pp. 16–19.

2. A. Manchester and A. Clauson, "1994 Spending for Food Away from Home Outpaces Food at Home," *FoodReview*, May/August 1995, pp. 12–15.

3. Observations for this section have been gleaned from M. Mogelonsky, *Everybody Eats: Supermarket Consumers in the 1990s*. Ithaca, NY: American Demographics Books, 1995.

4. *The Kiplinger Agriculture Letter*. Washington, DC: The Kiplinger Washington Editors, Inc., May 15, 1996, p. 4.

5. Federation of American Societies for Experimental Biology, Life Sciences Re-

search Office (LSRO). Prepared for the Interagency Board for Nutrition Monitoring and Related Research. *Third Report on Nutrition Monitoring in the United States: Executive Summary*. Washington, DC: U.S. Government Printing Office, 1995.

6. L.S. Sims, "Government Involvement in Nutrition Education: Panacea or Pandora's Box?" *Health Education Research* 5(4): 517–526, 1990.

7. L.S. Sims and S.K. Shepherd, *Further Exploration of Formatting, Structuring, and Sequencing of Nutrition Information for Household Food Managers*. Final Report submitted to the Human Nutrition Information Service (HNIS)/USDA, in partial fulfillment of FNS Contract No. 53–3198–4–66, 1987.

8. K. Glanz and C.L. Damberg, "Meeting our Nation's Health Objectives in Nutrition," *Journal of Nutrition Education* 19: 211–219, 1987.

9. N. Milio, "Promoting Health through Structural Change: Origins and Implementation of Norway's Farm-Food-Nutrition Program," *Social Science and Medicine* 15A: 721–734, 1981.

10. K.-I. Klepp and J.L. Forster, "The Norwegian Nutrition and Food Policy: an Integrated Policy Approach to a Public Health Problem," *Journal of Public Health Policy* 6: 447–463, 1985.

11. P. O'Brien, "Dietary Shifts and Implications for U.S. Agriculture," *American Journal of Clinical Nutrition* 61(suppl.): 1390S-1396S, 1995.

12. P.R. Thomas, ed., *Improving America's Diet and Health: From Recommendations to Action*. A report of the Committee on Dietary Guidelines Implementation, Food and Nutrition Board, Institute of Medicine. Washington, DC: National Academy Press, 1991.

13. A.P. Simopoulos, V. Herbert, and B. Jacobson, *Genetic Nutrition*. New York: Macmillan, 1993.

14. R. Leonard, "*Genetic Nutrition* Opens New Era in Food Policy," *CNI Nutrition Week*, June 18, 1993, pp. 4–5.

15. *Dietary Guidelines Focus Group Report*. Prepared for USDA's Center for Nutrition Policy and Promotion by Prospect Associates, Rockville, MD. August 18, 1995.

16. "Nutrition Promotion Ideas Often Lost on the Masses," as reported in *CNI Nutrition Week*, July 26, 1996, p. 6.

17. Thomas, *Improving America's Diet and Health*.

18. G.G. Harrison, "Reducing Dietary Fat: Putting Theory into Practice—Conference Summary," *Journal of the American Dietetic Association* 97(7): 593–596, 1997.

19. Ibid.

For Further Consideration

20. S.A. Neff and G.E. Plato, *Federal Marketing Orders and Federal Research and Promotion Programs*, USDA/Economic Research Service Report, AER-707. Washington, DC: U.S. Department of Agriculture, Economic Research Service, 1995, pp. 7–11.

21. "GAO Describes Agriculture Promotion Check-offs," *CNI Nutrition Week*, August 4, 1995, pp. 4–5.

22. O.D. Forker and D.J. Liu, "Commodity Promotion: Who Benefits and by How Much?" *Choices*, Third Quarter, 1989, pp. 8–11.

23. U.S. Code, Title 7 (Agriculture), Chapter 62, "Beef Research and Information,"

Section 2901, "Congressional Findings and Declaration of Policy," 1986.

5. GAO, "GAO Describes Agricultural Promotion Check-offs," p. 5.

6. "Using Semi-public Funds, Beef Industry Fixes Image," *CNI Nutrition Week*, October 4, 1991, p. 6.

7. "The Cattlemen's War on Fat," promotional sheet distributed by the National Cattlemen's Association, Washington, DC, November 1993.

8. C. Sugarman, "Pot Roast in a Flash and More," *Washington Post*, August 6, 1997, p. E1.

9. Dairy Promotion Programs, "The National Dairy Database" (on the World Wide Web), 1992, 9pp.

10. "Milk Industry Takes Step in the Right Direction," *Environmental Nutrition*, June 1995, p. 8.

11. "Promotion Board Expands Milk Mustache Campaign," *CNI Nutrition Week*, June 6, 1997, p. 3.

12. "Milk Processors Hope Ads Will Spur U.S. to 'Drink 3,' " *CNI Nutrition Week*, January 10, 1997, p. 3.

13. Estimated data obtained from Competitive Media Reporting, 1996.

Notes to Case Study 4

1. L.S. Sims, "The Ebb and Flow of Nutrition as a Public Policy Issue," *Journal of Nutrition Education* 15(4): 132–136, 1983.

2. Select Committee on Nutrition and Human Needs, United States Senate, *Dietary Goals for the United States*. Washington, DC: U.S. Government Printing Office, 1977.

3. A.S. Truswell, "Dietary Goals and Guidelines: National and International Perspectives," in *Modern Nutrition in Health and Disease*, ed. M.D. Shils, J.A. Olson, and M. Sheike, Chapter 93, vol. 2, 8th ed., Philadelphia: Lea & Febiger, 1994. pp. 1612–1625.

4. Ibid.

5. H.O. Kunkel and P.B. Thompson, "Interests and Values in National Nutrition Policy in the United States," *Journal of Agricultural Ethics* 1: 241–256, 1988.

6. U.S. Department of Health, Education, and Welfare, Public Health Service, *Healthy People: The Surgeon General's Report on Health Promotion and Disease Prevention*. DHEW (PHS) Publ. No. 79–55071, Washington, DC: U.S. Government Printing Office, 1979.

7. U.S. Department of Agriculture and U.S. Department of Health, Education and Welfare, *Nutrition and Your Health: Dietary Guidelines for Americans*. Home and Garden Bulletin No. 232, Washington, DC: U.S. Department of Agriculture, 1980.

8. C.A. Davis and E.A. Saltos, "The Dietary Guidelines for Americans—Past, Present, Future," *Family Economics and Nutrition Review* 9(2): 4–13, 1996.

9. Food and Nutrition Board, National Research Council, *Toward Healthful Diets*. Washington, DC: National Academy Press, 1980.

10. M. Nestle and D.V. Porter, "Evolution of Federal Dietary Guidance Policy: From Food Adequacy to Chronic Disease Prevention," *Caduceus* 6(2): 43–67, 1990.

11. J.E. Brody, "Sharp Departure: U.S. Study Sees No Cause for Limit on Cholesterol," *International Herald Tribune*, May 29, 1980, p. 7; N. Wade, "Food Board's Fat Report Hits Fire," *Science* 209: 248–250, 1980.

12. Hearings before the Subcommittee on Domestic Marketing, Consumer Relations, and Nutrition of the Committee on Agriculture, House of Representatives, 96th Congress, 2nd session, June 18 and 19, 1980. *National Academy of Sciences Report on Healthful Diets.* Washington, DC: U.S. Government Printing Office; Hearings before the Subcommittee on Agriculture, Rural Development and Related Agencies, Committee on Appropriations, 96th Congress, 2nd session, July 16, 1980. *Dietary Guidelines for Americans.* Washington, DC: U.S. Government Printing Office.

13. Truswell, "Dietary Goals and Guidelines," p. 1616.

14. M. Nestle, "Food Lobbies, the Food Pyramid, and U.S. Nutrition Policy," *International Journal of Health Services* 23(3): 483–496, 1993.

15. U.S. Senate Agricultural Appropriations Committee, Senate Report No. 96–1030, November 20, 1980.

16. "Olson Predicts Government Will Abandon Dietary Advice," *Food Chemical News*, September 15, 1980, p. 14.

17. U.S. Department of Agriculture and U.S. Department of Health and Human Services, *Nutrition and Your Health: Dietary Guidelines for Americans,* 2nd ed. Home and Garden Bulletin No. 232. Washington, DC: U.S. Department of Agriculture, 1985.

18. Dietary Guidelines Advisory Committee, *Report of the Dietary Guidelines Advisory Committee on the Dietary Guidelines for Americans.* U.S. Department of Agriculture, Human Nutrition Information Service, 1985.

19. Davis and Saltos, "The Dietary Guidelines for Americans," p. 6.

20. U.S. House of Representatives Conference Committee, 100th Congress, 1st session. H.R. 498, 1987.

21. Dietary Guidelines Advisory Committee, *Report of the Dietary Guidelines Advisory Committee on the Dietary Guidelines for Americans.* U.S. Department of Agriculture, Human Nutrition Information Service, 1990.

22. U.S. Department of Health and Human Services, Public Health Service, *The Surgeon General's Report on Diet and Health.* Washington, DC: U.S. Government Printing Office, 1988.

23. National Academy of Sciences, National Research Council, Food and Nutrition Board, *Diet and Health: Implications for Reducing Chronic Disease Risk.* Washington, DC: National Academy Press, 1989.

24. *National Cholesterol Education Program: Report of the Expert Panel on Population Strategies for Blood Cholesterol Reduction.* Bethesda, MD: Office of Prevention, Education and Control, National Heart, Lung, and Blood Institute of Health, U.S. Department of Health and Human Services, 1990.

25. U.S. Department of Agriculture and U.S. Department of Health and Human Services, *Nutrition and Your Health: Dietary Guidelines for Americans,* 3rd ed. Home and Garden Bulletin No. 232, Washington, DC: U.S. Department of Agriculture, 1990.

26. Ibid.

27. R.E. Leonard, "Federal Dietary Advice Weakens Health Reforms," *CNI Nutrition Week,* April 23, 1993, pp. 4–5.

28. Davis and Saltos, "The Dietary Guidelines for Americans," p. 7.

29. U.S. Department of Agriculture and U.S. Department of Health and Human Services, *Nutrition and Your Health: Dietary Guidelines for Americans.* 4th ed. Home and Garden Bulletin No. 232, Washington, DC: U.S. Department of Agriculture, 1995.

30. This quote was attributed to Dr. Marion Nestle in M. Burros, "In an About-

Face, U.S. Says Alcohol Has Health Benefits," *New York Times,* January 3, 1996, pp. A1, C2; S. Squires, "U.S. Guidelines Stress Food Variety, but Recognize Vegetarian Diet," *Washington Post*, January 3, 1996, p. A3; G. Cowley and A. Rogers, "Vats, Fats, and Rats," *Newsweek*, January 15, 1996, p. 56.

31. S. Palmer, "Food and Nutrition Policy: Challenges for the 1990s," *Health Affairs* 9(2): 94–108, 1990.

32. J. Kosterlitz, "The Food Lobby's Menu," *National Journal* 22(39): 2334–2338, September 29, 1990.

33. This quote was from "USDA's Not-So-Meaty Advice," by Colman McCarthy, *Washington Post*, January 9, 1996. Similar views are expressed in: M. Nestle, "Food Lobbies, the Food Pyramid, and U.S. Nutrition Policy," *International Journal of Health Services* 23(3): 483–496, 1993; C. Ireland, "The Politics of Nutrition," *Vegetarian Times*, no. 182, p. 54, October 1992.

34. Palmer, "Food and Nutrition Policy."

35. R.K. Manoff, *Social Marketing: New Imperative for Public Health*. New York: Praeger, 1985, pp. 64–84.

Notes to Case Study 5

1. M. Nestle, "Dietary Advice for the 1990s: The Political History of the Food Guide Pyramid," *Caduceus: Museum Journal of Health Sciences* 9(3): 136–153, 1993a.

2. M. Nestle, "Food Lobbies, the Food Pyramid, and U.S. Nutrition Policy," *International Journal of Health Services* 23(3): 483–496, 1993b.

3. M. DeC. Hinds, "Switch at Agriculture: Fewer Tips for the Cook," *New York Times*, August 30, 1982; S. Zuckerman, "Nutrition Education at USDA: Killing it Softly," *Nutrition Action* 11: 6–10, 1984.

4. F.J. Cronin, A.M. Shaw, S.M. Krebs-Smith, P.M. Marsland, and L. Light, "Developing a Food Guidance System to Implement the Dietary Guidelines," *Journal of Nutrition Education* 19: 281–301, 1987.

5. U.S. Department of Agriculture, Human Nutrition Information Service, Nutrition Education Division, *Developing the Food Guidance System for "Better Eating for Better Health," a Nutrition Course for Adults*. USDA Admin. Rept. No. 377, Washington, DC: U.S. Department of Agriculture, 1985.

6. Unless specific citations are specifically noted, this section is based on accounts given in the following references: S. Welsh, C. Davis, and A. Shaw, "Development of the Food Guide Pyramid," *Nutrition Today*, November/December 1992, pp. 12–23; J. Anderson, "U.S. Government Dietary Guidelines: Past Review and Present Opportunity," *Nutrition Update* (published by Nabisco Brands, Inc.) 3(1): 2–4, Spring 1993; M. Nestle, "Dietary Advice for the 1990s: the Political History of the Food Guide Pyramid." *Caduceus* 9(3): 136–153, 1993a.

7. From the Official Mission Statement of the Human Nutrition Information Service, U.S. Department of Agriculture, approved May 22, 1984.

8. This description of the process was described in an unpublished USDA staff memorandum, dated April 16, 1991, and published in Nestle, "Dietary Advice for the 1990s".

9. Recounted in the editorial, "What's Happening at USDA?" by Gerald F. Combs, a long-time USDA official shortly before his retirement. This account

appeared in Nutrition Notes, a publication of the American Institute of Nutrition, September 1991.

10. M. Burros, "Plain Talk about Eating Right," *New York Times Magazine*, Section 2, Good Health, October 6, 1991, p. 13.

11. This account was included in footnote 34 in M. Nestle, "Dietary Advice for the 1990s."

12. M. Nestle, "Dietary Advice for the 1990s," p. 146.

13. Ibid.

14. M. Burros, "U.S. Reorganizes Nutrition Advice," *New York Times*, April 28, 1992, p. A14.

15. M. Nestle, "Dietary Advice for the 1990s."

16. C. Sugarman, "The Lessons of the Pyramid," *Washington Post*, May 13, 1992.

17. C. Achterberg, "A Perspective: Challenges of Teaching the Dietary Guidelines Graphic," *Food and Nutrition News* 64(4): 23–26, September-October 1992; C. Achterberg, E. McDonnell, and R. Bagby, "How to Put the Food Guide Pyramid into Practice," *Journal of the American Dietetic Association* 94(9): 1030–1035, 1994.

18. M. Burros, "The Pyramid Draws Diners to Healthful Eating," *New York Times*, February 10, 1993, p. C4; W.C. Willett, F. Sacks, A. Trichopolou, et al., "The Mediterranean Diet Pyramid: A Cultural Model for Healthy Eating," *American Journal of Clinical Nutrition* 61: 14025–14065, 1995.

19. M. Burros, "When Pyramids Duel," *New York Times*, April 27, 1994, p. C4; M.W. Miller, "Call for a Daily Dose of Wine Ferments Critics," *Wall Street Journal*, June 17, 1994, pp. B1, 5; M. Burros, "The Pyramid That Calls for More Olive Oil," *New York Times*, March 29, 1995, p. C4.

Notes to Chapter 8

1. A. Adelson, "Advertising: California Takes on the Tobacco Industry with a $22 Million Campaign to Discourage Smoking," *New York Times*, April 4, 1997, p. C2.

2. P.A. Sabatier and H.C. Jenkins-Smith, eds., *Policy Change and Learning: An Advocacy Coalition Approach*. Boulder, CO: Westview Press, 1993.

3. N. Milio, *Nutrition Policy for Food-Rich Countries: A Strategic Analysis*. Baltimore: Johns Hopkins University Press, 1990, pp. 161–165.

4. P. O'Brien, "Dietary Shifts and Implications for U.S. Agriculture," *American Journal of Clinical Nutrition* 61(suppl): 1390S-1396S, 1995.

5. N. Milio, *Nutrition Policy for Food-Rich Countries*, p. 2.

6. B. Senauer, E. Asp, and J. Kinsey, *Food Trends and the Changing Consumer*. St. Paul, MN: Eagan Press, 1991, p. 281.

7. P. O'Brien, "Dietary Shifts and Implications for U.S. Agriculture."

8. M. Mills, *The Politics of Dietary Change*. Aldershot, England: Dartmouth Publishing, 1992, p. 136.

9. J. Price, "'Fat Tax' Demanded to Make Americans Lose Taste for Junk," *Washington Times*, July 1, 1997, p. A6.

10. T.L. Schmid, R.W. Jeffrey, J.L. Forster, B. Rooney, and C. McBride, "Public Support for Policy Initiatives Regulating High-Fat Food Use in Minnesota: A Multicommunity Survey," *Preventive Medicine* 18: 791–805, 1989.

11. J.D. Gussow and S. Akabas, "Are We Really Fixing Up the Food Supply?" *Journal of the American Dietetic Association* 93(11): 1300–1304, 1993.

12. P.R. Thomas, ed., *Improving America's Diet and Health: From Recommendations to Action.* A Report of the Committee on Dietary Guidelines Implementation, Food and Nutrition Board, Institute of Medicine. Washington, DC: National Academy Press, 1991, pp. 112–139.

13. P.M. Ippolito and A.D. Mathios, "Information, Policy, and the Sources of Fat and Cholesterol in the U.S. Diet," *Journal of Public Policy and Marketing* 13(2): 200–217, 1994.

Selected Bibliography

Nutrition Policy

Austin, J.E., and C. Hitt, *Nutrition Intervention in the United States*. Cambridge, MA: Ballinger Books, 1979.

Austin, J., and C. Overholt, "Nutrition Policy: Building the Bridge Between Science and Politics," *Annual Review of Nutrition* 8:1–20, 1988.

Davis, C.A. and E.A. Saltos, "The Dietary Guidelines for Americans—Past, Present, Future," *Family Economics and Nutrition Review* 9(2):4–13, 1996.

Federation of American Societies for Experimental Biology, Life Sciences Research Office (LSRO), Prepared for the Interagency Board for Nutrition Monitoring and Related Research, *Third Report on Nutrition Monitoring in the United States: Executive Summary*. Washington, DC: U.S. Government Printing Office, 1995.

Hutt, P.B., "A Brief History of FDA Regulation Relating to the Nutrient Content of Food," pp. 1–27. In *Nutrition Labeling Handbook*, ed. R. Shapiro. New York: Marcel Dekker, 1995.

Kessler, D.A., "The Federal Regulation of Food Labeling: Promoting Foods to Prevent Disease," *New England Journal of Medicine* 321(11): 717–723, 1989.

———, "The Evolution of National Nutrition Policy," *Annual Review of Nutrition* 15: xiii–xxvi, 1995.

Kunkel, H.O., and P.B. Thompson, "Interests and Values in National Nutrition Policy in the United States," *Journal of Agricultural Ethics* 1:241–256, 1988.

Milio, N., *Promoting Health through Public Policy*. Philadelphia: F.A. Davis, 1981.

———, *Nutrition Policy for Food-Rich Countries*. Baltimore: Johns Hopkins University Press, 1990.

Mills, M., *The Politics of Dietary Change*. Aldershot, England: Dartmouth Publishing, 1992.

National Academy of Sciences, National Research Council, Food and Nutrition Board, *Diet and Health: Implications for Reducing Chronic Disease Risk*. Washington, DC: National Academy Press, 1989.

Nestle, M., and D.V. Porter, "Evolution of Federal Dietary Guidance Policy: From Food Adequacy to Chronic Disease Prevention," *Caduceus: Museum Journal of Health Sciences* 6(2):43–67, 1990.

———, "Dietary Advice for the 1990s: The Political History of the Food Guide Pyramid," *Caduceus: Museum Journal of Health Sciences* 9(3): 136–153, 1993a.

———, "Food Lobbies, the Food Pyramid, and U.S. Nutrition Policy," *International Journal of Health Services* 23(3): 483–496, 1993b.

Nestle, M. and C. Woteki, "Trends in American Dietary Patterns: Research Issues and Policy Implications." In *Nutrition and Health: Topics and Controversies*, ed. F. Bronner, pp. 16–23. Boca Raton, FL: CRC Press, 1995.

Palmer, S., "Food and Nutrition Policy: Challenges for the 1990s," *Health Affairs* 9(2): 94–108, 1990.

Porter, D.V., and R. Earl, eds., *Nutrition Labeling: Issues and Directions for the 1990s*. Washington, DC: Institute of Medicine/National Academy of Sciences, 1990.

———, "Food Labeling Reform: The Journey from Science to Policy," *Nutrition Today* 28(5): 7–12, 1993.

Schmandt, J., R.A. Shorey, and L. Kinch, *Nutrition Policy in Transition*. Lexington, MA: Lexington Books, D. C. Heath, 1980.

Schmid, T.L., R.W. Jeffrey, J.L. Forster, B. Rooney, and C. McBride, "Public Support for Policy Initiatives Regulating High-Fat Food Use in Minnesota: A Multicommunity Survey," *Preventive Medicine* 18:791–805, 1989.

Select Committee on Nutrition and Human Needs, United States Senate, *Dietary Goals for the United States*. Washington, DC: U.S. Government Printing Office, 1977.

Sims, L.S., "The Ebb and Flow of Nutrition as a Public Policy Issue," *Journal of Nutrition Education* 15(4): 132–136, 1983.

———, "Nutrition Policy through the Reagan Era: Feast or Famine?" Presented for the Pew/Cornell Lecture Series on Food and Nutrition Policy. Ithaca, NY: Cornell University, November 1, 1988.

———, "Government Involvement in Nutrition Education: Panacea or Pandora's Box?" *Health Education Research* 5(4): 517–526, 1990.

———, "Public Policy in Nutrition: A Framework for Action," *Nutrition Today* 28 (2): 10–20, 1993.

Thomas, P.R., ed., Institute of Medicine, Committee on Dietary Guidelines Implementation, *Improving America's Diet and Health: From Recommendations to Action*. Washington, DC: National Academy Press, 1991.

Truswell, A.S., "Dietary Goals and Guidelines: National and International Perspectives." In *Modern Nutrition in Health and Disease*, ed. M.D. Shils, J.A. Olson, and M. Sheike, chapter 93, vol. 2, 8th ed. Philadelphia: Lea & Febiger, 1994, pp. 1612–1625.

U.S. Department of Health and Human Services, Public Health Service, *The Surgeon General's Report on Diet and Health*. Washington, DC: U.S. Government Printing Office, 1988.

Woteki, C.E., and P.R. Thomas, eds., *Eat for Life*. Washington, DC: National Academy Press, 1992.

Agriculture and Food Policy

Browne, W.P., *Cultivating Congress: Constituents, Issues, and Interests in Agricultural Policymaking*. Lawrence: University Press of Kansas, 1995.

———, *Private Interests, Public Policy, and American Agriculture*. Lawrence: University Press of Kansas, 1988.

Gussow, J.D., *Chicken Little, Tomato Sauce and Agriculture*. New York: Bootstrap Press, 1991.

Hadwiger, D.F., and W.P. Browne, eds., *The New Politics of Food*. Lexington, MA: Lexington Books, D.C. Heath, 1978.

Halcrow, H.C., *Food Policy for America*. New York: McGraw-Hill, 1977.

Hallberg, M.C., R.G.F. Spitze, and D.E. Ray, eds., *Food, Agriculture, and Rural Policy into the Twenty-First Century*. Boulder, CO: Westview Press, 1994.

Hansen, J.M., *Gaining Access: Congress and the Farm Lobby, 1919–1981*. Chicago: University of Chicago Press, 1991.

National Research Council, Committee on Technological Options to Improve the Nutritional Attributes of Animal Products, *Designing Foods: Animal Product Options in the Marketplace*. Washington, DC: National Academy Press, 1988.

O'Brien, P., "Dietary Shifts and Implications for U.S. Agriculture," *American Journal of Clinical Nutrition* 61(supplement):1390S-1396S, 1995.

Rapp, D., *How the U.S. Got into Agriculture . . . And Why It Can't Get Out*. Washington, DC: Congressional Quarterly, 1988.

"Results from the 1994 Continuing Survey of Food Intakes by Individuals (CSFII)," *What We Eat in America, 1994–96*. Washington, DC: USDA/ Agricultural Research Service, 1996.

Senauer, B., E. Asp, and J. Kinsey, *Food Trends and the Changing Consumer*. St. Paul, MN: Eagan Press, 1991.

Vetter, J.L., *Food Laws and Regulations*. Manhattan, KS: American Institute of Baking, 1996.

Public Policy (General)

Anderson, J.E., *Public Policymaking: An Introduction*. 3rd ed. Boston, MA: Houghton Mifflin, 1997.

Jones, C.O., *An Introduction to the Study of Public Policy*. 3rd ed. Monterey, CA: Brooks/Cole, 1984.

Kingdon, J.W., *Agendas, Alternatives, and Public Policies*. 2nd ed. New York: HarperCollins, 1995.

Meier, K.J., *Politics and the Bureaucracy*. 3rd ed. Belmont, CA: Wadsworth, 1993.

Palumbo, D.J., *Public Policy in America—Government in Action*. San Diego: Harcourt Brace Jovanovich, 1988.

Ripley, R.B., and G.A. Franklin, *Congress, the Bureaucracy, and Public Policy*. 5th ed. Belmont, CA: Wadsworth, 1991.

Rubin, B.R., *A Citizen's Guide to Politics in America: How the System Works—and How to Work the System*. Armonk, NY: M.E. Sharpe, 1997.

Sabatier, P.A., and H.C. Jenkins-Smith, *Policy Change and Learning: An Advocacy Coalition Approach*. Boulder, CO: Westview Press, 1993.

Index

About The Author

Currently a professor of human nutrition at the University of Maryland, College Park, Dr. Laura S. Sims previously served as dean of the College of Human Ecology at that same university from 1988 to 1992. Prior to that, she served for two years as administrator of the Human Nutrition Information Service, an agency within the U.S. Department of Agriculture. Before joining USDA, Dr. Sims was a faculty member at Pennsylvania State University for over ten years.

Dr. Sims holds a Ph.D. in nutrition from Michigan State University, an M.P.H. (Master of Public Health) in nutrition (with specialization in maternal and child health) from the University of Michigan, and a Bachelor of Science degree in nutrition and family studies from Pennsylvania State University.

Dr. Sims is 1997–98 president of the Society for Nutrition Education. She served as editor for the *Journal of Nutrition Education* from 1985 to 1988 and again as interim editor in 1995–96. Dr. Sims, a registered dietitian, was the chair of the Council on Research for the American Dietetic Association from 1987 to 1990, and, by virtue of this elected position, served on the boards of directors for the American Dietetic Association and its Foundation. Since 1990, she has served as a member of the board of directors of the Christian Children's Fund, and served from 1993 to 1996 as an appointed member of the Montgomery County (Maryland) Commission on Health.

Dr. Sims is the author of over sixty research publications and has served as principal investigator for a number of research projects. She has served on several national advisory boards and task forces, including the Institute of Medicine/Food and Nutrition Board's 1989–90 Committee on "Nutrition Components of Food Labeling" and the 1991 Committee on "State Food Labeling." She has been scientific advisor to the Food, Nutrition, and Safety Committee of ILSI-NF, and a member of the USDA's Human Nutrition Board of Scientific Counselors and the Advisory Board for "Project LEAN," sponsored by the Kaiser Family Foundation. In addition to serving on a number of NIH and USDA research review panels, she headed the research team that conducted the "National Assessment of Extension's Food and Nutrition Programs."

Dr. Sims's major scholarly and research interests currently focus on the study of domestic nutrition policy, effectiveness of public nutrition information strategies and delivery systems, psychosocial influences on food consumption behavior, and issues dealing with community nutrition program and delivery education.